Curriculum for the
Preschool – Primary Child
A Review of the Research

Curriculum for the
Preschool–Primary Child
A Review of the Research

Edited by
Carol Seefeldt

*University of
Maryland*

Charles E. Merrill Publishing Co.
A Bell & Howell Co.
Columbus, Ohio

Published by
Charles E. Merrill Publishing Co.
A Bell & Howell Co.
Columbus, Ohio 43216

This book was set in Peignot Demibold and Times Roman.
The production editor was Deborah Payne.
The cover was designed by Will Chenoweth.

International Standard Book Number: 0-675-08678-7
Library of Congress Catalog Card Number: 75-16644

3 4 5 6 7 8 9 10—79 78

Printed in the United States of America

Preface

Throughout the 1960s, education focused on the preschool and primary child. Sparked by the theories of Hunt, Bloom, Piaget, and others, who believed that mental growth is cumulative and that later intellectual development depends, in part, upon early educational experiences, early childhood education fostered. Intensified by the civil-rights movement, the cognitive growth of young children became the central concern of early childhood education. Head Start and other compensatory and intervention programs, as well as specific curriculum models designed to stimulate intellectual growth, were conceived during the 1960s.

Although research was conducted in other areas of the child's life, it was often overshadowed by the numerous studies exploring the effects of various approaches on the intellectual growth of young children. During the 1970s, a growing concern for the curriculum areas and other aspects of the child's life largely neglected during the 1960s has arisen.

The works of Eisner in art education and Jordan who is developing a process approach to curriculum; the research in early reading and social studies; the new concepts in mathematics education, movement exploration, and music education; and new understandings on the role of play are being observed with renewed interest and expectation.

To meet this interest, *Curriculum for the Preschool-Primary Child: A Review of the Research* has compiled the theoretical foundations and the current research in the content areas of the curriculum. The book examines past and current theory; research and practice in the curriculum areas of language, mathematics, science, reading, music, art, play, social studies, and the process approach to planning curriculum for preschool and primary age children. Each of the chapters reviews the research results available in the area. Conclusions are presented that direct attention to the implications for actual classroom experiences.

Curriculum for the Preschool-Primary Child: A Review of the Research does not emphasize the research resulting from compensatory or intervention programs for young children, nor is its primary purpose to review the literature on cognition or intellectual growth or to analyze the "model" programs that arose during the 1960s and continue today. Rather, the text discusses the ongoing research in curriculum content areas appropriate for all young children. Each of the chapters discusses a different curriculum area and has been written by an authority in the particular curriculum area. An overview of the learning theories that have influenced curriculum development is presented in the introduction. Although the text presents separate chapters on specific content areas of the curriculum, it recognizes the importance of an integrated program for young children.

Curriculum for the Preschool-Primary Child: A Review of the Research, with its strong theoretical and research base, is directed to the graduate or advanced undergraduate student in early childhood education. It should also prove to be a useful resource to those who are interested in curriculum development and research in early childhood education. Supervisors, curriculum planners, and the concerned classroom teacher will find it helpful in presenting information necessary to make program decisions and for planning actual curriculum.

Acknowledgements

Chapters contributed by

Nita Barbour
University of Maryland, Baltimore

Maureen A. Dietz
University of Maryland

Lydia A. Gerhardt
Wheelock College

Richard K. Jantz
University of Maryland

Martin L. Johnson
University of Maryland

Daniel C. Jordan
University of Massachusetts

Carol Seefeldt
University of Maryland

Shirley J. Shelley
University of Maryland

Acknowledgements

Dorothy D. Sullivan

University of Maryland

Dennis Sunal

University of Maryland

Bonnie Tyler

University of Maryland

John W. Wilson

University of Maryland

Contents

CHAPTER ONE

DETERMINING THE CURRICULUM

Carol
Seefeldt

Determining what to teach.

Who decides what will be taught to young children? How do teachers know what experiences to plan for children? The forces that determine the curriculum are perhaps more clearly evident in the field of early childhood education than in any other area. Throughout the history of early childhood education, social forces, philosophy of the nature of man, and learning theories have greatly influenced the curriculum.

A unique combination of theory and social philosophy, coupled with research, contributed to the 1960s being called the decade of early childhood education. For example, Bloom and Hunt built a strong theoretical case for the concept of the flexible IQ and provided justification for early learning experiences. The widely quoted statement, "Fifty percent of a person's mature IQ develops in the first four years of life," became the rationale for early childhood education. The crumbling concept of a person's having a fixed IQ was a major reversal in learning theory and led to the concept that one could improve a child's IQ by manipulating his total environment or enriching his preschool experience.

However, the theories of Bloom and Hunt might have remained only theories without the prevailing social philosophy of the 1960s. The increasing awareness of inequalities in our society and the gross differences of educational opportunities and achievement among different groups of children led to the development of the civil-rights movement. As a result of this awareness, society looked for ways to equalize opportunities and to solve the problems of the poor and discriminated; it decided that early educational experiences would help provide the answer. It was thought that early schooling would increase the child's cognitive functions, provide him with the tools necessary for success in our society, and prepare him to become a productive member of society.

In addition to the social philosophy of the 1960s and the theory of the malleability of the IQ, the shock of Sputnik was still present. With Sputnik whirring overhead, the idea of waiting for children to unfold no longer seemed to be as viable an educational goal as it once was. Educators were mandated to reexamine their curricula and to identify goals, processes and objectives of their programs. The famous Woods Hole Conference of 1959 in which scientists and educators met to discuss curriculum led to the idea that curriculum could be determined by identifying the structure of a discipline. If scientists could identify the underlying principles that gave structure to a subject, then educators would be able to determine the most fundamental understanding of that principle that could be achieved by the child.

The American Association for the Advancement of Science (AAAS) curriculum, introducing science as a process skill; the Science Curriculum Improvement Study (SCIS), several mathematics curricula; and the social studies, Man: A Course of Study resulted from the Woods Hole Conference. Following the conference, Bruner wrote *Towards a Theory of Instruction*, and his idea that any subject can be taught to any child at any age, as long as you approach it from the level of the child, became the rationale for much of the curriculum developed for young children during the 1960s. Every area of the curriculum was touched as educators attempted to redevelop it.

This was a period of awesome change for early childhood educators. Teachers did not have time to stop and catch their breath; there was no possibility of modifying the past. Rather than becoming breathless, early childhood educators analyzed these changes on the basis of existing child development theory, learning theories, research, and past experiences. The rampant innovations of the 1960s should be evaluated and analyzed with theories from the past.

Learning Theories

Numerous learning theories throughout the ages have influenced early childhood curriculum. Faculty psychology dating back to the eighteenth century is still alive in many preschools; this is exemplified by teachers who say, "the children must learn to sit, carry a tray, wait to go to the bathroom, and finish a task before beginning another." Although few would care to admit it, these statements are reminiscent of the learning theory that advanced the ideas that the more difficult school was, the better it would train the will of the children and that will power could best be fostered by accomplishing difficult and distasteful tasks. Other learning theories have an even more potent effect on curriculum in early childhood education.

Naturalistic Theory

"Learning through unfoldment" or the naturalistic theory of learning, dating back to the eighteenth century, continues to affect early childhood curriculum. Development of the naturalistic point of view is usually associated with Rousseau, Pestalozzi, and the founder of kindergarten, Froebel.

The overall philosophy of this theory is that all men are naturally good and at the same time active in relation to their environment. All men are assumed to be free, autonomous, and forwardly active persons, who are reaching from themselves to make their world. Unless children are corrupted by some influence from outside themselves, everything they do will be good. According to the naturalists, each child is free and his personal choice and responsibility account for his life. Since man is good and the environment is equally good, the only thing necessary for children to learn and develop is to be free in their natural environment. Learning does not require any direct teaching or interference. Rather than having a teacher develop behavioral objectives or impose his ideas and knowledge on a child, the child learns as he follows his own interests.

The naturalistic theory resulted in schools for young children that did not have prepared programs and carefully thought-out objectives. Large amounts of free time for play and for use of materials in a safe, stimulating environment characterized the curriculum. Teachers based their plans on the interests, impulses, and capacities of their specific group of children.

In each of the curriculum areas (i.e., art, science, math, language), there is at least one type of curriculum based on the theoretical foundation of the naturalistic theory. One approach to the mathematics curriculum is based on the principle that the curriculum should begin with the knowledge of the child and place upon him the responsibility to select and learn what he believes or feels is important. The nativistic approach to language development argues that the child is prewired for language and that language learning is really a process of growth and development in a natural environment. Several theories of child art express the view that children, left alone in a stimulating environment without any form of outside interference, will be able to achieve their full potential.

Behavioristic Theory

Behaviorism in its broadest sense refers to all conditioning theories. The works of Thorndike, Watson, and Hall, although differing on many points, could all fit under the umbrella term *behaviorism*.

In general, this theory views the child as being neither good or bad but rather as neutral. The child reasons, attends and is able to remember, and these attributes can be developed through conditioning, that is, the rewarding of desirable responses or behavior and punishment for undesirable responses.

Teaching, according to the behaviorists, is largely a matter of conditioning, and learning consists of specific bonds between a stimulus and a response. Much of the early experimental work of the behaviorists was conducted on animals that were taught to respond to specific stimuli. In these studies it was found that the more frequently a bond between stimulus and response was exercised, the more readily available it was for subsequent use. Extrapolating these findings to children, learning and teaching consisted of drills and exercises, with rewards for desired responses and punishment for the undesirable. The teacher determined what responses to reward and set the stage for the process of fixing the stimulus-response bonds. It was the teacher, not the child, who designed and determined the curriculum.

A revival of the behavioristic theory arose in early childhood education during the 1960s. Examples of the behavioristic theory of learning can be found in each curriculum area. Curriculum emphasizing the structure of a discipline, with stress on an organized, logical sequence to learning, is based on this theory. Programmed learning and teaching machines which require overt responses from the child and give immediate reward in the form of feedback are examples of the behavioristic theory of learning. The DISTAR program is one example of this type of curriculum. Children in DISTAR take only one step at a time, they do not move until they master that step, and they are immediately reinforced for proper responses.

The concept of reinforcement plays a large role in current behavioristic curricula. Some rewards consist of social praise, smiles, hugs, or verbal praise. Other psychologists advocate the use of more stable reinforcements, such as crackers, candy, toys, or tokens. Punishment, or negative reinforcement, may occur through some form of ignoring the child, rather than giving a direct reprimand.

The highly mechanical approach of the behavioristic theory, which leaves no room for children's feelings, sensitivities, intrinsic motivation, or sense of autonomy in learning, has not been widely accepted by early childhood educators. Educators perceive this theory as being restrictive in nature and presenting a mechanistic view of man. They believe that the theory is insufficient to explain man with his aspirations, will, freedom, dignity, and sense of purpose.

Others object to this theory because they believe it promotes conventional and conforming behavior and focuses on short-range, rather than long-range, goals and objectives. "While short-term change is easily observed and evaluated, there are seldom any attempts to study the long-term effects of these curricula. In the final analysis such programs may be based as much on ultimate faith as are many of the more traditional programs. The description of a program in psychological terminology and the great emphasis on the evaluation of effectiveness without analyzing ultimate goals may, in the long run, obscure the ultimate consequences of these programs" (Spodek, p. 49).

Gestalt Psychology

Gestalt psychologists see children as purposely interacting with their psychological environments. Gestalt psychologists think that a person's environment is psychological, consisting of what he makes of what is around him. Lewin, Koffka, Freud, and Combs could be called Gestalt psychologists. According to this theory, man has potential for good or bad and can choose. Man, as an active agent, can determine his own future. The Gestalt psychologists see learning as the ability to select and organize data, to discover relationships and general principles, and to form concepts and generalizations. Learning is perceived as being a nonmechanical development; it is believed to be a change in perception or a modification of life space.

"Life space" is a term used by Gestalt psychologists and is defined as containing the person and his total psychological and physical world where he is at that point in time. Life space is seen as a dynamic process of interacting experiences in which life spaces are changed to become more serviceable to the individual. In this process, learning is purposive, exploratory, imaginative, and individual.

Experience, to a behaviorist, is the conditioning process by which an organism either learns new responses or changes old ones as a result of stimuli. Gestalt psychologists use the term "experience" to describe a psychological event that involves a person's acting purposefully with anticipation of the possible consequences of his action. "Experience is interaction of a person and his perceived environment" (Bigge, p. 76).

Teachers who draw on the Gestalt theory are concerned with the problems of personal involvement and awareness. Their goal is to increase children's awareness of their environment, of themselves, and of their feelings. Children, according to Gestalt psychology, need to realize a need to learn something, and teachers attempt to arrange the teaching-learning environment so children will adopt new goals that are appropriate. Children are led to self-discipline and self-control as they assume responsibility for their own life.

Psychoanalytic Theory

Psychoanalytic thought has influenced, to a great degree, much of the early childhood curriculum. Through their work, Anna Freud, Lois Barclay Murphy, and others showed the importance of the emotional and affective life of the child in his education. The concerns of nursery school teachers for the feelings of children led to their general acceptance of the basic analytic beliefs.

Many kindergarten teachers had always accepted the role of play in the curriculum and psychoanalytic theory gave them a new rationale for play activities. Through play, the child could reveal his inner feelings, and he would be free to release his natural impulses so they would not be driven below the threshold of consciousness and leave dangerous residues. Teachers could find a rationale for many other practices of the nursery school in analytic thought. Allowing children to use fluid paints and materials in any way they desire, setting up the housekeeping corner, promoting dramatic play, and providing punching bags, clay, wood, or large muscle activities for the release of feelings, tensions, and hostility were supported by the analytic theory.

For many years preschool education was looked on as providing for the emotional and social needs of young children. Goals of preschool education were stated in terms of developing emotionally stable individuals. It was not until the 1960s that these goals were reexamined and concern for the intellectual as well as emotional aspects of children's growth were given equal consideration.

Cognitive Developmental Theories

New theories of learning greatly influenced the curriculum during the 1960s and have retained their influence in the 1970s. Many of the theories of cognition have been derived from those of Jean Piaget, who had been studying the cognitive functions of children for over thirty years, yet was relatively unknown in the United States until the early 1960s.

For Piaget, intellectual growth is a developmental process involving two interactive functions between an individual and his environment: (1) inward integration or organization called assimilation, and (2) outward adaptive coping called accommodation. Further development depends on these internal and external factors that equilibrate each other through the person's self-regulation and self-correction. Equilibrium is the point at which the processes of accommodation and assimilation achieve fruitful balance. The child's physical activities, environmental encounters, and social exchanges with peers are considered important to learning. However, many educators have designed curriculum, based on Piagetian thought, that ignores these factors.

According to Piaget and his colleagues, intelligence emerges from continuous transformations in the structure of logical thought. From birth to about eighteen to twenty-four months of age, the child is in the sensorimotor period of development. This period is followed by one of concrete operations which has three phases: a pre-conceptual period, two to four years of age; an intuitive phase, seven to eight years of age; and a third period of concrete operations. As the child repeatedly acts upon things and people, his thought becomes decentered from his perceptions and actions; and he can make logical deductions and generalizations.

Piaget's theories, coupled with the theoretical positions of Hunt and Bloom, have had major influences in the development of curriculum for young children. Because Piaget has not fully translated his theory into curriculum, there are wide differences among curricula based on his theory. The cognitively oriented curricula under the direction of Kamii, Weikart, and Lavatelli are examples of diverse curricula that are based on Piaget's work.

The place of Piaget's theory in curriculum development has been questioned. "Should it be used in such a direct manner for teaching? Or should it form part of the background understanding crucial for a teacher of young children?" (Weber, 1970, p. 86) As the work of Piaget is continually studied, educators should gain new insights that will answer questions that arise. Weber stated, "It is a difficult theory to deal with—one that will continuously make enormous demands upon the teacher—but one that will ultimately provide improved curricula for young children" (Weber, 1970, p. 87).

Child Growth and Development

"What is significant about child development across the decades is the trust that kindergarten leaders place in child development as the only basis for making curriculum decisions" (Weber, 1970, p. 177). At its worst, child development theories led teachers to quote standards for growth and wait for children to become ready, and at its best, child development theories caused the teacher to focus attention on the child, making the child the critical variable in the teaching-learning process.

Influenced by Darwin, Hall developed the theory that human development proceeds in a pattern of predetermined unfoldment. Hall believed that each stage of development was essential for behavior patterns to form. Gesell, one of Hall's students, capitalized on this idea and developed the maturational theory.

Gesell charted the normative behavioral development of children and presented his findings as standards for total growth, that is, intellectual, physical, social, and emotional growth. He believed that growth was a result of a more or less automatic unfoldment of behavior. Maturation became a powerful force in Gesell's theory and led to the hands-off approach in early childhood education. The idea that when a child reached sufficient maturity, learning, growth, and development would occur prevailed. There was no need for teaching since the child naturally passed through the ages and stages of growth. Curriculum for young children could be planned around these ages and stages.

Jersild defined the child development approach to the curriculum as "an effort to apply to the education of children the lessons learned from the study of children themselves. Research in child development has provided many findings with implications for education, but the child development approach does not represent merely a collection of facts; it represents a point of view, basic to this point of view is a spirit of inquiry and a desire to learn about the ways of children" (Jersild, p. 1).

Summary

Learning theories have had a strong influence on curriculum development in early childhood education. It is doubtful whether any one theory offers a sufficient base for curriculum development or decision making, especially in a pluralistic society. Each of the curriculum content areas presented in this text reflects a number of learning theories, and each reflects the social forces present during the past decade.

In general, two major types of curriculum, the behavioral and the developmental, are found. Both are based on the philosophy that children, to grow and develop and to become fully functioning members of a democratic society, require a preschool-primary experience that provides for the cognitive skill development as well as the affective, emotional, and social life of the child.

All of the theories mentioned in this chapter, with the exception of the behavioristic theory, could be termed "developmental" and can be cited as the basis for the traditional early childhood program and curriculum. The majority of programs and curricula for young children today are based, at least in part, on these theories. The child is a complete whole that cannot be separated into parts for cognitive, social, or emotional development, and the teacher can provide a curriculum that fosters this belief by allowing for large blocks of time to pursue a variety of activities. Social science, science, reading, leanguage, math, art, and music are integrated as a whole into a curriculum. Free play activities, in an enriched physical environment where the teacher can work with individual children in an emotionally rich, supportive warm social environment, typify the curriculum. Social skills are stressed, and great attention is given to the child's feelings.

The other major type of curriculum found today is the more structured, or behavioristic, curriculum. These programs, like the traditional early childhood programs, maintain that they foster all of the skills valued in society. However, they see children as separable into parts for the learning of academic, social, or physical skills. The child is believed to be an organism that learns and develops through specific stimuli-response bonds rather than from interaction with the environment. In these programs, the child's play is believed relatively unimportant and provides exercise rather than learning opportunities. Teachers work directly with children on teacher-directed tasks, and there are limited opportunities for children to interact socially or freely with the environment.

A knowledge of learning theories can be a helpful guide in analyzing curriculum development. Much of what is described as innovative in this text, when analyzed in view of learning theory, may be found to be an adaption of central ideas from the past. Curriculum innovations are meaningless without constant evaluation.

References

Bigge, L.M. *Learning Theories for Teachers*. New York: Harper & Row, Publishers, 1971.

Bloom, B.S. *Stability and Change in Human Characteristics*. New York: John Wiley & Sons, 1964.

Bruner J.E. *Toward a Theory of Instruction*. Cambridge: Harvard University Press, 1966.

Freud, A., and Damn, S. "An Exploration in Group Upbringing." *Psychoanalytic Study of the Child* 6(1951):127–68.

Gesell, A. *The First Five Years of Life*. New York: Harper & Row, Publishers, 1950.

Hall, S. *The Contents of Children's Minds*. Boston: Ginn and Co., 1920.

Hunt J.M. *Intelligence and Experience*. New York: The Ronald Press Co., 1961.

Jersild, A.T. *Child Development and the Curriculum*. New York: Teachers College Press, 1946.

Murphy, L.B. *The Widening World of Childhood*. New York: Basic Books, 1962.

Piaget, J. *The Origins of Intelligence in the Child*. New York: International University Press, 1952.

Spodek, B. "What Are the Sources of the Curriculum?" *Young Children* 26(1970):48–60.

Thorndike, E.L. *The Psychology of Learning*. New York: Teachers College Press, 1913.

Watson, J.B. *Behavior*. New York: Holt, Rinehart & Winston, 1965.

Weber, E. "The Function of Early Childhood Education." *Young Children* 28(1973):273.

Weber, E. *The Kindergarten: Its Encounter with Educational Thought in America*. New York: Teachers College Press, 1970.

CHAPTER TWO

LANGUAGE

NITA BARBOUR

School—a place to talk and someone to talk to.

In recent years linguists, educators, psychologists, sociologists, and biologists have given attention to the language development of the young child. Physical maturation, environment, and culture are elements being examined to determine the effect they have on language acquisition and development.

Language is probably the most important vehicle through which the child is educated and enculturated. Language is also a common vehicle through which teachers appraise the cognitive growth of the child. It would follow then that information gained from theory and research in language acquisition and development is vitally important for the early childhood educator. Therefore, it is not surprising that numerous programs in early childhood education with strong language components have been developed in the last decade. Many of these programs have been influenced by the differing theories and research of language acquisition and development.

As a result of the programs with research components, specific techniques have been found to facilitate specific language growth in some children; however, no one technique or program has been found to be superior to another. Knowledge gained from examining the various theories and techniques is indispensable to early childhood educators because as educators prepare curricula and programs to guide the child's growth, they need to be calculating the possible impact of these theories and techniques.

13

The manner in which the child acquires language is logically related to the specifics of linguistic information and the age at which he acquires certain linguistic patterns. Therefore, theories of language acquisition, research in the language growth of children, and the specifics of linguistic information have strong implications for curriculum designers and teachers as they seek ways to facilitate the language growth process in young children.

Theory

There are a number of theories of language acquisition and development. Among the theories described in this chapter are the nativist theory, the behaviorist theory, and the socialistic theory. According to the behaviorist theory, language acquisition basically results from a reinforcing environment. However, behaviorists do recognize that the infant must have minimal biological conditions before he can develop language. According to the nativist theory, on the other hand, language is fundamentally a process of internal growth and maturation. The nativists recognize, however, that the environment of an infant influences the particular style or mode that his language will take. The socialistic theory includes elements of the sociolinguistic and the interaction theories. The sociolinguistic theorists emphasize the social nature of language; that is, language growth depends upon the function and use of language in a particular setting. The interaction theorists realize the social nature of language but stress that language acquisition depends upon a type of interaction between the maturation process and the environmental factors of reinforcement. The differences in the various views center on the relative importance of either the environmental reinforcement or the maturation process in the child's acquisition of language.

The Nativist Theory

The nativist view is that man is "prewired" for language and that language development is a process of maturation. Lenneberg, from his research with normal and abnormal children, indicates that the onset of language is a regular and consistent event with children of all cultures and that other milestones in language development are attained in fixed sequence and at relatively constant ages (Lenneberg, 1967, pp. 125–26). He also notes that as children grow, there is a synchronization between their language development and their motor development (Lenneberg, 1971, p. 299). At the age of five months, for example, the baby starts to sit, using his hands for support. He also begins to reach out in front of himself for objects. At the same time his cooing sounds become a babbling of consonantal sounds. The child continues to develop, and by age two he starts to run and to climb down stairs with only one foot forward. His language development at this time is at the two-word phrase level (e.g., "me go," "car go," "daddy go") with a vocabulary of perhaps 300–400 words. He has at this time stopped babbling. Other stages showing relationships of language and motor development can be noted in Lenneberg's summary of the "Simultaneous Development of Language and Coordination" (Lenneberg, 1971, p. 299).

Support for this nativist theory has been gained by comparing research on Russian language acquisition with the research on American children. Slobin points out that early syntactic development in English and Russian looks very much alike. One similarity is that two-word sentences contain two classes (i.e., pivot and open class). In English, for example, "see daddy," "see car," "see baby," the "see" belongs to the pivot class and the "daddy," "car," "baby" belong to the open class. A second similarity Slobin noted is that the first three-word sentences a child uses are simple negations. English examples are "no more doggie," "no more car." Still another similarity is that in learning inflections, both Russian and English speaking children go through a stage of overgeneralization. For example, in English when the child first learns the plural form "boxes," he may use "car(z)es" even though he has previously used "cars" correctly. In English as the child learns the rule for inflecting past tense verb endings by adding "ed," he may inflect the irregular verbs (e.g., "satted," "risened," "swimmed," "runned") even though he may have previously used these verbs correctly. Although their grammatical rules differ, Russian children show the same tendency to overgeneralize when first learning a new rule.

Noam Chomsky, a renowned authority in the field of linguistics, approaches language development from a nativist view. He notes from his research that the child acquiring language often produces sentences or syntactical structures that are incorrect and not even heard in his environment. Chomsky explains that the child's ability to produce and understand these novel sentences is due to man's innate language capacity. Chomsky hypothesizes that man has a set of innate mechanisms which he calls the "language acquisition device" (Chomsky, 1965, pp. 30–33). This device purportedly provides the child with a preknowledge of language universals and the environment provides the model from which the child learns the unique rules of his own language.

This "language acquisition device" theory is further expanded by McNeill. He states that the language acquisition device is made up of two components: one is a preknowledge of language universals and the other is a set of procedures that enables the child to analyze the language he hears, so that from a small sample of language he is able to discern rules.

McNeill further explains that the child must learn not only those rules of "outer" structure (or those particular sentences a child hears) but also the basic structure from which all other sentence types may be generated. Language acquisition becomes a decoding-encoding process, and the child must acquire rules of transformation for this process. The basic structure is a kernel sentence or a simple-active-declarative sentence such as "There's a car," "The car broke," or "I see a car." These sentences can be transformed into negatives, interrogatives, or compound and complex sentences, such as "Is the car there?" "Where is the car?" "The car did not break," "The car is broken, but the truck is not broken."

Supporting McNeill's theory is an investigation of children's linguistic behavior conducted by Lois Bloom. In investigating the linguistic behavior related to the underlying meaning of language for the child, Bloom found that apparently even as early as single word utterances, children learn basic language structures (Bloom, 1970). It was shown that the grammatical function of a particular word in single utterance follows a particular developmental order; for example, the manner in which the child uses the word "mama" follows a developmental pattern. It is used first to mean "There is mama." Secondly, the child uses it to identify an object belonging to "mama," such as her hat. Next it is used in reference to an event in which "mama" was an agent (e.g., the child points to the door through which the mother has just passed and says "mama"). Finally, the word is used in reference to an event in which "mama" was an object (e.g., the child points to the cat's foot that just scratched his mother and says "mama").

The Behaviorist Theory

Behavioral theorists believe that significant others in the child's external environment model language behavior, reinforce the child's responses in various ways, and shape through reinforcing strategies these responses until they resemble the model. Since most behaviorists are reluctant to acknowledge the existence of internal behavior, they define language theories in terms of observable behavior in a stimulus and response situation.

With regard to language acquisition, the behaviorists presume that the only inborn mechanisms that a child possesses are those which enable him to make stimulus-response bonds and to articulate speech sounds. Skinner maintains that the only difference between other kinds of behavior and verbal behavior is that the latter is reinforced through the mediation of other persons (Skinner, pp. 21–28). Skinner describes several ways in which a speech pattern may arise. It may be learned as an *echoic* response that is in imitation of a heard stimulus, that the parent may reward if it is sufficiently similar to the stimuli. Language may be learned as a *mand*; that is, the child may make a random speech utterance that sounds enough like the current need of the child that the parent rewards the behavior by supplying the need. Language may also be acquired by a *tact;* that is, a child may make a particular verbal response while in the presence of or in contact with a given stimulus and is rewarded for doing so. According to Skinner, language is a collection of verbal operants acquired through stimulus-response-reward conditioning and emitted as a function of various sorts of stimuli.

Skinner's view of language development requires external reinforcement for the child to learn. Mowrer extends this theory to what he calls the "autism" theory (Mowrer, p. 80). The sounds a baby makes become secondary reinforcers, thus giving the child reinforcement when he babbles or later talks without need for constant adult reinforcement. Habituated to the use of language, the child recognizes its utility as a means of gaining control over his environment and in the process gains constant reinforcement.

Imitation, according to Peterson, is a necessary condition for language acquisition. The child who is unable to repeat or echo the sounds made by other persons does not develop speech adequately. He further maintains that if children are reinforced on some of their imitative responses, they will imitate other responses, thus generalizing imitative behavior and establishing an imitative repertoire. Peterson explains the child's expressing novel language behavior "as though he had learned rules" as a result of this generalized imitative repertoire. Thus, a child may act verbally as though he has learned a set of rules for language structure while his behavior may really be the product of the contingencies of reinforcement.

Experimenting with severely retarded children, Baer, Peterson, and Sherman supported the generalized reinforcement theory. The children in this study who could not learn any imitative behaviors were not able to learn to speak. On the other hand, the children who learned an imitative repertoire of nonverbal behaviors also learned to speak by imitating verbal sounds that were chained to the already learned imitative nonverbal behavior.

The habituation continues to occur, according to Staats, as the child grows older and learns the more complex structures of his language simply because parents and teachers continually reinforce the child by using language to control his environment. He points out that humans continually reward and punish each other through language and thereby influence each other's verbal behavior. Staats views language learning as a series of response chains which build on each other in a linear series of associations.

Braine maintains a more complicated behavioral pattern. He argues that language is not an accumulation of simple linear associations but is based upon learning the relative positions of the parts of larger constructions; thus language possesses a hierarchical structure determined by the location of a unit within the next larger unit. There are two levels of the hierarchy: within the sentence the units are primary phrases and within the primary phrase the ultimate units are morphemes.

In summarizing the nativist and behaviorist points of view, the nativists argue that instead of being taught, the child learns language rather effortlessly largely because of the innate capacities and maturational tendencies of the human being. In contrast, behaviorists assume that environmental factors in terms of reinforcement exert influence on language development. However, these two views converge and agree that language is acquired in a social context and that there are individual differences.

The Socialistic Theory

Piaget describes language as being the result of the biological interaction between man and his environment and an adaptation process that he calls *accommodation* and *assimilation*. He observed children passing through a number of developmental stages, each characterized by certain types of linguistic organization and behavior. Piaget maintains that language develops along with the child's capacity for logical thought, judgment, and reasoning and that it reflects these capacities. However, as the child's internal organization changes, he must interact with his environment and absorb these elements into his internal structure before the next stage takes place. Piaget bases his concept of the mind upon various hereditary elements specific to man. Thus, the linguistic developmental progress is caused by a combination of heredity, growth, and experience.

Vygotsky holds much the same view as Piaget with the exception that he does not view language and thought as being parts of the same process as does Piaget. According to Vygotsky, language and thought develop independently in early childhood and become interrelated as the child grows. Other Soviet psychologists' view of language relates more closely to this interaction process:

> Soviet psychologists have not been attracted by mechanistic and imitation-based, passive models of language acquisition. They see first language learning as a highly active, creative process, rivaling the productions of the poet and artist in subtlety and originality. (Slobin, 1966, p. 132)

Cultural Influences on Language

Other socialistic theorists view the social necessity of language as a fundamental factor in the development of specific patterns. In general, these theorists are not concerned with particular mechanisms of language acquisition. They argue that children learn language naturally and that their language is the particular language of the culture.

Sapir states that language is a guide to social reality and it is the manner in which the group views the real world. Language is primarily a cultural or social product. The regularity and formal development of language rests on considerations of both a biological and psychological nature.

Like Sapir, Whorf, who placed linguistic description in its sociocultural framework, emphasizes understanding language as a process through which the child learns to understand and function in his world. This view stresses the importance of the child's learning not only grammatical structures but also developing rules of linguistic codes for different social structures in which he must function.

Bernstein has done a major work in the sociolinguistic field. He has studied language samples from five subgroups in the culture and has described two general kinds of linguistic codes: restricted and elaborated. He maintains that the type of code used is related to social subgroups. The subculture is thus transmitted through these codes. Bernstein further explains that a relationship exists between family role systems and linguistic codes. The lower class uses a restricted code in which the family role system is positional or object oriented and present oriented. The middle class uses an elaborated code in which the family role system is personal or person oriented and future oriented (Bernstein, 1970).

In the lower-class code sentences tend to be short with many commands. There is a great emphasis on "do it because I said so," or a simple "shut up." A great emphasis is on the position or role in the family rather than on the value of the individual (e.g., "Kids don't talk," "Big boys don't cry.") Immediate reward and punishment is given so that expectancies are short, and it is hard to give up present gains or look for future rewards.

In the middle class code sentences tend to be long with greater complexity of structure than those of the lower-class code. Reasons are given for requests (e.g., "Please don't all talk at once." "I can't hear what anyone is saying."). The emphasis in the family is on the individual, each having status and rights (e.g., "I know it hurts when he hits you, but he didn't like it when you grabbed his toy."). Rewards and punishments are often delayed. Children's experiences are often organized toward future goals (e.g., "Let's practice the *s*, then you can learn to write your name on your paintings.").

Other researchers give support to Bernstein's code theory. Hess and Shipman; Greenberg and Formanch; Giebink and Marden; Osser, Wang, and Zaid; Plumer; and Jones in their studies found cultural differences in fluency and in grammatical usage.

There have been several studies of nonstandard English which confirm the sociolinguistic theories that there are differences in language along class structures. Baratz, Labov, and Stewart concur that there are grammatical and structural differences in dialects which reflect cultural influences. They point out that these grammatical differences are not inferior, only different. They refute the idea of verbal or cultural deprivation. These linguists assert that the nonstandard English dialect has a highly structured system.

Labov conducted research in south central Harlem and other ghetto areas between 1965-1968. He taped interviews with children eight to seventeen years old away from adult-dominated homes and schools. He analyzed the grammatical structure of the speech from these interviews. Labov compared the structural and functional differences betwen black, nonstandard English and standard English in the classroom. He found that the differences between black English and standard English are "extensions and restrictions of certain formal rules and different choices of redundant elements" (Labov, p. 185). For example, in standard English the progressive tense is expressed by using a form of *to be* and *ing* (e.g., I am going to the store) whereas in non-standard English the form of *to be* is dropped (e.g., I going to the store). In standard English the third person singular verb is formed by adding an *s* (e.g., he walks home). In nonstandard English, it is not obligatory (e.g., he walk home). The conditional in standard English is expressed by *whether* or *if* (e.g., I wondered if he asked to go). In black English the conditional is expressed by a change in word order (e.g., I wondered do he ask to go). Cazden states that

> views of cultural differences in child language are inadequate on two counts. First, they speak only of patterns of structural forms and ignore patterns of use in actual speech events. Second, they speak as if the child learns only one way to speak which is reflected in the same fashion and to the same extent at all times. (Cazden, 1970, p. 83)

There have been a few studies that indicate children do in fact speak differently in different situations. Fischer examined children's use of *ing* or *in* in various situations. He concluded that people adopt a particular variant primarily because it reveals how they feel about their status relative to another person.

Strandberg discovered that four- and five-year-old children talk more about a toy, or a silent film about that toy, then they do about a still photograph of it. However, there was no difference in either length or complexity of the responses. Strandberg and Griffith taught four- and five-year-old children to take pictures with a simple camera. The children were instructed to take specific pictures at first, but later they were allowed to take pictures of what they wished. When the children were asked to talk about the two sets of pictures, the investigator found that they talked more and used sentences of greater length and complexity when talking about the pictures they had selected themselves.

Cowan et al. presented elementary children of mixed socioeconomic status with ten colored pictures. They found that the length of the child's response and the effect of the particular picture upon him was positively correlated across age, sex, and socio-economic class. In her study Smith found that children eighteen to seventy months produced longer sentences in interaction with adults than at play with other children. Cowe recorded the conversation of kindergartners in nine activities; he concluded that the factors that seemed to influence the amount and complexity of speech were house-keeping, play and group discussion.

Luriia's study of retarded twins emphasizes the role that function plays in language development. Two retarded twins who used only gutterals to communicate with each other were separated. One received special language training. The other received only that language training that a relatively unstructured nursery school would provide. Although the twin that received special training made greater gains, it was evident from the study that special training played only a subsidiary role in language develop-ment, leaving the leading role to the need the twins felt for communicating and using language in a social setting.

Research in Language Acquisition and Development

Lenneberg summarized the studies that have been done on identifying the periods in which children progress from the babbling stage to using sentences. Most studies have concluded that between the ages of three and five the child acquires the basic structures of language. Lenneberg also noted that during this age period, the child is refining the complexity and the use of language. From the studies it appears that the first years of life are the most important in the child's language development.

Vocabulary

Vocabulary has been described as the raw material of language, and it has been studied by researchers for years. Johnson, Darley, and Spriestersbach stated:

> Children's knowledge of words has long served as an index of their language maturity. Investigators have based their judgments concerning progress in language development upon the age at which children first begin speaking intelligible words, the number of words they appear to know at any given age, and their ability to define use or indicate understanding of selected sample of words at various levels of difficulty. (Johnson, Darley, Spriestersbach, pp. 173–74)

Researchers sampled children's vocabulary in order to measure their language development. Summaries of the studies indicated that vocabulary increases rather slowly as the child first learns to say words, quite rapidly throughout the preschool period, and then more slowly until mental maturity is reached. (McCarthy has done an extensive review of this research.) Lenneberg related motor development to language development; he stated that the increase in vocabulary seemed to be related to the age of walking in individual children and that there seemed to be a plateau in language development during the mastery of a new skill (Lenneberg, 1967, p. 130). Welch's report showed that the greatest gains in vocabulary occur at eighteen to twenty-one months and again during the fourth year of life.

Smith, a pioneer investigator into the manner of vocabulary growth in young children, found that there is a marked increase in vocabulary of children as they increase in age. Additionally, McCarthy, utilizing a sampling of fifty consecutive statements, noted a marked increase with age in the mean number of total words as well as the mean number of different words. Templin studied both the vocabulary of recognition and the vocabulary of use in children of ages three to eight. Her findings indicated a continued, substantial increment with increase in age. Jersild and Ritzman, observing extensive examples of the conversations of a group of academically superior preschool children, reported a substantial increase in size of vocabulary with chronological and mental age.

Length of Response

Since Nice concluded that the mean length of response is an indication of the child's stage of linguistic development, the length of utterances has been used to determine differences in children's language development and maturity. McCarthy summarized the studies relating mean length of response to age differences. Though there are variations in the results reported and differences noted due to class distinctions, there appears to be a consistent increase in length of response due to age in all of the studies (McCarthy, 1954, pp. 520–23).

Some attempts have been made to correlate various measures of language development. Williams' study indicated a fairly high level of relationship between the measures of length and complexity of the sentences (McCarthy, 1954, pp. 520–23). The length of utterances has been found to correlate with specific grammatical features. Examples of these relationships are discussed in the Brown and Fraser and the Brown, Bellugi, and Cazden studies. They made careful analysis of the grammatical features of the language of the subjects and related the appearance of these specific features in the child's speech to the child's mean length of utterance. Brown and Fraser found that the initial use of the auxiliary verb in the child's speech is related to the length of utterance. In her study of negation, Bellugi discovered consistent relationships between length and complexity of utterances. She noted that the four stages of negation appeared in three children's languages whenever each child reached the same length of utterance. In her review of noun and verb inflections in the speech of three children, Cazden indicated that the complexity of these features and length do increase together but that it was not the same in all details for all children.

Complexity of Language

A review of the early studies on the complexity of language showed the appearance of the first sentence from the fifteenth to the twenty-sixth month in infants (McCarthy, 1954, p. 524). Nice outlined the stages in sentence formation from the single-word stage to complex sentences which appear as early as three years of age and which consist of approximately six to eight words (Nice, pp. 375–79). The complex sentences were characterized by an increased use of relational words and a fairly good mastery of inflections.

Braine investigated the earliest two-word combinations of normally developing children and he described the child's earliest grammar as containing pivot and open classes. Brown, Cazden, and Bellugi have attempted to describe the early grammatical stages of language acquisition. In stages I, II, and III children chiefly form simple sentences. There is little imbedding (e.g., The girl in the picture is pretty) or conjoining (e.g., The boy and the girl are going).

From the data gathered in the Brown, Bellugi, and Fraser studies, Cazden established stages of development for the acquisition of noun and verb inflections: plurals are formed before possessives; present progressives, before past and present indicatives. N. Chomsky developed a transformational grammar model which attempts to explain the grammatical differences that exist between the verbal behavior of the child and the underlying meaning. The model establishes base structures and kernel sentences from which all child sentences emerge. McNeill, using Brown's data and Chomsky's theory, proposed that the earliest grammatical structures a child forms are basic phrase structures or kernel sentences from which he eventually learns rules for transformations and novel utterances. Using these studies, Lee devised developmental type sentences to be used to determine the child's stage of language development. She classified sentences developmentally from two-word combinations to noun phrases, to constructions, to kernel sentences (i.e., simple-active-declarative), and finally to emerging transformations.

Researchers tend to concur that by age four children have mastered the basic rules of grammatical structures. This means that children can form simple, declarative sentences. However, researchers such as Menyuk, Chomsky, Fox, and Clay noted that children even as old as ten years are still developing syntactical maturity. For example, children at that age are still developing in their ability to form negative, passive, and imperative sentences. They are still learning the rules for inflecting various morphemes (e.g., box-boxes, ox-oxen, take-taken) (Menyuk, 1969). C. Chomsky cited in her study that children do not have a pronominal preference before 5.6 years of age. Researchers found considerable variation in the rate of acquisition in children's syntactical development, but they found that the order in which the children develop the particular structure is relatively stable.

Studies done in the 1930s, 1940s, and 1950s analyzed the complexity of sentence structure rather than specific linguistic features. However, these studies also indicated that children continue in language development until ten years of age.

Johnson, Darley, and Spriestersbach compiled the analyses from several of these studies and concluded the following:

1. The percentage of simple sentences increases with age.
2. As there is an increase in the use of compound and complex sentences, there is a decrease in the use of simple sentences.
3. Compound and complex sentences initially appear around two years of age and rise quickly until four to five years at which time they remain at about that level.
4. Elaborated sentences are rare in preschool children's speech and continue to increase until ten years of age.

Function of Language

Psychologists and sociologists are more interested in the function that language has for the child in his life than in the particular structural changes he makes. Attempts have been made to determine if the child's use of language changes as he grows and matures and what effect, if any, the environment has on this change.

From longitudinal observations of young children, Piaget classified child speech into egocentric and socialized speech (Piaget, 1955). In egocentric speech, the child talks only about himself, he never takes another person's point of view into account. In socialized speech, the child exchanges his thoughts with another. Piaget reported a higher percentage of egocentric speech in children between ages three to five and noted a definite socialization in the speech of children seven to eight years of age. McCarthy, Day, Smith, and Davis used techniques similar to those of Piaget but defined egocentric speech somewhat differently than he did; as a result, all four found less egocentric speech in children than did Piaget. It is important to note that each of these researchers did report that this type of speech decreases with age as socialized speech increases.

Piaget implied that adult speech is highly socialized and the child, as he matures, develops a more socialized function for speech. Vygotsky took a different view. From his research he postulated that the child's action language, describing, and defining what is happening, decreased when there was background noise, social isolation, or a lack of listeners (Vygotsky, p. 24). He maintained that the child first needs to express thoughts out loud but that as he grows older, he is able to internalize these thoughts. Thus, the egocentric speech of Piaget is viewed by Vygotsky as a precursor to verbal thought. The child's egocentric speech becomes internalized rather than changing to socialized speech.

Maturation and environment appear to play important roles in the development of the function of a child's language, according to Luriia. After he changed the environment of the retarded twins in his study, in three months time they showed a marked improvement in socialized speech and moved from speech connected with direct action to speech which could be used to plan an activity. McCarthy's summary indicated similar findings as to type of speech but related the change in function to age (McCarthy, 1954). She found that naming, a form of speech connected with direct action upon an object, is very prominent in the speech of eighteen-month-old children and decreases sharply with age. Corresponding to this decrease was an increase in the number of remarks associated with the situation and also in the child's ability to recall facts and relate them to present and future actions, a form of speech which can be used to plan an activity.

Children's questions have received considerable attention in the studies of Piaget, Davis, Smith and McCarthy. Most of the studies showed that preschool children's questions make up 10–15 percent of the conversation and that there is a slight, though irregular, increase with age (McCarthy, 1954). Davis and Piaget indicated that the form of the child's question changes as his age increases.

Piaget noted these changes in an earlier summary of children's questions. At a beginning stage up until about three years of age, the majority of the questions that children ask are in the form of "what" and "where" and relate simply to the name of objects or to the place of objects (e.g., What is that? Where is Mommy?). At the following stage, from two to three years of age, the majority of questions children ask are in the form of "why" questions and relate to seeking an explanation behind an action or event (e.g., Why are you ironing? Why is he jumping?). At a third stage, from three to seven years of age, there is a marked increase in questions using "how." These questions relate to seeking justification (e.g., How do you know the rain falls from the sky?).

Cazden, in an analysis of three children's speech, identified a sequential order for the questions these children learned to ask. The rate of development, however, varied considerably from child to child. Their questions developed from intonation questions to "yes-no" type questions to "what" questions. The function of questions also changed with age; children first used them to ask for names of objects, then for casual inquiry, and finally for justification.

Three children, in a study by Bloom, developed negation in a sequential order; first they expressed it as nonexistence, next as rejection, and finally as denial. Again the rate of acquisition varied among the three children but the order remained constant.

Effect of Classroom Climate on Language Development

In recent years a large number of early childhood education programs have been developed with strong language components. These programs have philosophies that range from behaviorist learning theory to Gestalt learning theory. A middle range philosophy attempts to use some of the behavioristic components but employs Piagetian elements or the richly responsive environments recommended in Montessori programs. Programs have been set up with clearly defined goals based on learning theory and research in the language development and cognitive growth of young children.

Many early childhood language programs adhere to the behaviorist theory. These programs imply that training procedures can affect language behavior. The teacher is the model and the initiator for language development. The child imitates, responds, and is reinforced for his response.

Behavioristic models, such as those developed by Bereiter and Englemann, Bushnell, and Risley, picture language development as being extremely important for the intellectual development of the child. In these programs language patterns are presented to the child in a structured setting and then these patterns are reinforced in a stimulus-response model. In general, results of the research on these model programs indicate that children who have participated in these programs for a year show increases in IQ and in certain areas of language usage. In the original research by Bereiter and Englemann fifteen children from culturally disadvantaged homes were selected. These children were taught structured lessons of fifteen to twenty minutes in duration in language, reading, and arithmetic. At the end of the year the children's scores on the Illinois Test of Psycholinguistic Abilities rose from one to one and one-half years below average to approximately average scores. The mean score on the Stanford-Binet IQ Test rose from the low 90s to slightly over 100. Children, after the preschool year, scored at the beginning first-grade level in reading and at the beginning second-grade level in arithmetic.

Hart and Risley and Reynolds and Risley studied the spontaneous speech of four and one-half-year-old culturally disadvantaged children over a three-year period. In the studies access to preschool materials during free playtime was available to the children contingent upon their use of noun-adjective-noun combinations and compound sentences. The control group of children was taught similar language skills in a group setting. At the end of the study the control group showed increases in language skills only in the group setting and not in its spontaneous language during free play. The experimental group showed significant increases in its use of nouns, adjective noun combinations, and compound sentences in its spontaneous language during free play.

In the cognitive-discovery methods language is viewed as an adjunct and help in developing logic and cognitive skills. The teacher's role is to model certain language and syntactical structures for the children; he should also elicit these structures, or an approximation of them, from the children. The environment of the classroom (including the teacher) must be responsive to the child; thus materials and equipment must be self-teaching. As the child acts upon his environment, the teacher provides the language model. Blank and Solomon, Karnes, Weikart, Lavatelli, Klaus and Gray, and Montessori describe these programs in their writings. The research indicated that children involved in these programs show some language growth and IQ gains.

Karnes, Zehrbach, and Teska gathered longitudinal data on preschool intervention programs designed to improve children's cognitive skills. Data were collected on sixty four-year-old children assigned to one of four classes; two classes were based upon a

Karnes model and two classes were based upon a traditional curriculum. The Karnes' program is a highly structured, highly specified program. All the program's activities are designed to improve specific deficits of disadvantaged children and provide motivation for successful learning. Children, in groups of five, are given specific instructions in the areas of their weaknesses. In the first year, the Karnes' program was more effective in promoting cognitive development, as reflected by the pupils' scores on the Stanford-Binet test. After three years, however, the differential effects of the program were not statistically significant.

Weikart's Perry School Project in Ypsilanti, Michigan was a two-year daily program for children in which weekly visits to the homes were conducted to involve parents in the educative process. The curriculum was derived mainly from Piagetian theory and focused on cognitive objectives. The program assumed that children learn by physically interacting with their environment. The children were exposed to a large variety of materials. As they physically interacted with these materials, the teacher explained to them what they were experiencing and encouraged the children to explain their actions. During the five years of the project, fifty-eight children attended the experimental program and sixty-five who did not attend preschool served as a control group (Weikart, Deloria, Lawson, 1974). Children in the experimental group showed significant improvement in cognitive and language growth, as measured by their scores on the Stanford-Binet, the Peabody Picture Vocabulary Test, and the Illinois Test of Psycholinguistic Abilities. This significant improvement continued into the second grade. At this point the significant differences between the two groups declined.

Sixty-one children in the Klaus and Gray Early Training Project for Disadvantaged Children were randomly assigned to one of three groups. Two groups of children were placed in summer intervention programs for four hours one day a week; they received follow-up weekly home visits by a trained home visitor when regular school was in session. The third group served as a control group which had no intervention. The children in the experimental group showed significant gains over the control group on the Stanford-Binet, the Peabody Picture Vocabulary Test, and the Illinois Test of Psycholinguistic Abilities.

A traditional nursery school based on Gestalt learning theory can be described as a child-centered program. In such a program, language is seen as developing along with social and physical development. In this type of school teachers tend to explain a great deal to children, question them, and extend their language usage rather than model language for the child. Children build and develop vocabulary and grammar as they are actively involved in play and extended experiences such as trips. The Tucson Educational Model (Hughes, Wetzel and Henderson, 1968), The British Infant School Model (Rogers, 1971), the Bank Street Model (Minuchin and Biber, 1968) and the Educational Developmental Model (Armington, 1968) are four examples of this type of program.

Comparison of Language Growth in Model Programs

Further research on the preceding and similar models has been done that contrasts one type of program with another. Day conducted a study contrasting the effects of language instruction in a Bereiter-Englemann program with that in a traditional program. Contrary to expected results, children in the Bereiter-Englemann program indicated no significant differences in their use of language in a test situation after the program.

Karnes did a three-year longitudinal study that contrasted the effect of five pre-school interventions: traditional, community integrated, Montessori, ameliorative (Karnes), and direct-verbal (Bereiter-Englemann) (Karnes, 1972). On the subtests of the Illinois Test of Psycholinguistic Ability, those children who showed the greatest deficit, when placed in the ameliorative group, showed the greatest gains in the first year of the program. There were no differences among the groups on the Peabody-Picture Vocabulary Test. At the end of kindergarten, the direct-verbal group was the only one that demonstrated a significant increase in language scores. However, at the end of the first grade there were no significant differences in the language scores for the groups.

Weikart compared three preschool curricula: the unit-based (traditional), the cognitively oriented (Weikart), and the language training (Bereiter-Englemann) (Weikart, 1970). He found no significant differences in language growth among the children in these programs. As all programs had high teacher involvement and a strong teacher belief in the philosophy of the program, Weikart concluded that program approach was not as important as teacher input. The United States Office of Education supported a large study to determine the effect of model type on child learning. The first reports indicated that the model type played no significant role in the child's language growth (Stanford Research Institute, 1971).

Specific Instruction and Language Growth

Numerous studies have been conducted to determine if specific language instruction has an effect upon child language growth. Some instruction has been based on materials in learning kits, such as the Peabody Language Development Kit. Jones instructed twenty-six Head Start children for fifty-six lessons using the Peabody Language Development Kit and found that their language abilities as tested on the Illinois Test of Psycholinguistic Abilities increased significantly. Mitchell did a similar study on Head Start children but provided only twenty-five treatment sessions. Her subjects increased in language development; however, these increases were not significant. Milligan used middle-class kindergarten children in a treatment period of twenty-four weeks. He found that students when given instruction in the Peabody Language Development Kit improved in their abilities to relate to spoken words through analysis and to express ideas in spoken words.

Other specific language instruction has been based on training children in specific ways or for a specific linguistic competence. Hart and Risley discovered that they could effectively increase children's use of adjectives in spontaneous speech by making preschool materials available to them contingent upon their use of the color's name. Reynolds and Risley greatly increased the verbalization of a black child who had a low frequency of talking by making his access to preschool materials and to adult social reinforcement contingent upon his verbalizations.

An early study by Dawe provided a special language training program for preschool and kindergarten children in an orphanage. A teacher worked with one or two children at a time reading stories to them, taking them on walks, and discussing events, words, or concepts with them. After approximately fifty hours of special training, this group of children showed significant gains in mean length of response and in complexity of sentences when compared with a matched group of children from the orphanage. Blank and Solomon and Southern devised specialized language programs through tutoring sessions. Blank and Solomon's tutored children made significant IQ gains, but Southern's tutored children made gains only on the verbal encoding task of the Illinois Test of Psycholinguistic Abilities.

Several studies have been done in which children were taught specific grammatical structures in formal lessons. In Yonemura's study, the children showed gains in grammatical usage when the utterances were taken from formal situations but they showed gains in the free-play situation only when using "what" in forming questions. Lindquist, Elardo, and Stern successfully taught special grammatical structures in short intensive lessons.

In their study, Cullinan, Jaggar, and Strickland used a literature-based oral language program to increase the ability of black children in kindergarten and grades one, two, and three to use standard English. The kindergarten children in the study showed significant gains in their increased use of the following standard English forms:

1. The presence of the copula (e.g., he *is* talking).
2. The use of *s* with the third person verb (e.g., he wears a tie).
3. The use of *s* in possessives (e.g., Tom's cousin).
4. The use of *s* in the plural (e.g., fifty cents).
5. The use of a single negation (e.g., he doesn't want *any*).
6. The use of *if* in its conditional (e.g., I don't care *if* he comes).

The manner in which the teacher talks to the children has been found to relate to certain language growth patterns in children. Levy, using the results of Head Start children on the Illinois Test for Psycholinguistic Abilities, analyzed the effect of teacher behavior on children's language development. Teachers who stressed response-reinforcement, modeling, and social-emotional relationships generally had students who scored high on all the Illinois Test of Psycholinguistic Abilities (ITPA) subtests except for the Verbal Automatic Subtest.

Barbour studied the relationship between teacher facilitative/directive verbal behavior and language development. She found no relationship between the child's vocabulary and function of language and the type of teacher verbal behavior. However, the teacher directive verbal behavior was significantly related to growth in the child's use of complex sentences.

Cazden postulated that the individual differences in the amount of talking young children do pose a specific problem for teachers because research indicates that adults tend to talk more to children who talk back. The teacher, because of his need for reinforcement, may unwittingly magnify the natural differences in the amount of verbalization children do. Talkers who are reinforced for talking by someone they like and trust will talk even more; nontalkers may be even less inclined to talk if they are ignored. Cazden suggested that teachers should be exceedingly careful as to how they distribute their attention.

Analyses of conversations between adults and children have indicated that neither correction of immature speech forms nor reinforcement of mature forms occurs with sufficient frequency to be a potent force in developing children's language. Cazden suggested that parents and teachers, busy and occupied with other things, do not focus attention on the child's acquisition of syntax. She concludes, "The child is offered a cafeteria, not a carefully prescribed diet. And seemingly impelled from within, he participates in the give and take of conversation with adults and other children as best he can from the very beginning, and in the process takes what he needs to construct his own language system" (Cazden et al. 1971, p. 68).

Many of the early intervention programs teach mothers how to instruct their children. In the Juniper Garden Parent-Teacher Cooperative Preschool in Kansas, the mothers were taught strategies for verbally interacting with their children. The mothers were also taught to increase the amount of praise they used with their children. The children in the study increased their scores on the Peabody Picture Vocabulary Test by an average of eighteen points (Risley).

In Levenstein's intervention programs, home visitors brought toys into children's homes and demonstrated to the mothers how to use these toys in a verbal interaction with their children. The mothers were made aware of the fact that they were the prime educators of their children. Children were pre- and posttested on the Cattell or Stanford-Binet Intelligence Scale and the Peabody Picture Vocabulary Test. After seven months of intervention, the experimental children showed a mean IQ gain of 17 points on the Cattell and Stanford-Binet and a gain of 12.2 IQ points on a Peabody Picture Vocabulary Test while the control group showed a mean IQ gain of 1 point on the Cattell and Stanford-Binet and a loss of 4 points on a Peabody Picture Vocabulary Test.

Karnes and her colleagues designed a program for instructing mothers of four-year-old children (Karnes, 1968). Mothers living in an economically depressed neighborhood attended weekly two-hour instructional meetings where they became involved in developing materials and learning strategies for using materials with their children. In addition to these meetings, teachers visited in the homes every two weeks to further demonstrate teaching techniques. At the end of twelve weeks, the children showed a significant IQ gain of seven points as compared to no difference from a control group of carefully matched children.

In an attempt to provide an enrichment program for school-age children who had completed Weikart's preschool program, a supplementary kindergarten intervention program was established (Radin). A home counselor visited the parents while the child was in school and suggested activities that paralleled the child's activities at school that the mothers could carry out with the child. The activities were strongly cognitive in nature, often focusing on Piagetian classification skills and seriation skills. Strong emphasis was given to helping the mother see herself as a prime resource in helping to educate her child. At the end of the school year, the children whose mothers participated in the program showed an IQ gain of fourteen points on the Stanford-Binet, which was a significantly larger gain than the control children who only attended kindergarten.

In general, teaching for a specific language change has an effect, at least temporarily, on the child's learning the specific structure. The teacher's talk and parent's talk can influence the children's talk. This influence is especially apparent when the child is guided in activities that are structured to develop language and thought. The results of a specific program type on children's language learning are less clear.

Curriculum Development: Design and Application

Behaviorist Theory and Curriculum

Many curriculum designs have been influenced by the theories of the behaviorists. In these programs, the child is viewed as a reactive organism, one whose characteristics are largely a product of environmental influences. Learning takes place when the child takes part in an activity with reinforcement (Bigge).

Bereiter and Englemann designed a total program, part of which consists of language development, on the behaviorist theory. The well-known program was designed for the economically disadvantaged because it is believed that the disadvantaged child must disregard his own language and learn standard English in order to survive in today's schools.

In this program, lessons in language development are carefully prestructured for the exact language behavior of the child. Behavioral outcome and objectives are carefully broken down to specific language behavior patterns. Teachers in this program use immediate reinforcement in the form of praise or teacher approval for correct answers. Tokens or other external reinforcers may be used if praise or teacher approval is felt to be insufficient.

Children are grouped, according to ability, in small groups and taught language lessons. The teacher directs the learning, and the child responds to his directions. Language is the means for cognitive development in this type of program, and social interaction is assumed to develop naturally without particular classroom attention.

Language lessons proceed in complexity from simple vocabulary development in complete sentences to correct statements of causal relationships. Rules of behavior are established so children will understand clearly the way they are expected to respond. For example, after certain signals are given by the teacher, the children will respond in unison. Other signals given by the teacher will indicate to the children that they are to respond individually. The children must always respond loud and clear. "Say it right" is a common rejoinder of the teacher.

A great deal of stress is placed not only on speaking correctly but also on listening carefully. To enhance listening skills, the teacher, after the children have learned a correct pattern, will play the "fooler game." The teacher will use an incorrect pattern in an attempt to "catch the student." The children learn not only the response but take over as the teacher and learn the questions as well. Examples of the patterns that the child learns are:

Teacher: This a car. (Child repeats the pattern.)
          This is not a car. (Child repeats the pattern.)
Teacher: Is this a car? (Holding up a car)
Child: Yes, this is a car.
Teacher: Is this a car? (Holding a truck)
Child: No, this is not a car.
Teacher: This is a vehicle. (Child repeats the pattern.)
          (Several objects that are vehicles are shown and this pattern repeated.)

Teacher: This fork is not a vehicle. (Child repeats the pattern.)
           (Several objects that are not vehicles are shown and this pattern repeated.)
Teacher: Is this car a vehicle?
Child: Yes, this car is a vehicle.
Teacher: Is this fork a vehicle?
Child: No, this fork is not a vehicle.

After practicing the patterns, the teacher gives a definition for a vehicle. He would say, "A vehicle has wheels, and you can ride in it or on it." If the children make a mistake and respond that a kite is a vehicle, then the teacher asks for the definition of a vehicle. He would then use the following practice:

Teacher: Does a kite have wheels?
Child: No.
Teacher: Do you ride in or on a kite?
Child: No.
Teacher: Is this kite a vehicle?
Child: No, this kite is not a vehicle.

These language skills of listening carefully and speaking correctly continue as the children have lessons in writing and reading.

Interactionist Theory and Curriculum

The influence of elements of the interactionist theories are found in some programs. These curricula, such as those designed by Weikart, Lavatelli, Montessori, Klaus, and Gray have been designed basically to stress the intellectual, cognitive, or thinking skills of the child. According to this theory, as the child matures biologically, he needs to manipulate and act upon his environment for new learning to occur. Since developmental growth takes place for different children at different times, designers of the curricula provide carefully sequenced, individualized, and self-pacing materials. The child may use these materials at his own skill level and proceed at his own pace. Children usually work alone or in small, self-selected groups, though there is a total planning and evaluation time.

In these programs, language learning is viewed as following the cognitive learning process. It is assumed that the preschool child already has the basic language structures and he must be taught how to use these structures as a function for intellectual growth. Weikart designed a "cognitively oriented program," having as its rationale the interactive learning theory (Weikart, 1971). In this program, direct language teaching is not done, and the child's verbal usage is seen as an indication that he has learned a concept. Language is the tool by which the child is led from motoric operations to verbal operations. The child must first be able to act on the teacher's instructions or to act on his environment before he can give a verbal response or explanation; thus language development as cognitive development goes through two periods. One is the motoric period in which the child interacts with his environment and the teacher either acts as a verbal instigator for this interaction or as a verbal interpreter. The other period is the verbal period in which the child uses language to interpret, evaluate, and integrate his own experiences and to communicate to his peers and adults; thus language becomes a function for social interaction.

In the verbal period, specific language lessons are not structured. However, the teacher teaches language through modeling, expanding, and questioning as the child interacts with his environment.

Example I:

> The teacher says, "Put your toy in your cubbie, John." John does not respond. The teacher takes John to the area, points out John's cubbie, and repeats the command. If John still does not respond, the teacher gently puts the toy in the cubbie and repeats the command; thus John would go through the motoric action of the teacher's verbalization.

Example II:

> The teacher says, "Bring me the hammer, John." The child looks bewildered. The teacher then takes the child to where the hammer is kept, gives the hammer to the child, and says, "This is a hammer." He shows the child at least one of its uses by saying, "You can put a nail in a piece of wood with a hammer. Can you tell me what this is now, John?" The child may or may not respond. Later, the teacher follows up to check that the child remembers the word when he hears it and uses it correctly.

The teacher expands language when the child gives incomplete or incorrect linguistic structures. An example follows:

> Child (As he/she is playing with the dolls): Baby sleep now.
> Teacher: Yes, the baby is sleeping now, isn't she?

The teacher uses questions to stimulate language development in the children. An example follows:

> Teacher: What will happen if we talk too loudly while the baby is sleeping? What will you do when the baby wakes?

The teacher plans specific concept lessons at both the motoric and verbal levels of operations. Thus, a lesson on seriation would begin with the children manipulating big objects and small objects. The teacher verbalizes the relationships and then the children begin to use the correct terms with the correct objects (Weikart, Rogers, Adcock, and McClelland).

Lavatelli developed a curriculum, based on Piagetian or interactionist philosophy, in which language development was also a part of the cognitive development. She suggested a systematic approach to the development of syntactical structures that was based on research in the field of developmental psycholinguistics. The procedure is a modeling-eliciting technique done both in structured lessons and during the time that children are engaged in spontaneous, self-directed activities. The following is an example of this curriculum:

In the structured lessons, the teacher is teaching the concept of high and low. The teacher models, "This chair is high," and "This chair is low." She elicits a response from the child by saying, "Tell me about the chair." If the child responds, "This chair is big," the teacher replies, "Yes, good, this chair is big, and it is also high." If the child does not respond, the teacher does not pressure him but waits until another time to check whether the concept of high was learned.

In spontaneous situations, the child's access to the use of desired materials could be contingent upon his use of specific vocabulary, a natural syntactical structure, or a social use of the language. As a child's language facility increases his access to the desired object rests on more complex language usage. In the Demonstration and Research Center for Early Education (DARCEE) program Klaus and Gray used the following technique:

Tricycles are available for children's outdoor play, but there are not enough for every child to have one. In the beginning of the year, a child would only have to be able to say "tricycle" to be permitted to have one. Later he would have to ask for a particular one: a red tricycle, the big tricycle, the tricycle with the green handlebars, etc. Later he would have to ask another child for a turn, thus learning that language is used to socially interact with another child. Then later the child would learn the traffic rules for the tricycle, and his continued use of the tricycle would be contingent upon his stating the rules and acting in accordance with them.

Some years ago, Montessori also recommended a modeling-eliciting technique in language development. She recommended that teachers use a simple but very direct approach to language instruction, using three stages of presentation: naming, recognition, and presentation. For example, as the child is working with musical bells, the teacher isolates the bells, the loudest tone and the softest tone. As she hits the bell she states, "This is soft," or "This is loud." In the second stage the teacher checks the child's understanding by asking him to hit the soft tone or to hit the loud tone. In the third stage the teacher checks the child's ability to say the word by hitting the bell and asking, "What tone is this?" The child receives reinforcement for using language by either teacher approval or use of desired object.

Cullinan, Jaggar, and Strickland suggested a language expansion technique using children's literature as the medium for a language development program. Children's books provide standard English patterns in meaningful contexts. The teacher reads stories to the children, and then they practice the patterns in a variety of ways.

Structured activities are provided by having the children repeat in unison the expressions and phrases said by the story characters, having children role play the parts of the characters, playing a game in which the children are asked to parrot exactly certain sentences from the text. The teacher would use structured activities to model certain syntactical structures that children are using incorrectly or are not using. She might model, for example, the plurals of words or the negation of "He doesn't see *any* houses."

Creative activities are provided by the teacher asking open-ended questions about the story and the children retelling the story, sometimes extending it or adding other sequels or endings, and the children dramatizing the story through puppetry or creative dramatics.

Nativist Theory and Curriculum

Nativist theories have influenced some language programs. Since language learning is an important part of the child's total development, language plays an important part in the curriculum of these programs. These programs are often referred to as the "traditional nursery school." The Bank Street model is one example of formalizing this approach (Biber, Shapiro, and Wickers). In programs of this type, the teacher interacts with the child as he experiences the life of the classroom and interprets the experiences he brings with him into the classroom. If the child does not have the vocabulary to name an object, the teacher provides him with the label. His role is to talk with the child, elicit his responses and perceptions of events, provide labels or models if necessary, extend his thinking by posing problems, and listen with care and interest to the child's responses.

An everyday occurrence such as arrival time, a special event such as a trip, or an occasional event such as cooking in the classroom are all used by the teacher in such a program to foster vocabulary development, increase syntactical development, and promote functional use of the language.

A child may arrive at school with a toy stethoscope that he received for his birthday. The teacher comments on it and asks if he knows what it is called. He supplies the word and shares it with a few children who may be interested. She might then ask the child, "How do you use it?" or "What do you hear?" modeling question forms. As the children play, two of them might start to fight over the stethoscope. The teacher might then suggest, "Tell him you would like to play with the stethoscope," or "Tell him you don't feel like sharing right now." She would thus be helping the children to understand that we use language to tell other people what we want and how we feel.

The teacher provides equipment or arranges the classroom in order to stimulate children to use language in a social context. In these programs, language development is not just a vehicle for cognitive development but an integrated part of the child's total development. Toy telephones may stimulate children to engage in two-way conversations. Certain arrangements in the housekeeping area can entice small groups of children to role play and interact. Large blocks, boxes, and planks can be arranged so that one child needs to ask another to help him to work, build, or move equipment. Games that require children to verbally interact should be available. Puppets and dress-up clothes that encourage children to role play or to participate in creative dramatics provide opportunities for language growth and development.

Storybooks are used to increase a child's vocabulary and use of language. Children are encouraged to answer questions about the story, to relate the story to their own experiences, to retell the story, to anticipate events in the story, and to fill in missing words as the teacher reads a familiar story.

In a day-care center or nursery school, children spend much time talking to one another. Suggestions for maximizing the value of talk among children come from sociolinguistic analyses of children's spontaneous speech. These studies indicate that children spend a great deal of time speaking for self-aggrandizement or raising their own status. Multi-age grouping, in which younger children are grouped with older ones, might encourage more of this type of speech. Materials for dramatization such as puppets, animals, or robots would provide the younger child with opportunities to express verbally his sense of superior status.

These studies also indicate that children utilize speech for explanations. Children's learning environments should be equipped with objects of considerable complexity. Old clocks, radios, vacuum cleaners, or television sets can be taken apart and put together while children explain what they are doing. The woodworking bench should have materials that can be used by children to make things that require children to explain what they are doing. Children can be taught to use most of the media hardware in a classroom, such as the tape recorder, the filmstrip machines, the record players, the film projectors; they can then teach other children to use the equipment, thus enhancing their receptive and oral language of explanation.

A third type of language that children use spontaneously in group settings is for aesthetic pleasure. Teachers can say and sing nursery rhymes, poems, ditties, and songs with children as they play. "One, two, buckle my shoe" can be chanted as children put on their shoes or as they count. Nursery rhymes such as "Rain, rain go away/ Come again some other day" or "The north wind doth blow/And we should have snow/And what will poor Robin do then" introduce a new charm to the weather. Lines from poems such as "Oh, how I love to go up in the swing/Up in the air so blue" by Robert Louis Stevenson, "Halfway down the stairs/Is a stair/Where I sit" by A. A. Milne, and "It was laughing time and the tall Giraffe/Lifted his head and began to laugh" by William Jay Smith can be recited with children as they play and laugh in the classroom. Children can add their own rhymes. Musical instruments that the children can use themselves encourage children to use language in a rhythmic way. These nursery rhymes, poems, ditties, and songs train the child's ear, challenge his imagination, and introduce him to the aesthetic quality of the English language.

Conclusions

Curricula have been designed on the behaviorist, the interactionist, and the nativist theories of language development. In developing techniques for these programs, some of the designers have relied on the research that indicates the stages of language development. However, whatever the technique or philosophical base, all programs stress the importance of language development as a base for important learning to take place in other curriculum areas. An increase in vocabulary, syntactical complexity, and functional use of language are certainly important in helping children develop reading, writing, math, science, music, and art skills. Research has not proven that any one technique or method is superior to another. It does point out that with careful planning, diligence, and interest, teachers and parents can and do enhance the language development of the young child.

References

Armington, D. "The ECD Head Start Approach." ERIC Reference PS 003–877, September, 1968.

Baer, D.; Peterson, R.; and Sherman, J. "The Development of Imitation by Reinforcing Behavioral Similarity to a Model." *Journal of Experimental Analysis of Behavior* 10(1967): 405–16.

Barbour, N.H. "Relationship of Change in Child Language to Nursery School Climate as Determined by Teacher Verbal Behavior." Ph.D. dissertation. University of Maryland, 1973.

Baratz, J. "Language and Cognitive Assessment of Negro Children: Assumptions and Research Needs." Unpublished manuscript. San Francisco: Center for Applied Linguistics, 1968.

Baratz, J. and Pavich, E. "Grammatical Construction in the Language of the Negro Preschool Child." Paper presented at the National Meeting of the American Speech and Hearing Association, 1967.

Bereiter, C. and Englemann, S. *Teaching Disadvantaged Children in the Preschool.* Englewood Cliffs, N.J.: Prentice-Hall, 1966.

Bernstein, B. "Social Class Linguistic Codes and Grammatical Elements." *Language and Speech* 5(1962):221–40.

———. "A Sociolinguistic Approach to Socialization with Some Reference of Educability." In *Language and Poverty: Perspectives on a Theme*, edited by F. Williams. Chicago: Markham Publishing Co., 1970.

Biber, B.; Shapiro, E.; and Wickens, D. *Promoting Cognitive Growth: A Developmental Interaction Point of View*. Washington, D.C.: Publications Department, National Association for the Education of Young Children, 1971.

Bigge, M.L. *Learning Theories for Teachers*. New York: Harper & Row, Publishers, 1964.

Blank, M. and Solomon, F. "A Tutorial Program to Develop Abstract Thinking in Socially Disadvantaged Preschool Children." *Child Development* 39(1968):379–89.

Bloom, L. "Language Development: Form and Function in Emerging Grammars." Unpublished doctoral dissertation. Columbia University, 1968.

———. "Semantic Features in Language Acquisition." Paper presented at the Conference on Research in the Language of the Mentally Retarded at the Bureau of Child Research. University of Kansas, February, 1970.

Braine, M. "On Learning the Grammatical Order of Words." *Psychological Review* 70(1963): 345–48.

Brown, R., and Fraser, C. "The Aquisition of Syntax." In *The Aquisition of Language*, edited by J.R. Hill. *A Monograph of the Society for Research in Child Development* 29:43–79. Lafayette, Ind.: Child Development Publication, 1964.

Brown, R.; Cazden, C.; and Bellugi, U. "The Child's Grammar from I to III." *The 1967 Minnesota Symposium on Child Psychology*. Minneapolis: University of Minnesota Press, 1969.

Bushnell, D.; Worbel, P.; and Michaelis, M. "Applying Group Contingencies to the Classroom Study Behavior of Preschool Children." *Journal of Applied Behavior Analysis* 1(1968):55–61.

Cazden. C. "The Acquisition of Noun and Verb Inflections." *Child Development* 39(1968): 433–48.

———. *Child Language and Education*. New York: Holt, Rinehart & Winston, 1972.

———. "Children's Questions: Their Forms, Function and Role in Education." *Young Children* 25(1970):202–20.

———. "The Neglected Situation in Child Language Research and Education." In *Language and Poverty: Perspectives on a Theme*, edited by F. Williams. Chicago: Markham Publishing Co., 1970.

Cazden, C.; Baratz, J.; Labov, W.; and Palmer, F. "Language Development in Day-Care Programs." In *Day Care: Resources for Decisions*, edited by E.H. Grotberg. Washington, D.C.: Office of Economic Opportunity, 1971.

Chomsky, C. *The Acquisition of Syntax in Children From 5 to 10*. MIT Research Monographs LVII. Cambridge: M.I.T. Press, 1970.

Chomsky, N. *Aspects of the Theory of Syntax*. Cambridge: M.I.T. Press, 1965.

Cowan, P.A. et al. "Mean Length of Spoken Response as a Function of Stimulus, Experimenter and Subject." *Child Development* 38(1967):191–203.

Cowe, E. "A Study of Kindergarten Activities for Language Development." Unpublished doctoral dissertation. Columbia University, 1967.

Cullinan, B.; Jaggar, A.; and Strickland, D. "Language Expansion for Black Children in the Primary Grades." *Young Children* 29(1974):98–114.

Davis E. "The Form and Function of Children's Questions." *Child Development* 3(1932):57–74.

Dawe, H. "A Study of the Effect of an Educational Program upon Language Development and Related Mental Functions in Young Children." *Journal of Experimental Education* 11(1942):200–209.

Day, D.E. "The Effects of Different Language Instruction on the Use of Attributes by Pre-kindergarten Disadvantaged Children." Paper presented at American Educational Research Association. Chicago, February, 1968.

Elardo, R. "The Experimental Facilitation of Children's Comprehension and Production of Four Syntactic Structures." Paper presented at AERA. New York, February, 1971.

Englemann, S. *Preventing Failure in the Primary Grades*. Chicago: Science Research Association, 1970.

Fischer, J. "Social Influences on the Choice of a Linguistic Variant." *Word* 14(1958):47–56.

Fowler, W. "Cognitive Learning in Infancy and Early Childhood." *Psychological Bulletin* 59(1962):116–52.

Giebink, J.W., and Morden, M. "Verbal Expression, Verbal Fluency and Grammar Related to Cultural Experience." *Psychology in the Schools* 5(1968):365–68.

Greenberg, S., and Formanck, R. "Social Class Differences in Spontaneous Verbal Interactions." Paper presented at the American Educational Research Association. New York, February, 1971.

Hart, B.M., and Risley T.R. "Establishing Use of Descriptive Adjectives in the Spontaneous Speech of Disadvantaged Preschool Children." *Journal of Applied Behavior Analysis* 1(1968):109–20.

Hess, R., and Shipman, V. "Early Experience and the Socialization of Cognitive Modes in Children." *Child Development* 36(1965):869–86.

Hughes, M.; Wetzel, R.; and Henderson, R. "The Tucson Education Model," ERIC Reference EP 033–753, 1968.

Jersild, A., and Ritzman, R. "Aspects of Language Development: The Growth of Loquacity and Vocabulary." *Child Development* 9(1938):256.

Johnson, W.; Darley, F.; and Spriestersbach, D.C. *Diagnostic Methods in Speech Pathology*. New York: Harper & Row, Publishers, 1963.

Jones, E. "The Effects of a Language Development Program on the Psycholinguistic Abilities and IQ of a Group of Preschool Disadvantaged Children." Unpublished doctoral dissertation. University of Arkansas, 1970.

Jones, P. "Home Environment and the Development of Verbal Ability." Paper presented at the American Educational Research Association. New York, February, 1971.

Karnes, M. "A Quarter of Century of Research with Young Handicapped and Low Income Children at the Institute for Research on Exceptional Children at the University of Illinois." Paper presented at the Second Human Blumberg Symposium at Johns Hopkins University. Baltimore, April, 1972.

———. "Research and Development Program on Preschool Disadvantaged Children." Final Report, University of Illinois, Contract No. OE6–10–235. United States Office of Education, 1969.

Karnes, M.B.; Studley, W.M.; Wright, W.R.; and Hodgins, A.S. "An Approach to Working with Mothers of Disadvantaged Preschool Children." *Merrill Palmer Quarterly* 14(1968): 174–84.

Karnes, M.B.; Zehrbach, R.R.; and Tesha, J.B. "The Karnes' Preschool Program: Rationale, Curricula Offerings and Follow-up Data." In *A Report on Longitudinal Evaluation of Preschool Programs, Volume I, Longitudinal Evaluations,* edited by Sally Ryan. Washington, D.C.: Department of HEW, Publication No. (OHD), 1974.

Klaus, R.A., and Gray, S. "The Early Training Project for Disadvantaged Children: A Report after Five Years." In *Language Remediation for the Disadvantaged Child,* edited by M.A. Brottman. *A Monograph of the Society for Research in Child Development* 33. Lafayette, Ind.: Child Development Publication, 1968.

Labov, W. "The Logic of Nonstandard English." In *Language and Poverty: Perspectives on a Theme,* edited by F. Williams. Chicago: Markham Publishing Co., 1970.

LaCivita, A.F.; Kean, J.M.; and Yamamoto, K. "Socioeconomic Status of Children and Acquisition of Grammar." *Journal of Educational Research* 40(1966):71–74.

Lavatelli, C. *Piaget's Theory Applied to an Early Childhood Program.* Boston: American Science and Engineering, 1970.

Lee, L. "Developmental Sentence Types: A Method for Comparing Normal and Deviant Syntactic Development." *Journal of Speech and Hearing Disorders* 31(1966):313–30.

Lenneberg E. *Biological Foundations of Language.* New York: John Wiley & Sons, 1967.

———. "The Natural History of Language." In *Human Development and Cognitive Processes,* edited by J. Eliot. New York: Holt, Rinehart & Winston, 1971.

Levenstein, P. "Cognitive Growth in Preschoolers through Verbal Interaction with Mothers." *American Journal of Orthopsychiatry* 40(1970):426–32.

Levy, A. "The Effects of Teacher Behavior on the Language Development of Head Start Children." Unpublished doctoral dissertation. Case Western Reserve University, 1968.

Lindquist, M.L. "Teaching Specific Skills in Language and Cognition to Disadvantaged Preschoolers." Unpublished doctoral dissertation. University of Wisconsin, 1969.

Luriia, A., and Yudovich F. *Speech and the Development of Mental Processes in the Child.* London: Staples Press, 1959.

McCarthy, Dorothea. "Language Development in Children." In *Manual of Child Psychology,* edited by L. Carmichael. New York: John Wiley & Sons, 1954.

———. *The Language Development of the Preschool Child.* University of Minnesota Institute of Child Welfare Monograph IV. Minneapolis: University of Minnesota, 1930.

McNeill, Dan. "Developmental Psycholinguistics." In *The Genesis of Language: A Psycholinguistic Approach,* edited by F. Smith and G. Miller. Cambridge: M.I.T. Press, 1966.

Menyuk, P. *Sentences Children Use.* M.I.T. Research Monographs III. Cambridge: M.I.T. Press, 1969.

Milligan, J. "A Study of the Effects of a Group Language Development Program upon the Psycholinguistics Abilities of Normal Kindergarten Children." Ph.D. dissertation. University of Kansas, 1967.

Minuchin, P., and Biber, B. "A Child Development Approach to Language in the Preschool Disadvantaged Child." In *Language Remediation for the Disadvantaged Child,* edited by M.A. Brottman. *A Monograph of the Society for Research in Child Development* 33. Lafayette, Ind.: Child Development Publication, 1968.

Mitchell, R. "A Study of the Effects of Specific Language Training on Psycholinguistic Scores of Head Start Pupils." Ph.D. dissertation. Florida State University, 1967.

Montessori, M. *Doctor Montessori's Own Handbook.* New York: Schocken Books, 1965.

Mowrer, O.H. *Learning Theory and the Symbolic Process.* New York: John Wiley & Sons, 1960.

Nice, Margaret. "Length of Sentences as a Criterion of a Child's Progress in Speech." *Journal of Educational Psychology* 16(1925):370–79.

Osser, H.; Wang, M.; and Zaid, F. "The Young Child's Ability to Imitate and Comprehend Speech: A Comparison of Two Subcultural Groups." *Child Development* 40(1969): 1063–75.

Peterson, R. "Imitation: A Basic Behavioral Mechanism." *Journal of Applied Behavior Analysis* 4(1971):1–9.

Piaget, J. *The Language and Thought of the Child*. New York: The Noonday Press, 1955.

————. *The Origin of Intelligence in Children*. New York: W.W. Norton & Co., 1952.

Plumer, D. "Parent-Child Verbal Interaction: A Study of Dialogue Strategies and Verbal Ability." Paper presented at the American Educational Research Association. New York, February, 1971.

Radin, N. "The Impact of a Kindergarten Home Counseling Program." *Exceptional Children* 36(1969):251–56.

Reynolds, N., and Risley, T. "The Role of Social and Material Reinforcers in Increasing Talking of a Disadvantaged Preschool Child." *Journal of Applied Behavior Analysis* 1(1968): 253–62.

Risley, T. "Learning and Lollipops." *Psychology Today* 1(1967):28–65.

Rogers, V. *Teaching in the British Primary Schools*. New York: The Macmillan Co., 1971.

Sapir, E. "The Status of Linguistics as a Science." *Language* 5(1929):207–14.

Shriner, T.H., and Miner, L.E. "Morphological Structures in the Language of Disadvantaged and Advantaged Children." *Journal of Speech and Hearing Research* 11(1968):605–10.

Skinner, B.F. *Verbal Behavior*. New York: Appleton-Century-Crofts, 1957.

Slobin, D. "The Acquisition of Russian as a Native Language." In *The Genesis of Language: A Psycholinguistic Approach*, edited by F. Smith and G.A. Miller. Cambridge: M.I.T. Press, 1966.

Smith, M. "A Study of Some Factors in Influencing the Development of the Sentence in Preschool Children." *Journal of Genetic Psychology* 46(1935):182–212.

Southern, M.L. "Language-Cognitive Enhancement of Disadvantaged Preschool Children through Modeling Procedures." Unpublished doctoral dissertation. Stanford University, 1969.

Staats, A. "Linguistic-Mentalistic Theory versus an Explanatory S-R Learning Theory of Language Development." In *The Ontogenesis of Grammar: A Theoretical Symposium*, edited by D. Slobin. New York: Academic Press, 1971.

Stanford Research Institute. *Implementation of Planned Variations in Head Start: Preliminary Evaluation of Planned Variations in Head Start According to Follow-through Approaches (1969-1970)*. Menlo Park, Calif.: Stanford Research Institute, 1971.

Stern, C., and Bryson, J. "Competence versus Performance in Young Children's Adjectival Comparative." *Child Development* 1(1970):1197–1201.

Stewart, W. "Nonstandard Speech Patterns." *Baltimore Bulletin of Education* 43(1966):52–65.

Strandberg, T.E. "An Evaluation of Three Stimulus Media for Evoking Verbalization from Preschool Children." Master's thesis. Eastern Illinois University, 1969.

Strandberg, T.E., and Griffith, J. "A Study of the Effects of Training in Visual Literacy on Verbal Language Behavior." Unpublished paper. Eastern Illinois University, 1968.

Templin, Mildred. *Certain Skills in Children*. Minneapolis: University of Minnesota Press, 1957.

Vygotsky, L.S. *Thought and Language*. Cambridge: M.I.T. Press, 1962.

Weikart, D. "A Comparative Study of Three Preschool Curricula." In *The Disadvantaged Child: Issues and Innovations*, edited by J. Frost and G. Hawkes. Boston: Houghton Mifflin Co. 1970.

———. *Preschool Intervention: Preliminary Report of the Perry Preschool Project*. Ann Arbor, Michigan: Campus Publishers, 1967.

Weikart, D.P.; Deloria, D.J.; and Lawson, S. "Results of a Preschool Intervention Program." In *A Report on Longitudinal Evaluation of Preschool Programs, Volume I, Longitudinal Evaluations*, edited by S. Ryan. Washington, D.C.: Department of HEW, Publication No. (OHD), 1974.

Weikart, D.; Rodgers, L.; Adcock, C.; and McClelland, D. *The Cognitively Oriented Curriculum*. Washington, D.C.: Publications Department National Association of Education for Young Children, 1971.

Welch, L. "The Genetic Development of the Associational Structures of Abstract Thinking." *Journal of Genetic Psychology* 56(1940):175–206.

Whorf, B.L. "Science and Linguistics." In *Thought and Reality: Selected Writings of Benjamin Lee Whorf*, edited by J. Carroll. Cambridge: M.I.T. Press, 1956.

Yonemura, M. "A Study of the Ability of Nursery and Kindergarten Children from Low Economic Backgrounds to Develop More Adequate Language Skills through a Special Language Program." Unpublished doctoral dissertation. Columbia University, 1965.

CHAPTER THREE

Reading

Dorothy D. Sullivan

Reading—as good as a miracle.

Theoretical Base of Reading

Any compilation of the theory and research related to reading in the decade of the seventies will reveal dramatic differences from the previous decades in respect to what is being theorized, as well as new directions in what is being researched and important challenges to traditional approaches to research. The objective of this chapter is to focus upon key aspects of the theories and research that have direct implications for those involved in facilitating the moving-into-reading process of children. There is a basic assumption, however, that such a pulling together of significant aspects of the reading field in this context of the young child is done within the broad overview of the total reading spectrum of an effective adult reader. The goal is that a child as he moves through the grades not only *can* read but *does* read in order to meet his responsibility as a participating citizen and to develop and enrich his growth professionally and personally. It is also an objective of this chapter to direct the reader to other sources that elaborate upon the areas of reading research presented here.

History of Reading Research

The field of reading has an impressive body of literature to draw upon. The literature and research in reading since the 1880s has come from a number of disciplines—psychology, neurology, sociology, linguistics, and others. A number of interdisciplinary studies have been conducted on the learning-to-read process and its effect on the reader. The multidimensional aspects of this field can be sorted into those relating to the reading process, those focusing on the reader, and those pertaining to reading instruction.

To determine what is the current state of the art and science of reading instruction, it is essential to understand the nature of the reading act. A clear concept of the reading process is not just an academic concern. According to Clymer, "A teacher's definition of reading influences every action he takes in the classroom" (Clymer, p. 8). Understanding the reading process can help the administrator and the teacher to plan goals for instruction, select materials and instructional methods, and evaluate progress and achievement.

The professional literature lends credence to the statement that changes in curriculum goals and instruction in reading have reflected an evolving definition of the reading process through the years. The sources for developing definitions of reading have been the theories and knowledge of many disciplines. At the turn of the century, E.B. Huey wrote that reading was a psycho-physiological process that was "almost as good as a miracle." Definitions of the reading process have taken on the narrowed or elaborated dimensions of the disciplines that originated the definition. "Reading is a complex process involving the interaction and integration of ocular, perceptual, associative, and motor abilities" (Masland and Cratty, p. 141). According to Gibson's linguistic definition, as a child begins his progression from spoken language to written language, his reading is essentially a decoding process with these three phases: learning to differentiate graphic symbols, learning to decode letters to sounds, and using progressively high-order units of semantic and syntactic structure. While Goodman states, "Reading, like listening, is a receptive psycholinguistic process," he goes on to describe a totally involving, and evolving, process that reflects a loosening of linguistic theory of language (Goodman, 1970, p. 129). According to Goodman, when a person sees language in its graphic form, he has to build meaning of the printed passage through a series of predictions, samplings, selections, guesses, and confirming activities in which meaning is both input (meaning of syntactic and semantic elements of the words and sentences) and output (meaning of the passage).

A sociolinguist's definition would specifically provide for group and individual differences of the processor that effect the decoding of the graphic symbol and bring meaning to it (Entwisle). A summation of the aspects of reading by Stauffer reflects the process operating within the context of the "total personality," a concept that is familiar to early childhood educators:

> It would follow, then, that reading is a mental process requiring accurate word recognition, ability to call to mind particular meanings, and ability to shift or associate meanings—until the constructs or concepts presented are clearly grasped, critically evaluated, accepted and applied, or rejected. This means that knowledge gained through reading can increase understanding, and in turn, influence social and personal adjustment, enrich experience, and stimulate thinking. (Stauffer p. 16)

In addition to such definitions, there have been many other influences on the educator in planning reading programs. The range of influences is evident in this statement:

> These influences include opinions of parents or the teacher next door, personal experiences of the teachers, hortatory articles in professional journals, accounts of action research or how we did it in a particular situation, careful descriptions of applied research in classroom and individual situations, and scholarly accounts of basic investigations in laboratory and other settings. (Russell and Fea, p. 865)

For several decades efforts have been made to report the ever-growing body of research in the field of reading and to organize it into meaningful units for use by educators and researchers. Published studies have been annotated, indexed, and stored for retrieval by a number of annual summaries, the most familiar being the series initiated by William S. Gray (1925).[1] The Educational Resources Information Center (ERIC) was established in 1966 to supplement existing information systems by providing a broader index of research and current practices.[2] Other major attempts to make a comprehensive analysis of educational theory and research relating to reading were made by the American Educational Research Association[3] and the National Society for the Study of Education.[4] The International Reading Association, in cooperation with Educational Resources Information Center/Clearinghouse on Retrieval of Information and Evaluation on Reading (ERIC/CRIER) and ERIC Clearinghouse on Reading and Communication Skills (ERIC/RCS), has initiated several interpretive studies of research through a Reading Information Series as well as other publications including bibliographies, monographs, and interpretive papers on specific reading areas.[5]

The accumulative literature on reading reflects several significant developments in the views on child growth and development and education. Gesell was the notable spokesman for the early views of "intrinsic growth," "neural ripening," or "unfolding behavior." During the fifties there was a gradual increasing interest in the concept of cognitive processing and language development of children within the context of nurturing their environment. The accomplishments of Bruner, Hunt, Bloom, Piaget, and Ausubel relating to these latter views were of tremendous importance for education in general. Later, they and others such as Fowler, Deutsch and Cicarelli, Evans, and Schiller had particular impact on preschool and primary grade programs and their focus on concept development and language activities. Those in the field of reading were drawn into these developments through the cognitive and language processing components of reading.

In the fifties, there were also inquiries into the current education of children and preparation of teachers; the impetus came from an increasing emphasis on effective education for broader ranges of the population. Reading instruction was one of the prime targets resulting from both of these developments in the sixties. Government and foundation funds became available to survey educational practices in the education of reading teachers methods for teaching beginning reading, and research in reading and its influence on practice. Conant and Austin and Morrison helped to determine the beliefs and current practices of reading instruction and teacher preparation. The effect of the theorists and the studies of the current practices in reading instruction was inevitable and immediate.

With a greater understanding of child growth and development and a more comprehensive defining of the reading process, many new approaches to reading instruction were initiated during the sixties. Changes in existing programs and innovations in methods, materials, and classroom organization for moving children into reading were often developed with the guidance of linguists, learning psychologists, and sociologists. Their orientation was sometimes interdisciplinary. They focused their approaches on the reading act, the teaching act, or the reader—alone or in combination. There were linguistic programs, modified alphabets, and programmed instruction for beginning reading. There was perceptual, language development, and perceptual-motor training for both preschool and primary grade children. Both new and existing methods and materials that have been designed for moving children into reading at the primary grade level were utilized with preschool-age children.[6] Increased federal funding of education opened the market for published materials. Many large companies spent vast sums of money on experimental programs for reading instruction. From this avalanche of updated and new programs came the need to determine the nature and components of these programs and to assess their effectiveness; at this point in time, their success no longer was measured only with the children of middle socioeconomic levels to which so many traditional education practices had been geared. Research during the fifties and sixties was often unrelated or lacked the rigors of carefully defined populations, procedures, or control of significant variables along with criterion measures of reliability or validity; such research was a source of confusion and frustration for educators trying to develop effective reading instruction programs and for researchers trying to advance the science of reading. Russell and Fea indicated their concern for this problem by stating, "The amount and variety of materials available in this area make an evaluation of the research and practice doubly necessary if an adequate basis for fruitful new research on reading is to be laid" (p. 865).

During this period, Chall made a comprehensive assessment of reading instruction. She examined both the instructional methods and materials for beginning reading and the research that supported or negated these approaches. Reviewing the research on reading instruction from 1910 to 1965, Chall encountered the myriad problems of analyzing research. Simultaneously, the U.S. Office of Education (USOE) First-Grade Reading Studies were launched; these studies consisted of a body of research on beginning reading instruction that could be correlated by the control of certain variables and have conclusions that could be generalized to larger populations because of the scale of the twenty-seven studies involved, each with approximately one thousand children. Findings of these investigations will be discussed in this chapter under the heading "Reading Programs."

Theoretical Models for Research

The abundant accumulation of piecemeal, though comprehensive, research in reading and relevant disciplines by the sixties indicated an even greater need to evaluate, organize, and synthesize this body of knowledge into inclusive and refined conceptualizations of reading or models. Such models were to provide help in further efforts to understand reading behavior, a framework for research hypotheses, and ultimately more than piecemeal guidelines for moving all children into reading and into refining their skills as they move into adult reading.

One of the earliest and most ambitious efforts to develop a theoretical model of the reading process was made by Holmes in his Substrata-Factor Theory of Reading. This theory provides a structure of working systems that denotes not only the interrelationship of skills but also the hierarchical relationship of major skills with minor subskills. The substrata factors are considered to be "neurological subsystems of brain-cell assemblies, containing various kinds of information, such as memories for shapes, sounds, and meanings of words and word parts, as well as memories for vicarious and experiential material, conceptualizations, and meaningful relationships stored as substantive verbal units in phrases, idioms, sentences, etc. . . . These substrata factors are tied together in a working system and as their interfacilitation in the working system increases, the efficiency of the child's reading increases" (Holmes, 1970, p. 188).

Attempts to isolate factors through statistical analysis resulted in a delineation of certain important factors that operate when speed and power of reading are considered. While Holmes' original work focused on college level reading, further work by Holmes and Singer with the Substrata-Factor Theory at the elementary grade levels supported the concept of the developmental integration of substrata factors. From empirical evidence, it was found that there are gradual changes that occur in the substrata-factor organization; in regard to speed of reading, a predominance of visual perceptual abilities was noted at the third grade level while a balance of visual perceptual and word meaning factors emerged at the sixth grade level (Singer).

Other theoretical models were developed that reflected psycholinguistic aspects of the communication process. Besides Goodman's model that was referred to earlier, R.B. Ruddell developed the Systems of Communication Model in which he used transformational and semantic theories to encompass the variables of surface and deep structure, lexical meaning, short- and long-term memory, as well as affective and cognitive strategies. Venezky and Calfee's Reading Competency Model focuses on the dual functions of forward scanning (a chunking and tagging process to find the largest unit that can be identified) and integration; this syntactic-semantic integration may utilize phrases, words, letter strings, or single letters.

Because of the complex nature of these models, the reader is directed to *Theoretical Models and Processes of Reading,* edited by Singer and Ruddell, for an in-depth description of the theoretical basis of these models along with a graphic presentation of them. This volume also presents a number of useful papers that relate to linguistic, perceptual, and cognitive components in reading as well as affective factors.

A major program to develop research-oriented models of reading was initiated in 1970 by the United States Office of Education and scholars in reading and related disciplines. The initial thrust of the Convergence Application Planning Team (Gephart) was to disseminate the knowledge base dealing with learning to read, the reading process, and models of the reading process from members of the various disciplines through the Targeted Research and Development Program on Reading (TRDPR) (Kling, Geyer, and Davis). This approach was taken on the assumption that improvement in teaching requires a clear understanding of what is being taught. After a literature search of some eight thousand documents in the areas of language development related to reading, learning to read, and the reading process, various teams of scholars were to build a comprehensive or partial model of the processes in these areas or in a combination of the three. Hypotheses and tests were to be formulated so that the models could be refined and their basic assumptions tested. It was felt that the knowledge generated from such an integrated framework of research would have potential benefit for the field by minimizing redundancy in research, facilitating ongoing research, and identifying gaps in our present knowledge. The goal of TRDPR was to establish a meaningful and workable definition of the reading process and all its components in order to bring meaningful and workable changes to reading instruction. The first phase of TRDPR was completed with the publishing of a series of reports. Later references will be made to those findings that are relevant, but a brief noting here of the nature of their reports might be useful.

In the area of language development as related to reading, Athey (1971) examined psychological models of language acquisition that related language growth to the emergence of cognitive maturation. Wardhaugh reviewed linguistic models of language acquisition. Entwisle described the relatively new field of sociolinguistics that, while itself lacking a defined model, recognized that existing models of language development did not account for variation among groups of learners or the social contexts of the reading process. In the area of the reading process, the reports included an analysis of eight comprehensive and partial models related to the reading process (Geyer, 1972), components of sensation and perception in reading (Schiffman), modeling effects of oral language on reading language (Weaver and Kingston), psychometric dimensions of comprehension and reading (Davis), cognitive skills in reading (Mackworth, N.H.), and models of the reading process of learners and "skilled readers" (Mackworth, J.F.). In the area of learning to read, Williams (1973) reviewed the variety of theories and models of reading acquisition from psychological and linguistic viewpoints. Bloom (1973) presented an operant perspective of the learning-to-read process. Gillooly examined the influence of writing system characteristics on learning to read. Samuels (1973) dealt with success and failure in the learning-to-read process.

The result of this comprehensive project is apparent in Athey's statement:

> The fact is that reading is a very complex phenomenon, and we need more understanding of all the elements—perceptual, cognitive, affectual, linguistic, and others—before we can begin to bridge the gap between theory and practice. The second point, which emerges from the first, is that, given this complexity, the goal of constructing a single model of the reading process that can take cognizance of all the above factors is far from being accomplished. (Athey, 1971, p. 86)

Athey goes on to discuss the prematureness and inappropriateness of trying to integrate models at this time when many are in a state of "becoming." The usefulness of TRDPR has been to bring together the various disciplines to organize the present state of knowledge and to provide coherence and direction for the next generation of theorists, researchers, and educators.

It is hoped that the reader will approach the remaining part of the chapter with the view that what is known about the reading process is useful but that it is not ultimate and final and that much remains to be done through research to bring the components of the reading process into harmony with the reader through appropriate reading curriculum to facilitate the learning-to-read process.

Research in Reading

This portion of the chapter will focus on the most pertinent research that provides some direction for developing answers to such questions as *when* and *how* to help children move into reading so that they not only can read successfully but do so to extend their experiences. This will be done within the framework of the reading process, the reader, and reading instruction. This framework operates from the assumption that reading is a multidimensional process with interacting components.

The Reading Process

The components of the reading process will be presented within a two-phase framework, the decoding process and the meaning process. Elements of each phase will be dealt with within the context of physical, psychological, and environmental influences on these phases. The decoding phase pertains to the identification-recognition process whereby the grapheme elements are identified and then recognized in a grapheme-phoneme correspondence of letters, words, syllables, and sentences. The meaning phase is the process whereby meaning is attributed to the graphic symbol, based on the past experiences of the reader. Reading, therefore, consists of decoding the printed symbol and then making that symbol meaningful to the reader. There is interaction between the decoding and the meaning phases.

In the decoding phase, the getting meaning process contributes to the identification-recognition process of the printed symbol, particularly as the reader matures. The most notable research effort in this area was done by Goodman (1970), described earlier; his work clearly demonstrated this interaction process that has come to reflect the generative linguistic views of N. Chomsky and Halle and the sociolinguist viewpoint expressed by Entwisle. Goodman's psycholinguistic studies indicated that the reader utilizes the language structure he has, which is an outgrowth of his environment, to select graphic cues of the reading material in the identification-recognition process. For an in-depth analysis of the psycholinguistic approach to reading, you are referred to *Understanding Reading* by F. Smith.

Likewise, the decoding-meaning interaction is evident in the phase in which the reader utilizes his experiences with his environment for the cognitive processing of concepts. The sensory channels utilized in decoding the printed symbol are also active in the cognitive or meaning process and include sight, sound, touch, and the kinesthetic sensorimotor functions (Sullivan and Humphrey). This viewpoint of the distinct but interacting decoding and meaning phases has been characterized as being analytic in nature and is different from that of linguists such as Bloomfield, Carroll, Gibson (1962, 1963, 1968), and LeFevre. Their view is that the first phase of discriminating the grapheme-phoneme correspondence is synthetic in nature and operates separately and precedes the second phase of bringing meaning to the graphic symbol. Fries took a modified approach between the two; he emphasized the grapheme-phoneme correspondence task but within some element of meaning. This basic difference in interpreting the reading process has direct impact on beginning reading programs. It also led to the Chall and USOE first-grade studies along with the initiation of the TRDPR literature search for developing a research model from which new knowledge could be generated to bring answers to the divergent views in the area of the reading process.

Decoding the Graphic Symbol.   In decoding there are essentially two components, the visual act of receiving the graphic symbol and then the act of processing that symbol into a sound-symbol correspondence. It is generally agreed that the visual and auditory modes are the key sensory channels in arriving at the grapheme-phoneme correspondence. The various types of graphic cues have been the focal point of much theory and research. Cue utilization approaches have been broadly categorized as being analytic or synthetic. The analytic cue approach involves the recognition of wholes as meaningful units which are then analyzed for the important elements. The synthetic cue approach utilizes the individual elements to build recognition of the whole. Within each cue approach, there are further differentiations as to size of unit (i.e., letters, syllables, whole words, thought units, or sentences), depending on the orientation. There are theories on the interacting of these approaches in the decoding process. Research has sought to verify these theorized approaches and the instructional programs that have resulted from these theories. As the research is examined relating to the sensory components in the decoding process, these cue approaches are evident.

   Visual perception.   Visual perception includes acuity, discrimination, memory, and sequence. While acuity is a physiological fact that can be improved in certain circumstances, other elements of visual perception respond to training. According to Spache and Spache, the visual task calls for "an orientation to left and right, up and down, front and back; accurate binocular shifts from point to point; accurate focus and accommodation to distance; and a fine degree of parallel and coordinated action of both eyes, or binocular coordination" (Spache and Spache, p. 198). This visual-motor component depends on intact ocular and neurological systems. The research in this area has focused basically on the number and duration of fixations during the visual-motor act in relation to age, reading maturity, purpose for reading, and the nature of the material. A recent study by Nodine and Lang supported the earlier research that eye movement patterns are an effect of the cognitive processing used in the particular reading situation. Useful references for this aspect of visual perception include Anderson and Dearborn, Gilbert, Taylor, Morris (1959), Vernon, Gray (1960), Smith and Dechant, Tinker, and Lott (1969). Geyer (1970) related the research to models of the reading process.

   Visual perception is based on sensorimotor experiences that depend on eye-hand coordination, left-right body orientation, and other visual spatial abilities including sequencing. Visual perception skills are considered when an attempt is made to show a sequential development with optimum performance, as when a child can trace, copy, or match shapes; reproduce limited types of shapes from memory; and discriminate differences of word forms (Ilg and Ames). Numerous studies (e.g., Hinds, Cox and Hambly, Goins, and Halgren) have found that aspects of visual perception can be improved through training. The major areas of such training in visual perception include directionality, eye-hand coordination or ocular motility, and form discrimination of objects, designs, and wordlike forms.

In regard to visual discrimination, two general types of graphic cue systems were noted among first graders, one by which children recognize and hold the total configuration or symbol in mind and one by which they utilize discriminating details (Goins). Rystrom found in working with children in kindergarten through the primary grades that their visual discrimination of letters alone and in words increased significantly through the grades. However, no pattern of mastery of uppercase and lowercase letter names in relation to visual discrimination could be identified at any level from kindergarten through third grade (Smythe, Stennett, Hardy, and Wilson, 1970–71). Another study of children's responses indicated two types of letter confusion, reversal or rotated letters and a lack of identification of significant elements in words (Rystrom). The importance of single letter and letter details in recognition of words rather than just whole word recognition by kindergarten children was supported in the studies of Muehl, King (1964), Marchbanks and Levin, Samuels and Jeffrey, and Yawkey.

In working with first graders, Wylie and Durrell found that whole words were more easily identified than separate vowels in phonograms. Some phonograms were easier to recognize than others. Long vowels were easier to recognize than short, though not significantly. There were no differences in the recognition of the silent *e* and vowel digraph phonograms. Single consonant endings were easier to perceive than consonant blend endings. It was also determined that high-frequency phonograms were learned more readily than low-frequency ones. Several studies concluded that children learn to search for invariant patterns or regularities as cues to word recognition (Lott, Smith, and Cronnell; Gibson, 1970). Gibson also concluded that children must make their own discovery of such patterns before they can transfer word recognition strategies to the identification of new words. An earlier study, which examined pronounceable letter combinations from a child's language phonogram patterns, noted that these combinations aided in the recall of letters within clusters (Gibson, Pick, Osser, and Hammond). When children were confronted with high- and low-similarity words, it was found that the rate of success in word recognition depended on the degree of similarity with high-similarity words for them to perceive (Otto and Pizillo).

A series of studies provided evidence that repeated exposures to a word aid in the speed of recognition and that the recognition of uppercase letters facilitated the recognition of lower-case letters (Haber, 1965; Haber and Hershenson; Hershenson and Haber; Standing, Sell, Boss, and Haber; Haber, Standing, and Boss).

Several studies focusing on the errors in the oral reading of children attempted to identify cues that young children utilize from graphic and contextual information (MacKinnon; Clay; Goodman, 1969; Goodman and Burke; Biemiller; Weber). There was general agreement that contextual constraints on word recognition are refined gradually. Goodman's work in this area resulted in the development of a taxonomy of reading errors or miscues from which verification could be made that reading is more than matching letter sounds or identifying words; he found that reading is a complex process by which decoding is directed by a variety of grapho-phonic, syntactic, and semantic events. Barr examined the effect of training on the types of reading errors and concluded that different instructional methods entailing different strategies of word recognition do influence differentially the pattern of word recognition errors. Barr stressed the need for longitudinal studies to determine "whether changes in reading strategies are a function of experience with words and/or of direct instruction" (Barr, p. 528).

Individual differences have been found to effect the decoding process. Several studies attempted to examine the differences of children's processing of graphic symbols. Goins found some children look at pictures as wholes while others match details, a finding similar to that of Rudisill (1956) in a study of the rates of recognition of flashing digits and phrases. Hartley (1970), in working with first graders, determined that for the optimal learning of maximum and minimum contrast words, it is essential to match mode of training (i.e., words only, words plus picture, or words with context clues) to the child's sex as well as high and low ability levels. It was found that boys achieved higher scores than girls on graphic words plus context clues with maximum contrast. Girls scored higher than boys on words only with minimum contrast. However, the evidence is not conclusive as to the relative usefulness of pictures in establishing sound-symbol correspondence. When Samuels (1970) reviewed earlier studies on the effects of pictures on learning to read, he concluded that pictures interfere with the acquisition of sight vocabulary. Petty (1939) noted from a study of first graders that low ability readers used the general shape or analytic method while high ability readers used key letters or letter arrangements in a synthetic approach. Elkind, Larson, and VanDoorninck found that good readers were significantly more successful in the perceptual-decentration task than poor readers; they concluded that training in sound-symbol relationships should begin as early as kindergarten.

Several studies have been concerned with the cognitive style of an individual and its relationship to the learning-to-read process. Kagan found that the reflection-impulsivity dimension of first graders affected their word recognition. Lesiak reported that reflective girls who were in the first grade performed better in word recognition as well as comprehension and critical reading, while no significant differences were noted between impulsive and reflective boys in word recognition and comprehension. It was further concluded that cognitive style was more important for the learning-to-read process since the impulsive-reflective dimension had no significant relationship with later reading achievement. Watson noted significant relationships between field dependence-independence and reading achievement at the primary grade level. Field independence, the ability to keep an object separate from its surrounding field, related positively with reading achievement. Rosenfield and Santostephano, Rutledge, and Randall also found that cognitive style does relate to the selecting, organizing, and processing of graphic symbols. Blanton and Bullock, in reviewing the research relating cognitive style to reading behavior, found positive relationships reported in the research but concluded it was difficult to generalize from the limited research to date and suggested some directions for further work in this area. They discussed the role cognitive style may have on reading models in general.

Studies have shown that specific discrimination training is effective with young children. Studies on the relative effectiveness of different methods of instruction have also indicated the need to consider factors relating not only to the reading process but also to the reader. Popp; Staats, Minke, Finley, Wolf, and Brooks; and Jeffrey and

Samuels concluded from their studies on kindergarten children that specific discrimination training was effective. In word attack instruction, high ability first graders responded best to a letter-combination approach whereas low ability children responded best to a single-letter approach (Sullivan, Okada, and Niedermeyer). Williams (1969) sought to determine the effect of the timing of training and method of training on children's visual discrimination and reproduction of letterlike symbols. Timing of training, the first month of school or three-fourths through the school year, produced significant differences among training methods only in the early training groups, which indicated age was an important factor in instruction.

It was found that the ability to discriminate letters can be facilitated by the method of presentation. Distinctive letters can be presented simultaneously whereas similar letters that are more difficult to discriminate should be presented successively (Williams and Ackerman). "Errorless" discrimination of letters by kindergarten children can be facilitated by a "faded stimuli" method, involving fading techniques of the nondiscriminating stimulus (Karraker and Doke). Skailand tested four types of language-unit training with kindergarten children. The methods were essentially synthetic, similar spelling patterns, contrasting spelling patterns, and the whole word or sight approach. Both spelling pattern methods facilitated the recall of items, but there were no significant differences for transfer to other words.

In a study of prekindergarten and kindergarten children as to the type of visual discrimination training (i.e., whole word, sounding out words, isolated letter sounds) and its transfer effect to new words or word components, no significant differences were found by Marsh and Sherman. Della-Piana and Endo indicated that some of the problems inherent in the type of study utilized, in which transfer effects were assessed immediately following training, might be solved with a longitudinal study to determine if significant differences did exist. Potts and Savino examined the effectiveness of two instructional methods; one emphasized grapheme-phoneme relationships and one was a whole word approach. The more effective program incorporated the phonics training.

Auditory perception.   The evidence on the relative contribution of auditory and visual discrimination to the grapheme-phoneme correspondence process is not conclusive. Auditory cues in the grapheme-phoneme correspondence include letter names and sounds of single letters or groups of letters; these are often referred to as phonics skills. Auditory acuity, discrimination, memory, and sequence are aspects of auditory perception. Harrington and Durrell found that auditory and visual discrimination and phonic ability are more important than mental age for learning to read. Auditory acuity studies indicate that high pitch acuity loss relates to children's reading achievement in the primary grades (Henry). It was found that loss of high-frequency hearing is more frequent among boys than girls (Dahl). Auditory memory span for vowels increases until age ten while memory span for consonants increases to age twelve (Metraux); this may indicate consonants are more difficult to distinguish.

According to Robinson (1946), auditory discrimination has been considered to be a more positive factor than acuity in the learning-to-read process. Efforts to relate auditory discrimination to reading achievement have been conclusive. Studies have indicated the value of teaching letter names and sounds (Kingston; Durrell and Murphy, 1963; Barrett; Lowell). In a longitudinal study, Morency found low but significant correlations between first-grade auditory test scores and third-grade reading achievement. Sapir found that young children are able to discriminate sounds more easily in the beginnings of words and syllables. Brown, in his work with preschoolers, examined the effects of one or two phonemes on either side of the break in blending training; he found that syllables were easier to blend than phonemes, overall vowel-consonant training seemed to be more effective, syllable or phoneme training did not transfer well to the other, and optimal training of phonemes and syllables would involve easy to hard within-syllable or phoneme training, with syllable and phoneme training interspersed.

A recent study testing the auditory discrimination performance of primary grade children in quiet listening situations as opposed to noisy listening conditions supported previous research that there is a significant difference between the results of children in the situations, particularly for those identified as retarded readers (Nober). It was questioned whether tests of auditory discrimination, usually administered in quiet settings, can serve as adequate predictors of auditory discrimination. Researchers have posed questions about the measurement of auditory discrimination with the tests being used. These problems in testing have been the concern of Buktenia; Smythe, Hardy, Stennett, and Wilson; McNinch; and Risko.

Numerous studies have focused on the amount of phonics instruction that would be desirable. The studies of Mulder and Curtin and Rudisill (1957) supported the conclusions of earlier research that methods of phonics instruction produce differing results and that moderate amounts of phonics instruction are helpful.

Multisensory perception. Research does not clearly indicate the relative importance of any one or a combination of sensory modalities for the decoding process. Furthermore, the evidence is not available as to whether utilizing modal preference enhances reading achievement. The individual differences of the learner are significant interacting factors that must be determined.

King and Muehl's study of modal combinations for teaching grapheme-phoneme correspondence of whole words to kindergarten children found that discrimination of similar words needs additional modality cuing such as pictures rather than spoken word alone. Fillmer and Linder noted that with black second graders from low socioeconomic levels, total auditory methods were less effective than a total visual or an auditory-visual approach. In noting that training in either the auditory or visual modality improves recognition through that channel, Postman and Rosenzweig reported that the transfer effects from visual training to auditory recognition are greater than the reverse.

In respect to the utilization of auditory or visual modality preference, Bateman (1968) found that the placement of first graders in an auditory or visual method according to their modality strength did not produce significant gains in reading achievement. It was concluded that the auditory method was favored for all groups. Bruininks came to similar conclusions regarding the ineffectiveness of using the modality strength of economically disadvantaged boys. Studies by Otto as well as Cooper and Gaeth indicated preferred modality may vary with age. It was also found that motivational and attentional factors may govern the effective use of a given modality (Walters and Kosowski, Birch, and Olson and Pau).

Another concern has been "modal shifting." Jones made a thorough summary and analysis of the research concerned with the effect of the interrelatedness of the auditory and visual modes and reading achievement through intersensory transfer, perceptual shifting, and modal preference. His general conclusions were that it is highly probable that intersensory transfer (i.e., the ability to associate verbal and visual stimuli) is related to success in reading but its relationship to intelligence, age, and grade level is not clearly defined. Conclusions in the area of intersensory perceptual shifting (i.e., the ability to shift attention rapidly from one modal source of input to another) could not be drawn because of the limited number of studies.

In the area of modal preference, significant interactions were not found. In this area not only was modal preference focused upon but also the effectiveness of bimodal versus monomodal presentation of verbal material. In regard to the lack of significance, Jones concluded, "Perhaps the greatest weakness of modal preference research, then, is the failure to admit that possibly there is no discrete *auditory approach* or *visual approach* to learning to decode printed words. The findings in the area of intersensory integration would seem to support the latter explanation" (Jones, p. 36). Another important point made by Jones was that until researchers assess the optimum learning mode for each individual, the superiority of bimodal or monomodal verbal stimuli will not be determined.

Minimum attention has been given to the kinesthetic modality as a channel in the decoding process. Schonnell, Eberl, and Morris (1959) have cited the usefulness of the kinesthetic and tactile elements of tracing in the "Fernald" method, a method generally reserved for clinical cases of reading disability. Several recent studies employed kinesthetic and tactile elements in the decoding process. Linn and Ryan found that teaching letter names and sounds through tracing and vocalizing along with visual study was effective with first graders. Segal included kinesthetic elements in one of his varying modality approaches to the grapheme-phoneme correspondence and found that different approaches produced significantly varying performance results among kindergarten children from low socioeconomic backgrounds.

The effectiveness of another kinesthetic approach, the echoic response, is inconclusive at this point. McDowell and Neville found no significant differences in groups using an oral or echoic response approach in the decoding process. Braun, however, reported the auditory stimulus-echoic response approach was superior to an auditory-visual approach, particularly with low ability kindergarten children.

Bringing Meaning to the Graphic Symbol. While decoding the graphic symbol is essential, the reading process is one of obtaining the meaning intended by the author. The limitations placed on this aspect of reading would be the experiences of the reader that in turn are affected by factors such as maturity, mental ability, and the environment. These interrelating factors affect the reader's language development, conceptual development, and cognitive processing. Reading is a process of *bringing* meaning to the graphic symbol. Acquisition of meaning involves an accumulation of percepts, concepts, and vocabulary from a multisensory base that feeds into an increasingly more complex cognitive processing as the reader matures. Bloom's Taxonomy of Educational Objectives has served as a useful referent in structuring components of cognitive processing in reading. Elements in the comprehension processing of grapheme-phoneme correspondences have been identified as the following:

1. Recognition of symbolic units such as combinations of letters in syllables and words, sentences, and paragraphs

2. Divergent production in which a set of given facts or ideas are used in original or creative ways
3. Convergent production by which isolated facts or ideas are taken and generalizations made from them
4. Evaluation or a comparative or critical approach to the material (Guilford, 1960)

Research in the areas of language and cognitive development has served as a major source of direction for those in the field of reading. However, since these areas of research will be dealt with in the chapters on math, science and social studies, this chapter will recognize the importance of the research relating to these components of the meaning process and cite only a few important studies in reading comprehension for the primary grades. A thorough presentation on reading comprehension and related research can be found in Russell and Fea's "Research on Teaching Reading."

While the linguistic elements such as letters, phoneme patterns, syntax, and semantics have been researched in terms of their usefulness to grapheme-phoneme correspondence, several studies have focused on larger units of syntactic structure and semantics to determine their effect on the readability of material. Bormuth's research on reading comprehension resulted in an effort to develop a taxonomy of skills with observable features that for the most part could be manipulated both instructionally and experimentally. Bormuth's purpose was to identify linguistic features that affected comprehension. In working with fourth-grade children, he utilized the linguistic structural categories of syntactic relationships within sentences, anaphoric expressions (i.e., word or phrase that substitutes for an antecedent), and intersentence syntax in constructing questions to assess factual comprehension. It was concluded that the linguistic features incorporated in the questions produced different performances and there might be a hierarchical relationship (Bormuth; and Bormuth, Carr, Manning, and Pearson).

In a study with five-year-old children who could not read, Hatch, Sheff, and Chastain found that transformations related to comprehension; sentences with subject-verb order were understood significantly better than ones with verb-subject order. They found that deletions increased the difficulty of comprehension. When third graders were given word problems to read in arithmetic, they understood significantly better those problems that presented parallel information rather than those that presented reverse information. An example of a parallel presentation is, If John started out with three coins and he found two coins, how many coins did he end up with? A reverse presentation is, How many coins did John end up with if he found two coins and he started out with three coins? (Rosenthal and Resnick) These studies indicated that the readability of the material was considered a significant factor in comprehension. Such studies focused on the awareness of the reading comprehension tasks confronting children and providing guidance in handling language structures with which they are not familiar.

Another significant component in reading comprehension is the importance of a meaningful vocabulary as verbal tools in conceptualizing. The studies in language recognize the factors such as socioeconomic status, experience, and intelligence that affect children's vocabularies. Research has consistently provided evidence of the relationship between vocabulary strength and success in reading. Research has shown

that an ability to determine precise meaning is related to an ability to read with comprehensioin (Dunkel; Hunt, 1953; and Reed and Pepper). In relation to this essential component is the problem of verbalism whereby a child uses a word or concept symbol with little understanding or a completely wrong concept. Many studies tried to handle vocabulary in ways that facilitate comprehension by considering the syntactic and semantic load of a passage. Control of vocabulary has been an approach utilized by publishers of basal readers. Numerous studies have been made to determine the familiarity children have with the words they are to meet in their reading material. Present studies in vocabulary indicate children will encounter many new words in the books used for reading instruction and in the content areas (Stauffer, 1966; Johns; and Cohen and Kornfeld). Vocabulary needs to be considered not just in terms of developing decoding skills for word recognition but also in terms of these words being meaningful in order to help children bring meaning to their reading. It is a matter of facilitating comprehension through language and concept development with multi-sensory, concrete, or vicarious experiences. Studies by Humphrey and Moore, with third-grade children utilizing motor-oriented reading content, and Humphrey, utilizing active games, showed that using motor learning helps the child develop meaning from graphic symbols.

Other studies examined reading instruction materials for theme and content having to do with race, environment, occupations, and outcomes and noted there is now more material appearing with which more children can identify (Blom, Waite, and Zimet; Collier; Waite, Blom, Zimet, and Edge, 1967; Waite, 1968). Wiberg, however, found there was a significant difference in the story content of primers from twelve popular reading series and the library choices of first graders from a middle- and upper-middle-class suburban school; the primer stories centered mainly on child and child-adult interactions whereas the story content of the child-selected library stories centered on animals, make-believe, and inanimate objects. There were also significant differences of content between checked-out and nonchecked-out library books. Confirming earlier studies, it was found that boys prefer boy-oriented activity stories while no such preference was shown by girls. Such studies confirm that simply because a child can decode a series of words, he will not automatically understand them and have interest.

A final area of significance in reading comprehension that has little research to guide or support it is that of critical reading emphasis in the primary grades. There needs to be research at the primary grade levels to provide information as to what critical reading should be at these grade levels and the most appropriate ways of developing this component of reading comprehension. At this point, the work of the cognitive theorists provides the most insight into the problem. Some elaboration on this aspect of comprehension can be found in the works of Johnson and Petty (1956).

The Reading Process and the Reader

From the research, it is evident that several factors—vocabulary development, conceptual development, and cognitive processing—have been correlated with effective reading. Studies have further shown that variables such as intelligence, physical capacities, home environment, sex, and personality factors interact with these factors;

some of these factors may compound the problems or advantages for children learning to read.

Intelligence. In addition to numerous earlier studies that found intelligence correlated with performance in reading are those by Hanson and Robinson as well as Mortenson. Gray (1960) in his review of research reported .40 to .60 correlations between intelligence and reading achievement. However, the limitation of the intelligence factor has been noted in several studies; for example, Harrington and Durrell concluded that auditory and visual discrimination and phonic ability are more important than mental age for learning to read.

Physiological Factors. Physiological aspects relating to reading achievement include perceptual and neurological deficits as well as general physical condition. A useful reference for a review of the research in these areas is *Psychology in Reading* (Smith and Dechant, pp. 120–82).

    Visual. Visual defects that are most frequently associated with progress in reading include farsightedness, binocular incoordination, fusion difficulties, and aniseikonia (Robinson, 1946; Eames, 1948, 1957; Steinberg and Rosenberg).

    Auditory. The relationship between auditory factors such as acuity and reading has been established by research that indicates not only the deaf but also the hard-of-hearing children are handicapped in education, and reading specifically (Waldman, Wade, and Aretz; Sheridan; and Fiedler). The relationship between children's listening and reading was also established by Durrell and Murphy (1953) and Reynolds. McNinch's recent review of the research in auditory perception is a useful reference.

    Speech. There is little evidence of any relationship between speech defects and reading achievement. Bond (1935) noted no significant differences among good and poor readers regarding the presence of speech defects. He observed that over one-third of the poor oral readers who were good silent readers did have speech defects; in contrast, good oral readers who were poor silent readers displayed no speech defects. Eames (1950) made a comprehensive review of the relationship between articulatory disorders and reading achievement.

    Neuro-physiological. The neuro-physiological structure is an area in which basic integrity is essential for success in learning to read. Money offers a comprehensive review of this area relating to the nature of dyslexia and its identification. Bateman (1971) also provides specific examples of learning-to-read problems inherent in children with neurological disorders.

The Home Environment. Socioeconomic levels of children were correlated with their "readiness" for reading and reading achievement levels in the primary grades (Justman; Hanson and Robinson; Fillmer and Kahn; Morris, Pestaner, and Nelson; Mortensen; Oakland; Miller, 1969; Miller, 1970; Chomsky, 1972). Home environment has been related to the language development of children in numerous studies, but some of these studies have also noted its relationship to readiness for reading and reading achievement in terms of the amount of prereading activities present in the home (Durkin, 1966; Miller, 1969; Chomsky, 1972; Miller, 1970). Perhaps the most significant study of the relationship between home and parent involvement and reading achievement was Durkin's study. Significant factors were not socioeconomic level, parent occupation, or the child's intelligence but rather the interaction between parents and their children, with parents answering the preschooler's questions about written words and providing opportunities for the child to identify written words with alphabet books and other printed materials. Durkin and Sutton found that children who read before the first grade maintain their advantage as they progress through the grades. Parental verbal interaction and demonstration of affection were also related to successful reading achievement (Milner). Della-Piana, Stahlmann, and Allen reviewed the research relating specific parental characteristics to the reading achievement of children and the effect of parental involvement in treatment programs. They concluded that while positive relations and significant differences were noted in the studies, the results indicate the need for the coordination of further research to identify conditions under which treatments are differentially effective.

Sex Differences. Positive relationships between sex differences usually favoring girls in the early years of reading instruction have been considered more as environmental and cultural differences by Gates (1961) and supported by Prescott and Wozencraft.

Personality. A relationship between some personality factors of young children and reading achievement has been positively correlated. Grimes and Allinsmith, in examining the relationship between anxiety and impulsivity personality characteristics and method of instruction, found highly anxious and compulsive children achieved better in structured settings with a phonics method while those who were characterized as high anxiety and low compulsive performed lower in the unstructured setting of the whole-word method of instruction. Haywood, in a study of the motivational orientation of elementary school children, reported that overachievers in reading were intrinsically motivated and underachievers, extrinsically motivated. Kagan noted that those children characterized as reflective made fewer errors in word recognition than those identified as impulsive. In a study focusing on independence personality characteristics, Hoffman reported some relationship between the development of independence, having to do regular chores, and being allowed to make purchases in stores, and success in reading. Mason and Blanton found low but positive correlations between interest in reading and reading achievement.

While research provides evidence of the extreme complexity of the reading process and of the fact that the process is unique for each reader, there is an overall general schema of decoding and comprehending the graphic symbol. However, perceptual and cognitive factors do not allow a precise, single pattern for decoding the graphic symbol, and comprehension is an accumulation of the reader's experiences. As a learned skill, the essential components of the reading process are not the product of natural maturation but are the result of training. Implications from existing research indicate a continued need for examining the reading process and structuring a research model by which variables can be identified and their relations determined with greater specificity so that appropriate instruction can be developed for all children.

Assessment in Reading

The impact of the nature-nurture issue to assure children success in learning and the psychological testing movement led to efforts to identify readiness for reading instruction. The use of the mental age concept was championed by Morphett and

Washburne. The appearance of reading readiness tests were attempts to provide teachers and administrators with objective data from which decisions could be made as to the best time to initiate reading instruction. The use of readiness tests has been questioned increasingly over the past decade (Durkin, 1967; Dykstra; Farr). Factors affecting success in reading go beyond visual and auditory perception, left-to-right visual scan, grapheme-phoneme relationships, and phoneme blending—the most frequent content of reading readiness tests (Rude). According to Rude, the one skill most consistently measured is letter recognition and it remains as the most valid predictor of success from readiness tests. However, research has indicated the complexity of bringing meaning to a decoded graphic symbol. The components call for teacher awareness of the language and experiences of the child, his modality for learning, his cognitive style for processing perceptual stimuli as well as his attitude about himself and learning to read.

Because of the limitations of readiness tests, efforts have been directed to the utilization of a series of tests for a composite predictor (deHirsche, Jansky, and Langford; Panther; Kaufman and Kaufman). A follow-up study of the *deHirsch Predictive Index* supported the results of other studies that stronger correlations are obtained from the use of several performance criteria (Askov, Otto, and Smith). Among additional tests that have been used are the Wepman, the Bender, the Frostig, and the Illinois Test of Psycholinguistic Abilities (ITPA). Reviews of the research on the Frostig test are found in Leeds and on the ITPA in Bateman (1965). Teacher judgments have also been found to be useful in identifying the strengths and needs of children (Ebbesen; Zaruba; Shinn; Ferinden and Jacobson; Tobiesson, Duckworth, and Conrad). A useful reference of measures for assessing prereading skills is found in Pikulski.

A major concern is that there needs to be recognition that readiness in one or two skills as measured on reading readiness tests does not assure success in learning to read. Individuals, each with unique profiles of development, necessitate a more open concept of readiness. Durkin has stated:

> Most children are neither totally ready nor totally unready for reading. Such an awareness ought to encourage schools to give up the idea that getting ready to read and beginning to read occur at separate points on a time line as well as the related practice of having a readiness program followed by a reading program. (Durkin, 1972, p. 59)

Another important point is that readiness should be viewed in relation to the instructional task. Instruction, by being adapted to the capacity of the learner, can then assure readiness, or capacity, to handle the instructional task (Durkin, 1970 b). Gates' study challenging the mental age concept concluded:

> The study emphasizes the importance of recognizing and adjusting to individual limitations and needs . . . rather than merely changing the time of beginning. It appears that readiness for reading is something to develop rather than merely to wait for. (Gates and Bond, p. 684)

Not only must assessment in terms of the instructional task be multidimensional but it needs to be made early in order that instructional methods can be adapted to assure the child success in the learning-to-read process. A useful summary of the problems in assessment in reading can be found in the works of Farr and Durkin (1968).

Reading Programs

Preschool Programs. During the sixties, an increasing interest in effective ways of moving children into reading led to a number of preschool programs with a particular focus on activities related to skills that are essential in the reading process. These programs were utilized at both the nursery and kindergarten levels with positive and generally significant results. Some programs emphasized language development and cognitive processing (Morrison and Harris; Karnes, Wollersheim, Stoneburner, Hodgins, and Teska; Ayers and Mason; McConnell, Horton, and Smith; Durkin, 1970c; Hayes and Dembo; O'Donnell, 1971). Head Start programs were also representative of this approach (Hyman and Kliman; Ramsey and Boercker; Clasen, Spear, and Tomaro; Willmon; Cawley, Burrow, and Goodstein; Love and Stallings). Stanchfield (1971) reported on a broader language arts kindergarten program that included activities in listening comprehension, auditory and visual discrimination, oral language skills, motor-perceptual skills, and sound-symbol relationships. Her conclusions were that such a program facilitated progress in the learning-to-read process. Hillerich and Sutton reported favorable results from early reading activities. Sutton's study discussed the use of informal activities with materials which provided incidental opportunities for exploration in reading. Other programs utilized traditional reading readiness programs including visual discrimination of graphemes through workbook activities (Langston; Kelley and Chen; Singer, Balow, and Dahms; French; Perlish; Fowler, 1971).

Special preschool programs included those that were highly structured. Prendergast found no significant differences favoring the Montessori nursery school from conventional upper-middle-class nursery schools except on the children's eye-hand coordination on the Peabody, the Frostig, and the Boston Sound Picture Discrimination Test. Latent gains in word recognition in first grade were evident in children who had visual perceptual training in kindergarten (Faustman). In a study of kindergarten children, one group was given Frostig's "formal" visual training program materials and another group was given an adaptation of Frostig's program in informal game-like materials; both groups made significant gains on the Frostig test, but there was no significant difference between the gains. There were also no significant differences on reading readiness scores with the two types of materials. However, if attitudes toward the learning task are to be considered, it was noted that the children in the formal Frostig program seemed to gain skill in paper and pencil tasks, learned to follow directions and respond correctly to assignments but that "many had to be continually encouraged or reprimanded to continue to work in the books" (Church, p. 364).

Perceptual-motor programs in kindergarten programs produced mixed correlations. Occasionally, such training related positively with performance in the visual-motor area but with no significant differences on readiness or reading achievement tests (Beaupre and Kennard; Falik; Stone and Pielstick; Sheffer; Pryzwansky). Fisher and Turner found that one-half year of perceptual-motor training for advantaged children was as effective as a year's program for economically disadvantaged kindergarten children in relation to intelligence and reading readiness measures with an increasing latent effect.

According to a study by Goralski and Kerl, kindergarten children in classes having aides made greater gains in reading readiness scores. It was found that underprivileged and average boys tend to learn better with a letter and word recognition program on a Computer Assisted Instruction (CAI) terminal than do girls (Green, Henderson, and Richards). A study on the effect of the television program *Sesame Street* on disadvantaged Head Start children in kindergarten with follow-up activities both at home and at school indicated they had significantly higher reading readiness scores than those who had regular letter, language, and listening activities in kindergarten (Sprigle).

The most publicized preschool projects have been the Denver kindergarten project (Brzeinski; McManus), the Comparing Reading Approaches in First-Grade Teaching (CRAFT) program (Morrison and Harris), and the Head Start programs. All produced evidence that programs focusing on a reading skills foundation are effective but the positive gains achieved by the children are not maintained if there is no follow-up or related instructional program in the first grade. Traditional beginning reading programs or even more recently developed programs are not automatically appropriate for first-grade children who have had earlier experiences in beginning reading skills. Since there are differential results from the programs, there is a need to select or adapt a curriculum according to the needs of the children. Unfortunately, it has been found that mass instruction in the same reading program is an increasing occurrence at the preschool level (Karnes, Wollersheim, Stoneburner, Hodgins, and Teska; and Cohen, 1969). Research evidence of developmental differences among children at this age level indicates that flexibility in the curriculum is needed to ensure appropriate learning-to-read activities.

Primary Grade Programs.   As indicated previously in this chapter, reading instruction innovations followed the new concepts of language and cognitive development in children. The updated and new programs reflected the full range of theoretical approaches to the grapheme-phoneme correspondence process. There were completely synthetic programs in which children learned vowels and consonants and then blended them into phonogram patterns. There were programs utilizing modified alphabets to facilitate the grapheme-phoneme correspondence. The use of the child's own language and experiences for initial reading materials evolved to help establish the grapheme-phoneme correspondence. Traditional basal programs adopted phonics with varying degrees of emphasis. Linguistic programs that appeared showed varying degrees of compromise between the decoding, the meaning, and the decoding-meaning approaches to grapheme-phoneme correspondence.

The broad range of instructional programs emphasizing opposing theories of the learning-to-read process has been both confusing and frustrating to educators, particularly with the increasing pressures of the public as to the quality of the reading "product" of the school systems. From this instructional morass, the Chall and USOE first-grade studies sought to come up with some answers as to *what* method *works*. Chall sought to determine the objectives and actual techniques utilized in the varied instructional methods as well as what research there was to support the use of these methods. Categorizing the types of different instructional programs was difficult because it was found teachers often adapt or add techniques to adjust instruction to the children. It was also difficult to assess the claims of effectiveness of programs because of the numerous problems inherent in behavioral research. Chall's conclusions supporting the importance of phonics in beginning reading instruction have been generally confirmed by the USOE first-grade studies. However, the nature of the USOE studies makes their findings of particular significance to the questions of *what* and *how* of reading instruction.

USOE first-grade studies. Initiated during the 1964–65 school year, the U.S. Office of Education first-grade studies involved a nationwide effort to conduct a broad-based coordinated group of twenty-seven studies, with approximately one thousand children in each study, in which certain pupil, teacher, class, school, and community variables would be controlled so that inclusive generalizations might be made from the research. Fourteen of the studies were extended through the second and third grades so that longitudinal effects of the reading instruction methods could be determined. Reports from the first year of the project noted that teacher effectiveness was a significant factor with greater differences within methods than between methods (Bond, 1966). The final report at the completion of the third-grade longitudinal studies noted that different methods yield different outcomes with children of varying abilities. Comparing the basal programs and their variations with the Lippincott system and initial teaching alphabet (i/t/a), it was concluded that an emphasis on specific discrimination skills benefits the beginning reading process and that the use of phonic instruction increases word recognition, phonics, and spelling. The writing component of several of the programs was considered effective. Positive attitudes and reading habits tend to be established with basal programs (Bond and Dykstra).

The effectiveness of an emphasis on phonics in beginning reading instruction has also been reported by Henderson, Sparks and Fay, Wollam (1961), Bliesmer and Yarborough (1965), Gurren and Hughes (1965), Potts and Savino, and Sabaroff. It is important to recognize that such studies define phonics instruction in many different dimensions.

Reading instruction personnel. The importance of the teacher has been further supported by the CRAFT project. Harris and Morrison reported from a longitudinal study of two instructional approaches to teaching of reading that differences within methods were greater than between approaches. Ramsey evaluated three grouping procedures for teaching reading and concluded that the influence of the teacher is greater than method, material, or plan of organization. Artley summarized studies on the teacher variable in reading instruction and concluded that improved teaching results in improved reading. Parents have been found to be useful in the instructional process. In a kindergarten maintenance program by parents during the summer with structured reading practice, extending the Southwest Regional Laboratory's first year reading program, those children whose parents participated regularly progressed more. It was reported that the parents of the poorer readers did not participate to the extent that the parents of better readers did (Sullivan and Labeaune). Cramer found significant gains in reading achievement of children who had the help of parent tutors who received thirty-five hours of training in tutoring techniques. Another source of tutors yielded positive results in reading achievement. McWhorter and Levy had economically disadvantaged college-bound students with reading problems work with primary grade retarded readers from inner-city schools; both groups profited from the program in terms of reading achievement.

   Token reinforcement techniques.   Innovations in beginning reading instruction based on theories of learning have taken the form of behavioral management through extrinsic reinforcement by tokens. Several studies reported positive effects with the use of token reinforcement in beginning reading instruction (Staats, Minke, Finley, Wolf, and Brooks; Heitzman; Winett, Richards, and Krasner; Hamblin and Hamblin).

   Grouping for instruction.   The effect of organizational grouping procedures on reading achievement has been the focus of several studies. Cartwright and McIntosh reported grouping procedures whereby economically disadvantaged children received reading instruction within heterogeneous classrooms, homogeneous classrooms on the basis of IQ, or ungraded team-teaching situations. There were no significant differences among the groups in reading achievement although mean scores favored the heterogeneous grouping in grades one and two. Grouping by the child's sex for first- and second-grade reading instruction yielded no significant differences in gains or achievement in reading (Tagatz; Stanchfield).

   Perceptual training.   Specialized programs in visual perception and perceptual-motor training have been utilized in the primary grades with inconclusive results. Generally, those studies assessing the effectiveness of visual perceptual training with the Frostig Program on reading achievement reported no significant gains (Rosen; Jacobs, Wirthlin, and Miller; Fortenberry). Two studies reported that those most in need of visual perceptual training benefit the least from the program in terms of reading achievement (Wiederholt and Hammill; Gamsky and Lloyd). Two studies focusing on perceptual-motor training yielded more positive results in relation to gains in readiness and achievement scores in reading (McCormick, Schnobrich, and Footlik; Collins and Bidle). No measurable effect of visual-tactual training on first-grade reading achievement was found although a positive gain in nonlanguage mental maturity function was reported (Lloyd). Another study with first graders used a linguistic phonic teaching approach combined with a typing program; the results in reading achievement and spelling favored the added typing program (Bernazza, Bloomer, and Cline).

   Programmed instruction.   Other innovative beginning reading instruction programs have focused on the use of a programmed format, some assisted by computers or other mechanized aids. One study found no significant differences in children's reading achievement after the use of programmed materials as a supplement to basal reading instruction (Hammill and Mattleman). Automated instruction programmed on the Edison Responsive Environment Learning System (ERE) was compared with a nonautomated program utilizing an electric typewriter, slide projector, and tape recorder. Both programs used the same visual and oral materials. Second- and third-grade readers of at least one year of retardation demonstrated significant gains in reading achievement with the ERE (Frazier and Zaslav). A group of students using one computer assisted first-grade reading program reported significantly higher performance in word recognition than those not using the program (Hartley, 1971). In two studies, Atkinson found in working with culturally disadvantaged first graders of average or better than average IQ that the Stanford CAI Project reading program, which focuses on grapheme-phoneme correspondence of letter combinations, produced significantly higher mean scores in all areas of reading except comprehension. Useful references for the Stanford CAI Reading Program are Atkinson and Paulson as well as Fletcher and Atkinson. Other programmed approaches include Project PLAN (Program for Learning in Accordance with Needs), which has been reported by Wright, and the Individually Prescribed Instruction (IPI) program of the Learning Research and Development Center at the University of Pittsburgh, which has been described by Beck and Bolvin. The impact of such approaches to beginning reading instruction is yet to be felt on the educational scene. One of the major problems in terms of the feasibility of such methods is their cost.

It is evident from the research that the "product" of the instructional program depends on the view one takes of the reading process and the consequent skills emphasis resulting from that view. It is further recognized that physiological, psychological, and environmental factors of the individual are significant variables in the learning-to-read process. The answer has not been found as to *what* and *how* and *when* for all children. But the research does provide some direction, both for instructional programs and areas of further research.

Implications for the Reading Curriculum

The readiness definition of Durkin (1972) is one of the most fruitful approaches to the problem of *when* children should be moved into reading. Building on Ausubel's concept of readiness as "the adequacy of existing capacity in relation to the demands of a given learning task" (Ausubel, p. 246), Durkin proposes that identifying a child's capacity or readiness to handle the learning-to-read process depends on the method of instruction that will be used. Durkin goes on to propose that one of the best ways of determining a child's adequacy of handling a task is to give him opportunities to attempt informal activities using the task. Then, from observing what the child does or does not do, the nature of what the next learning activity should be can be determined. This approach appears to be appropriate, particularly in light of the limited usefulness of existing readiness tests for prediction purposes and from the evidence of the diverse types of skills needed for specific instructional approaches. Furthermore, beginning reading experiences can thus be placed in a natural, meaningful learning environment as these activities emerge from the experiences which take place in the classroom.

As described by Durkin, beginning reading activities take on the full dimensions of the reading process—both decoding and meaning. Reading instruction is providing opportunities for the child to stroke the *cat's sleek black fur* and note the *soft pads* on *his feet;* to see *his yellow eyes* that are the *same color* as the *yellow butterfly,* and *yellow butter,* and *yellow buttercups;* or to print his name on his picture. The teacher can also ask questions such as, Does anyone have a name that starts with the same letter as Bill's? or What is the name of the letter at the beginning of these names that are printed on the board—Bill, Barbara, Bobby? Beginning reading instruction then emerges in a structured but natural environment. This means that children move into reading from language and concept developing activities to recording their experiences in story form, to collecting words for listening and looking at letter elements, to reading and writing their own stories, and finally to reading and enjoying a book.

Beginning reading activities proceed through a developmental sequence geared to modality and a graphic-cue system that works for the child. This does not mean there are twenty-five instructional methods in the classroom. It means that if a general program is adapted based on the teacher's understanding of the components of the learning-to-read process through diagnostic teaching procedures, the teacher will note which children are not responding to that particular method. Adapting to the specific needs of a child might be through individual or small group activities using techniques by which he can be successful with the possible supervision of an aide or tutor. Such a reading program does entail the teacher to become knowledgeable about the dimensions of the decoding process, to recognize that children use more than one cue system, to realize that reading is a "meaning" process from which the reader can extend his experiences. To accomplish the latter, words must come "alive" for the reader through "quality" experiences.

In the primary grades, the need for the diagnostic teaching approach becomes even greater. Many gains achieved from preschool programs have been lost as children moved into reading programs that did not take advantage of their earlier reading experiences. An even greater need for diagnostic teaching is evident for those children who made minimum progress or who lacked the opportunity to participate in early reading activities during the preschool years; these children need a different program than the one geared for the children who had early reading instruction.

In terms of *how,* beginning reading instruction is not synonymous with a primer or a workbook. It is a series of planned activities, both formal and informal, that help children focus on auditory and visual components of their language. It can be done by a variety of means. Basic principles of learning and what is known about child growth and development can also serve as additional guidelines for the teacher. Using the preschool and primary grade children's curiosity and love for the active, the teacher can enhance the learning-to-read process. Dramatic and creative play, active games, examining the environment through all the senses and attaching words to these experiences and grouping and categorizing by colors, shapes, number, composition, and use can provide the language and concept development needed to facilitate reading. Perceptual-motor developmental activities can help the child's orientation to his environment. Specific activities in visual and auditory discrimination of letters, words, and sentences can and should be structured.

A language arts approach to beginning reading is becoming increasingly recognized as the approach that provides for the multidimensional aspects of reading. From the research on language and concept development and the positive correlations of these areas with success in reading, from what is known about the learning process, and from child growth and development patterns, the language arts approach appears to be the most natural setting for beginning reading instruction. In this approach, the basal reader and workbook become only a part of a total communication process that builds on the listening and speaking skills of children and is reinforced through writing. The language arts approach focuses on meaningful communication tasks evolving from a natural setting of needing and wanting to know. The program evolves from the strengths and needs of the children. The *what* in a beginning reading program depends on the children who are enrolled in that program. Early and Durkin have described such programs.

Research needs are limitless as continued efforts are directed to finding out more about matching appropriate methods of instruction to the individual. The goals of reading instruction are to produce readers who have independence in word recognition as well as critical and creative readers who *can* and *do* read.

Notes

1. The Summaries were continued annually in the *Elementary School Journal* from 1926 to 1932 and in the *Journal of Educational Research* from 1933 to 1960. Helen P. Robinson and others assumed responsibility for these annual summaries that then appeared in the International Reading Association's publications, *The Reading Teacher* from 1961 to 1964 and the *Reading Research Quarterly* from 1965 to the present. The complete collection of studies is housed in the William S. Gray Memorial Collection of Scientific Studies in the University of Chicago Library.

2. ERIC's Clearing House on Reading and Communication Skills is sponsored by the National Conference of Teachers of English in cooperation with the National Institute of Education of the United States Office of Education. ERIC includes not only published research but also USOE programs and project reports, information on doctoral dissertations relating to reading, and materials not regularly circulated such as conference proceedings and curriculum guides. The works of Olson and Rupley as well as O'Donnell are useful references as to the use of ERIC/RCS for purposes of disseminating research on specific aspects of reading for the educator and the researcher.

3. AERA's four editions of the *Encyclopedia of Educational Research* published in 1941, 1950, 1960, 1969; their *Handbook of Research on Teaching* (Gage); and *Second Handbook of Research on Teaching* (Travers) provide an informative and useful analyses of the research in reading and reading instruction and related fields.

4. The Society published their first yearbook on reading, *Report of the National Committee on Reading* in 1924. *The Teaching of Reading: A Second Report* appeared in 1937. Others related to early childhood reading include *Reading in the Elementary School* published in 1956 and *Development in and through Reading* published in 1961.

5. Publications of IRA can be obtained from their headquarters located at Six Tyre Avenue, Newark, Delaware, 19711.

6. Aukerman's *Approaches to Beginning Reading* is a useful reference with a description of some one hundred beginning reading instruction programs other than the traditional basal material. This reference includes origins of each approach as well as descriptions of methods and materials with illustrations of essential features of each program.

References

Anderson, I.H., and Dearborn, W.F. *The Psychology of Teaching Reading.* New York: The Ronald Press Co., 1952.

Artley, A.S. "The Teaching Variable with Teaching of Reading." *Reading Teacher* 23(1969): 239–48.

Askov, W.; Otto, W.; and Smith, R. "Assessment of the deHirsch Predictive Index Tests of Reading Failure." In *Some Persistent Questions on Beginning Reading,* edited by R.C. Aukerman. Newark, Del.: International Reading Association, 1972.

Athey, I.J. "Affective Factors in Reading." In *Theoretical Models and Processes of Reading,* edited by H. Singer and R.B. Rudell. Newark, Del.: International Reading Association, 1970.

———. "Language Models and Reading." *Reading Research Quarterly* 7(1971):16–110.

Atkinson, R.C. "Instruction in Initial Reading under Computer Control: The Stanford Project." *Journal of Educational Data Processing* 4(1967):175–92.

———. "Computerized Instruction and the Learning Process." *American Psychologist* 23(1968):225–39.

Atkinson, R.C., and Paulson, J.A. "An Approach to the Psychology of Instruction." Technical Report 157. Stanford, Calif.: Institute for Mathematical Studies in the Social Sciences, 1970.

Aukerman, R.C. *Approaches to Beginning Reading.* New York: John Wiley & Sons, 1971.

Austin, M.C., and Morrison, C. *The First R: The Harvard Report on Reading in Elementary Schools.* New York: The Macmillan Co., 1963.

Ausubel, D.P. "Viewpoints from Related Disciplines: Human Growth and Development." *Teachers College Record* 60(1959):245–54.

Ayers, J.B., and Mason, G.E. "Differential Effects of Science: A Process Approach upon Change in Metropolitan Readiness Test Scores among Kindergarten Children." *Reading Teacher* 22(1969):435–39.

Barr, R.C. "The Influence of Instructional Conditions on Word Recognition Errors." *Reading Research Quarterly* 7(1972):509–29.

Barrett, T.C. "Visual Discrimination Tasks as Predictors of First-grade Reading Achievement." *Reading Teacher* 18(1965):276–82.

Bateman, B. *The Illinois Test of Psycholinguistic Abilities in Current Research: Summaries of Studies.* Urbana: University of Illinois Press, 1965.

———. "The Efficacy of an Auditory and a Visual Method of First-grade Reading Instruction with Auditory and Visual Learners." In *Perception and Reading,* edited by H.K. Smith. *Proceedings of the International Reading Association* 12(1968):105–12.

Bateman, B., ed. "Learning Disorders." *Reading* 4(1971):293–383.

Beaupre, R.G., and Kennard, A. "An Investigation of Pre- and Post-Metropolitan Readiness Test Scores for Differing Motor Education Programs." *Illinois School Research* 5(1968): 22–25.

Beck, I.L., and Bolvin, J.O. "A Model of Nongradedness: The Reading Program for Individually Prescribed Instruction." *Elementary English* 46(1969):130–35.

Bernazza, A.M.; Bloomer, R.; and Cline, M. "An Experimental Test of a First-grade Reading-Typewriter Program." In *Reading: Process and Pedagogy,* edited by G.B. Schick & M.M. May. *Nineteenth Yearbook of the National Reading Conference* 1(1971):34–38.

Biemiller, A. "The Development of the Use of Graphical and Contextual Information as Children Learn to Read." *Reading Research Quarterly* 6(1970):75–96.

Birch, R.W. "Attention Span, Distractibility, and Inhibitory Potential of Good and Poor Readers." Ph.D. dissertation, University of Wisconsin, 1967.

Blanton, W.E., and Bullock, M.A. "Cognitive Style and Reading Behavior." *Reading World* 12(1973):276–87.

Bliesmer, E.P., and Yarborough, B.H. "A Comparison of Ten Different Beginning Reading Programs in First Grade." *Phi Delta Kappan* 56(1965):500–504.

Blom, G.E.; Waite, R.R.; and Zimet, S.F. "Ethnic Integration and Urbanization of a First-grade Reading Textbook: A Research Study." *Psychology in the Schools* 4(1967):176–81.

Bloom, R.D. "Learning to Read: An Operant Perspective." *Reading Research Quarterly* 8(1973):147–66.

Bloom, B.S. *Stability and Change in Human Characteristics.* New York: John Wiley & Sons, 1964.

Bloom B.S., ed. *Taxonomy of Educational Objectives. Handbook I: Cognitive Domain.* New York: Longmans, Green and Son, 1956.

Bloomfield, L. "Linguistics and Reading." *Elementary English* 19(1942):125–30, 183–86.

Bond, G.L. *The Auditory and Speech Characteristics of Poor Readers.* New York: Teachers College Press, 1935.

———. "First-grade Reading Studies: An Overview." *Elementary English* 43(1966):465.

Bond, G.L., and Dykstra, R. *Coordinating Center for First-grade Reading Instruction Programs.* Final Report, Cooperative Project No. X–001. Minneapolis: University of Minnesota, 1967a.

———. "The Cooperative Research Program in First-grade Reading Instruction." *Reading Research Quarterly* 2(1967b):1–142.

Bormuth, J.R. "An Operational Definition of Comprehension Instruction." In *Psycholinguistics and the Teaching of Reading,* edited by K.S. Goodman and J.T. Flemming. Newark, Del.: International Reading Association, 1969.

Bormuth, J.R.; Carr, J.; Manning, J.; and Pearson, D. "Children's Comprehension of Between- and Within-Sentence Syntactic Structures." *Journal of Education Psychology* 61(1970): 349–57.

Braun, C. "Interest-loading and Modality Effects on Textual Response Acquisition." *Reading Research Quarterly* 4(1969):428–44.

Brown, D.L. "Some Linguistic Dimensions in Auditory Blending." In *Reading: The Right to Participate,* edited by F.P. Greene. Twentieth Yearbook of National Reading Conference 2(1971):227–36.

Bruininks, R.H. "Teaching Word Recognition to Disadvantaged Boys." *Journal of Learning Disabilities* 3(1970):28–37.

Bruner, J.S. *The Process of Education.* Cambridge, Mass.: Harvard University Press, 1960.

Brzeinski, J.E. "Beginning Reading in Denver." *Reading Teacher* 18(1964):16–21.

Buktenia, N.A. "Auditory Discrimination: A New Assessment Procedure." *Exceptional Children* 38(1971):237–40.

Carroll, J.B. "The Analysis of Reading Instruction: Perspectives from Psychology and Linguistics." *Theories of Learning and Instruction,* edited by E.R. Hilgard. Sixty-third Yearbook of the National Society for the Study of Education, Part II. Chicago: The University of Chicago Press, 1964.

Cartwright, G.P., and McIntosh, D.K. "Three Approaches to Grouping Procedures for the Education of Disadvantaged Primary School Children." *The Journal of Educational Research* 65(1972):425–29.

Cawley, J.F.; Burrow, W.H.; and Goodstein, H.A. "Performance of Head Start and Non-Head Start Participants at First Grade." *Journal of Negro Education* 39(1970):124–31.

Chall, J.S. *Learning to Read: The Great Debate.* New York: McGraw-Hill Book Co., 1967.

Chomsky, C. "Stages in Language Development and Reading Exposure." *Harvard Educational Review* 42(1972):1–33.

Chomsky N. "Phonology and Reading." In *Basic Studies on Reading,* edited by H. Levin and J.P. Williams. New York: Basic Books, 1970.

Church, M. "Does Visual Perceptual Training Help Beginning Readers?" *Reading Teacher* 27(1974):361–64.

Cicarelli, V.G.; Evans, J.W.; and Schiller, J.S. "The Impact of Head Start: A Reply to the Report Analysis." *Harvard Educational Review* 40(1970):105–29.

Clasen, R.E.; Spear, J.E.; and Tomaro, M.P. "A Comparison of Relative Effectiveness of Two Types of Preschool Compensatory Programming." *Journal of Educational Research* 62(1969):401–5.

Clay, M.M. "The Reading Behavior of Five-year-old Children: A Research Project." *New Zealand Journal of Educational Studies* 2(1967):11–31.

Clymer, T. "What Is Reading? Some Current Concepts." *Innovation and Change in Reading Instruction.* Sixty-seventh Yearbook of the National Society for the Study of Education, Part II. Chicago: The University of Chicago Press, 1968.

Cohen, S.A. *Teach Them All to Read.* New York: Random House, 1969.

Cohen, S.A., and Kornfeld, G.S. "Oral Vocabulary and Beginning Reading in Disadvantaged Black Children." *Reading Teacher* 24(1970):33–38.

Collier, M. "An Evaluation of Multi-ethnic Basal Readers." *Elementary English* 44(1967): 152–57.

Collins, W., and Bidle, R. "Motor Fitness Training and Reading Readiness: A Causal Relationship." *Illinois School Research* 8(1971):13–15.

Conant, J.B. *The Education of American Teachers.* New York: McGraw-Hill Book Co., 1963.

Cooper, J.C., and Gaeth, J.H. "Interactions of Modality with Age and with Meaningfulness in Verbal Learning." *Journal of Educational Psychology* 58(1967):41–44.

Cox, B.J., and Hambly, L.R. "Guided Development of Perceptual Skill of Visual Space as a Factor in the Achievement of Primary Grade Children." *American Journal of Optometry and Archives of American Academy of Optometry* 38(1961):433–44.

Cramer, W. "My Mom Can Teach Reading Too!" *Elementary School Journal* 72(1971):72–75.

Dahl, L.A. *Public School Audiometry: Principles and Methods.* Danville, Ill.: Interstate Printers & Publishers, 1949.

Davis, F.B. "Psychometric Research on Comprehension in Reading." *Reading Research Quarterly* 7(1972):628–78.

deHirsch, K.; Jansky, J.J.; and Langford, W.S. *Predicting Reading Failure.* New York: Harper & Row, Publishers, 1966.

Della-Piana, G.M., and Endo, G.T. "Reading Research." *Second Handbook of Research on Teaching.* A project of the American Educational Research Association. Chicago: Rand McNally & Co., 1973.

Della-Piana, G.M.; Endo, G.T.; Stahlmann, R.F.; and Allen, J.E. "Parents and Reading Achievement: A Review of Research." *Elementary English* 45(1968):190–200.

Desberg, P., and Berdiansky, B. *Word Attack Skills: Review of Literature.* Inglewood Calif.: Southwest Regional Laboratory, 1968.

Deutsch, C.P., and Deutsch, M. "Brief Reflection on the Theory of Early Childhood Enrichment Programs." In *Early Education,* edited by R.D. Hess and R.M. Bear. Chicago: Aldine Publishing Co., 1968.

Deutsch, M. "The Role of Social Class in Language Development and Cognition." *American Journal of Orthopsychiatry* 35(1965):78–88.

Dunkel, H.B. "Testing the Precise Use of Words." *College English* 5(1944):386–89.

Durkin, D.D. *Children Who Read Early.* New York: Teachers College Press, 1966.

————. "Informal Techniques for the Assessment of Prereading Behavior." In *The Evaluation of Children's Reading Achievement,* edited by T.C. Barrett. Newark, Del.: International Reading Association, 1967.

————. "A Language Arts Program for Pre-First Grade Children: Two-Year Achievement Report." *Reading Research Quarterly* 5(1970):534–65.

————. *Teaching Them to Read.* Boston: Allyn & Bacon, 1970a.

————. "What Does Research Say about the Time to Begin Reading Instruction?" *Journal of Educational Research* 64(1970b):52–56.

————. *Teaching Young Children to Read.* Boston: Allyn & Bacon, 1972.

————. "When Should Children Read?" In *Innovation and Change in Reading Instruction,* edited by H.M. Robinson. The Sixty-seventh Yearbook of the National Society for the Study of Education, Part II. Chicago: The University of Chicago Press, 1968.

Durrell, D.D., and Murphy, H.A. "The Auditory Discrimination Factor in Reading Readiness and Reading Disability." *Education* 73(1953):556–60.

————. "Boston University Research in Elementary School Reading, 1933–1963." *Journal of Education* 146(1963):3–53.

Dykstra, R. "The Use of Reading Readiness Tests for Prediction and Diagnosis: A Critique." In *The Evaluation of Children's Reading Achievement,* edited by T.C. Barrett. Newark, Del.: International Reading Association, 1967.

Eames, T.H. "Comparisons of Eye Conditions among 1,000 Reading Failures, 500 Ophthalmic Patients, and 150 Unselected Children." *American Journal of Ophthalmology* 31(1948): 713–17.

————. "The Relationship of the Central Vision Field to the Speed of Visual Perception." *American Journal of Ophthalmology* 43(1957):279–80.

————. "The Relationship of Reading and Speech Difficulties." *Journal of Educational Psychology* 41(1950):51–55.

Early, M. "Components of a Language Arts Program in the Primary Grades." In *Some Persistent Questions on Beginning Reading,* edited by R.C. Aukerman. Newark, Del.: International Reading Association, 1972.

Ebbeson, J.A. "Kindergarten Teacher Rankings as Predictors of Academic Achievement in the Primary Grades." *Journal of Educational Measurement* 5(1968):259–64.

Eberl, M. "Visual Training and Reading." In *Clinical Studies in Reading,* II. Supplementary Monograph, 1953, 77:141–48.

Elkind, D.; Larson, M.; and Van Doorninck, W. "Perceptual Decentration Learning and Performance in Slow and Average Readers." *Journal of Educational Psychology* 56(1965): 50–56.

Entwisle, D.R. "Implications of Language Socialization for Reading Models and for Learning to Read." *Reading Research Quarterly* 7(1971):111–67.

Falik, L.H. "The Effects of Special Perceptual-Motor Training in Kindergarten on Reading Readiness and on Second-grade Reading Performance." *Journal of Learning Disabilities* 2(1969):395–402.

Farr, R. *Reading: What Can Be Measured?* Newark, Del.: International Reading Association, 1969.

Faustman, M.N. "Some Effect of Perception Training in Kindergarten on First-grade Success in Reading." In *Perception and Reading,* edited by H.K. Smith. *Proceedings of the International Reading Association,* 12(1968):99–101.

Ferinden, W.E., and Jacobson, S. "Early Identification of Learning Disabilities." *Journal of Learning Disabilities* 3(1970):589–93.

Fiedler, M.F. "Teacher's Problems with Hard-of-Hearing Children." *Journal of Educational Research* 42(1949):618–22.

Fillmer, H.T., and Kahn, H.S. "Race, Socioeconomic Level, Housing, and Reading Readiness." *Reading Teacher* 21(1967):153–57.

Fillmer, H.T., and Linder, R. "Comparison of Auditory and Visual Modalities." *Education* 91(1970):110–13.

Fisher, M.D., and Turner, R.V. "The Effects of a Perceptual-Motor Training Program upon the Academic Readiness of Culturally Disadvantaged Kindergarten Children." *Journal of Negro Education* 41(1972):142–50.

Fletcher, J.D., and Atkinson, R.C. "An Evaluation of the Stanford CAI Program in Initial Reading (Grades 1 through 3)." Unpublished manuscript, Stanford University, 1971.

Fortenberry, W.D. "An Investigation of the Effectiveness of a Special Program upon the Development of Visual Perception for Word Recognition of Culturally Disadvantaged First-grade Students." In *Reading: Process and Pedagogy,* edited by G.B. Schick and M.M. May, *Nineteenth Yearbook of the National Reading Conference* 1(1971):141–45.

Fowler, W. "A Developmental Learning Strategy for Early Reading in a Laboratory Nursery School. *Interchange* 2(1971):106–25.

———. "The Effects of Early Stimulation." In *Early Education,* edited by R.D. Hess and R.M. Bear. Chicago: Aldine Publishing Co., 1968.

Frazier, R.I., and Zaslav, S.S. "An Automated and Non-Automated System of Teaching." *Reading Teacher* 24(1970):115–19.

French, V.R. "A Study of Student Achievement under Two Contrasting Kindergarten Programs." *Illinois School Research* 5(1969):13–18.

Fries, C.C. *Linguistics and Reading*. New York: Holt, Rinehart & Winston, 1962.

Gage, N.L., ed. *Handbook of Research on Teaching*. Chicago: Rand McNally & Co., 1963.

Gamsky, N.R., and Lloyd, F.W. "A Longitudinal Study of Visual Perceptual Training and Reading Achievement." *Journal of Educational Research* 64(1971):451–54.

Gates, A.I. "The Necessary Mental Age for Beginning Reading." *Elementary School Journal* 37(1937):497–508.

———. "Sex Differences in Reading Ability." *Elementary School Journal* 51(1961):431–34.

Gates, A.I., and Bond, G.L. "Reading Readiness." *Teachers College Record* 37(1936): 679–85.

Gephart, W.J. "The Targeted Research and Development Program in Reading: A Report on the Application of the Convergence Technique." *Reading Research Quarterly* 5(1970): 505–23.

Gesell, A. *The First Five Years of Life*. New York: Harper & Row, Publishers, 1940.

———. *Infancy and Human Growth*. New York: The Macmillan Co., 1928.

———. *The Mental Growth of the Preschool Child*. New York: The Macmillan Co., 1925.

Gesell, A., and Ilg, F. *The Child from Five to Ten*. New York: Harper & Row, Publishers, 1946.

Gesell, A., and Thompson, H. "Learning and Growth in Identical Twin Infants." *Genetic Psychology Monographs* 6(1929):1–124.

Geyer, J.J. "Comprehensive and Partial Models Related to the Reading Process." *Reading Research Quarterly* 7(1972):541–87.

———. "Models of Perceptual Processes in Reading." In *Theoretical Models and Processes of Reading*, edited by H. Singer and R.B. Ruddell. Newark, Del.: International Reading Association, 1970.

Gibson, E.J. "Learning to Read." *Science* (1965) pp. 1066–72. Also in H. Singer and R. Ruddell (Eds.) *Theoretical Models and Processes of Reading*. Newark, Delaware: International Reading Association, 1970, pp. 315–34.

———. "The Ontogeny of Reading." *American Psychologist* 25(1970):136–43.

Gibson, E.J.; Pick, A.; Osser, H.; and Hammond, M. "The Role of Grapheme-Phoneme Correspondence in the Perception of Words." *American Journal of Psychology* 75(1962): 554–70.

Gibson, E.J.; Osser, H.; Schiff, W.; and Smith, J. "An Analysis of Critical Features of Letters, Tested by a Confusion Matrix." In *A Basic Research Program on Reading* (Cornell University and United States Office of Education Cooperative Research Project No. 639). Ithaca, N.Y.: Cornell University, 1963.

Gibson, E.J.; Schapiro, F.; and Yonas, A. "Confusion Matrixes for Graphic Patterns Obtained with Latency Measure." In *The Analysis of Reading Skill: A Program of Basic and Applied Research* (Cornell University and United States Office of Education, Final Report, Project No. 5–1213). Ithaca, N.Y.: Cornell University, 1968.

Gibson, E.J.; Schurcliff, A.; and Yonas, A. "Utilization of Spelling Patterns by Deaf and Hearing Subjects." In *Basic Studies in Reading*, edited by H. Levin and J.P. Williams. New York: Basic Books, 1972.

Gilbert, L.C. "Functional Motor Efficiency of the Eyes and Its Relation to Reading." *University of California Publication in Education* 11(1953):159–232.

Gillooly, W.B. "The Influence of Writing System Characteristics on Learning to Read." *Reading Research Quarterly* 8(1973):167–98.

Goins, J.T. *Visual Perceptual Abilities and Early Reading Progress.* Supplemental Educational Monographs, No. 87. Chicago: University of Chicago Press, 1958.

Goodman, K.S. "Analysis of Oral Reading Miscues: Applied Linguistics." *Reading Research Quarterly* 5(1969):9–30.

———. "Claremont Reading Conference." *Reading Conference Yearbook* 34(1970):125–35.

———. "Dialect Barriers to Reading Comprehension." *Elementary English* 42(1965):853–60.

Goodman, K.S., and Burke, C.L. "A Study of Oral Reading Miscues that Result in Grammatical Re-transformations. (Final report covering Contract No. OEG-0-8-070219-2806(010), Project No. 7–E) Washington, D.C.: United States Department of Health, Education and Welfare, 1969.

Goodman, K.S., and Flemming, J.T., eds. *Psycholinguistics and the Teaching of Reading.* Newark, Del.: International Reading Association, 1969.

Goralski, P.J., and Kerl, J.M. "Kindergarten Teacher Aides and Reading Readiness in Minneapolis Public Schools." *Journal of Experimental Education* 37(1968):34–38.

Gray, W.S. *Summary of Investigations Relating to Reading.* Chicago: University of Chicago Press, 1925.

———. "Reading." In *Encyclopedia of Educational Research,* edited by C.W. Harris. 3d ed. New York: The Macmillan Co., 1960.

Green, D.R.; Henderson, R.L.; and Richards, H.C. "Learning to Recognize Words and Letters on a CAI Terminal. In *Reading and Realism,* edited by J.A. Figurel. *Proceedings of the International Reading Association* 13(1969):658–64.

Grimes, J.W., and Allinsmith, W. "Compulsivity, Anxiety, and School Achievement." *Merrill-Palmer Quarterly* 7(1961):248–71.

Guilford, J.P. "Frontiers in Thinking That Teachers Should Know About." *Reading Teacher* 13(1960):176–82.

Gurren, L., and Hughes, A. "Intensive Phonics versus Gradual Phonics in Beginning Reading: A Review." *Journal of Educational Research* 58(1965):339–47.

Haber, R.N. "Effect of Prior Knowledge of the Stimulus on Word-Recognition Processes." *Journal of Experimental Psychology* 69(1965):282–86.

Haber, R.N., and Hershenson, M. "Effects of Repeated Brief Exposures on the Growth of a Percept." *Journal of Experimental Psychology* 69(1965):40–46.

Haber, R.N.; Standing, L.; and Boss, J. "Effects of Position and Typeface Variation on Perceptual Clarity." *Psychonomic Science* 18(1970):91–92.

Halgren, M.R. "Opus in See Sharp." *Education* 81(1961):369–71.

Halle, M. "Some Thoughts on Spelling." In *Psycholinguistics and the Teaching of Reading,* edited by K.S. Goodman and J.T. Fleming. Newark, Del.: International Reading Association, 1969.

Hamblin, J., and Hamblin, R.L. "On Teaching Disadvantaged Preschoolers to Read: A Successful Experiment." *American Educational Research Jurnal* 9(1972):209–16.

Hammill, D., and Mattleman, M. "An Evaluation of a Programmed Reading Approach in the Primary Grades." *Elementary English* 46(1969):310–12.

Hanson, E., and Robinson, H.A. "Reading Readiness and Achievement of Primary Grade Children of Different Socioeconomic Strata." *Reading Teacher* 21(1967):52–56.

Harrington, Sr., M.J., and Durrell, D.D. "Mental Maturity versus Perception Abilities in Primary Reading." *Journal of Educational Psychology* 46(1955):375–80.

Harris, A.J., and Morrison, C. "The CRAFT Project: A Final Report." *Reading Teacher* 22(1969):335–40.

Hartley, R.N. "Effects of List Types and Cues on the Learning of Word Lists." *Reading Research Quarterly* 6(1970):97–121.

———. "A Method of Increasing the Ability of First-grade Pupils to Use Phonetic Generalizations." *California Journal of Educational Research* 22(1971):9–16.

Hatch, E.; Sheff, J.; and Chastain, D. *The Five-Year-Old's Comprehension of Expanded and Transformed Conjoined Sentences.* Inglewood, Calif.: Southwest Regional Laboratory, 1969.

Hayes, M.E., and Dembo, M.H. "A Diagnostic-Prescriptive Approach to Preschool Education." *Psychology in the Schools* 8(1971):37–40.

Haywood, H.C. "Motivational Orientation of Overachieving and Underachieving Elementary School Children." *American Journal of Mental Deficiency* 72(1968):662–67.

Heitzman, A.J. "Effects of a Token Reinforcement System on Reading and Arithmetic Skills Learnings of Migrant Primary School Pupils." *Journal of Educational Research* 63(1970): 455–58.

Henderson, M. *Progress Report of Reading Study: 1952–55.* Champaigne, Ill.: Illinois Board of Education, 1955.

Henry, S. "Children's Audiograms in Relation to Reading Attainment: I. Introduction to and Investigation of the Problem." *Journal of Genetic Psychology* 70(1947):211–31.

———. "Children's Audiograms in Relation to Reading Attainment: II. Analysis and Interpretation." *Journal of Genetic Psychology* 71(1947):3–63.

Hershenson, M., and Haber, R.N. "The Role of Meaning in the Perception of Briefly Exposed Words." *Canadian Journal of Psychology* 19(1965):42–46.

Hillerich, R.L. "Pre-Reading Skills in Kindergarten: A Second Report." *Elementary School Journal* 65(1965):312–17.

Hinds, L.R. "Longitudinal Studies of Certain Visual Characteristics, Readiness, and Success in Reading." In *Reading in a Changing Society.* Newark, Del.: International Reading Association, 1959.

Hoffman, E. "Pre-Kindergarten Experiences and Their Relationships to Reading Achievement." *Illinois School Research* 8(1971):6–12.

Holmes, J.A. "The Substrata-Factor Theory of Reading: Some Experimental Evidence." In *New Frontiers in Reading. Proceedings of the International Reading Association,* 1960. Also in *Theoretical Models and Processes of Reading,* edited by H. Singer and R.B. Ruddell. Newark, Del.: International Reading Association, 1970.

Holmes, J.A., and Singer, H. *The Substrata-Factor Theory: Substrata Factor Differences Underlying Reading Ability in Known Groups.* Washington, D.C.: United States Office of Education, 1961.

Huey, E.B. *The Psychology and Pedagogy of Reading.* New York: The Macmillan Co., 1908.

Humphrey, J.H. "Comparison of the Use of Active Games and Language Workbook Exercises as Learning Media in the Development of Language Understandings with Third-Grade Children." *Perceptual and Motor Skills* 21(1965):23–26.

Humphrey, J.H. and Moore, V.D. "Improving Reading through Physical Education." *Education* 80(1960):559–61.

Hunt, J.M. *Intelligence and Experience.* New York: The Ronald Press Co., 1961.

————. "The Psychological Basis for Using Preschool Enrichment as an Antidote for Cultural Deprivation." *Merrill-Palmer Quarterly* 10(1964):209–48.

Hunt, J.T. "The Relation among Vocabulary, Structural Analysis, and Reading." *Journal of Educational Psychology* 44(1953):193–202.

Hyman, I.A., and Kliman, D.S. "First-Grade Readiness of Children Who Have Had Summer Head Start Programs." *Training School Bulletin* 63(1967):1963–67.

Ilg, F.L., and Ames, G. "Developmental Trends in Reading Behavior." *Journal of Genetic Psychology* 76(1950):291–312.

Jacobs, J.N.; Wirthlin, L.D.; and Miller, C.B. "A Follow-up Evaluation of the Frostig Visual-Perceptual Training Program." *Educational Leadership* 26(1968):169–75.

Jeffrey, W.E., and Samuels, S.J. "Effect of Method on Reading Training on Initial Learning and Transfer." *Journal of Verbal Learning* 6(1967):354–58.

Johns, J.L. "The Dolch Basic Word List—Then and Now." *Journal of Reading Behavior* 3(1970–71):35–40.

Johnson, M.S. "Readiness for Critical Reading." *Education* 73(1953):391–96.

Jones, J.P. *Intersensory Transfer, Perceptual Shifting, Modal Preference, and Reading.* Newark, Del.: International Reading Association, 1972.

Justman, J. "Academic Aptitude and Reading Test Scores of Disadvantaged Children Showing Varying Degrees of Mobility." *Journal of Educational Measurement* 2(1965):151–55.

Kagan, J. "Reflection Impulsivity and Reading Ability in Primary Grade Children." *Child Development* 36(1965):609–28.

Karnes, M.B.; Wollersheim, J.; Stoneburner, R.; Hodgins, A.; and Teska, A. "An Evaluation of Two Pre-School Programs for Disadvantaged Children: A Traditional and a Highly Structured Experimental Pre-School." *Exceptional Children* 34(1968):667–76.

Karraker, R.J., and Doke, L.A. "Errorless Discrimination of Alphabet Letters: Effects of Time and Method of Introducing Competing Stimuli." *Journal of Experimental Education* 38(1970):29–35.

Kaufman, A.S., and Kaufman, N. "Tests Built from Piaget's and Gesell's Tasks as Predictors of First-Grade Achievement." *Child Development* 43(1972):521–35.

Kelly, M.L., and Chen, M.K. "An Experimental Study of Formal Reading Instruction at the Kindergarten Level." *Journal of Educational Research* 60(1967):624–29.

King, E.M. "Effects of Different Kinds of Visual Discrimination Training on Learning to Read Words." *Journal of Educational Psychology* 55(1964):325–33.

King, E.M., and Muehl, S. "Different Sensory Cues as Aids in Beginning Reading." *Reading Teacher* 19(1965):163–68.

Kingston, Jr., A.J. "The Relationship of First Grade Readiness to Third and Fourth-Grade Achievement." *Journal of Educational Research* 56(1962):61–67.

Kirk, S.A., and McCarthy, J.J. "The Illinois Test of Psycholinguistic Abilities—An Approach to Differential Diagnosis." *American Journal of Mental Deficiency* 66(1961):399–412.

Kling, M.; Geyer, J.J.; and Davis, F.B. "Proposal for TRDPR Project No. 2, Literature Search." New Brunswick, N.J.: Graduate School of Education, Rutgers University, 1970.

Langston, G. "Achievement of Gifted Kindergarten and Gifted First-Grade Readers." *Illinois School Research* 3(1966):18–24.

Leeds, D.S. "Summary of Research Abstracts—Frostig Developmental Test of Visual Perception." *Journal of the Reading Specialist* 9(1970):125–37.

LeFevre, C.A. *Linguistics, English, and the Language Arts*. Boston: Allyn & Bacon, 1970.

Lesiak, J.F. "The Relationship of the Reflection-Impulsivity Dimension and the Reading Ability of Elementary School Children at Two Levels." Ph.D. dissertation, The Ohio State University, 1970.

Linn, J.R., and Ryan, T.J. "The Multi-Sensory-Motor Method of Teaching Reading." *Journal of Experimental Education* 36(1968):57–59.

Lloyd, B. "The Effects of Programmed Perceptual Training on the Reading Achievement and Mental Maturity of Selected First-Grade Pupils: A Pilot Study." *Journal of the Reading Specialist* 6(1966):49–55.

Lott, D. *Visual Word Recognition: Its Implications for Reading Research and Instruction*. Inglewood, Calif.: Southwest Regional Laboratory, 1969.

Lott, D.; Smith, F.; and Cronnell, B. *Functional Equivalence of Feature Combinations in the Visual Identification of Words*. Inglewood, Calif.: Southwest Regional Laboratory, 1968.

Love, H.D., and Stallings, S.G. "A Comparison of Chidren Who Attended Project Head Start Not Having a Follow-through Program and Children Who Attended Project Head Start Having a Follow-through Program." *Education* 91(1970):88–91.

Lowell, R.E. "A Factor Analysis of Reading Readiness Tests." *Journal of the New England Reading Association* 5(1970):28–30.

MacKinnon, A.R. *How Do Children Learn to Read?* Ontario, Canada: Copp Clark, 1959.

Mackworth, J.F. "Some Models of the Reading Process: Learners and Skilled Readers." *Reading Research Quarterly* 7(1972):701–33.

Mackworth, N.H. "Seven Cognitive Skills in Reading." *Reading Research Quarterly* 7(1972):679–700.

Marchbanks, G., and Levin, H. "Cues by Which Children Recognize Words." *Journal of Educational Psychology* 56(1965):57–61.

Marsh, G., and Sherman, M. *Transfer from Word Components to Words and Vice Versa in Beginning Reading*. Inglewood, Calif.: Southwest Regional Laboratory, 1970.

Masland, R.L., and Cratty, B.J. "The Nature of the Reading Process, the Rationale of Non-Educational Remedial Methods." In *Reading Forum*, edited by E. Calkins. NIMOS Monograph No. 11, National Institute of Health, 1971.

Mason, G.E., and Blanton, W.E. "Semantic Constructs and Beginning Reading." In *Reading: Process and Pedagogy*, edited by G.B. Schick and M.M. May. *Nineteenth Yearbook of the National Reading Conference* 1(1971):39–45.

McConnell, F.; Horton, K.B.; and Smith B.R. "Language Development and Cultural Disadvantagement." *Exceptional Children* 35(1969):597–606.

McCormick, C.C.; Schnobrich, J.N.; and Footlik, S.W. "The Effect of Perceptual-Motor Training on Reading Achievement." *Academic Therapy Quarterly* 4(1969):171–76.

McDowell, E.E. "A Programmed Method of Reading Instruction for Use with Kindergarten Children." *Psychological Record* 18(1968):233–39.

McManus, A. "The Denver Pre-Reading Project Conducted by WENH-TV." *Reading Teacher* 18(1964):22–26.

McNinch, G. "Auditory Perceptual Factors and Measured First-Grade Reading Achievement." *Reading Research Quarterly* 6(1971):472–92.

McWhorter, K.T., and Levy, J. "The Influence of a Tutorial Program upon Tutors." *Journal of Reading* 14(1971):221–24.

Metraux, R.W. "Auditory Memory Span for Speech Sounds: Norms for Children." *Journal of Speech Disorders* 9(1944):31–38.

Miller, W. "Certain Home Environmental Factors and Children's Reading Readiness." *Illinois School Research* 7(1970):30–34.

Miller, W.H. "An Examination of Children's Daily Schedules in Three Social Classes and Their Relation to First-Grade Reading Achievement." *Wisconsin State Reading Association News* 12(1969):2–10.

Milner, E. "A Study of the Relationship between Reading Readiness in Grade One School Children and Patterns of Parent-Child Interaction." *Child Development* 22(1951):95–112.

Money, J., ed. *Reading Disability: Progress and Research Needs in Dyslexia.* Baltimore: The Johns Hopkins Press, 1962.

Morency, A. "Auditory Modality, Research, and Practice." In *Perception and Reading,* edited by H.K. Smith. *Proceedings of the International Reading Association* 12(1968):17–21.

Morphett, M.V., and Washburne, C. "When Should Children Begin to Read?" *Elementary School Journal* 31(1931):496–503.

Morris, J. "Teaching Children to Read." *Educational Research* 1(1959):38–49.

Morris, J.; Pestaner, M.; and Nelson, A. "Mobility and Achievement." *Journal of Experimental Education* 35(1967):74–80.

Morrison, C., and Harris, A.J. "Effect of Kindergarten on the Reading of Disadvantaged Children." *Reading Teacher* 22(1968):4–9.

Mortensen, W.P. "Selected Pre-Reading Tasks, Socioeconomic Status, and Sex." *Reading Teacher* 22(1968):45–49, 61.

Muehl, S. "The Effects of Visual Discrimination Pretraining on Learning to Read a Vocabulary List in Kindergarten Children." *Journal of Educational Psychology* 51(1960):217–21.

————. "The Effects of Visual Discrimination Pretraining with Word and Letter Stimuli on Learning to Read a Word List in Kindergarten Children." *Journal of Educational Psychology* 52(1961):215–21.

Mulder, R.F., and Curtin, J. "Vocal Phonetic Ability and Silent Reading Achievement." *Education Digest* 21(1956):46–47.

Neville, M.H. "Effect of Reading Method on the Development of Auditory Memory Span." *Reading Teacher* 22(1968):30–35.

Nober, L.W. "Auditory Discrimination and Classroom Noise." *Reading Teacher* 27(1973):288–91.

Nodine, C.F., and Lang, N.J. "Development of Visual Scanning Strategies for Differentiating Words." *Developmental Psychology* 5(1971):221–32.

Oakland, T. "Relationships between Social Class and Phonemic and Non-Phonemic Auditory Discrimination Ability." Paper presented at the meeting of the American Educational Research Association, Los Angeles, Calif., February 1969.

O'Donnell, B. "ERIC/RCS." *Reading Teacher* 27(1974):874–76.

O'Donnell, C.M. "The Effectiveness of an Informal Conceptual Program in Developing Reading Readiness in the Kindergarten." In *Language, Reading and the Communication Process,* edited by C. Braun. Newark, Del.: International Reading Association, 1971.

Olsen, T., and Rupley, W.H. "ERIC/RCS." *Reading Teacher* 26(1973):866–72.

Olson, D.R., and Pau, A.S. "Emotionally Loaded Words and the Acquisition of a Sight Vocabulary." *Journal of Educational Psychology* 57(1966):174–78.

Otto, W. "The Acquisition and Retention of Paired Associates by Good, Average, and Poor Readers." *Journal of Educational Psychology* 52(1961):241–48.

Otto, W., and Pizzillo, C. "Effect of Intralist Similarity on Kindergarten Pupils' Rate of Word Acquisition and Transfer." Paper presented at the meeting of the American Educational Research Association, New York, February 1971.

Panther, E.E. "Prediction of First-Grade Reading Achievement." *Elementary School Journal* 68(1967):44–48.

Perlish, H.N. "Early Reading via Television." *Educational Television International* 4(1970): 110–15.

Petty, M.C. "An Experimental Study of Certain Factors Influencing Reading Readiness." *Journal of Educational Psychology* 30(1939):215–30.

Petty, W. "Critical Reading in the Primary Grades." *Elementary English* 33(1956):298–302.

Piaget, J. *The Language and Thought of the Child.* Rev. ed. London: Routhledge & Kegan Paul, 1959.

———. *Six Psychological Studies.* New York: Random House, 1967.

Pikulski, J.J. "Assessment of Pre-Reading Skills: A Review of Frequently Employed Measures." *Reading World* 13(1974):171–97.

Popp, H.M. "The Measurement and Training of Visual Discrimination Skills Prior to Reading Instruction." *Journal of Experimental Education* 73(1967):91–100.

———. "Visual Discrimination of Alphabet Letters." *Reading Teacher* 17(1964):221–25.

Postman, L., and Rosenzweig, M.R. "Perceptual Recognition of Words." *Journal of Speech and Hearing Disorders* 22(1957):245–53.

Potts, M., and Savino, C. "The Relative Achievement of First Graders under Three Different Programs." *Journal of Educational Research* 61(1968):447–50.

Prendergast, R. "Pre-Reading Skills Developed in Montessori and Conventional Nursery Schools." *Elementary School Journal* 70(1969):135–41.

Prescott, G.A. "Sex Differences in Metropolitan Readiness Test Results." *Journal of Educational Research* 48(1955):605–10.

Pryzwansky, W.B. "Effects of Perceptual-Motor Training and Manuscript Writing on Reading Readiness Skills in Kindergarten." *Journal of Educational Psychology* 63(1972):110–15.

Ramsey, W.S. "An Evaluation of Three Methods of Teaching Reading." In *Challenge and Experiment in Reading,* edited by J.A. Figurel. *Proceedings of the International Reading Association* 7(1962):153.

Ramsey, W.S., and Boercker, M. "The Influence of a Head Start Program on Reading Achievement." In *Forging Ahead in Reading,* edited by J.A. Figurel. *Proceedings of the International Reading Association* 12(1968):513–18.

Reed, J.C., and Pepper, R.S. "Interrelationship of Vocabulary, Comprehension and Rate among Disabled Readers." *Journal of Experimental Education* 25(1957):333–37.

Reynolds, M.C. "A Study of Relationships between Auditory Characteristics and Specific Silent Reading Abilities." *Journal of Educational Research* 46(1953):439–49.

Risko, V.J. "Relate Auditory Discrimination to Reading Achievement." *Reading World* 13(1973):43–51.

Robinson, H.M. "Factors Which Affect Success in Reading." *Elementary School Journal* 55(1955):263–69.

———. *Why Pupils Fail in Reading.* Chicago: University of Chicago Press, 1946.

Rosen, C.L. "An Experimental Study of Visual Perceptual Training and Reading Achievement in First Grade." *Perceptual and Motor Skills* 22(1966):979–86.

Rosenfield, S.S. "The Effect of Perceptual Style in Word Discrimination Ability of Kindergarten Children." Ph.D. dissertation, University of Wisconsin, 1967.

Rosenthal, D.J., and Resnick, L.B. "The Sequence of Information in Arithmetic Word Problems." In preparation, 1971. Cited in "Reading Research" by Della-Piana, G.M. and Endo, G.T., 1973.

Ruddell, R.B. "Psycholinguistic Implications for a Systems of Communication Model." In *Psycholinguistics and the Teaching of Reading,* edited by K.S. Goodman and J.T. Fleming. Newark, Del.: International Reading Association, 1969. Also in *Theoretical Models and Processes of Reading,* edited by H. Singer and R.B. Ruddell. Newark, Del.: International Reading Association, 1970.

Rude, R.T. "Readiness Tests:Implications for Early Childhood." *Reading Teacher* 26(1973): 572–80.

Rudisill, M. "Flashed Digit and Phrase Recognition and Rate of Oral and Concrete Responses: A Study of Advanced and Retarded Readers in the Third Grade." *Journal of Psychology* 42(1956):317–20.

———. "Interrelationships of Functional Phonic Knowledge, Reading, Spelling, and Mental Age." *Elementary School Journal* 57(1957):264–67.

Russell, D.H., and Fea, H.R. "Research on Teaching Reading." In *Handbook of Research on Teaching,* edited by N.L. Gage. Chicago: Rand McNally & Co., 1963.

Rystrom, R. "Evaluating Letter Discrimination Problems in the Primary Grades." *Journal of Reading Behavior* 1(1969):38–48.

Sabaroff, R.E. "A Comparative Investigation of Six Reading Programs: Two Basal, Four Linguistic." *Education* 91(1971):303–14.

Samuels, S.J. "Effects of Pictures on Learning to Read, Comprehension and Attitudes." *Review of Educational Research* 40(1970):397–407.

———. "Success and Failure in Learning to Read: A Critique of the Research." *Reading Research Quarterly* 8(1973):200–239.

Samuels, S.J. and Jeffrey, W.E. "Discriminability of Words, and Letter Cues Used in Learning to Read." *Journal of Educational Psychology* 57(1966):337–40.

Santostephano, S.; Rutledge, L.; and Randall, D. "Cognitive Styles and Reading Disability." *Psychology in the Schools* 2(1965):57–62.

Sapir, S.G. "Auditory Discrimination with Words and Nonsense Syllables." *Academic Therapy* 7(1972):307–13.

Schiffman, H.R. "Some Components of Sensation and Perception for the Reading Process." *Reading Research Quarterly* 7(1972):588–612.

Schonnell, F.J. *Psychology and Teaching of Reading.* 3d ed. Edinburgh: Oliver & Boyd, 1951.

Segal, M. "An Experimental Study in Perceptual Modality Training." *Journal of Reading Behavior* 3(1970–71):22–34.

Sheffer, M.J. "A Study of the Effect of a Program of Visual-Motor-Tactile Skills Development on Standardized Readiness Test Performance." *Reading Research Quarterly* 3(1969): 28–35.

Sheridan, M.D. *The Child's Hearing of Speech.* London: Meuthuen & Co., 1948.

Shinn, B.M. "A Study of Teacher Judgement and Readiness Tests as Predictors of Future Achievement." *Illinois School Research* 6(1969):12–15.

Singer, H. "A Developmental Model for Speed of Reading in Grades Three through Six." *Reading Research Quarterly* 1(1965):29–49. Also in *Theoretical Models and Processes of Reading,* edited by H. Singer and R.B. Ruddell. Newark, Del.: International Reading Association, 1970.

Singer, H.; Balow, J.H.; and Dahms, P. "A Continuum of Teaching Strategies for Developing Reading Readiness at the Kindergarten Level." In *Forging Ahead in Reading,* edited by J.A. Figurel. *Proceedings of the International Reading Association* 12(1968):463–68.

Skailand, D.B. "A Comparison of Four Language Units in Teaching Beginning Reading." Paper presented at the meeting of the American Educational Research Association, New York, February 1971.

Smith F. *Understanding Reading.* New York: Holt, Rinehart & Winston, 1971.

Smith, H.P., and Dechant, E.V. *Psychology in Teaching Reading.* Englewood Cliffs, N.J.: Prentice-Hall, 1961.

Smythe, P.; Hardy, M.; Stennett, R.; and Wilson, H. "Developmental Patterns in Elemental Reading Skills: Phoneme Discrimination." *Alberta Journal of Educational Research* 18(1972):59–67.

Smythe, P.; Stennett, R.; Hardy, M.; and Wilson, H. "Developmental Patterns in Elemental Skills: Knowledge of Uppercase and Lowercase Letter Names." *Journal of Reading Behavior* 3(1970–71):24–33.

Spache, G.D., and Spache, E.B. *Reading in the Elementary School.* Boston: Allyn & Bacon, 1969.

Sparks, P.E., and Fay, L.C. "An Evaluation of Two Methods of Teaching Reading." *Elementary School Journal* 57(1957):386–90.

Sprigle, H.A. "Can Poverty Children Live on 'Sesame Street'?" *Young Children* 25(1971):202–16.

Staats, A.W.; Minke, K.; Finley, J.; Wolf, M.; and Brooks, L. "A Reinforced System and Experimental Procedure for the Laboratory Study of Reading Acquisition." *Child Development* 35(1964):209–31.

Stanchfield, J.M. "The Development of Pre-Reading Skills in an Experimental Kindergarten." *Elementary School Journal* 71(1971):438–47.

———. "Differences in Learning Patterns of Boys and Girls." In *Self and Society,* edited by M.P. Douglass, *Yearbook of the Claremont Reading Conference* 32(1968):218–27.

Standing, L.; Sell, C.; Boss, J.; and Haber, R. "Effect of Visualization and Subvocalization on Perceptual Clarity." *Psychonomic Science* 18(1970):89–90.

Stauffer, R.G. *Directing Reading Maturity as a Cognitive Process.* New York: Harper & Row, Publishers, 1969.

———. "A Vocabulary Study Comparing Reading, Arithmetic, Health and Science Texts." *Reading Teacher* 20(1966):141–47.

Steinberg, P.M., and Rosenberg, R. "Relationship between Reading and Various Aspects of Visual Anomalies." *Journal of American Optometric Association* 26(1956):444–46.

Stone, M., and Pielstick, N.L. "Effectiveness of Delacoto Treatment with Kindergarten Children." *Psychology in the Schools* 6(1969):63–68.

Sullivan, D.D., and Humphrey, J.H. *Teaching Reading through Motor Learning.* Springfield, Ill.: Charles C. Thomas, Publisher, 1973.

Sullivan, H.J., and Labeaune, C. "Parents: Summer Reading Teachers!" *Elementary School Journal* 71(1971):279–85.

Sullivan, H.J.; Okada, M.; and Niedermeyer, F. "Learning and Transfer under Two Methods of Word Attack Instruction." *American Educational Research Journal* 8(1971):227–39.

Sutton, M.H. "Children Who Learned to Read in Kindergarten: A Longitudinal Study." *Reading Teacher* 22(1969):595–602, 683.

Tagatz, G.E. "Grouping by Sex at the First and Second Grade." *Journal of Educational Research* 59(1966):415–18.

Taylor, S.E. *Eye-movement Photography with the Reading Eye.* Huntington, N.Y.: Educational Development Laboratories, 1958.

Tinker, M.A. *Bases for Effective Reading.* Minneapolis: University of Minnesota Press, 1965.

Tobiessen, J.; Duckworth, B.; and Conrad, W. "Relationships between the Schenectedy Kindergarten Rating Scales and First-Grade Achievement and Adjustment." *Psychology in the Schools* 8(1971):29–36.

Travers, R.M.W., ed. *Second Handbook of Research on Teaching.* Chicago: Rand McNally & Co., 1973.

Venezky, R.L. and Calfee, R.C. "The Reading Competency Model." In *Theoretical Models and Processes of Reading,* edited by H. Singer and R.B. Ruddell. Newark, Del.: International Reading Association, 1970.

Vernon, M.D. "The Perceptual Process in Reading." *Reading Teacher* 13(1959):2–8.

Waite, R.R. "Further Attempts to Integrate and Urbanize First-Grade Reading Textbooks: A Research Study." *Journal of Negro Education* 37(1968):62–69.

Waite, R.R.; Blom, G.; Zimet, F.; and Edge, S. "First-Grade Reading Textbooks." *Elementary School Journal* 67(1967):366–74.

Waldman, J.L.; Wade, F.; and Aretz, C. *Hearing and the School Child.* Washington D.C.: Volta Bureau, 1931.

Walters, R., and Kosowski, I. "Symbolic Learning and Reading Retardation." *Journal of Consulting Psychologists* 27(1963):75–82.

Wardhaugh, R. "Theories of Language Acquisition in Relation to Beginning Instruction." *Reading Research Quarterly* 7(1971):168–94.

Watson, B.L. "Field Dependence and Early Reading Achievement." Ph.D. dissertation, University of California at Los Angeles, 1969.

Weaver, W.W., and Kingston, A.J. "Modeling the Effects of Oral Language upon Reading Language." *Reading Research Quarterly* 7(1972):613–27.

Weber, R.M. "A Linguistic Analysis of First-Grade Reading Errors." *Reading Research Quarterly* 5(1970):427–51.

Wiberg, J.L., and Trost, M.A. "A Comparison between the Content of First-Grade Primers and the Free Choice Library Selections made by First-Grade Students." *Elementary English* 47(1970):492–98.

Wiederholt, J.L., and Hammill, D.D. "Use of the Frostig-Horne Visual Perception Program in the Urban School." *Psychology in the Schools* 8(1971):268–74.

Williams, J.P. "Learning to Read: A Review of Theories and Models." *Reading Research Quarterly* 8(1973):121–46.

————. "Training Kindergarten Children to Discriminate Letterlike Forms." *American Educational Research Journal* 6(1969):501–14.

Williams, J.P., and Ackerman, M.D. "Simultaneous and Successive Discriminations of Similar Letters." *Journal of Educational Psychology* 62(1971):132–37.

Willmon, B. "Parent Participation as a Factor in the Effectiveness of Head Start Programs." *Journal of Educational Research* 62(1969):406–10.

Winett, R.A.; Richards, C.; and Krasner, L. "Child-monitored Token Reading Program." *Psychology in the Schools* 8(1971):259–62.

Wollam, W.A. "A Comparison of Two Methods of Teaching Reading." Ph.D. dissertation, Western Reserve University, 1961.

Wozencraft, M. "Sex Comparisons of Certain Abilities." *Journal of Educational Research* 57(1963):21–27.

Wright, C.E. "Project PLAN Progress Report." *Education* 90(1970):261–69.

Wylie, R.E., and Durrell, D.D. "Teaching Vowels through Phonograms." *Elementary English* 47(1970):787–91.

Yawkey, T.D. "Reading Training and Rural Disadvantaged Five-Year-Old Children." *Reading World* 13(1973):128–40.

Zaruba, E. "Objective and Subjective Evaluation at Grade One." *Reading Teacher* 22(1968): 50–54.

chapter four

Social Studies

Richard K. Jantz

Mapping their world with blocks.

Various approaches have been suggested as a basis for organizing curriculum in social studies. Weikart et al. suggested a cognitively oriented curriculum. Bruner advocated a process approach with an emphasis on skill development. Kohlberg and Mayer discussed cognitive development as being the aim of education. Jarolimek considered understandings, attitudes, and skills important areas for social studies education. The 1971 National Council for the Social Studies publication, *Social Studies Curriculum Guidelines,* listed knowledge, abilities, valuing, and social participation as categories for curriculum sources. The Center for Education in the Social Sciences and the Social Science Education Consortium identified the nature of students, the nature of learning, the nature of society, and the nature of knowledge as sources of social studies curriculum (Taylor and Haas, 1973).

Hymes in discussing children under six emphasized the importance of building self-concepts and social learnings. He asserted a healthy child is "a child who feels pleased with himself and pleased with others, a child who can live with himself and live with others" (Hymes, p. 331). Stant recommended a social studies program for nursery school and kindergarten children that focused on social adjustments whereby the child learned about himself and others. Johnson stressed social learnings and growth stages as part of the nursery school curriculum. Leeper et al. considered the formation of attitudes in young children one of the important aspects of social studies programs for three, four, and five year olds.

Spodek has identified a succession of goals for kindergartens over the past one hundred years (Spodek, 1973, pp. 192–95):

1. Kindergartens to Teach Philosophic Idealism
2. Kindergartens to Americanize Immigrant Children
3. Kindergartens to Build "Proper Habits"
4. Kindergartens to Provide Emotional Prophylaxis
5. Kindergartens to Provide a Vestibule for the Grades
6. Kindergartens to Present the Content of School Subjects
7. Kindergartens to Develop "Learning How to Learn" Skills

In projecting new social studies programs for young children, Spodek (1974) suggested adopting a Piagetian framework stressing goals in the areas of physical knowledge, social knowledge, logico-mathematical knowledge including spatiotemporal knowledge, and representation or expression.

Preston and Herman reported on newer programs in elementary social studies. They found that "newer programs incorporate intellectually substantial concepts and generalizations; they cover fewer topics, giving the child the experience of learning about selected aspects of society in depth; and they provide him with the opportunity to make some discoveries through his own efforts and to work out some explanations of social phenomena himself" (Preston and Herman, p. 47).

With a variety of approaches available around which to organize a social studies curriculum in early childhood, the teacher must become an educational decision maker in formulating a social studies program. The intent of this chapter is to provide the teacher with some of the theoretical background and a sampling of the research for some of the areas that have been identified as important to nursery school and primary grade social studies programs.

The first section relates to the broad area of understandings and cognitive development and focuses on concept formation in young children. The second section contains discussions on thinking, problem solving, inquiry, and decision-making skills, based upon the process approach. The third and fourth sections rely heavily on a Piagetian cognitive developmental framework and describe map and globe skills and time and chronology skills, respectively. Section five combines cognitive, affective, and behavioral components into a description of the formation of attitudes and prejudices in young children. This section is followed by one on the self-concept of the child and how this concept expands to include others. Section seven augments the previous sections to include social learning theory. The final section is on moral development about which Kohlberg has said, "Let me turn now from cognitive to moral stages which I think are of even greater significance to social studies education" (Kohlberg, 1973, p. 372).

Concept Formation

Gagné proposed a hierarchy of eight learning types with the attainment of concepts (Type 6) being a prerequisite to principle learning (Type 7) or problem solving (Type 8).

Concept learning could be defined as "putting things into a class and responding to the class as a whole" (Gagné, p. 126). Gagné further stated that "the great value of concepts as means of thinking and communicating is the fact that they have concrete references" (Gagné, p. 138). Learning a concept also means learning to respond to stimuli in terms of abstracted properties such as color, shape, position, or number as opposed to concrete physical properties such as specific wavelength or particular intensities. By combining the concrete references with the abstracted properties, a child "is able to identify a class of objects that differ from each other physically in infinite ways" (Gagné, p. 47).

Concepts represent characteristics of events, rather than a particular event. This permits the identification of particular attributes of concepts. Kagan identified four important qualities of a concept: degree of abstraction, complexity, differentiation, and centrality of dimension (Kagan, p. 87). A concept may be very concrete, such as a dog or a cat, or abstract, such as justice or corruption. Concepts that are dependent upon few dimensions such as smoke are less complex than concepts that rely upon many dimensions such as the concept of society. There is also a range in concepts in terms of differentiation. The concept "house" can take many forms and is highly differentiated. The basic set of qualities that represent rain has little variation that is typical of limited differentiated concepts. Kagan stated that "some concepts derive their essential meaning from one or two central dimensions; other concepts rest on a set of dimensions that are of equal importance in defining them" (Kagan, p. 88). The concept of living animal rests equally upon the various life processes such as assimilation, reproduction, and respiration while the concept "infant" is determined by the central dimension of age.

Bruner et al. indicated that several characteristics can be combined to form broad classes of concepts. For example, the concept of distance is based upon a starting point and a stopping point and the span in between. Distance would be considered a relational concept. Relational concepts identify particular associations such as the associations between people like in-laws, cousins, uncles, or grandmothers. Concepts involving time or combinations of time and distance such as miles per hour, light-years, or longitude are also relational concepts. These types of concepts are rather difficult for children to learn.

Another category of concepts suggested by Bruner is disjunctive concepts. These involve either-or types of judgments. For example, academic achievement could be considered as either the grade level one is in or one's performance on a standardized test. An out in baseball may be either a third strike on the batter or a fly ball caught by the opposing team. Learning the various criteria and the exceptions that might constitute a disjunctive concept makes the acquisition of these types of concepts difficult for young children.

A third class of concepts mentioned by Bruner is conjunctive concepts. Conjunctive concepts combine characteristics in an additive manner, such as in a play area, math corner, or doll house. The word *and* is important in formulating conjunctive concepts. Concepts in this class may be complex and abstract; examples are international cold war, socioeconomic status, or differentiated school staff.

Taba suggested that the development of concepts consists of three processes: the differentiating of the properties or characteristics of objects and events, such as differentiating the materials of which houses are built from other characteristics of houses; grouping; categorizing and labeling (Taba, 1965, pp. 534–42). (See Taba et al. 1971 for instructional strategies based upon these processes.)

In addition to the processes involved in the development of concepts, there is some indication that children pass through age-related stages in early concept formation. Piaget (1954) reported that with increasing age, the child moves from an egocentric universe revolving around his perceptions and actions to an objective world independent of his will. The development of the concepts of object, space, time, and causality are essential in moving into an objective world.

Welch and Long examined the formation of concepts in terms of hierarchies. They found that young children could understand the genus-species relationship even though they might not have been able to verbalize the relationship. They identified a series of stages that a child passes through in formulating concepts in terms of hierarchies. The first grasp of simple genus-species relationships such as cats and dogs are animals appears about the twenty-sixth month. The second stage in the understanding of hierarchies occurs around four and one-half years of age. Children comprehend food-meat-ham and food-fruit-orange relationships; or people-man-father and people-lady-nurse hierarchies. In the final stages of understanding higher-order hierarchies, children can handle from four or five up to eight or nine steps.

Banks proposed that hierarchies of concepts could be used to create curriculum units for social studies (Banks, 1973b, pp. 77–85). Key concepts from various disciplines such as anthropology, history, geography, sociology, political science, or economics might serve as organizing concepts in social studies instruction. Taba et al. (1971) suggested that eleven key concepts could serve as the basis for an entire elementary social studies program. These concepts were causality, conflict, cooperation, cultural change, differences, interdependence, modification, power, societal control, tradition, and values.

Spodek believed that social science concepts could be learned by kindergarten pupils (Spodek, 1963, pp. 253–56). He tested this idea and concluded:

1. Kindergarten children can begin to develop significant social science concepts.
2. Kindergarten children bring a background of knowledge with them to school.
3. Kindergarten children gather information in many ways.
4. Kindergarten children can deal with ideas over long periods of time.
5. Kindergarten children use the tools of the social scientist.
6. Kindergarten children transfer their understanding in approaching new situations.

The research on the teaching of concepts in social studies was reviewed by Decaroli. He disclosed that children at the kindergarten level and higher were able to utilize the basic processes of concept formation. A critical variable in concept development was the degree of abstraction of the concept; the more concrete the examples, the easier it was to learn the concept. Decaroli provided a series of questions to guide the analysis of a concept (Decaroli, p. 332):

1. What kind of concept is it? What is the rule that could be followed to decide whether or not a given instance is an example of the concept?

2. What are the critical or relevant attributes of the concept? What things need to be observed by pupils in order to successfully identify an instance of the concept?
3. What examples can I choose that will highlight these relevant attributes? Which ones will minimize irrelevant attributes?
4. What examples can I make available that are not instances of the selected concept?
5. Can I find a range of examples of this concept, some of which are more concrete than others or more familiar to pupils?
6. What other concepts are related to this one? Which of these are prerequisite to learning the selected concept? Are these prerequisites present among pupils?

Schwab and Stern investigated the effects of variety on the learning of social studies concepts by preschool children. They discovered that superior learning occurs with the presentation of fewer concepts. McKinney and Golden concluded "that many abstract concepts can be taught more efficiently through an appropriate activity which requires the child's direct experience as opposed to methods which rely solely on verbal and symbolic modes of presentation" (McKinney and Golden, p. 176). Rogers and Layton found that first-grade children could conceptualize social studies topics but that they changed little in their ability to conceptualize between the first and third grade. Lowry reported that many second graders knew key social studies concepts for that grade prior to instruction. Other studies (Brown, Larkins and Shaver, and Spears) indicated that basic economic concepts could be taught to first graders. Inquiries (Goldstein, Portugaly, and Sheridan) acknowledged that primary grade children had some concepts relating to maps and globes and the study of geography. Towler and Nelson disclosed, however, that most children do not develop a concept of scale before age ten or eleven. Mugge (1968) detected that many first graders had difficulty with concepts relating to geography, political science, economics, and time as it related to history.

Martorella stated that "while concept learning as an objective is currently receiving considerable emphasis in the social studies literature and in the descriptive literature accompanying curricular materials, little evidence has been experimentally adduced concerning how students systematically learn social science concepts" (Martorella, pp. 888–90). Martorella has listed several categories in which research relating to concepts in the social studies is needed:

1. Types of concepts
2. Complexity of critical attributes
3. Effects of extraneous or distracting material
4. The hierarchical relationship of concepts
5. Relationship of concepts to nonconcepts

Several social studies projects have incorporated concepts from the various social sciences as part of their primary grade emphasis (see *Social Education*, November 1972 for a brief review of twenty-six different social studies projects). The Materials and Activities for Teachers and Children (MATCH) project was developed by the

Boston Children's Museum. The project relies heavily upon inquiry techniques and concepts from anthropology, sociology, geography, and history. The Concepts and Inquiry program developed as the Greater Cleveland Social Studies project also utilizes the inquiry approach and emphasizes concepts from history and geography as well as some from other social science disciplines. Project Social Studies developed at the University of Minnesota is an interdisciplinary program stressing concepts from anthropology, sociology, and geography and inquiry strategies. The Taba program in social studies uses questions to promote thinking and contains concepts from anthropology, economics, geography, history, political science, psychology, and sociology.

Other social science projects tend to emphasize a single discipline. There are several projects that focus on concepts for the primary grades. Senesh's economic program, Our Working World, centers around the basic needs of man—food, clothing, and shelter. Both large and small group instruction employing role playing, class discussions, and committee work are included. The Georgia Anthropology Project introduces the concept of culture to kindergartners and first graders and the methodology of archeology to second graders. The project is organized around a deductive approach to instruction. Concepts are first presented and then followed by readings and discussions. The Lincoln Filene Center for Citizenship and Public Affairs has developed a program based upon concepts from political science. The program for the primary grades is based upon intergroup relations. It investigates human behavior and why groups, individuals, and cultures differ. Attention is given to areas such as discrimination, prejudice, poverty, and race relations. The program centers upon active student involvement with an emphasis on inductive methodology.

Thinking, Problem Solving, Inquiry, and Decision Making

Dewey stated that thinking "converts action that is merely appetitive, blind, and impulsive into intelligent action" (Dewey, p. 17). Thinking frees the individual from impulse reactions so that he can plan deliberate courses of action. Thinking is regulated by its purpose such that "the nature of the problem fixes the end of thought, and the end controls the process of thinking" (Dewey, p. 15). Dewey blended these principles into a process that is referred to as reflective thinking.

The process originates with a doubt, a concern, or some perplexity that serves as the guiding factor throughout the thinking process. A tentative plan is formulated to account for the peculiarities in question and to offer some possible suggestions for solutions; this is sometimes referred to as the formation of a hypothesis. An intellectual search, including some suspense, takes place and the information is processed and analyzed. Judgments are made based upon the examination and testing of the information obtained in relationship to past experiences and previous knowledge (Dewey, Chapter One).

The process of reflective thinking outlined by Dewey is not to be construed as an irreversible sequence of steps but as a series of actions aimed at the discovery of information that will resolve the doubt or confusion.

To be genuinely thoughtful, we must be willing to sustain and protract that state of doubt which is the stimulus to thorough inquiry, so as not to accept an idea or make positive assertion of a belief until justifying reasons have been found. (Dewey, p. 16)

Russell viewed thinking as a process that included materials, motives, and abilities. The materials of thinking include images, concepts, sensations, memories, and perceptions. Motives for thinking are determined by values, attitudes, and feelings. Abilities in thinking produce ease and precision in problem situations. The thinking process consists of problem solving, inductive thinking, discovery, and critical thinking. These factors can be ordered into the following series of steps (Russell, p. 16):

1. The child's environment stimulates mental activity.
2. The orientation or initial direction of thinking is established.
3. The search for related materials takes place.
4. There is a patterning of various ideas into some hypothesis or tentative conclusions.
5. The deliberative, or critical, part of the thinking process is developed.
6. The concluding stage of the thinking process takes place when the selected hypothesis is tested.

Other investigators have developed processes ranging between three and nine steps for problem solving (see Russell, p. 256). These steps do not tend to be rigid following a uniform pattern; they vary depending upon the problem. For example, Humphrey provided a six-step process for directed thinking with the order of the steps involving trial and error, association and images, and a flash of insight differing as the problem under investigation changed.

Lastrucci described some of the basic assumptions underlying the scientific method. Gee and Batten related some of the principles of the scientific method to social science research and methods. Kerlinger applied these processes to educational and psychological inquiry. Goldmark discussed the role of inquiry in the social studies curriculum, and Dunfee and Sagl formulated processes of problem solving for social studies programs in the elementary school.

Problem solving occurs when a person desires to obtain a specific goal but does not have direct access to it. The solution to a problem can be obtained in a number of ways depending upon the past experiences and learning of the subject. Kagan indicated that the problem-solving process usually follows a set sequence. The child first must understand the problem and be able to hold elements of it in his memory while he investigates possible solutions. He then evaluates and forms a hypothesis in the next phase of the problem-solving process. The child chooses a solution and implements it in the final step.

Sagl discussed the relationship between problem solving and inquiry. Problem solving relates to finding a solution to a particular problem. Inquiry relates to the obtainment of knowledge that can be used to formulate social theory. Banks agreed with this distinction when he stated, "The building of social theory is the primary goal of social inquiry" (Banks, 1973b, p. 43).

The scientific procedure tends to be cognitively oriented. In the social sciences decision making often utilizes inquiry as a part of a process that incorporates both cognitive and affective judgments. Banks indicated that social science inquiry differed from decision making because in inquiry knowledge is produced while in decision making knowledge is selected, synthesized, and applied. Banks combined these principles to formulate a decision-problem model (Banks, 1973b, p. 29). One branch of this model utilizes social knowledge obtained from inquiries by social scientists or one's own social inquiry. The other branch employs a value inquiry process resulting in value clarification. The value component and the knowledge component are blended to reach a rational decision that is followed by intelligent social action.

Stevenson developed a reciprocal interaction analysis system that can be used in examining teacher influences on the decision-making behavior of nursery school-age children. The Categories for the Observation of Decision-Making Elements (CODE) system were used with a taxonomy of teacher behaviors that might influence the behaviors of the children. The major categories of the CODE system were (1) attending, (2) focusing on a problem, (3) assisting, (4) informing, (5) extending, (6) prescribing and describing, (7) predicting, (8) intending-choosing, (9) appraising, and (10) mystifying. Stevenson found that teachers scored highest in categories 4, 6, and 9 while children scored highest in categories 2, 4, and 8. Both teachers and children scored low in category 7.

Crabtree designed a study with two groups of second-grade pupils to test the effects of teacher structuring on their thinking. She discovered that children exposed to highly structured discussions exhibited more convergent thinking while those exposed to jointly structured discussions produced more frequent examples of divergent thinking.

Lewis observed the behavior of elementary social studies teachers in terms of the reflective thinking model proposed by Dewey. She found the problem approach in use but that the solutions tended to be the judgments of teachers because the reflective processes were not discussed with the pupils.

Almy and Cartwright examined young children's problem-solving abilities through block building activities. Children between two and three years of age often built structures and then named them while older children often named the structure first and then built it.

Other studies (Hazlitt; Heidbreder; and Isaacs) found that children as young as three could solve problems that dealt with concrete, personal, and immediate situations. Research has indicated that verbalization and the ability to generalize relate to the concreteness or the abstractness of the problem-solving situation (Biber et al.; Hildreth; Long and Welch; and Ray). The problems approach was also found to be effective in the development of abstract concepts and critical thinking skills. (Jones, 1964; Possien; Rapparlie; and Suchman).

Elkind (1967) reviewed some of the research relating to cognition in early childhood. In terms of problem solving, he found that both trial-and-error learning and insight could be observed in the thinking processes of the young child even though the young child had difficulty in verbalizing his behavior. He stated:

> Reasoning is implicit in his actions but he cannot verbalize the relationship he has constructed. By the age of six or seven, however, the child can reason in his head, and this is in part due to internalization of language. (Elkind, 1971, p. 46)

Research on problem solving comparing insight and trial-and-error learning is conflicting. Some studies (Jones, 1932; Ling; and Mattheson) asserted that problem solving by young children was principally trial-and-error learning. However, Alpert had different conclusions. She had preschool children use sticks, boxes, and chairs to obtain prizes. In analyzing the problem-solving behavior of these children, she reported that approximately 70 percent of the time children made their solutions on the basis of sudden insight, gradual insight, or immediate insight. Anderson found a wide range of problem-solving behaviors in young children. In approximately 60 percent of the cases, their behavior was systematic, explorative, or eliminative. In about 30 percent of the cases, their behavior was aimless, blundering, or somewhat erratic. Harter worked with three to six year olds and found that as children grow older, they increasingly rely upon mental manipulation of materials rather than upon trial-and-error learning.

Russell summarized some of the research on problem solving with young children and found that (Russell, pp. 228–29):

1. there is probably no "age of reason" that children must attain before they can do problem solving
2. the problem-solving ability of children, especially preschool children, should not be compared with their verbal abilities
3. the roles of trial and error and of insight in children's problem solving vary with the nature of the problem and with the purpose of the subject
4. rather than indicating that one type of behavior, such as trial and error, is particularly typical of problem solving, the evidence suggests that even young children are capable of a wide variety of activities in solving problems
5. children are often impetuous in their problem solving, jumping from an awareness of the problem to some solution without any intervening steps, influenced by their emotional reactions rather than by a knowledge of logical steps in thinking
6. there is some evidence that children do not solve complex problems in a series of organized steps; therefore, insight may occur in different parts of the solving process
7. problem-solving ability increases with age in terms of both speed and accuracy

Taba stated, "All intellectual skills and abilities from concept formation to problem solving are likely to be identified with thinking" (Taba, 1962, p. 215). Taba (1963) employed a multi-dimensional analysis of taped classroom transactions to examine teacher influences upon children's thinking. She found that teacher behavior had an enormous influence upon children's thinking. This lead to certain assumptions about thinking and the teaching of thinking (Taba et al., 1971, p. 11):

1. Thinking involves an active transaction between an individual and the data with which he is working.
2. The teacher cannot "give" students the ability to think.
3. All school children are capable of thinking at abstract levels, though the quality of individual thinking differs markedly.

4. All subjects offer an appropriate context for thinking.
5. Teachers can develop precise teaching strategies that will encourage and improve student thinking.

McAndrew investigated the problem-solving abilities of children three to six years of age She found that the type of questions asked influenced the thinking behavior of children. Bloom developed a taxonomy of cognitive objectives that can be used as the basis for structuring questions requiring higher level thinking. Fraenkel suggested that pupil responses relate to the questions teachers ask. He proposed a taxonomy of questions that include a "classification in terms of the purposes which teachers might have, the actions required or desired of students, and the types of questions which teachers would accordingly ask" (Fraenkel, p. 177).

In promoting thinking in young children, we should remain conscious of their cognitive and affective development and not expect a level of thinking in advance of their present capabilities. Reflective thinking has been considered an advanced mental process that is often compared to Piaget's formal level of operations. Kohlberg asserted, "Social science and legal disciplines, as patterns of thought, are extensions of a natural mode of thought, that of formal operations. They are not really relevant models of thought for children at an earlier stage" (Kohlberg, 1973, p. 372).

Maps and Globes

Piaget and Inhelder stated that a child can effectively comprehend the complexity of maps and their systems of coordinates only after he has reached the formal operation stage. They believed that children advance through a series of cognitive developmental stages in formulating concepts of place and space.

Copeland outlined these stages of development in relationship to map making with a two-dimensional layout (Copeland, pp. 280–85). In Stage 1 the child uses the concepts of proximity and enclosure to locate objects. During Stage 2, which normally occurs between four and seven years of age, the child begins to develop reference points and locates items by left, right, in front of, and behind. A child in Stage 3 has no difficulty in locating or placing items on the two-dimensional drawing.

A more difficult place and space task for the child is the reproduction of a complete map layout when provided with a model to follow. A child in Stage 1 can only construct a crude approximation. During Stage 2, the child begins to locate items but has no real reference point and has difficulty in utilizing the space at his disposal. In Stage 3, which occurs at age seven or eight, he can locate all positions but has difficulty in preserving distance between objects; towards the end of this stage, the child can establish correct distances by actual measurements. At Stage 4 the child is operating at the formal operation level; he no longer needs concrete measuring devices to position objects correctly but "he now has in his mind abstract coordinates (one vertical and one horizontal) intersecting at the center of the model as the best means of reproducing the model" (Copeland, p. 285).

Mitchell in her work with young children found progressive stages of development based upon children's professed interests in their environment. These stages were similar to Piaget's in progression. For example, between ages five and six children crudely placed familiar objects in space relationships. At approximately age eight, children began to relate the object orientations to distance, and at about age eleven, children started to work on relationships expressed through abstractions.

Skill Development in Social Studies, the thirty-third yearbook of the National Council for the Social Studies, promotes basic map skills that should be taught throughout the primary grades. In the section on maps and globes, Kennamer stated "it is this enlarging personal world that makes necessary the development of a sense of place and space" (Kennamer, p. 169). The following skills were suggested as the basis for interpreting maps and globes:

1. To orient the map and to note directions
2. To recognize the scale of a map and to compute distances
3. To locate places on maps and globes
4. To express relative location
5. To read map symbols
6. To compare maps and to make inferences (Kohn, 1953)

Subskills have been identified for each of these broad areas. Johns and Fraser prescribed an appropriate grade level for the introduction through readiness activities, the systematic development, and the reteaching for maintainence of each of these subskills. Most of the specific skills for the early and late primary grades are proposed at the readiness level rather than the systematic development level. Joyce developed a similar schema for grade placement of map and globe skills.

In relation to skill development, Howe (1931) investigated children's knowledge of direction. After analyzing the responses of over 1,300 children in kindergarten to grade 6, he concluded that children did not know directions and they did not acquire them incidentally. In a later study involving intensive instruction, he disclosed (Howe, 1932, p. 210):

1. Children can systematically and accurately acquire a clear concept of directions in space.
2. Children should be taught directions outside of the classroom in order to exclude the probability of association with local objects.
3. Though it may in some instances be desirable to begin instruction in the latter part of the second grade, evidence points to the third grade as the most favorable period of comprehension.

Other map and globe skills have been taught to primary grade children. Bamberger showed that unit pictographs and developmental picture charts as they relate to graphical interpretation can be used in the first grade. Savage and Bacon taught symbolic map skills to first graders and revealed that they have the skill and sophistication to begin on a more abstract level than was previously thought. McAulay's study demonstrated that second graders can use maps to secure information. Kilman reported that with instruction, fourth graders can use directions, map guides, legends, and map scales and draw reference from maps.

Preston and Herman identified common errors in the maps drawn by young children (Preston and Herman, p. 432):

1. Omissions—for example, terraces or bridges

2. Distortion of shapes
3. Disregard of directional relationships
4. Separation of continuous areas
5. Disregard of natural law

Other studies have proposed that the mastery of certain skills in relation to maps and globes be delayed until after the primary grades. Lee and Stampfer found erroneous and inadequate knowledge on the part of primary grade children; they recommended that directional skills be extended to the upper primary grades. Miller (1967) discovered that most children at the age of twelve had developed the concept of perspective but that few children in the primary grades were able to coordinate perspectives. Sorohan studied children's obtainment of interpretive map skills such as the ability to read scales, grids, symbols, and legends. He concluded that even though these skills were often taught at an earlier age, mastery did not occur until about the fifth grade.

The development of specific concepts is important in the acquisition of map and globe skills. Hanna et al. stated that "geographers agree that what is most needed in the early years is to help children build clear images of the immediate environment and accurate concepts in relation to their first-hand experiences" (Hanna et al., p. 111). They strongly urged that the geographic concepts developed be viewed in terms of biopsychological considerations. Complex terms such as longitude, which involves concepts of both time and distance, should not be taught until the later elementary grades. Towler and Nelson in their study of spatial concepts in children concluded that most children do not develop a concept of scale before the age of ten or eleven. Preston found that spatial concepts in third graders were poorly developed and confused.

However, some concepts can be taught at an earlier age. Portugaly found that kindergarten pupils can develop a basic understanding of geography terms such as earth and sun as well as terms relating to seasonal characteristics. Goldstein examined the land and form concepts held by first graders. He indicated that they entered school with more knowledge than was expected. Verbalization of a concept, however, does not guarantee that the child can associate the terminology with the map symbol. Gengler studied the use of map terminology in relationship to map symbols. He found that 85 percent of the sixth graders in his study were unable to identify a cape on a map. Every child could verbalize a definition of a valley but only 49 percent of them could identify one on a map.

Carr, Wesley, and Murra reviewed the research on the teaching of maps and globes prior to 1950. Their findings are still pertinent. They concluded:

1. Children make numerous errors in trying to read maps.
2. The reading of maps must be taught specifically and concretely.
3. Pupils can be taught to read maps with a fair degree of accuracy.
4. Without guidance pupils do not know whether the word or the dot indicates the location of a city on a map.
5. The use of a scale of miles and reading the directions, the direction of river flow, and the key symbols for locating a place on a map all require specific instruction.

6. The use of outline maps is an effective aid to learning.
7. Real maps and hypothetical maps both have teaching values.
8. Children do not require a knowledge of directions until they study geography.
9. Terms such as zone, latitude, and longitude require specific teaching.
10. Numerous studies prove that an ignorance of common geographic facts is widespread.
11. Geographic errors common among pupils are also common among teachers.
12. Many students have not mastered the simplest descriptive ideas to be gained from a map by the time they enter junior high school.
13. Teachers should not take for granted pupils' ability to read maps.
14. It is doubtful that teaching difficult concepts relating to the sphericity of the earth is productive before the sixth or seventh grade.

Towler believed that in terms of teaching map and globe skills, we really do not know "what to teach, when to teach it, or how to teach it" (Towler, p. 893). He felt that this was due, in part, to our ignorance of the child's obtainment of mapping skills. His research supported Piaget's developmental theory, particularly the relationship of egocentrism as related to the development of map skills. Towler differed from Piaget in that he assigned specific ages to particular stages. Towler expressed a need for research with a focus on

1. Developing a valid and reliable test of egocentrism.
2. Determining the exact relationship between egocentrism and map reading ability.
3. Developing a method of helping a child to become less egocentric at a very early age.

He advised that without research "we will continue to plunge blindly along, attempting to teach map-reading skills with an almost total disregard for the pupil's stage of psychological readiness" (Towler, p. 898).

In addition to *Skill Development in Social Studies* by the National Council for the Social Studies, Mitchell's book, *Young Geographers,* and Hanna's book, *Geography in the Teaching of Social Studies: Conceptual Skills,* provide concepts and skills that are appropriate for the primary grades as well as teaching strategies for the obtainment of these concepts and skills.

Time and Chronology

The underlying principles of time and chronology are formulated upon abstract relational concepts that are difficult for children to obtain, but about which children often ask questions at a very early age. Hess and Croft reported some of the types of questions children ask in relationship to time (Hess and Croft, p. 197). They are as follows:

Is today a long time?
How old will I be when I am forty?
How much time is ten o'clock?
What does four-thirty mean?

When will it be tomorrow?
Mark, a five year old, was asked, "How long is a day?" He replied, "It's today until you get
to tomorrow!" He was then asked, "How long is that?" Mark replied, "Today is when you
get up and you play and you eat lunch and you play some more and you go to school and
you come home and it's nice outside and then it's night and you go to sleep and when you
wake up it's tomorrow!"

Elkind identified clock time, calendar time, and psychological time as three important areas for the development of time concepts in young children (Elkind, 1971, pp.
54–55). Clock time is based upon the formation of time intervals such as hour and
minute. Young children soon learn that these terms have definite meanings; and by
the time they reach kindergarten age, they are using these terms in their conversations
even though an internalization of the duration of the interval has not yet been
developed.

Springer described the development of clock time in four to six year olds. Children
first begin to associate activities with the regular daily class schedule. (This may be
one rationale for placing the daily schedule on the blackboard.) Soon they associate
this schedule and time by the clock. Then they develop concepts of hour, half-hour,
and quarter-hour. Later children begin to set the hands of cardboard clocks to
specific times. These types of activities precede the development of the understanding
of the function of both hands on the clock. In her study of telling time by kindergartners, Stephens concluded that specific instruction was more successful than
incidental instruction in developing concepts of clock time in young children.

Ames revealed that children first learn to respond to time concepts and then learn to
use these concepts themselves, and finally understand the concept to the extent that
they can correctly answer questions relating to the concept. Ames also found that four
year olds can distinguish between morning and afternoon, five year olds can tell
which day it is, and seven year olds can tell clock time in the conventional sense.

Calendar time is formulated upon the temporal or sequential order of events.
Calendar time includes as a basis the development of indefinite time concepts such as
first, last, next, later, sooner, before, and after. The development of these indefinite
time concepts in children is accomplished primarily by experiences. Kim, who was
two and one-half years old, was beginning to develop the concept of later. One night
Grandmother called on the telephone and Kim asked if she could visit Grandma. She
was told that she could go later. Her previous experiences with the concept *later* meant
never. Even though things were promised to her in the future, she was unable to
associate an event by the time they actually occurred with the previous promise. Kim,
now age three, when told something will take place later, wants to know "how soon
later" or "how far later."

The development of calendar time in young children is also exemplified in many
children's books. Very young children often hear fairy tales that begin with the familiar phrase, "once upon a time," which reflects an indefinite time concept of past. In
the later elementary school grades, children's stories reflect a more definite relationship to calendar time. *Across Five Aprils* by Irene Hunt begins, "Ellen Creighton and
her nine-year-old son, Jethro, were planting potatoes in the half-acre just south of

their cabin that morning in mid-April, 1861; they were out in the field as soon as breakfast was over and Southern Illinois at that hour was pink with sunrise and swelling redbud and cluster of bloom over the apple orchard across the road" (Hunt, p. 7).

With the onset of their development of calendar time, children begin to form concepts of week, month, year, and seasons that eventually lead to the development of a true historical perspective. Spiro indicated that attempts to develop a chronological perspective through systematic training should be delayed until about the seventh grade. Kelty had earlier asserted that it was doubtful that the teaching of chronology in historical periods was effective prior to the sixth grade. Mugge (1963) reported that second graders had little grasp of time and place concepts. However, Wesley believed that the later development of historical time concepts in children did not preclude the teaching of time as opposed to chronology (Wesley, p. 362). He felt that there were many time concepts that were not chronological which children could learn in the primary grades.

The third area that Elkind identified as being important for the development of time concepts is psychological time. Piaget identified stages of development of time concepts in young children that are closely related to his stages of cognitive development leading to formal operations.

Piaget indicated that there are two types of time concepts exhibited by young children. There is intuitive time that is "limited to successions and durations given by direct perception," and operational time that uses logic as a basis for the operational understanding of time (Piaget, 1971, p. 2). Piaget believed time to be the coordination or coseriation of at least two motions.

Piaget examined the concept of time by investigating the concepts of succession, duration, and simultaneity. Piaget stated "but if time as we suggest is the operational coordination of the motions themselves, then the relations between simultaneity, succession, and durations must first be constructed one by one" (Piaget, 1971, p. 3). Simultaneity can be considered as a sychronism. For example, if a child looks at two different clocks, each clock should be telling the same time and measuring the same time periods. Succession can be considered as a sequencing of events and duration, as identifying the same period of elapsed time. For an in-depth discussion of these principles from a logico-mathematical perspective, see Piaget's book, *The Child's Conception of Time.*

Copeland applied Piaget's theory of the development of time concepts to children's perceptions of time in terms of age. He found that children at Stage 1 have primitive intuitions of their age in terms of a sibling's age. During Stage 2, some children did not realize who was born first, but they did know that the age difference between them remained the same. Other children could identify who was born first but felt that as a younger sibling grew, he would become older than the other because he would become bigger than the other. Children at Stage 3 on were at the formal operations level. They could understand the idea of succession of events in time in terms of order of births (e.g., If I am older, I must have been born first) and the idea of duration or conservation of age differences (e.g., If I am five years older, I will always be five years older) (Copeland p. 181). For additional teaching implications of Piaget's research on time, see Copeland's chapter on time, pp. 166–82.

Dunfee reported "a review of the studies of time concepts seems to indicate that children may be able to understand time and chronology concepts at an earlier age than previously predicted and that many children are receptive to planned instruction in these areas" (Dunfee, 1970, p. 29). In 1950, Carr, Wesley, and Murra, as a result of their review of the research on time, recommended certain guideposts in teaching time concepts:

1. Children at any grade level can develop concepts of time; but since the child's maturation is important, the teacher must carefully consider it when instruction is to be undertaken.
2. There is little if any use in teaching chronology before the child is about twelve years old.
3. The use of time lines and time charts before junior high school is largely a fruitless effort.
4. Students must be given specific instruction designed to improve their understanding of time concepts and practice in the use of these concepts if they are to improve measurably; this instruction must provide active use of time expressions.
5. Exact dates and other specific references to time are superior to general time references in terms of economy of learning and total grasp of chronology.
6. The memorizing of specific date-event relationships and associations without relating dates to one another is almost universally condemned.

Preston and Herman stated that the development of time concepts or time relationships in the elementary school has a four-fold responsibility (Preston and Herman, pp. 318–19). First, it should help children to form an understanding of terms that designate temporal units. This may be accomplished by activities such as putting the day of the week, the date, and the daily schedule on the chalkboard.

Second, it should help children to think of an event as part of a chronological series. Readiness for this is exemplified by teacher's statements such as:

1. When you go home at noon . . .
2. This morning we will . . .
3. After reading class . . .
4. First let's finish this, then we will . . .
5. Billy is first, then Martha, then John . . .

The concept of a chronological series of events can also be accomplished through the use of time lines. Typical time lines used in the early school years include (Preston and Herman, p. 319):

1. A series of pictures of children of various ages to show their progression from birth to their present age.
2. A series of pictures to show the child's daily routine. Each picture depicts an event such as eating breakfast or arriving at school.

3. A line drawn along a lengthy stretch of chalkboard divided to show the weeks and months of the school year. It provides the opportunity to enter words or sketches to record significant school events as they occur.
4. The rearrangement of a calendar by clipping it so that the dates of a month run in a continuous horizontal line.

A third major responsibility for developing time concepts is to help children think of the separation of an event from the present in measured units. This can quite often be accomplished by the use of cardboard clocks with moveable hands. The teacher may set one clock at 9 A.M. and state, "This is when the school day begins." He may then set the other clock at 10 A.M. and state, "This is time for cookies and milk." At 10 o'clock he would indicate that one hour has passed.

A fourth responsibility is to help children form an understanding of the differences in duration of various historical periods. This requires fully developed time concepts and is a skill that tends to be refined in the upper elementary, junior high, and high school grades.

Spieseke provided some directions in relationship to the sequencing of time skills based upon developmental and maturational considerations. He suggested

1. mastering the telling of time by the clock;
2. understanding the days, weeks, months, and years as expressed by the calendar;
3. establishing a framework for time relationship;
4. developing a meaningful vocabulary of definite and indefinite time expressions;
5. coping with time concepts in reading and listening situations;
6. relating dates to personal experiences and to life span; and
7. placing related events in chronological order.

For additional skills relating to time and chronology and for recommendations as to readiness levels, systematic development and reteaching for maintenance, see Johns and Fraser.

Attitudes and Prejudices

Attitudes are hypothetical constructs that can be inferred by a person's verbal expressions or overt behavior. They refer to "certain regularities of an individual's feelings, thoughts, and predispositions to act toward some aspect of his environment" (Secord and Backman, p. 97). Attitudes are composed of cognitive, affective, and behavioral components. For example, one's attitude towards big cities might be inferred as negative if he makes statements of dislike for the sounds and smells of the city, makes objective statements about the tax burden of supporting big cities, and refuses to drive into the city from his suburban environment.

One approach to studying attitudinal change is to focus on the behavioral component. Katz identified four major functions of attitudes. The utilitarian function is tied directly to rewards and punishments; favorable attitudes are developed towards those objects, events, or people that offer some form of reward, and negative attitudes are developed towards those things that bring a form of punishment to the individual. A second function is that of the ego-defense role; negative attitudes toward others are often developed to protect one from the disparity of his own situation. A third function of attitudes relates to value expression; individuals often gain satisfaction from expressing attitudes that relate to their personal value system and enhance their self-concept. The knowledge role is the fourth major function of attitudes. Attitudes are formed or changed to develop internal consistency and harmony within the individual. This fourth function is similar to the dissonance theory that focuses on the cognitive component of attitudes.

According to the cognitive-dissonance theory of attitudinal change, a person who makes a public statement contrary to his personal belief will create dissonance or conflict within himself. In order to remove this internal discomfort, he must modify his attitude to make it more consonant with his public statement. Festinger stated that the existence of cognitive dissonance was psychologically uncomfortable for an individual and served as motivation for change. The dissonance theory can be summarized as follows (Festinger, p. 31):

1. There may exist dissonant or "nonfitting" relations among cognitive elements.
2. The existence of dissonance gives rise to pressures to reduce the dissonance and to avoid increase in dissonance.
3. Manifestations of the operation of these pressures include behavior changes, changes of cognition, and circumspect exposure to new information and new opinion.

Festinger proposed a theory of attitudinal change based upon cognitive dissonance. Rosenberg proposed changing attitudes by focusing upon the affective components of attitudes as they related to one's value system. By changing the affective component, an affective-cognitive inconsistency would be created resulting in a drive towards a resolution of the internal conflict. By linking this drive towards one's value system, which includes whole classes of objects including many different attitudes, a single attitude could be changed.

Kelman formulated a theory of attitudinal change reflecting both permanent and temporary changes that are tied to social influences. The concepts of compliance, identification, and internalization were important in the process of changing opinion. Compliance occurs "when an individual accepts influence from another person or from a group because he hopes to achieve a favorable reaction from the other" (Kelman, p. 62). For example, beginning teachers often modify their statements in the teacher's lounge as part of a socialization process of becoming part of the group. At first this modification may be temporary, but over a period of time it may become a permanent part of the teacher's behavior. Identification occurs when "an individual adopts behavior derived from another person or a group because this behavior is associated with satisfying a self-defining relationship to this person or group" (Kelman, p. 63). For example, children often model the behavior of parents or significant adults in their environments by conforming to their expectations and later adopting their prejudices. Internalization occurs when "an individual accepts influences because the induced behavior is congruent with his value system" (Kelman, p. 65). In this instance the induced behavior is intrinsically rewarding. For example, a preservice teacher might volunteer to tutor a child in social studies because this is consistent with one of the values to which he subscribes—that children should be helped and encouraged to learn.

Prejudice and discrimination are both closely linked to the formation and changing of attitudes as they relate to groups of people. Prejudice has been considered as an attitude that "predisposes a person to think, perceive, feel, and act in favorable or unfavorable ways towards a group or its individual members" (Secord and Backman, p. 412). Discrimination has often been referred to as the overt expression of prejudice. The concept of perceiving as it relates to the formation of stereotypes is important in terms of forming prejudices. Secord and Backman identified three important characteristics of stereotyping (Secord and Backman, p. 412):

1. Persons are categorized according to certain identifying characteristics.
2. Perceivers agree on the attributes that the persons in the category possess.
3. A discrepancy exists between attributed traits and actual traits.

The attitudes and prejudices children develop are often modeled after the behavior exhibited by significant adults in their immediate environment. Wisniewski identified some prejudices that teachers have towards urban areas (Wisniewski, p. 7). He stated, "those social studies teachers who are afraid to go into downtown areas are hardly objective observers of the urban milieu. Their prejudices and fears outweigh rationality. . . . the mood of pessimism toward cities reflects racial and social class biases that are neither subtle nor pleasant" (Wisniewski, p. 7). Coates investigated white adult behavior towards black and white children and indicated that the adults rated black children more negatively than white children.

Children develop attitudes at a young age, and parents are important in the development of these attitides (Yawkey; Roff). Children often model political attitudes after those of their parents. Geletka investigated the political awareness of preschool children through their knowledge of concepts such as the president, policeman, White House, vote, election, and government. She concluded that five year olds were more politically aware than four year olds. She identified the family as the main agent for the preschool child's politicalization. Other studies have also indicated that the family plays an important role in the politicalization of young children (Cleary; Dawson and Prewitt; Hess and Torney; and Langdon).

Easton and Hess reported that children between three and thirteen years of age are most receptive to the development of political attitudes. They found that early political concepts included simple ideas of government as reflected by concepts of the president and policemen. Jaros also found that young children have developed some concept of the president.

Schnepf discovered that Negro children held positive attitudes towards the law but a negative trend in terms of age towards police and freedom. Greenberg also reported that black children are less supportive of the political system and express more dissatisfaction for government and political officials than white children. Sica investigated the political orientation of Mexican-American children compared to the orientation of Anglo-American children and found them to be more cynical about the responsiveness of government; they also expected unfair treatment from judges and policemen.

Evidence shows that children also develop racial attitudes at an early age. Cantor used a conflict paradigm to study race awareness in second-grade children. He found that more children choose white for good and black for bad than would be expected by chance.

McMurtry and Williams employed reinforcement techniques to weaken white children's association of positive characteristics with light-skinned human figures and to strengthen their associations of positive characteristics with dark-skinned figures. Katz (1973) modified racial attitudes through a perceptual differentiation technique in which children learned distinctive names for photographs of faces of people of other races. Hohn also found perceptual training to be useful in studying racial preferences of kindergarten children. Ward and Braun's study of racial preferences revealed that black children are reversing the trend of choosing white models and rejecting dark models; they concluded that this reversal reflects a more accepting incorporation of racial identity and pride within a black child's self-concept.

For a detailed description of prejudice and self-concept, see *The Black Self-Concept* by Banks and Grambs. Additional insight might be gained from Clark's book, *Prejudice and Your Child*, or Goodman's *Race Awareness in Young Children*. For discussions relating to social studies on topics such as racism, cultural pluralism, social justice, ethnic minority cultures, white ethnic groups, and women's rights, read the forty-third Yearbook of the National Council for the Social Studies; this yearbook, edited by Banks, contains concepts and strategies for teaching ethnic studies.

Self-Concept

It has been suggested that self-concept is the single most important factor affecting behavior. Individuals have the capability to perceive themselves as objects and to develop a set of feelings and cognitions about themselves consisting of cognitive, affective, and behavioral components. Self-concept is an abstraction, an organization of ideas. Combs, Avila, and Purkey defined self-concept as "all those aspects of the perceptual field to which we refer when we say 'I' or 'me'. It is the organization of perceptions about self which seems to the individual to be who he is" (Combs, Avila, and Purkey, p. 39).

Combs et al. identified several major principles relating to self-concept (Combs et al., pp. 43–60). The first is that self-concept determines behavior. It provides a filtering system through which everything is perceived, evaluated, and understood. Self-concept influences behaviors such as school performance, levels of aspiration, and mental health. Self-concept has a circular effect in that "it corroborates and supports the already existing beliefs about self and so tends to maintain and reinforce its own existence" (Combs et al., p. 44). This self-corroborating characteristic pertains to both positive and negative self-concepts, making it difficult for self-concepts to change once they have been established. This self-perpetuating characteristic is also apparent in social problems in which individuals "are caught in a vicious circle in which their experiences seem always to confirm their unhappy or disasterous concept of self. . . . How to help these and thousands of other desperate victims of their own perceptions off the treadmill of self-corroboration is one of the great problems faced by our generation" (Combs et al., pp. 46–47).

A second major principle is that self-concept is learned. At an early age the child begins to distinguish between "me" and "not me." A child's interactions with his world and other individuals have an important influence on the development of a self-concept. Children learn who and what they are by their interactions with important people in their environments. These important people are often referred to as significant others, and it is from "interactions with such people, each of us learns that he is liked or unliked, acceptable or unacceptable, a success or failure, respectable or of no account" (Combs et al., p. 48). Changes in self-concept occur slowly as an accumulation of many experiences repeated over a long period of time. A traumatic event becomes important only because of its explicitness of implicit feelings experienced over long periods of time. Once established, the self-concept has a high degree of permanence and stability.

A third major principle relates self-concept and self-report. Self-concept is what a person believes that he is while self-report is what he tells others. The self-concept is not open to direct examination but can only be inferred by one's behavior. Neither an inferred self-concept based upon observable behavior nor a self-reported self-concept is a precise measurement of a person's real self, but both can be useful tools for obtaining information. (See Wylie, p. 24 for the limitations of self-report studies of self-concept.)

A fourth major principle relates self-concept to the helping professions. Combs et al. state, "Any aspect of human personality which affects behavior so fundamentally as the self-concept must be of vital concern to workers in the helping professions" (Combs et al., p. 55). Teachers are in the profession of helping children and can be effective agents in changing their self-concept. The theoretical basis for a helping profession is that self-concept can be learned; therefore, it can be taught despite "the high degree of permanence characteristic of its central aspects" (Combs et al., p. 58).

Purkey reviewed the theories on the development of the self and identified the following characteristics as being most important (Purkey, p. 13):

1. The self is organized and dynamic.
2. To the experiencing individual, the self is the center of his personal universe.
3. Everything is observed, interpreted, and comprehended from a personal vantage point.
4. Human motivation is a product of the universal striving to maintain, protect, and enhance the self.

For detailed theories of the development of self, see the works of Allport; Bettelheim; Hamachek; Jersild; May; Maslow; Mead; Montague; and Rogers.

There are indications that the development of a mature self is an intricate process involving the consolidation of the past and an orientation to the future. As a child becomes increasingly aware of others, his self-awareness expands. Gesell and Ilg have identified growth gradients associated with the development of self (Gesell and Ilg, pp. 318–25):

3 Years --Sense of "I" becomes stronger
3½ Years --Beginning of temporary attachments to one playmate, often of the opposite sex

4   Years --Expanding sense of self indicated by bragging, boasting, and out-of-
        bounds behavior
5   Years --Rather impersonal age; self and others taken for granted
6   Years --Center of his own universe; is expansive, undiscriminating
7   Years --More aware of and withdrawn into himself
8   Years --More outgoing, contacting people and places
9   Years --A "change for the better," less tension; life simpler

Stant described a similar set of stages typical of nursery-school-age children (Stant, pp. 6–7). She identified the child of two or three years of age as usually playing alone and seldom working cooperatively with other children. At this age children often work beside each other with little interplay or conversation. The child is still learning about himself and might be considered to be at a "me" stage. At about age four, a child begins to play more with others and often develops a friendship with another child. Group play is most often limited to two or three. "Me" is still important, but the child begins to see advantages in cooperation. At approximately age five, the play group expands to four or five children, and the child becomes more sociable in his behavior.

In a review of child development research, Yarrow summarized several factors that were influential in a child's labeling himself as masculine or feminine (Yarrow, p. 151). A child's identification with parental or surrogate parental models, acquisition of sex-typed skills, and sex role congruent experiences were all important factors in his identification of self as masculine or feminine in nature.

Swift offered several suggestions for nursery school teachers to enhance the self-concept of their pupils. One of these suggestions was for the teacher to serve as a model for the group in establishing relationships with an individual member. If a teacher developed a positive relationship toward a child, then the group would also model this behavior toward the child. Other suggestions for enhancing the self-concept of pupils were as follows:

> The teacher can increase the child's self-confidence by helping him develop skills and to experience successes that will add to his feeling of personal worth. She can help him increase his social perceptiveness through discussion of incidents that occur in the classroom. (Swift, pp. 277–78)

Purkey reviewed the research on self-concept in relationship to the task of the teacher. He concluded that "what the teacher believes about himself and about his students, and his attitudes towards students are more important than techniques and materials" (Purkey, p. 65). He reported that a child's success in school is related to his self-concept, but he cautioned against assuming a cause and effect relationship.

Elkind identified a variety of factors affecting the self-concept of young children (Elkind, 1971, pp. 23–37). Factors in the home situation such as parent-child relationships, birth order, and sibling relationship all affect a child's self-concept. Factors relating to school such as peer relationship and teacher-pupil interaction affect a child's self-perceptions. The factors of race, religion, and socioeconomic status are other salient determinants of a child's self-concept. Peer acceptance was felt to be important in the development of self-concept but "more rigorous evidence on the nature of this relationship needs to be obtained" (Campbell, p. 307).

For a comprehensive review of the research on self-concept prior to 1960, see Wylie's text, *The Self-Concept: A Critical Survey of Pertinent Research Literature.*

Social Learning

The development of the self-concept cannot be separated from one's increasing awareness of others in society. In this expansion of the self-concept, a child moves from an egocentric to a more cooperative, societal orientation. This requires an understanding on the part of the teacher of not only where a child is but also where a child is going on this egocentric to cooperative continuum.

Erikson suggested that to "understand either childhood or society, we must expand our scope to include the study of the way in which societies lighten the inescapable conflicts of childhood with a promise of some security, identity, and integrity" (Erikson, p. 277). To assist us in this task, Erikson has identified ego qualities associated with critical periods of development that reflect a child's movement toward a cooperative orientation within society. In describing these stages, Erikson identified both a positive and negative trait with promises and dangers for the child. He referred to these stages as the "eight ages of man" (Erikson, pp. 247–69). They are as follows:

1. Basic Trust vs. Basic Mistrust
2. Autonomy vs. Shame and Doubt
3. Initiative vs. Guilt
4. Industry vs. Inferiority
5. Identity vs. Role Confusion
6. Intimacy vs. Isolation
7. Generativity vs. Stagnation
8. Ego Integrity vs. Despair

Several of these stages parallel the nursery school and primary school periods. Stage 2 might be referred to as the holding on and letting go stage. Outer control must be firm and reassuring while at the same time permitting a child to assert his autonomy by letting go into his environment. This firmness must protect the child from meaningless and arbitrary experiences of shame and early doubt. The development of self-control without a loss in self-esteem enables the child to develop a lasting sense of pride and good will. If a child experiences too much control by outsiders or a feeling of loss of self-control, he will develop a lasting propensity for doubt and shame. Erikson felt this stage became "decisive for the ratio of love and hate, cooperation and willfullness, freedom of self-expression and its suppression" (Erikson, p. 254). During this stage the child may develop ideas of the principles of law and order while at the same time realize a danger of strict adherence to the letter rather than the spirit of the law; these ideas may have an influence on his adult life.

In Stage 3 the child has abundant energy and is actively involved with life. Because of this involvement a sense of guilt sometimes develops over the "goals contemplated and the acts initiated in one's exuberant enjoyment of new locomotor and mental powers" (Erikson, p. 255). The child becomes cooperative in his play with others and begins to model the behavior of significant adults. Social institutions offer children of this age "an economic ethos, in the form of ideal adults recognizable by their uniforms and their functions, and fascinating enough to replace, the heroes of picture books and fairy tales" (Erikson, p. 258). During this stage the child may develop a sense of moral responsibility while at the same time become aware of the danger that "even moral man's initiative is apt to burst the boundaries of self-restriction, permitting him to do to others, in his or in other lands, what he would neither do nor tolerate being done in his own home" (Erikson, p. 258); these ideas that the child forms during this stage may have an influence on his adult life.

During Stage 4 children receive some form of systematic instruction. They become part of the school culture and must become workers and potential providers. They face the dangers of inadequacy and inferiority in meeting their assigned tasks. During this stage a child begins to develop a sense of division of labor and of a differentiated system of opportunities and rewards. During this stage the child may develop ideas of a technological culture while at the same time realize the danger that if man "accepts work as his only obligation, and 'what works' as his only criterion of worthwhileness, he may become the conformist and thoughtless slave of his technology and of those who are in a position to exploit it" (Erikson, p. 261); these ideas may have an influence on his adult life.

One important aspect of these stages of man proposed by Erikson is the identification of ideal adults by young children. Social learning theory is premised upon the learning of novel responses through imitative learning or modeling behavior.

The acquisition of novel responses has traditionally depended upon the expectation that such behavior would be reinforced and the value of the reinforcer to the subject (Rotter). Novel responses have been explained by Skinner as being successive approximations that never suddenly emerge but are outcomes of operant conditioning through relatively prolonged processes.

Miller and Dollard believed that novel responses could be acquired through observational learning. They viewed imitation as a special form of instrumental conditioning with social cues serving as discriminating stimuli. In this form of social learning, the responses of the learner are differentially rewarded depending upon the imitation of the model presented.

Bandura and Walters suggested that social learning can occur even without immediate imitation and reinforcement. A learner's behavior can be modified by vicarious reinforcement where the model under observation is rewarded. This principle of learning through observations of models without direct reward has important implications for affective relationships within a classroom.

Secord and Backman have identified a number of principles, advanced by various researchers, accounting for the choice of a model for identification (Secord and Backman, p. 532):

1. Secondary reinforcement. A person is chosen as a model because he frequently rewards the learner.
2. Vicarious reinforcement. A person is chosen as a model because he receives rewards that are experienced vicariously by the learner.
3. Withholding of love. A person is chosen as a model because the learner fears that otherwise the person will withhold his love.
4. Avoidance of punishment. A person is chosen as a model because the learner fears that the person will otherwise injure him.

5. Status envy. A person is chosen as a model because he is envied as a recipient of rewards from others.
6. Social power. A person is chosen as a model because he has the power to reward (but does not necessarily reward the learner).
7. Similarity to learner. A person is chosen as a model because the learner perceives that he has a trait similar to one of his own.

Most children tend to imitate the responses of successful models, and they are often rewarded for this behavior by the model. Social behavior patterns are often determined by a system of differentiated rewards coupled with the influence of the model.

Other studies (Bryan; Masters) indicated that children's altruistic behavior is affected by adult modeling. Hapkiewicz found boys to be more aggressive than girls in their behavior after being exposed to aggressive cartoons.

In studies of modeling behavior, there appears to be some indication that seven year olds learn more from observational learning than do four year olds (Hartup and Coates; Joslin, Coates, and McKown). However, other studies do not support this contention (Grusec; Rosenhan and White).

Past experiences and the present situation do affect the development of social behavior patterns. The past social history of a child may modify his susceptibility to social learning through modeling behavior. Children with strong dependency habits, for example, are more easily influenced by modeling behavior than those children who are more independent in their actions. Children with past histories of failure or who have been subjected to negative reinforcement of independent behavior are more likely to be influenced by the rewards offered by the model. Children who have been exposed to an emotional or deprivation situation are often more susceptible to imitative learning.

Punishment is used less often to produce avoidance responses to situational cues in social learning than to inhibit responses that children have already acquired. Model behavior that permits aggressiveness and then punishes the child for imitating that behavior often results in aggressiveness on the part of the child. Nonpermissiveness of aggression without punishment when aggression does occur tends to create less aggressive children (Walters and Demkow).

The social developments described in the eight ages of man by Erikson and the social learning theory of Bandura and Walters were similar to those proposed by Gesell and Ilg. The development of a more cooperative orientation in children and the importance of the modeling role of the teacher were depicted by Gesell and Ilg; they outlined growth gradients for teacher-child and child-child interpersonal relationships (Gesell and Ilg, pp. 351–56). (See chart on p. 108)

Bossard identified the preschool play group as the first peer group of a child (Bossard, p. 539). He suggested that a child's school adjustment might be related to his associations with the peer group. The peer group influences a child's social development by emphazing the rights of others, controlling its members, acting as a security device, providing a cultural entity, and determining personality roles.

The effects of the peer group and the age of the children have also been investigated in relationship to social learning. Murray combined conservers and nonconservers in a group problem-solving situation. All subjects made significant gains in conservation behavior and in explanations for their judgments. Rardin and Moan found that popularity with peers was closely related to measures of social development. Peters

Age	Teacher-Child	Child-Child
3 years	Child likes to talk to teacher conversationally; he likes to help teacher.	Cooperative play begins to replace parallel play. Child begins to share.
4 years	Child enjoys taking on a teacher or mother role with new or shy children.	Child will share or play cooperatively with special friends.
5 years	Child likes teacher; he quotes him as an authority.	Child prefers playmates of his own age; he plays well with other children especially if groups are small.
6 years	Child likes to conform to teacher's demands; he may even like discipline. He is in awe of teacher; the teacher's word is law.	Child has marked interest in making friends, having friends, being with friends; he cannot bear to lose games and will cheat if necessary to win.
7 years	Child has more personal relationship crushes. The teacher is really paramount in school.	Child begins to be aware of friends' attitudes as well as their actions; he is learning to lose but must win in the end.
8 years	The teacher is less personally important. The child is pleased at the idea of teacher making a mistake.	The childs' group play is better; he is more cooperative, less insistent on having his own way; he worries less about behaviors of others.

and Torrance examined the block building behavior of children, age two to six, who were placed in same-sex dyads; they found the dyadic interaction facilitative to block building for only the six year olds.

Vance applied some of the principles of social learning theory to guidance for young children. She suggested using principles of positive reinforcement in developing desirable patterns of behavior in preschool-age children and the principles of extinction to eliminate undesirable patterns of behavior in them. Counter-conditioning was discussed as a means of helping children overcome apprehensions such as fear of the dark, fear of strange people, or fear of animals. Vance concluded that the principle of social learning theory could be used in preschool programs to establish goals such as increasing or decreasing socially assertive responses, decreasing fear of specific objects or people, increasing social skills, decreasing some aggressive responses, and increasing sharing with one's friends.

Brown and Elliott utilized principles of social learning theory to reduce aggression in nursery school children. They concluded, "There seems to be little doubt that ignoring aggressive responses and attending cooperative ones had reliable and significant effects upon the behavior of the children" (Brown and Elliott, p. 107).

Kounin and Obradovic suggested that effective classroom management techniques could be developed to promote an effective classroom ecology (Kounin and Obradovic, p. 131). They applied these techniques to the group rather than to individuals. The authors reached the following conclusions:

1. Specific teacher techniques, which can be delineated, do determine how children behave in a classroom.
2. These techniques are group management techniques.
3. They have about the same effect upon emotionally disturbed children as upon nondisturbed children.

Doland and Adelberg studied sharing behavior in preschool children. Girls appeared to be more receptive to modeling behavior than boys while both groups made gains in sharing under conditions of social reinforcement. Dreman and Greenbaum studied the sharing of candies by kindergartners under conditions where the giver knew and did not know the receiver. They found boys to be less sharing than girls, particularly when the identity of the sharer of the candy was not known. Langlois et al. found five year olds responded with higher levels of social behavior when the partner was of the same sex rather than of the opposite sex.

Classroom teachers need to be constantly aware of the role they play as models for children to imitate. Aggressive behavior on the part of the teacher can cause a rippling effect resulting in aggressive behavior on the part of their children. Verbal rewards and encouragement by the teacher towards child's relationships with his peers can often make the transition from an egocentric to a cooperative orientation more pleasant for all of those involved in the social learning of children.

Moral Development

The Greek philosophers reflected upon and discussed the role of moral education for the young children of their time. They reflected on the moral growth of children, particularly their ability to practice, demonstrate, and develop moral tenets. They discussed the role of the teacher as a moral model for children to emulate. Protagoras argued that virtue was developmental in nature and that a child should be exposed to alternative courses of action as a part of this developmental process; he stated:

> Education and admonition commence in the first years of childhood and last to the very end of life. Mother and nurse and father and tutor are vying with one another about the improvement of the child as soon as ever he is able to understand what is being said to him: he cannot say or do anything without their teaching him and setting forth to him that this is just and this is unjust; this is honourable; that is dishonourable; this is holy, that is unholy; do this and abstain from that. (Cahn, p. 41)

Over the centuries philosophers and educators have been concerned with the moral education of young children; this concern has been reflected in long-term goals such as the one Kant proposed about imparting "to man a value with regard to the whole human race" (Cahn, p. 185). Kant suggested that the accomplishment of such long-term behavior must begin with a readiness for moral growth that is established during the early years of schooling. This requires insight on the parts of both teachers and parents; otherwise, faults might develop within the child against which future influence of education would be powerless. Kant cautioned that discipline and moral education are not synonymous but that moral education was concerned with the dignity of man. Kant suggested that one approach to early moral training is the formation of character through an examination of rules. Kant stated:

> In moral training we should seek early to infuse into children ideas as to what is right and wrong. If we wish to establish morality, we must abolish punishment. Morality is something so sacred and sublime that we must not degrade it by placing it in the same rank as discipline. The first endeavor in moral education is the formation of character. Character consists in readiness to act in accordance with 'maxims.' At first they are school 'maxims,' and later rules. 'Maxims' are also rules, but subjective rules. They proceed from the understanding of man. If we wish to form the characters of children, it is of the greatest importance to point out to them a certain plan, and certain rules. (Cahn, p. 194)

Durkheim discussed moral education as it related to the socialization of the young child into adult society. Durkheim felt that there was a need for a sociological approach to education and that this approach was functional in nature. He believed that schools must be the guardians of the national character and that education should provide answers to the vital needs of society. He defined education as the socialization of each new generation.

> Education is the influence exercised by the adult generation on those that are not yet ready for social life. Its object is to arouse and to develop in the child a certain number of physical, intellectual, and moral states which are demanded of him by both the political society as a whole and the special milieu for which he is specifically destined. (Durkheim, 1956, p. 71)

One important aspect of his definition is the role of the child in the educational process. The child must be socialized to meet the demands of his "special milieu" and the state. Moral education was considered of the greatest importance in meeting these demands. Durkheim distinguishes two stages in childhood: an early period dominated by the family, and a later period influenced by the elementary school. He said, "Contrary to the all too popular notion that moral education falls chiefly within the jurisdiction of the family, I judge that the task of the school in the moral development of the child can and should be of the greatest importance" (Durkheim, 1961, p. 18).

Durkheim believed that the fundamental element of morality was the spirit of discipline and contended that there were two elements of this spirit: the preference for regularity of existence, and the moderation of desires and self-mastery. The child, he felt, was lacking in his development of both of these elements. Childish behavior is characterized by complete irregularity. Children shift with extraordinary speed from one activity to another, from one idea to another, or from one feeling to another. A child does not recognize normal limits to his needs; and when he wants something, he neither restrains himself nor readily complies when someone else imposes limits on him. He does not operate by nor conform to adult logic.

Durkheim suggested that whenever "two groups of people having unequal cultures come into continuous contact with one another, certain feelings develop that prompt the more cultivated group—or that which deems itself such—to do violence to the other" (Durkheim, 1961, p. 193). He used this theory to explain why a child, representing an inferior cultural position, is punished by a teacher, representing a superior cultural position.

Durkheim perceived moral sensitivity as one of the most delicate sentiments and felt that it should be a guardian against misdeeds and eliminate the need for punishment. He thought that the infliction of punishment contributed to future lapses in behavior. If punishment was used, he suggested a period of silent reflection between the misdeed and actual punishment. He cautioned against dispassionate punishment for fear that all emotion might be removed from the act, thereby draining it of all moral content.

The logical counterpart of punishment would be reward. Durkheim considered reward as an instrument of intellectual culture that is used to stimulate the qualities of intelligence. Since Durkheim defined education as a socialization process, he expressed the idea that children should not be rewarded for moral conduct when adult society does not reward the same behavior.

Although a child may be inconsistent in his behavior, he cherishes his own habitual ways. Repetitions become patterned ways of doing things and give order to the child's world. Durkheim saw this as a kind of general law of humanity for the child. He imagined that through the application of this, the basis for a moral order could be established (Durkheim, 1961, p. 138).

In addition to establishing a basis for moral order, Durkheim pictured the need to establish a base for moral authority. He was a believer in secularism in education and suggested that moral education could best be taught in the public schools rather than in parochial ones. McDonough contrasted Durkheim's view of moral education with that of the Catholic Church.

> The Durkheimian and Catholic forms of moral education have diametrically opposed theologies. There is an unbridgeable gulf between a guiding principle that seeks to attach the child to a secularized social group with his whole being and the one that attempts to bring the creature into a more intimate relationship with his Creator. (McDonough, p. 25)

According to Durkheim, moral discipline was not instituted for the benefit of a Supreme Being but rather for the benefit of man. He conceived authority as being granted to an individual through his relationship with other men; these other men elevated an individual to the position of a superman. To Durkheim, authority was a matter of opinion. He considered opinion a collective thing and, for this reason, pictured moral authority as being social in nature. He explained that society was a rational replacement for God and was the basis for moral authority (Durkheim, 1961, p. 91).

Durkheim believed that one of the primary tasks of education was to establish within the child those forces basic to moral life through rational expression rather than through mythical symbols. He felt that the socialization of each new generation must be linked with the preceding generations and that a child, upon entering the adult society, should be aware of the legacy of those who preceded him. The child should be able to connect the past, and its basic moral forces, to contemporary conditions.

In recent years, research of developmental psychologists has provided additional insight as to the moral growth of young children. A study of the "stage" theory of moral thinking might serve as the basis for a program of moral education for the nursery school and primary school child. Piaget (1965) and Kohlberg (1963) are two developmental psychologists who have suggested a developmental approach to moral thinking.

According to Piaget, young children exhibit two major levels of moral thinking. He identified these two levels as a morality of constraint and a morality of cooperation with the shift from one level to the next level of moral thinking occurring around the end of the primary grades.

> Society is the sum of social relations, and among these relations we can distinguish two extreme types: relations of constraint, whose characteristic is to impose upon the individual from outside a system of rules with obligatory content, and relations of cooperation whose characteristic is to create within people's minds the consciousness of ideal norms at the back of all rules. Arising from the ties of authority and unilateral respect, the relations of constraint therefore characterize most of the features of society as it exists, and in particular the relations of the child to its adult surrounding. Defined by equality and mutual respect, the relations of cooperation, on the contrary, constitute an equilibrious limit rather than a static system. (Piaget, 1965, p. 395)

Piaget's two levels of moral thinking can be contrasted by examining the perceptions of children in relationship to the concepts of control, justice, and responsibility. A child operating within a morality of constraint views duty as obeying authority. He defined good as obedience to rules which are accepted as dictates and not analyzed. A child operating within a morality of cooperation perceives control as a concept mutually agreed upon with his peers or with adults whom he perceives as near equals. At this level the child modifies rules by agreement, and he is less constrained by adults who determine rules for children.

Within a morality of constraint, a child perceives justice as a strict following of the letter of the law. The child sees justice as punitive in nature and develops anxieties concerning acts of forbidden behavior. Within a morality of cooperation, he considers a form of restitutive justice focusing upon the spirit of the law rather than the exact letter of the law. At this level the child exhibits a concern for inequalities and social injustices.

Within a morality of constraint, children have an objective view of responsibility associated with an egocentric orientation. At this level the child focuses on final outcomes and intentions or motives, for actions by others are not considered. As the child moves to a subjective view of responsibility, he considers the motives prompting action by others. The child accepts the rights of others to their opinions at the level of morality of cooperation.

Kohlberg identified six stages of moral development with justice as the core for moral action. He suggested that with this orientation towards justice, teachers need not be concerned with being accused of indoctrinating children.

> First, it is nonindoctrinative because it is not addressed to transmitting specific value-content but to stimulating a new way of thinking and judging. Second, it is nonindoctrinative because it is not imposing something alien in the student. Movement to the next

stage is movement in a direction natural to him; it is movement in the only direction he can go. Finally, it is not indoctrinative because the core of moral stages is a sense of rights and justice. (Kohlberg, 1973, p. 374)

Kohlberg identified the following six stages of moral development (Kohlberg, 1972, pp. 11–12):

Stage 1. Punishment and obedience orientation
Stage 2. Instrumental relationist orientation
Stage 3. Interpersonal concordance or "good boy-nice girl" orientation
Stage 4. "Law and Order" orientation
Stage 5. Social-contract legalistic orientation
Stage 6. Universal ethical principle orientation

Turiel suggested that movement from one stage of moral thinking to the next has the following characteristics (Turiel, p. 750):

1. a recognition of the inadequacies of the existing mode of thinking and a concomitant questioning of that mode
2. an attempt to construct a new mode of thinking
3. only an intuitive understanding of the new mode and, therefore, a tension existing between the old and the new which is manifested in conflict and fluctuation
4. a consequent attempt to subordinate the earlier mode of thinking into the new mode which, ultimately, results in the integration of a new view of the earlier mode into the more advanced mode

For an in-depth discussion of stage transition in moral development, see Turiel's review in *The Second Handbook of Research on Teaching.*

Other researchers (Henschel; Hogan; Lerner; and McRae) supported the stage theory of moral development. Studies have found that children have differentiated rates of acquiring higher levels of moral principles (Boehm; Durkin; Dlugokinski and Firestone; Harrower; Jantz; Schleifer and Douglas; and Shantz).

The role of moral education in the public school has been discussed by other writers (see Educational Policies Commission; Ekstein; Goldsmith; Meek; Jantz and Fulda; Duffey; Weaver; and Gantt).

Other investigators (e.g., Buchanan and Thompson; Costanzo et al.; and Gutkin) examined the effects of intent and consequences on children's moral judgments. Their findings tend to support Piaget's division of an objective and subjective view of responsibility in young children.

The stage theory of moral development in young children can provide the nursery school and primary school teacher with a set of objectives in moral education for the classroom. Recognition of the various stages of moral thinking can assist the teacher in providing readiness to facilitate the movement of children from one stage to the next. The goals of moral education for the nursery and primary school then revolve around enabling children to recognize the inadequacies of their existing mode of moral thinking and structuring environment and learning situations that enable children to construct higher levels of moral thinking.

Summary

In the development of a social studies curriculum for nursery school and primary school children, the classroom teacher is constantly faced with a variety of decisions relating to the content to be covered and the learning experiences employed in the obtainment of that content by his pupils. This chapter has attempted to provide the teacher with some theoretical and research bases for consideration in the selection and development of a social studies curriculum.

The formation of concepts in young children is extremely important to the social studies program. Teachers select concepts from a variety of social science disciplines and need to be concerned with the types and qualities of these concepts. For example, a complex, conjunctive concept such as political corruption is beyond the experience range of most primary grade children.

Concept development is also important to skill development in social studies. Young children can readily cope with time concepts such as hour or day but have considerable difficulty with abstract, relational concepts such as longitude or latitude. Thinking and problem solving are dependent upon children knowing the attributes of the concepts involved with these processes.

Concept development is essential to the formation of attitudes and prejudices in young children. A child's self-concept has great influence upon his success or failure in the school environment. The development of the concept of justice is vital to the moral growth of children.

Thinking processes, particularly as they relate to cognitive development, and social learning processes, especially identification and modeling behavior, are essential to social studies programs for young children. These processes, concept formation, and the development of a positive self-concept are all interrelated; this indicates a need for a social studies program concerned with the total development of the child.

References

Allport, G.W. *Becoming*. New Haven: Yale University Press, 1955.

Almy, M.C. "Are They Too Young for Problem Solving?" *Progressive Education* 27(1950): 148–51.

Alpert, A. "The Solving of Problem Situations by Pre-School Children: An Analysis." *Teachers College Contributions to Education*, No. 323, 1928.

Ames, L.B. "The Development of the Sense of Time in Young Children." *Journal of Genetic Psychology* 68(1946):97–125.

Anderson, J.E. *Psychology of Development and Personal Adjustment*. New York: Holt, Rinehart & Winston, 1949.

Bamberger, C.F. *Interpretation of Graphs at the Elementary School Level*. Educational Research Monographs 13. Washington, D.C.: Catholic University of America, 1941, 62 pages.

Bandura, A., and Walters, R. *Social Learning and Personality Development*. New York: Holt, Rinehart & Winston, 1963.

Banks, J., ed. *Teaching Ethnic Studies*. Forty-Third Yearbook of the National Council for the Social Studies. Washington, D.C.: National Council for the Social Studies, 1973a.

————. *Teaching Strategies for the Social Sciences: Inquiry, Valuing, and Decision Making.* Reading, Mass.: Addison-Wesley Publishing Co., 1973b.

Banks, J., and Grambs, J., eds. *Black Self-Concept.* New York: McGraw-Hill Book Co., 1972.

Batten, T.F. *Reasoning and Research: A Guide for Social Science Methods.* Boston: Little, Brown and Company, 1971.

Bettelheim, B. "Where Self Begins." *Child and Family* 7(1968):5–12.

Biber, B.; Black, I.; Murphy, L.; and Woddcock, L. *Life and Ways of the Seven to Eight Year Old.* New York: Basic Books, 1952.

Bloom, B., ed. *Taxonomy of Educational Objectives: The Classification of Educational Goals, Handbook I: Cognitive Domain.* New York: David McKay Co., 1956.

Boehm, L. "The Development of Conscience: A Comparison of American Children of Different Mental and Socioeconomic Levels." *Child Development* 33(1962):575–90.

Bossard, J.H.S., and Boll, E.S. *The Sociology of Child Development.* 3d ed. New York: Harper & Row, Publishers, 1960.

Brown, H. "Basic Economic Concepts Taught in Public Elementary Schools at Louisiana, 1967–1968." *Dissertation Abstracts* 29(1968):135A.

Brown, R., and Elliott, R. "Control of Aggression in a Nursery School Class." *Journal of Experimental Child Psychology* 2(1965):103–7.

Bruner, J. *The Process of Education.* Cambridge, Mass.: Harvard University Press, 1961.

————. *Towards a Theory of Instruction.* Cambridge, Mass.: Harvard University Press, 1966.

Bruner, J.; Austin, G.; and Goodnow, J. *A Study of Thinking.* New York: John Wiley & Sons, 1956.

Bryan, J.H. "Model Affect and Children's Imitative Altruism." *Child Development* 42(1971): 2061–65.

Buchanan, J.P., and Thompson, S.K. "A Quantitative Methodology to Examine the Development of Moral Judgment," *Child Development* 44(1973):186–89.

Cahn, S.M. *The Philosophical Foundations of Education.* New York: Harper & Row, Publishers, 1970.

Campbell, J. "Peer Relations in Childhood." In *Review of Child Development Research,* edited by M. Hoffman and L. Hoffman. New York: Russell Sage Foundation, 1964.

Cantor, G.N. "Use of a Conflict Paradigm to Study Race Awareness in Children." *Child Development* 43(1972):1437–42.

Carpenter, H. *Skill Development in Social Studies,* 33rd Yearbook of the Social Studies. Washington, D.C.: National Council for the Social Studies, 1963.

Carr, E.R.; Murra, W.F.; and Wesley, E.B. "Social Studies." In *Encyclopedia of Educational Research,* 2d ed., edited by W.S. Monroe. New York: The Macmillan Co., 1950.

Cartwright, S. "Blocks and Learning." *Young Children* 29(1974):141–46.

Clark, K. *Prejudice and Your Child.* Boston: Beacon Press, 1963.

Cleary, R. *Political Education in the American Democracy.* Scranton: Intext, 1971.

Coates, B. "White Adult Behavior toward Black and White Children." *Child Development* 43(1972):143–54.

Combs, A.; Avila, D.; and Purkey, W. *Helping Relationships: Basic Concepts for the Helping Professions.* Boston: Allyn & Bacon, 1971.

Copeland, R. *How Children Learn Mathematics: Teaching Implications of Piaget's Research.* New York: The Macmillan Co., 1974.

Costanzo, P.R.; Coie, J.D.; Franill, D.; and Grumet, J.F. "A Reexamination of the Effects of Intent and Consequence on Children's Moral Judgments." *Child Development* 44(1973): 154–61.

Crabtree, C. "Effects of Structuring on the Productiveness of Children's Thinking." *The Journal of Experimental Education* 36(1967):1–13.

Dawson, R., and Prewitt, K. *Political Socialization.* Boston: Little, Brown and Co., 1969.

Decaroli, J. "Concept Teaching." *Social Education* 37(1973):331–33.

Dewey, J. *How We Think.* Boston: D.C. Heath & Co., 1933.

Dlugokinski, E., and Firestone, I.J. "Congruence among Four Methods of Measuring Other-Centeredness." *Child Development* 44(1973):304–8.

Doland, D.J., and Adelberg, K. "The Learning of Sharing Behavior." *Child Development* 38(1967):695–700.

Dreman, S.B., and Greenbaum, C.W. "Altruism or Reciprocity: Sharing Behavior in Israeli Kindergarten Children." *Child Development* 44(1973):61–68.

Duffey, R. "Moral Education and the Study of Current Events." *Social Education,* in press.

Dunfee, M. *Elementary School Social Studies, A Guide to Current Research.* Washington, D.C.: Association for Supervision and Curriculum Development, NEA, 1970.

Dunfee, M., and Sagl, H. *Social Studies through Problem Solving.* New York: Holt, Rinehart & Winston, 1966.

Durkheim, E. *Education and Society.* Translated by S. Fox. New York: The Free Press, 1956.

———. *Moral Education.* Translated by E. Wilson and H. Schnurer. New York: The Free Press, 1961.

Durkin, D. "Children's Concepts of Justice: A Comparison with the Piaget Data." *Child Development* 30(1959):59–67.

Easton, D., and Hess, R. "The Child's Political World." *Midwest Journal of Political Science* 6(1962):229–46.

Educational Policies Commission. *Moral and Spiritual Values in the Public Schools.* Washington, D.C.: National Education Association, 1951.

Ekstein, R. "Origins of Values in Children." *Educational Leadership* 21(1964):523–26.

Elkind, D. "Cognition in Infancy and Early Childhood." In *Infancy and Early Childhood,* edited by Y. Brackbill. New York: The Free Press, 1967.

———. *A Sympathetic Understanding of the Child Six to Sixteen.* Boston: Allyn & Bacon, 1971.

Erikson, E.H. *Childhood and Society.* 2d ed. New York: W.W. Norton & Co., 1963.

Festinger, L. *A Theory of Cognitive Dissonance.* New York: Harper & Row, Publishers, 1957.

Fraenkel, J. *Helping Students Think and Value: Strategies for Teaching the Social Studies.* Englewood Cliffs, N.J.: Prentice-Hall, 1973.

Gagné, R. *The Conditions of Learning.* New York: Holt, Rinehart & Winston, 1965.

Gantt, W. "Teacher Accountability for Moral Education." *Social Education,* in press.

Gee, W. *Social Science Research Methods.* New York: Appleton-Century-Crofts, 1950.

Geletka, J. "The Political Awareness of Preschool Children." Master's thesis, University of Maryland, 1973.

Gengler, C.R. "The Application of Geographical Terms to Map Symbolism." *The Journal of Geography* 66(1967):394–96.

Gesell, A., and Ilg, F. *The Child from Five to Ten.* New York: Harper & Row, Publishers, 1946.

Goldmark, B. *Social Studies: A Method of Inquiry.* Belmont, Calif.: Wadsworth Publishing Co., 1968.

Goldsmith, C. "Begin Early." *Childhood Education* 40(1964):341.

Goldstein, P. "Concepts of Landforms and Waterforms of Children Beginning First Grade." *Dissertation Abstracts* 27(1966):1199–A–1200–A.

Goodman, M.E. *Race Awareness in Young Children.* New York: The Macmillan Co., 1964.

Greenberg, E. "Black Children and the Political System." *Public Opinion Quarterly* 34(1970): 333–45.

Grusec, J.E. "Power and the Internationalization of Self-Denial." *Child Development* 42(1971):93–105.

Gutkin, D.C. "The Effect of Systematic Story Changes on Intentionality in Children's Moral Judgments." *Child Development* 43(1972):187–95.

Hamachek, D.E., ed. *The Self in Growth, Teaching and Learning.* Englewood Cliffs, N.J.: Prentice-Hall, 1965.

Hanna, P.; Davies, G.; Farrar, C.; and Sabaroff, R. *Geography in the Teaching of Social Studies: Concepts and Skills.* New York: Houghton Mifflin Co., 1966.

Hapkiewicz, W.G., and Roden, A.H. "The Effect of Aggressive Cartoons on Children's Interpersonal Play." *Child Development* 42(1971):1583–85.

Harrower, M.R. "Social Status and the Moral Development of the Child." *British Journal of Educational Psychology* 4(1930):75–95.

Harter, G.L. "Overt Trial and Error in Problem Solving of Preschool Children." *Journal of Genetic Psychology* 38(1930):361–72.

Hartup, W.W., and Coates, R. "The Role of Imitation in Childhood Socialization." In *Early Experience and the Processes of Socialization,* edited by R.A. Hoppe, G.A. Milton, and E.C. Simmel. New York: Academic Press, 1970.

Hazlitt, U. "Children's Thinking." *British Journal of Psychology* 20(1930):354–60.

Heidbreder, E. "Problem Solving in Children and Adults." *Journal of Genetic Psychology* 35(1928):522–45.

Henschel, A. "Relationship between Values and Behaviors: Developmental Hypothesis." *Child Development* 42(1971):1997–2007.

Hess, R., and Torney, J. *The Development of Political Attitudes in Children.* New York: Doubleday & Co., 1968.

Hess, R.D., and Croft, D.J. *Teachers of Young Children.* Boston: Houghton Mifflin Co., 1972.

Hildreth, G.H. "Puzzle Solving with and without Understanding." *Journal of Educational Psychology* 33(1942):595–604.

Hoffman, M., and Hoffman, L., eds. *Review of Child Development Research.* New York: Russell Sage Foundation, 1964.

Hogan, R. "Moral Conduct and Moral Character: A Psychological Perspective." *Psychological Bulletin* 79(1973):217–32.

Hohn, R.L. "Perceptual Training and Its Effects on Racial Preferences of Kindergarten Children." *Psychological Reports* 32(1973):435–41.

Howe, G.F. "A Study of Children's Knowledge of Directions." *Journal of Geography* 30(1931): 298–304.

———. "Teaching Directions in Space." *Journal of Geography* 31(1932):209–10.

Humphrey, G. *Directed Thinking.* New York: Dodd, Mead & Co., 1948.

Hunt, I. *Across Five Aprils.* Chicago: Follett Publishing Co., 1964.

Hymes, J. *The Child under Six.* Englewood Cliffs, N.J.: Prentice-Hall, 1961.

Isaacs, S.S. *Intellectual Growth in Young Children.* New York: Harcourt Brace, 1930.

Jantz, R. "An Investigation of the Relationship between Moral Development and Intellectual Development in Male Elementary School Children." *Theory and Research in Social Education* 1(1973):75–81.

Jantz, R., and Fulda, T. "The Role of Moral Education in the Public Elementary School: A Developmental Approach." *Social Education,* in press.

Jarolimek, J. *Social Studies in Elementary Education.* 4th ed. New York: The Macmillan Co., 1971.

Jaros, D. "Children's Orientation towards the President: Some Additional Considerations and Data." *The Journal of Politics* 29(1967):368–87.

Jersild, A. *In Search of Self.* New York: Teachers College Press, 1952.

Johns, E., and Fraser, D. "Social Studies Skills: A Guide to Analysis and Grade Placement." In *Skill Development in Social Studies,* 33rd Yearbook of the National Council for the Social Studies, edited by H.M. Carpenter. Washington D.C.: National Council for the Social Studies, 1963.

Johnson, H. *Children in "The Nursery School."* New York: Agathon Press, 1973.

Jones, H.E. "Learning in Young Children: An Experimental Study." *California Parent-Teacher* 8(1932):8–9.

Jones, R. "Relationships between Two Modes of Social Studies Instruction." Ph.D. dissertation. University of California, Berkeley, 1964.

Joslin, D.; Coates, B.; and McKown, A. "Age of Child and Rewardingness of Adult Model in Observational Learning." *Child Study Journal* 3(1973):115–24.

Joyce, W.W. "The Development and Grade Placement of Maps and Global Skills in the Elementary Social Studies Program." *Dissertation Abstracts* 25(1965):6434–35.

Kagan, J. *Understanding Children: Behavior Motives and Thought.* New York: Harcourt Brace Jovanovich, 1971.

Katz, D. "The Functional Approach to the Study of Attitudinal Change." *Public Opinion Quarterly* 24(1960):163–204.

Katz, P.A. "Stimulus Predifferentiation and Modification of Children's Racial Attitudes." *Child Development* 44(1973):232–37.

Kelman, H. "Processes of Opinion Change." *Public Opinion Quarterly* 25(1961):57–78.

Kelty, M.G. "Time Expressions Comprehended by Children of the Elementary School." *Elementary School Journal* 25(1925):522–28, 607–18.

Kennamer, L. "Developing a Sense of Place and Space." In *Skill Development in Social Studies,* 33rd Yearbook of the National Council for the Social Studies, edited by H.M. Carpenter. Washington, D.C.: National Council for the Social Studies 1963.

Kerlinger, F.N. *Foundations of Behavioral Research: Educational and Psychological Inquiry.* New York: Holt, Rinehart & Winston, 1967.

Kilman, M.C. "Some Factors Related to Map-Reading Ability of Fourth Grade Pupils." *Dissertation Abstracts International* 30(1969):1751–A.

Kohlberg, L. "Comments on 'The Dilemma of Obedience'." *Phi Delta Kappan* 55(1974):607+.

———. "Developments of Moral Character and Moral Ideology." In *Review of Child Development Research,* edited by M. Hoffman and L. Hoffman. New York: Russell Sage Foundation, 1964.

———. "Moral Development and Identification." In *Child Psychology—the Sixty-Second Yearbook of the National Society for the Study of Education.* Chicago: The National Society for the Study of Education, 1963.

———. Moral Development and the New Social Studies." *Social Education* 37(1973):369–75.

———. "Understanding the Hidden Curriculum." *Learning* 1(1972):10–14.

Kohlberg, L., and Mayer, R. "Development as the Aim of Education." *Harvard Educational Review* 42(1972):449–96.

Kohn, C.F. "Interpreting Maps and Globes." In *Skills in Social Studies,* edited by H. Carpenter. Twenty-Fourth Yearbook of the National Council for the Social Studies. Washington, D.C.: National Council for Social Studies, 1953.

Kounin, J., and Obradovic, S. "Managing Emotionally Disturbed Children in Regular Classrooms: A Replication and Extension." *The Journal of Special Education* 2(1968):129–35.

Kurtines, W., and Greif, E. "The Development of Moral Thought: Review and Evaluation of Kohlberg's Approach." *Psychological Bulletin* 81(1974):453–70.

Langdon, K. *Political Socialization.* New York: Oxford University Press, 1969.

Langlois, J.H.; Gottfried, N.W.; and Seay, B. "The Influence of Sex of Peer on the Social Behavior of Preschool Children." *Developmental Psychology* 8(1973):93–98.

Larkins, G., and Shaver, J.P. "Economics Learning in Grade One: The Use of Assessment Studies." *Social Education* 33(1969):958–63.

Lastrucci, C.L. *The Scientific Approach: Basic Principles of the Scientific Method.* Cambridge, Mass.: Schenkman Publishing Co., 1963.

Lee, J.R., and Stampfer, N. "Two Studies in Learning Geography: Implications for the Primary Grades." *Social Education* 30(1966):627–28.

Leeper, S.; Dales, R.; Skipper, D.; and Witherspoon, R. *Good Schools for Young Children.* 3d ed. New York: The Macmillan Co., 1974.

Lerner, E. *Constraint Areas and the Moral Judgment of the Child.* Menosha, Wis.: Banta Publications, 1937.

Lewis, G.M. "Problem-solving Opportunities in Fifth Grade Social Studies: An Observational Study." *Dissertation Abstracts* 28(1968):4534–A.

Ling, B.C. "The Solving of Problem Situations by the Pre-School Child." *Pedagogical Seminary and Journal of Genetic Psychology* 68(1946):3–28.

Long, L., and Welch, L. "Influences of Levels of Abstractness on Reasoning Abilities." *Journal of Psychology* 13(1942):41–59.

Lowry, B.L. "A Survey of the Knowledge of Social Studies Concepts Possessed by Second Grade Children Previous to the Time These Concepts Are Taught in the Social Studies Lessons." *Dissertation Abstracts* 24(1963):2324.

McAndrew, M.B. "An Experimental Investigation of Young Children's Ideas of Causality." *Studies in Psychology and Psychiatry* 6(1943):66.

McAulay, J.D. "Some Map Abilities of Second Grade Children." *Journal of Geography* 61(1962):3–9.

McDonough, G. "Emile Durkheim and Moral Education." *The Catholic Educational Review* 65(1967):21–40.

McKinney, J.D., and Golden, L. "Social Studies Dramatic Play with Elementary School Children." *Journal of Educational Research* 67(1973):172–76.

McMurtry, C.A., and Williams, J.E. "Evaluation Dimension of the Affective Meaning System of the Preschool Child." *Developmental Psychology* 6(1972):238–46.

MacRae, D., Jr. "A Test of Piaget's Theories of Moral Development." *Journal of Abnormal and Social Psychology* 49(1954):14–18.

Martorella, P. "Classroom Concept Learning: Issues and Research Perspectives." *Social Education* 35(1971):888–92.

Maslow, A.H. *Toward a Psychology of Being.* New York: Van Nostrand Reinhold Co., 1962.

Masters, J.C. "Effects of Social Comparison upon the Imitation of Neutral and Altruistic Behaviors by Young Children." *Child Development* 43(1972):131–42.

Mattheson, E. "A Study of Problem-solving Behavior in Pre-School Children." *Child Development* 2(1931):242–62.

May, R. *Man's Search for Himself.* New York: W.W. Norton & Co., 1953.

Mead, G.H. *Mind and Society.* Chicago: University of Chicago Press, 1934.

Meek, C.R. "Personal Value Systems and Education." *Peabody Journal of Education* 42(1965): 225–28.

Miller, J.W. "Measuring Perspective Ability." *The Journal of Geography* 66(1967):167–71.

Miller, N.E., and Dollard, J. *Social Learning and Imitation.* New Haven: Yale University Press, 1941.

Mitchell, L.S. *Young Geographers.* New York: Bank Street College of Education, 1934.

Montague, A. *Man in Process.* New York: Mentor Brooks, 1961.

Muessig, R., and Rogers, V. "Developing Competence in Group Participation and Human Relations." In *Skill Development in Social Studies,* 33rd Yearbook of the National Council for the Social Studies, edited by H. Carpenter. Washington, D.C.: National Council for the Social Studies, 1963.

Mugge, D. "Are Young Children Ready to Study the Social Sciences?" *The Elementary School Journal* 68(1968):232–40.

———. "Precocity of Today's Young Children: Real or Wishful?" *Social Education* 27(1963): 436–39.

Murray, F.B. "Acquisition of Conservation through Social Interaction." *Developmental Psychology* 6(1972):1–6.

Peters, R.W., and Torrance, E.P. "Dyadic Interaction of Preschool Children and Performance on a Construction Task." *Psychological Reports* 30(1972):747–50.

Piaget, J. *The Construction of Reality in the Child.* New York: Basic Books, 1954.

———. *The Moral Judgment of the Child.* New York: The Free Press, 1965.

———. *The Child's Conception of Time.* New York: Ballantine Books, 1971.

———. and Inhelder, B. *The Child's Conception of Space.* New York: Humanities Press, 1963.

Portugaly, D. "A Study of the Development of Disadvantaged Kindergarten Children's Understanding of the Earth as a Globe." *Dissertation Abstracts,* 28(1968):4056-A.

Possien, W.M. "A Comparison of the Effects of Three Teaching Methodologies on the Development of the Problem-solving Skills of Sixth Grade Children." Ph.D. dissertation, University of Alabama, 1965.

Preston, R. "Implications of Children's Concepts of Time and Space." *Social Studies* 36(1945): 219.

Preston, R., and Herman, W. *Teaching Social Studies in the Elementary School.* 4th ed. New York: Holt, Rinehart & Winston, 1974.

Purkey, W. *Self-Concept and School Achievement.* Englewood Cliffs, N.J.: Prentice-Hall, 1970.

Rapparlie, E.B.R. "Descriptive Analysis of a Problem-solving Approach to the Teaching of Critical Thinking with Primary Children." *Dissertation Abstracts* 30(1969):221-A.

Rardin, D.R., and Moan, C.E. "Peer Interaction and Cognitive Development." *Child Development* 42(1971):1685-99.

Ray, J.J. "The Generalizing Ability of Dull, Bright, and Superior Children." *Peabody College for Teachers Contributions to Education,* No. 175, 1936.

Roberts, K.E. "The Ability of Preschool Children to Solve Problems in Which a Simple Principle of Relationship is Kept Constant." *Journal of Genetic Psychology* 40(1932):118-35.

Roff. M. "Intra-Family Resemblance in Personality Characteristics." *Journal of Psychology* 30(1950):199-227.

Rogers, C.R. *On Becoming a Person.* Boston: Houghton Mifflin Co., 1961.

Rogers, V., and Layton, D. "An Exploratory Study of Primary Grade Children's Ability to Conceptualize Based upon Content Drawn from Selected Social Studies Topics." *Journal of Educational Research* 59(1966):195-97.

Rosenberg, M.J. "A Structural Theory of Attitude Dynamics." *Public Opinion Quarterly* 24(1960):319-40.

Rosenhan, D., and White, G.M. "Observation and Reversal as Determinants of Prosocial Behavior." *Journal of Personality and Social Psychology* 5(1967):424-31.

Rotter, J.B. *Social Learning and Clinical Psychology.* Englewood Cliffs, N.J.: Prentice-Hall, 1954.

Russell, D.H. *Children's Thinking.* New York: Ginn and Co., 1956.

Sagel, H. "Problem Solving, Inquiry, Discovery?" *Childhood Education* 43(1966):137-41.

Savage, T.V., and Bacon, P. "Teaching Symbolic Map Skills with Primary Grade Children." *Journal of Geography* 68(1969):491-97.

Schleifer, M., and Douglas, V.A. "Moral Judgments, Behaviour and Cognitive Style in Young Children." *Canadian Journal of Behavioural Science* 5(1973):133-44.

Schnepf, V. "A Study of Political Socialization in a Subculture: Negro Children's Knowledge of and Attitudes toward the Police, Law, and Freedom." Ph.D. dissertation, University of Illinois, *Dissertation Abstracts,* 27(1967):2016-A.

Schwab, L., and Stern, C. "Effects of Variety on the Learning of a Social Studies Concept by Pre-School Children." *The Journal of Experimental Education* 38(1969):81-86.

Secord, P., and Backman, C. *Social Psychology.* New York: McGraw-Hill Book Co., 1964.

Shantz, D.W., and Voydanoff, D.A. "Situational Effects on Retaliatory Aggression at Three Age Levels." *Child Development* 44(1973):149-53.

Shaver, J.P., and Larkins, A.G. "Research on Teaching Social Studies." In *Second Handbook of Research on Teaching,* edited by R. Travers. Chicago: Rand McNally & Co., 1973.

Sheridan, J.M. "Children's Awareness of Physical Geography." *Journal of Geography* 67(1968):82–86.

Sica, M.G. "An Analysis of the Political Orientations of Mexican-American and Anglo-American Children." Educational Resource Information Center ED 066 418. Urbana and Champaign, Ill.: University of Illinois, 1972.

Skinner, B.F. *Science and Human Behavior.* New York: The Macmillan Co., 1953.

Sorohan, L.J. "The Grade Placement of Map Skills According to the Mental Ages of Elementary School Children." Ph.D. dissertation, Ohio State University, 1962.

Spears, S. "Children's Concept Learning in Economics under Three Experimental Curricula." *Dissertation Abstracts* 28(1968):2462–A.

Spieseke, A. "Developing a Sense of Time and Chronology." In *Skill Development in Social Studies,* 33rd Yearbook of the National Council for the Social Studies, edited by H.M. Carpenter. Washington, D.C.: National Council for the Social Studies, 1963.

Spiro, P. "Chronology: A Blind Spot in the Social Studies." *High Points* 30(1948):25–30.

Spodek, B. "Developing Social Science Concepts in the Kindergarten." *Social Education* 27(1963):253–56.

———. "Needed: A New View of Kindergarten Education." *Childhood Education* 49(1973): 191–97.

———. "Social Studies for Young Children: Identifying Intellectual Goals." *Social Education* 33(1974):40–45.

Springer, D. "Development in Young Children of an Understanding of Time and the Clock." *Journal of Genetic Psychology* 80(1952):83–96.

Stant, M. *The Young Child: His Activities and Materials.* Englewood Cliffs, N.J.: Prentice-Hall, 1972.

Stephens, L.E. "What Concepts of Telling Time Can Be Developed by Kindergarten Children?" *Dissertation Abstracts* 25(1964):1793.

Stevenson, C.A. *The Development of an Instrument to Examine Teacher Influences on Decision-making Behaviors of Children Ages Three to Five,* Unpublished Ph.D. dissertation, University of Maryland, 1973.

Suchman, R. "Inquiry Training in the Elementary School." *Science Teacher* 27(1960):42–47.

Swift, J. "Effects of Early Group Experiences in the Nursery School and Day Nursery." In *Review of Child Development Research,* edited by M. Hoffman and L. Hoffman. New York: Russell Sage Foundation, 1964.

Taba, H. *Curriculum Development: Theory and Practice.* New York: Harcourt Brace Jovanovich, 1962.

———. "Thought Processes and Teaching Strategies in Elementary School Social Studies." Paper presented at American Educational Research Association meeting in Chicago, February 13, 1963.

———. "The Teaching of Thinking." *Elementary English* 42(1965):534–42.

Taba, H.; Durkin, M.; Fraenkel, J.; and McNaughton, A. *A Teacher's Handbook to Elementary Social Studies: An Inductive Approach.* Reading, Mass.: Addison-Wesley Publishing Co., 1971.

Taylor, B., and Haas, J. *New Directions: Social Studies Curriculum for the 70s.* Boulder: Center for Social Science Education and Social Science Education Consortium, 1973.

Towler, J. "Egocentrism: A Key to Map-Reading Ability?" *Social Education* 35(1971):893–98.

Towler, J.O., and Nelson, L.C. "The Elementary School Child's Concept of Scale." *Journal of Geography* 67(1968):24–28.

Turiel, E. "State Transition in Moral Development." In *Second Handbook of Research on Teaching,* edited by R. Travers. Chicago: Rand McNally & Co., 1973.

Vance, B.J. "Social Learning Theory and Guidance in Early Childhood." *Young Children* 2(1965):30–42.

Walters, R., and Demkow, L. "Timing of Punishment as a Determinant of Resistance to Temptation." *Child Development* 34(1963):207–14.

Ward, S.H., and Braun, J. "Self-Esteem and Racial Preference in Black Children." *American Journal of Orthopsychiatry* 42(1972):644–47.

Weaver, V.P. "Moral Education and the Study of U.S. History." *Social Education,* in press.

Weikart, D.P.; Rodgers, L.; Adcock, C.; and McClelland, D. *The Cognitively Oriented Curriculum.* Washington, D.C.: Educational Resource Information Center and National Association for the Education of Young Children, 1971.

Welch. L., and Long, L. "The Higher Structural Phases of Concept Formation." *Journal of Psychology* 9(1940):59–95.

Wesley, E.B. *Teaching Social Studies in Elementary Schools.* Lexington, Mass.: D.C. Heath & Co., 1946.

Wisniewski, R., ed. *Teaching about Life in the City.* 42d Yearbook of the National Council for the Social Studies. Washington, D.C.: National Council for the Social Studies, 1972.

Wylie, R. *The Self-Concept: A Critical Survey of Pertinent Research Literature.* Lincoln: University of Nebraska Press, 1961.

Yarrow, L. "Separation from Parents During Early Childhood." In *Review of Child Development Research,* edited by M. Hoffman and L. Hoffman. New York: Russell Sage Foundation, 1964.

Yawkey, T. "Attitudes towards Black Americans Held by Rural and Urban White Early Childhood Subjects Based upon Multi-Ethnic Social Studies Materials." *Journal of Negro Education* 42(1973):649.

chapter five

Science

**Maureen A.
Dietz
Dennis W.
Sunal**

Messing around is science.

Introduction

Since the end of the 1950s a small revolution has taken place in science, technology, and education. We have added to our cultural knowledge vast amounts of information about our world and universe, new designs for investigators, and new information about how we learn. Journals disseminating this information have doubled over the past fifteen years. However, there are still many gaps in the reporting of this information, even though a number of retrieval sources, such as annotated bibliographies, digests of science education research over the past fifty years, and abstracts of research meetings and the Educational Resources Information Center of the National Institute of Education, (ERIC/SMEAC [Educational Resources Information Center/Science, Mathematics, Environmental Education Analysis Center]) have been used.

The early childhood educator encounters a virgin field in developing new theory with respect to science learning. The past fifteen years has included the beginning of the development of curricula in the area of science education. Yet, do we know how to develop curricula? We have tried to identify areas of the young child's life that have not been investigated. These investigations and research indicated areas that need to be treated together and considered in light of established learning theory. But how should all of this information affect the everyday school life of a child? It is hoped that these questions and many more will be given partial answers in the pages ahead.

This chapter is divided into five sections: Definitions of science and justification of science education in the young child's curriculum, theoretical basis for science learning, summary and analysis of the empirical data over the last ten to fifteen years, implications of theory and research for curriculum development and implementation, and a general summary with observations and inferences. Within each section opening remarks are intended to tie together the previous section(s) and what is to come.

Science and Its Place
in the Early Childhood Curriculum

What Is Science?

This question can be answered in many ways. We could consider what science is not. On the other hand, we could survey scientists and ask them their opinion; or we could pose this question to science teachers from the preschool to the university level. Whatever approach we take, the important thing is that we do answer the question at the very beginning of our discussion of science in early childhood education.

Let us first turn to the writings of famous scientists and scientific philosophers. Definitions of science by different scientific philosophers have been formulated in a variety of ways. Some define science as a product; that is, a set of facts, concepts, and conceptual schemes that are recorded and passed on to posterity. Such thinking is reflected in the definition of science as an interconnected series of concepts and conceptual schemes that develop as a result of experimentation and observation and are fruitful for further experimentation and observation (Conant). This same general idea of science as a set of interpretations of the universe makes it possible for recordable facts to be summed up in an economical fashion (Pearson; Kemeny). Science is considered a complete and interwoven taxonomy that can reduce our physical and biological world to simple relations (Nagel; Blin-Stoyle).

Science is a body of useful and practical knowledge. According to this definition, when science is used in the classroom, it is a series of object lessons about a piece of granite, an old wasp's nest, an acorn, or a tulip. It is the names of the parts of grasshoppers or of a flowering plant. It is learning to identify twenty trees, twenty insects, twenty flowers, or twenty anything (George). Science is an achievement and not a method of achieving.

Some philosophers consider science as mostly a process, that is, a way of thinking, a way of arriving at new knowledge. Science for these people is a way of finding out about our environment (Schwab). The scientist begins with a search for truth and continues this search on and on. Science is a creative art; it explains the environment but does not attempt to control it. It is a continuous search for unity in the wide variety of nature (Bronowski). Science is mainly a method of achieving. A classroom using this definition as a basis for instruction would be open and child centered; such a classroom would use science only as a vehicle for obtaining skills and thus be clearly distinguishable from classrooms where science is primarily a product.

A third group of philosophers view science as both a product and a process. Some have expressed these two sides of science by speaking of science as being both static and dynamic. The static view considers science an achievement and not a method. The dynamic view considers it a continuous living process (Brown). If a person is observing what is happening in the world and formulating the simplest set of suppositions to explain these happenings, he is doing science (Durrell). Science involves the process of verification as well as the process of discovery (Schwab). Such definitions consider the nature of what science produces and the process by which this product is obtained (Moe; Robinson; and Campbell). A classroom interpretation of this definition is that science is the study of problems found wherever we live, the finding of answers to specific questions we formulate, and learning concepts so that these concepts can help to solve problems. Science is both achieving and achievement. The effectiveness of this definition was addressed in a review of research by Ramsey and Howe. They concluded that pupil activity and experiments were important prerequisites for the effective learning of science concepts.

We can also look for an answer to our original question by considering the definitions of science that reflect collaborative thinking, that is, definitions formulated jointly by groups of scientists and educators. One such group stated that science can be taught as activity and as content, as process and as product (NSTA [National Science Teachers Association] Curriculum Committee and the Conference on Science Concepts). Science can also be considered in a rather global sense as rational inquiry and as such all things that man questions—religious, aesthetic, or literary—are considered (Educational Policies Commission, NEA-AAAS).

We can gain an appreciation of science by looking at it through the eyes of the nonscientist. We can view it as a body of useful and practical knowledge and a method of obtaining more knowledge (Campbell). The nonscientist appears to view science as a product of the human nature of the scientist or as continuing case studies from history (Maslow; Brown). Three human activities are seen as coming together to create a science: the creation of principles, the formation of hypotheses, and the observation of facts (Moe).

We can also gain an appreciation of science by comparing it with other disciplines. Can medicine, mathematics, engineering, or history be called a "science" according to any of the preceding definitions? No, not if these disciplines control the environment rather than create it. This would involve process differences. They would then constitute technology. The theme running through the preceding definitions is that science creates. It involves a specific product as well as the process of discovery and validation in the empirical world. Science as a creation and a creative act is distinguishable from other nontechnological disciplines.

Hence, science is mainly a product for some, a process for others, and both a product and a process for others. Science is creative and yet pragmatic; science is not technology since it creates and does not simply control the environment. Science is not activity for activity's sake. The scientist is active at something and for some reason. In order to give a rationale for teaching science, a definition of science is necessary. As the basis for the following section, science for the young child is defined as being mainly a method of achieving and, to a much lesser degree, a useful set of achievements.

Why Should We Teach Science in Early Childhood Education?

In an attempt to justify why science should be a part of the curriculum for early childhood education, we will look at the historical development of early childhood education as it coincides with the historical development of science education. Secondly, we
will investigate how others have justified science as being part of the curriculum.
Lastly, we will discuss the kinds of thinking processes educators most commonly investigate.

Historically, an interest in the study of children developed in the eighteenth century
and an interest in the young child began in the middle of the nineteenth century. Hall,
Freud, and Darwin were psychologists and scientists who first generated child development theories which, by suggesting ideas and by arousing disbelief and resistance, had the capacity to generate research. G. Stanley Hall, who founded the child
study movement, believed that the child repeats the evolution of the race and re-
capitulates the mental processes of the past. Freud postulated a psychoanalytic
concept of child development. He regarded a child primarily as a complex energy
system which maintains itself by means of transactions with the external world.
Darwin's theory of evolution stimulated the measurement of individual differences in
abilities and the functional value of psychological processes. These theories have
courted in various ways the attention of American educators over the past one
hundred years.

Educators in Europe were led by the teaching theory of Pestalozzi. Pestalozzi felt
that the learning environment was built around sense perception and activity. Pestalozzi influenced others, such as Froebel and Montessori. In America,
Pestalozzi's influence was not felt until after 1860, most notably through Froebel and
his kindergarten. Froebel was concerned with the education of children ages three
through seven years. He observed children and found that in their play activities, they
responded to sense perceptions and to activity within their environment. Through his
observations he found agreement with Pestalozzi's conclusions concerning children's
behaviors. Froebel developed educational principles with a child-centered orientation
based upon the spontaneous nature of children in which play was paramount (Cole).

An environment organized around sensory experiences was a major basis for
Montessori's activities for young children. This environment emphasized individual
freedom of action within it, guided by the child's spontaneous development. Her
emphasis on deriving educational practices from the children's natural interests in
their environment linked her to Pestalozzi's theories (Kilpatrick). In the United States
concern for young children seemed to vanish at the turn of the century until the 1960s
with the growth of Montessori nursery schools and when the Head Start program
became the first large federally funded project intended to aid the education of the
young child (Caldwell).

From the time of the Middle Ages, science was always a part of the gentleman's
education. A tradition was established of allowing the older student to experience the
enjoyment of science. However, when men such as Pestalozzi brought people's attention to the young child and how he should be educated, experiences with the world
around the child and experiences with nature were incorporated into his schooling.

Until recently, science education in America was reserved for the upper elementary,
junior, and senior high school student. Science was taught principally through

memorization of facts with minor emphasis on science processes. In the late 1950s and early 1960s pressures resulting from expanding national awareness and concerns in science, changing school population and role which school plays in society, technological advances, and government funding policies brought important changes in science education. These changes first involved science curriculum materials (Shulman and Tamir). Later changes involved instructional methodology, classroom materials and construction, and eventually the relationship between science and nonscience subjects taught.

Federally funded projects were begun at the high school level to assist students and high school teachers alike in thinking scientifically. In the early 1960s the concept of federally funded projects was extended into the elementary school, and in the 1970s it was successfully extended to kindergartens and nursery schools (Pierce). The kind of science developed in the funded projects in early childhood and elementary education is based on the hands-on, activities approach paralleling the learning principles advocated by the early educators.

How can we justify the incorporation of science into the early childhood curriculum? One investigation into the evolution of science in the curriculum over the past ten years indicated a growth in the opinion of early childhood educators that science should be taught to preschool-age children (Riechard). It can also be shown that science activities are a part of and are increasing in number within each of the federally funded curriculum projects now on the market (Benson). There has also been an increase in the number of studies revealing what young children know about nonscience and science topics, and there appears to be some direct links between these two kinds of topics (Lawson; Peterson and Lowery). Ramsey and Howe, in a review of research studies performed during the 1960s, indicated that a variety of objectives can be obtained through elementary school science programs. These include reading readiness, concepts, creativity, and inquiry skill objectives.

Others have justified the preschooler's exposure to science by surveying the stated objectives of federally funded projects (e.g., Head Start, Early Admissions, and the USOE-Ford Foundation-Carnegie Corporation project for the use of television) (Bennett). These objectives range from teaching the child how to think to providing experiences that can be used as a foundation for future educational growth. Internationally, the incorporation of science into the early childhood curriculum has been reported in a variety of sources (Nizova; Larat; Osiyale; Plowden on Primary Schools). Comber and Keeves confirmed, in a research report on science education in nineteen countries, the importance of exposure to science learning in the preschool years.

A survey of the research on cognition in early childhood education over the past ten years has revealed some interesting coincidences with the research on science education during that same period. Topics that are identified as science topics can also be found in the early childhood research. Liquid volume, rotation of objects, and problem solving using physical objects are just a few (Gruen; Charlesworth and Zahn; O'Brien and Shapiro). Others have been concerned with natural behaviors fostering independence and interaction with the physical environment and how this trait is associated with nonverbal ability (Pedersen and Wender).

Piaget is one of the most outstanding figures influencing science education today. Early childhood and science educators have explored Piaget's theories concerning the structuring of conservation of number, weight, volume and length by children from forty-nine to sixty-two months of age (Griffiths et al.; Delancy; Gruen). Piaget, who agrees with Bruner's emphasis on early readiness, has played an important role in the justification of introducing science in early childhood education (Shulman and Tamir).

In the previous discussion science was defined in various ways but all definitions could be included on the continuum between product and process and involved science as a creative, dynamic act of thinking. Researchers have spent much time investigating various factors that help or hinder this thinking act in young children. Their investigation, for example, has questioned the parts humor, freehand drawing, memory, and even testing play in the child's cognitive processes (Zigler; Sundberg and Ballinger; Neimark and Lewis). Attempts have also been made through observation to determine how the young child classifies and the relationship between the class a child selects and its subclass (Flavell). In general, a model of cognition and an enlightenment about the child's ability to use intellectual processes involved in conceptualization could emerge from this joint interest between science and early childhood educators.

Theoretical Bases

Evidence has been presented from historical events, other writers, and similarities in the research endeavors of science educators and early childhood educators to support the notion that science should be included in the educative experiences of the young child. It can also be stated that young children should learn science because it helps to develop their cognitive processes better than most other content areas of the curriculum. Children learn how to question, evaluate, and formulate theories when they study science. From the previous discussion describing the definition of science for the young child, we are now able to infer learning theories and describe methods of education that match both definition and theory.

Early learning philosophers ignored the young child. But as time went on, they began to insist that adults must be concerned with the needs and interests of the child and must provide an environment in which he can learn.

Contemporary theorists and researchers have impressed upon us the need for learning by discovery. This method of learning appears to be most appropriate when the child attempts to understand the physical world around him. The child can solve problems about what he sees, hears, touches, tastes, and feels if he can have some firsthand experience with his world under the guidance of adults.

Theories from the Fifteenth to the Nineteenth Centuries

There is a temptation to look only at the theories of child development experts such as Piaget, Bruner, and Gagné whose methods of teaching are currently exerting much influence on the kind of science being taught to preschool, primary, and elementary school children. One could sum up the current methods of teaching science as "learning by discovery." Like most ideas, this one also has a history. Just where to start in tracing that history should be determined by why the material is being compiled and written. Since we are interested mainly in research, its basis and outcomes, it appears useful to identify the twentieth century proponents of this idea and indicate those sages from the past whose theories significantly influenced contemporary leaders.

In 1904 Boole wrote an expose on learning and thinking that has an amazing similarity to the learning theory that is the basis of science education today (Taba, 1963). Around that time, other persons, such as Montessori and Dewey and the school of Gestalt psychologists, believed and preached that learning is synonymous with thinking which is synonymous with active discovery of relationships and organizing principles.

The evolution of these ideas began with Renaissance and Reformation thinkers such as Montaigne (1533–1592), Rabelais (1483–1553), and Mulcaster (1530–1611). Phrases such as "learning by doing," "learning should be enjoyable," and "education must be adapted to the needs of the students" were originally coined by these philosopher-educators. During the Age of Enlightenment, the seventeenth and eighteenth centuries, Locke and Rousseau added to their predecessors' ideas. Locke more fully developed the notion that experience, not innate ideas, is the basis of knowledge. Rousseau was one of the first to take a real interest in the infant, age birth to five years. Although he only recommended that the child be allowed to develop physically during these early years and did not recommend formal schooling, his theory brought about the child-centered schools of the eighteenth and nineteenth centuries.

In the Age of Idealism Pestalozzi (1746–1827) refined the notion of "learning by discovery." He believed that the child must have firsthand experiences with objects so that his senses perceive the object in order to learn; he did not believe that the teacher should teach the child words and hope he would understand the concept. The teacher must go from the known to the unknown. Pestalozzi was the first educator to define a psychologically oriented sequence of experiences and the first to make a systematic study of child growth. He inspired Froebel, Herbart, and Fichte.

The kindergarten, conceived for children ages three to seven, and the child-centered curriculum are two of Froebel's (1782–1852) lasting contributions to both science and early childhood education. In his child-centered curriculum each content area, as well as being related to the program's objectives, must be planned with the individual differences of each child in mind. Natural science, music, art, mathematics, and so forth were to be included in the curriculum. The introductions of many contemporary science projects contain many statements similar to these ideas expressed by Froebel.

Theories of Modern and Contemporary Times

Modern educators include those persons who made their major contributions during the early twentieth century. Montessori began her work with mentally retarded children and later became interested in infants. Her influence can be seen in today's science curriculum in that she advocated that a teacher's first concern should be the needs and interests of the child. She felt that individualized instruction and sensory training helped the child to abstract ideas and to conceptualize.

Montessori stressed the breaking down of skills and conceptual learning into carefully ordered activities. For example, the child studied gradations of the color blue through attempts to arrange a set of blue rectangles from the lightest to the darkest shade of blue. Each child progressed through sets of preplanned activity as the teacher judged the child ready to progress and as the child desired to try the next activity. Children in a Montessorian program learn by manipulating materials until they have mastered them (Glaser et al.).

The Montessorian concentration upon performance is similar to Dewey's emphasis on "learning by doing" (Kohlberg). Some of Dewey's basic themes were "begin where the child is," "recognize individual differences," and "seek growth within the in-dividual." Dewey insisted that education in science should begin with the familiar phenomena encountered in the home, garden, fields, and woods. Experience of this kind yields the subject matter which increasingly can be treated by the methods of observation, reflection, and testing. In *My Pedagogic Creed* Dewey stated that in-structional method is reducible to the question of the order of development of the child's powers and interests. The division of subject matter and methods is not real for the learner; instead, there exists a single continuous interaction of a great diversity of energies, a learning by doing (Dewey). Finally, the Gestalt psychologists introduced "insight"—the moment of discovering, organizing one's conceptual scheme, and "meaning." If we put the theories of these people or the theories of persons close to their school of thought into practice, we can improve our teaching and improve the ability of children to learn science (Kuhn).

In the contemporary theorist group there are two or three major contributors and at least one countermovement person notable for his objections to "learning by dis-covery." Based on their research, several science educators wrote exposes to make the education community aware of "learning by discovery." However, once an educa-tional theory is implemented in the classroom, there seem to be as many interpreta-tions of that theory as there are classrooms. The terms used to describe what we are doing take on many meanings. If we all agree that science is a process and a product, is it an end or a means or both? (Newport) The more a term is used, the more con-fusion it seems to generate. For example, it is now necessary to distinguish inquiry from discovery and from an investigation approach to science teaching (George et al.).

Changes in the definition of science after the late 1950s had great consequences for educators (Schwab). Prior to 1957 science knowledge meant finding new and more complex concepts; after 1957 inquiry became important as theory was translated into action (Suchman). Questions focused on pupils examining and reconstructing theories, on teachers examining and reconstructing their teaching techniques, and on scientists examining their methods of reconstructing theories (Fish and Goldmark).

Studies were conducted that showed that only a certain amount of permissiveness should exist in the classroom for effective problem solving to occur (Suchman). Lansdown and Dietz investigated and found that free experimentation with structured materials leads to a more personal discovery of science facts and concepts. Therefore, there must be a combination of focus and freedom in the classroom. When children were confronted with a science experiment but were free to do anything at all they liked with it, it was found that they needed direction (Butts). When this study was replicated with half the subjects in a planned guidance program and half with no planned guidance, the results of the earlier study were confirmed (Butts and Jones). It is not simply "learning by discovery" but learning through guided discovery that produces cognitive growth in science.

Through anecdotal records, tape recordings, and children's written materials, evidence was collected showing that the child's immediate experience with his environment provides him with the materials for concept development (Garone). Certain conditions were found to be necessary for inquiry teaching or learning by discovery (Suchman). To inquire, children must be faced with an inconsistency; the climate of inquiry must be free; and children must be able to test ideas against empirical events.

There have in addition been extensive discussions of the role of concepts in teaching science to young children (Navak). These writings disclose a transition on the part of scientists as to their understandings of the nature of science from a body of facts to an emphasis on major themes of science. The writings also helped in the National Science Teachers Association's (NSTA) efforts in concept identification and the role of concepts in planning instruction as evidenced in NSTA's position statement on school science education for the 70s, published in the *Science Teacher,* November 1971.

One proponent of a theory that is counter to "learning by discovery" is Ausubel. He argues that as the sophistication of the learner increases, the necessity for discovery learning decreases. Learning by discovery is time consuming and using it exclusively will greatly reduce the scope of learning (Ausubel, 1968).

Intuitive or subverbal understanding is acquired by performing certain operations such as comparing. Only after students have mastered operationally the meaning of a generalization, principle, or rule are they ready to verbalize it. He believes that any science curriculum must be concerned with the systematic presentation of an organized body of knowledge as an explicit end in itself. As science instruction progresses throughout the grades, it should be vertical; that is, each new presentation should build upon concepts already formed (Ausubel, 1960). Instructional sequence begins with a set of organizing statements at a level of abstraction higher than what must be learned subsequently. Ausubel calls such statements "advance organizers." These organizers are expositorily taught to the learners as the first step in a unit of instruction. They are not to be discovered as would occur in learning by discovery. Curricula in science must be concerned with more than the mere development of inquiry skills in which subject matter content is only incidental (Ausubel, 1963).

In general, Ausubel makes a sharp dichotomy between content and process. He believes that the teacher imparts content in the classroom-lecture situation while the laboratory is the place for processes to be learned or refined. This is the principle function of the laboratory. Whatever the person's existing cognitive structure is at any given moment will be the principle factor influencing the learning and retention of meaningnful new material (Ausubel, 1963, 1960).

Ausubel's philosophy of learning theory has been used to support the argument against "activities science," that is, those activities which do not concern themselves with physical or biological ideas. The influence of Ausubel is felt in many published science curricula; an example is *Concepts in Science,* edited by Paul Brandwein.

Some of the major contributors to the theory that science is the acquisition of process skills and that the way to accomplish this is learning by discovery are Bruner, Gagné, and Piaget. Bruner chaired the important Woods Hole Conference that was called just after Sputnik was launched in 1957. During this conference scientists and psychologists gathered to address the then perceived lack of intellectual thrust found in American schools at that time. The outcome of this conference signaled that a change process was occurring which was to turn the federally sponsored research institutions, such as AAAS (American Association for the Advancement of Science) and its subunits, away from their primary goal and plunge them into the business of curriculum development, teaching techniques, and student learning.

Unlike Ausubel, Bruner believed that the structure of science is taught through conceptual schemes. When a child understands this structure, he can proceed on his own to discover more about science. This structure has three elements. The first includes facts, observations, measurements, and theories. The second involves process or the interaction of fitting new observations into the existing framework. The third element includes conceptual schemes, the underlying principles of science which have been central to the reorientation of science curriculum (Bruner, 1960). Thus, when scientists identify a set of fundamental ideas in science, they have defined the structure of science. Bruner declared that this structure can be taught to any child at any stage of development; that is, ideas can be reduced to a form that young students can grasp. However, teaching things at certain times is better than at other times.

As Bruner later observed, these ideas about student learning supposed a middle-class value oriented population, that is, students who had developed a strong emphasis on analytic skills and a desire to learn. In a review of the science curriculum developed between 1960 and 1970, it was found that the particular curriculum emphasis used crippled the capacity of children in the lowest socioeconomic levels to participate at full power in our society and it did so early and effectively (Gil). At this point in time, Bruner believes curriculum development must deemphasize building structures and put vocation and intention back into the process of education (Bruner, 1971). Proceeding from the known to the unknown, learning the heuristics of discovery, and improving the technique of inquiry should depend upon practice in inquiry (Bruner, 1961). These principles of Bruner's philosophy can be seen today in the science units that are part of the Elementary Science Study (EES) curriculum.

Gagné published his theory of inquiry in the mid-1960s which is best described in the *Conditions of Learning* published in 1970. Gagné believed that one can infer whether a student is or is not capable of employing the methods of scientific inquiry by observing designated, specific behaviors. He termed these "terminal behaviors." Thus, we find Gagné influenced curriculum aims in the direction of teaching the student the processes of science and to develop science-relevant inquiry skills.

A second aspect of his learning theory is instructional conditions. These are sets of conditions that are used to bring about a change in the student's capability. These conditions include all the events, the teacher, fellow students, the classroom, the laboratory, etc., impinging upon the student that help him move from one set of abilities to another. Gagné gave education behavioral objectives that are so familiar in science and other fields today. Gagné's terminal activities were behavioral objectives (Gagné, 1966).

Gagné's learning theory is a cumulative process. For any task, one first identifies competencies that are subordinate to the task. The competencies are then described in behavioral terms. Lastly, these competencies are taught in sequence. There have been a few research studies conducted to determine the validity of Gagné's theory as it applies to science learning. One study explored the competencies that are prerequisite to learning and applying principles related to density and specific gravity (Capie and Jones). By applying density principles to novel situations, the experimenters wished to observe if there was any hierarchy among the prerequisites they had identified. The results were inconclusive. They stressed that extreme care should be taken in the development of instruments and that further hierarchical analysis is needed.

Another area where Gagné's theory has been applied is in the ability of preservice teachers to plan and execute sequenced science activities (Trojcak). She found that the amount of planning and the testing of activities while they are being developed has a direct effect on the amount of student learning.

Piaget has had extensive influence on how young children learn and most especially on how young children learn science. Piaget's learning theory is a cognitive development theory as contrasted with the cumulative learning process of Gagné. For the purposes of the discussion that follows, it is assumed that the reader is familiar with the major aspect of Piaget's theory. There are many well-written articles on Piaget that may be of interest to the teacher of young children (e.g., Duckworth; Flavell; and Chittenden). Some of Piaget's own writings can be found in paperback (Piaget; Inhelder and Piaget). It is also possible to find sopohisticated treatment of Piaget's theory (Bybee and McCormack; Furth, 1969).

Piaget's theory can be seen in many aspects of science learning and teaching. His genetic epistemology has been used to develop a model for criterion-based assessment (Raven and Guerin). It has also been used to develop a scale of mental development. These studies have indicated that criterion-based assessment of science content is a function of the levels of logical operation being used in the assessment of a given student at a specific development stage.

His theory forms a basis of curriculum development and reform (Case). Piaget's findings concerning children's mental structures being less adequate and less complex than those of adults have shown that these uncomplicated structures can actively interfere with the acquisition of a more sophisticated structure. There is now evidence to suggest that classroom activities need careful planning and execution in sequencing and reducing complexity (Ramsey and Howe). Care should be exerted to uncover spontaneously acquired notions or skills that may interfere with the one being taught.

Piaget has generated about equal proportions of controversy and contribution in the field of science education. His claims about what children can and cannot do have prompted many researchers to replicate situations in which his findings can be re-affirmed or disclaimed. According to Piaget, most kindergarten children are pre-operational, and a few are concrete operational and thus can conserve. Results of the effects of experiences upon the conservation ability of children have been studied. School experiences that are culturally related or socioeconomically determined do cause marked variations in the age at which a child can conserve (Greenfield et al.; Almy et al.). Likewise, language development is related to conservation ability (Wohwill and Lowe; Furth, 1969). The interactive effects of these variables can significantly help or hinder the young child in transition between preoperational and concrete operational thought processes.

Starting with the premise that the concrete operational child is incapable of using quantitative proportional reasoning since he has not developed the formal operational schema of proportion, one study found that after training and retraining the young child did demonstrate some understanding of proportion (Boulanger). Harding and Jones considered Piaget's five stages of a child's explanation of the cause of cloud movement. Piaget had found that the child at age five explains such causes through magic; the child at age six explains them through God or large men; at age seven, self is responsible; wind is the cause of cloud movement for eight year olds but the wind comes from the clouds themselves; at age nine the child gives the correct answer. This study found that these mean ages would change if the interrogator was dressed in a clerical garb.

Colton and Butts investigated the role one of the cognitive process skills plays in helping the preoperational child in grades one through three acquire concrete operational thought. The concrete operational task of predicting floating objects was the center of their investigation. Long- and short-term instruction as well as no instruction was given to the children. Both first and third graders that had experience with the short-term instructional program made significant gains on the performance of concrete operational tasks. The no treatment groups made no gains at all. Third graders with long-term instruction could do the concrete operational task of predicting, while the first graders could not.

McClure studied the effect of training on students who could not conserve mass with children ranging in age from 79 to 108 months. The children were given practice with symbols for "less than," "more than," and "equal to." In a second training session the children used concrete objects, plastic holders and dowel sticks, classified according to length and diameter. Objects were classified by unequal lengths and unequal diameters, with diameter decreasing as length increased. The outcome recommended that teachers do the following to teach the conservation of mass:

1. Use three-dimensional devices.
2. Pretest first and second graders so you know where they are.
3. Let children make conservation discoveries on their own.

Camp investigated relations between selected conservation tasks and drawings made from memory by primary school children and found that the quality of the child's memory is related to his intellectual structure. The Science Curriculum Improvement Study (SCIS) and the Nuffield Science 5/13 program are primarily based on aspects of Piaget's developmental theory.

Lately, researchers have been combining theories in an attempt to find if such combinations produce more student learning in science. According to Piaget, primary-age children are often in a preoperational stage of development. Many science concepts and principles are so abstract that only those students who have arrived at a formal operational level can understand them. One question that has been asked is, Can science instruction based on the task analysis theory of Gagné lead to the acquisition of the ability to perform certain Piagetian volume tasks that have been characterized as requiring formal operational thought for their solution? (Howe and Butts) The results of the study indicated that the ability to perform volume tasks is related to age.

Empirical Data—Summary and Analysis

Science Skills

In terms of Ausubel's model of learning, improving inquiry skills requires improving the cognitive structure relevant to a specific problem area. On this issue Gagné's views are close to Ausubel's. However, Gagné emphasizes that knowledge and knowing strategies are not all that is required for problem solving. To be an effective problem solver, the individual must somehow acquire masses of organized intellectual skills (Gagné, 1970). Piaget's writings also stress that strategies children use for problem solving depend on years of cognitive accommodation and assimilation.

Kindergarten children who are allowed to manipulate science materials attain process skills better than those who do not manipulate materials (MacBeth and Fowler; Denner and Cashdan). However, children in the primary grades show no difference in acquiring these same skills if they manipulate or do not manipulate science materials. When asked to solve a problem using dry cells, wires, and two light bulbs, primary grade children exhibited the same kind of behavior as did older elementary grade children (Felen and Moser).

Based on Piaget's theory one would expect that the young child can attain the cognitive skills of observing, classifying, comparing, sorting, and communicating. If children are equally skilled in observing, will they make a significantly greater number or variety of observations with a familiar object than with a novel object? (Barufaldi, 1972) A difference was found between their ability to observe a single object and their ability to compare these single objects with each other. When presented with different visual stimuli, that is, solid objects, photographs of these objects, and drawings, there was again a difference in the visual observations and comparisons made by primary grade children (Barufaldi, 1972). These findings were substantiated when the primary child's ability to observe and classify was studied to determine if any relation existed between these two skills (Barufaldi, 1973). Third-grade boys showed greater precision in observing to distinguish objects than first-grade boys; the classification skills of these two groups did not differ.

Once the child has made many observations, he begins to use data processing skills. One such skill is classifying. Classificatory behavior seems to be preliminary and necessary for effective conceptualization (Lowery and Allen). Various attempts have been made to determine what attributes of objects a young child focuses on in order to find the general category in which to place several objects. Studies have been conducted to determine what strategies children without training employ and what strategies children with training employ (Raven). When asked to sort colored paper shapes, first graders tend to classify according to shape and not by color (MacBeth). They also identify large classes of dimensions such as shape and size and rules conventionally used in science classification when asked to group science-related objects into subsets as an aspect of classifications (Weinbrenner). The importance of this strategy was found to be quite profound in research on teaching and transfer of seriation tasks with first-grade children (Pidilla and Smith). Successful performance on the seriation tasks was generally achieved with the use of a relatively systematic strategy. This suggests the feasibility of teaching children strategies for this and other tasks as well as the potential for transfer of strategies across content. The effects of an inquiry training program were found to be a significant help to kindergarten inner-city children learning to classify (Galbally).

Science Content Knowledge

Research indicates that science concepts are achieved by young children with and without training. When Klein gave children written tests and individual oral interviews, he found that differences in levels of understanding of selected science concepts appear to have some relation to socioeconomic factors. Also, cultural differences in the ability of second-grade children to process science information and to solve science problem-solving tasks appear to exist (Felen and Moser).

A first-grade child's achievement in science learning can be predicted when his mental ability scores of logical reasoning and memory are available (Poole and Feldhusen). The student's positive self-image and likelihood of success also play important parts as predictors of success and behavior (Matthews et al.). When first graders were examined for knowledge of smells, air, and the difference between solids, liquids, and air, it was found that many first graders can attain these concepts often thought to be too difficult for them to comprehend (Hibbard and Novak). This suggests that the young child's attainment ability of other concepts judged to be too difficult for them should be examined. Also, performance of young children in noting properties of as well as experiences with plants can be improved with instruction (Oelerich).

Researchers in science education have been concerned about various elements in the child's learning environment that can have an effect on his achievement. Individual versus group instruction was studied to determine which was better for third graders to master physical concepts in the Science Curriculum Improvement Study (SCIS) second-grade unit called Interaction and Systems (Gallagher). It was found that the choice of instructional mode altered the nature of what was learned and the nature of the learning experience. Primary grade teachers are an important source of information about the learning environment. Teachers identified a lack of equipment and appropriate curriculum guides as well as teachers not being aware of available resources as the top factors for not initiating a good science program (Carr and Emlaw). The amount of time teachers give students to respond to questions has a significant bearing on helping the child to reason (Garigliano). When the child can manipulate the rate, number of repetitions, and amount of direct hands-on experience, he can master science concepts more easily (Hibbard).

Performance versus verbal ability was studied by Crumbs. Low and high verbal ability kindergarten through grade two students were tested in classrooms with heavy emphasis upon the use of concrete materials and little formal instruction in reading and writing a number of concepts. After two years no significant difference was found in the achievement scores in reading, spelling, or arithmetic between the treatment and control groups. Increasing relationships have been found to exist between learning and cognition with an increase in age of children in verbal and visual tasks (Empfield).

The success of TV programs such as *Sesame Street* and *The Electric Company* has had a direct impact on science learning in young children. TV lessons are as effective as classroom lessons in helping first graders develop classifying skills, and television can motivate students to continue experiments after the program is over (Galey).

Attitudes toward Science

Teachers and curriculum developers need to know the preferences, attitudes, and curiosity of the young child with respect to science. Since it is difficult for young children to express themselves, an indirect approach to discovering their attitudes seems appropriate in research. Children's drawings of scientists have given some clues to what constitutes science for young children (Uhlhorn). The kind of things children draw, that is, the background and the kind of science done in the picture, help the researcher infer what science is to the children.

Several attempts have been made to use different types of instruments to determine what kind of interest in science young children have (Ballow; Peterson and Lowery). Questionnaires, free-time sketches, reading preferences, and colored drawings have been used. Also, studies have been made using these instruments to determine the relationship between interest in science activities and achievement or ability in simple cognitive skills used in that area of activities. Sunal, using pictures of various science activities with second-grade students found no correlation between achievement or skill ability and interest in science activities. It has also been thought that perhaps a child's handling of three-dimensional objects would give an accurate picture of his attitude toward science and of his concept of science itself. Children who were given thirty real objects and thirty black and white pictures of these objects selected animals, pictures of things in motion, and pictures of planets as the "science" things that interested them (Zapata).

By presenting children with an assortment of keys and a puzzle box secured by three padlocks, Peterson showed that problem solving and curiosity were not correlated. However, successful solutions to the problem were associated with Piaget's stages of development. Finally, the new science projects, Elementary Science Study (ESS), Science—A Process Approach (SAPA), and SCIS, as well as local science curricula, do contribute to a child's development of a positive understanding and attitude toward science (Jenkins). Ability in achieving skills or science concepts appears to be a poor prediction for attitudes. Instead, curricula incorporating high interest and creative materials may be the best way of fostering favorable attitudes and curiosity in children.

When children are young, it appears very important that they be given the opportunity to handle materials and have many firsthand experiences. However, when the child enters kindergarten, he appears able to grasp some semiabstract concepts without handling materials. A child's ability to understand science ideas appears to be influenced by socioeconomic factors, his logical reasoning ability, his memory, and his self-image. What children consider as part of science and how much interest they have in science are two additional elements that help the teacher and the curriculum planner arrange an interesting program for young children.

Both science skill and concept learning are directly influenced by the type of environment in which children learn. Individual versus group instruction, equipment or lack of it, and performance tasks versus verbal tasks are just a few elements in the learning environment where research has only just begun.

Implications for Curriculum Planning

In the United States there now exist three federally funded science curricula that have been widely adopted (Lockard). They are Science—A Process Approach (SAPA), Science Curriculum Improvement Study (SCIS), and Elementary Science Study (ESS). During the past ten years, these programs have had a significant impact on elementary and early childhood education. Because of their large scale, much of the information written about and research performed on science curricula have involved these programs. These programs have been used with a variety of different children, for example, urban, rural, disadvantaged and exceptional children (Lockard).

SAPA, sponsored by the American Association for the Advancement of Science (AAAS), held its first planning sessions in 1962. The purpose of the project is to show a broad concern for science education at all levels, including curriculum development for grades K–16 and for teacher preparation. The AAAS group, using Gagné's developmental theory, believed that young children could begin a stepwise development of skills in activities used in scientific investigation (Gagné, 1966). Throughout the program, learning experiences were selected that would help the child develop skills in using the processes of science. In this program the skills of observing, using space/time relationships, classifying, and using number are presented to the child. The child learns a great variety of science content since the unit's organization is centered around the process skills and not around one or two specific science concepts; that is, it is not a unit on plants or on animals, but a unit on observing, classifying, and so forth. In the kindergarten unit the child has experiences with colors, shapes, textures, size, temperature, leaves, nuts or shells, and many other scientific things. The first grader is expected to be able to communicate, observe and describe change, and interpret symbols. He is given experience with animal shapes, footprints, variations in seed shapes, the force of gravity, and reactions. The second-grade and third-grade programs build upon the previous years and, in addition, encourage the children to infer, describe, and identify variables. The science content found in these two grades includes growing plants, constructing and interpreting maps, dropping objects, and bouncing balls (Xerox).

Extensive program evaluation was carried out when it was being written (Livermore). This well-organized evaluation of results reporting success with large numbers of children has continued over the years. Some variables within the SAPA kindergarten and primary grade programs, such as teacher-pupil behavior and testing format, have been investigated (Hall; Walbesser and Carter). Since 1970 an extensive look has been taken at many factors relating to the project (e.g., Ransom).

In development at the same time was the ESS project. This project was sponsored partially by the National Science Foundation and partially by small grants from a variety of agencies (Lockard). The purpose of the original project writers was to develop more meaningful science materials and to have open-ended rather than teacher- or testbook-directed materials. Careful attention was given to all materials used so that all equipment looked like materials which are normally accessible to children in their own environment. The project has developed investigations for children in grades K–8 (Rogers).

Topics are not restricted to one specific grade level. Attributes Games and Problems (Eggs and Tadpoles, Tangrams, and Growing Seeds) are appropriate for grades K–8; Brine Shrimp for grades 1–7; Butterflies and Changes, grades 1–4, and so forth (McGraw-Hill, 1968). The units in this project are organized around science concept topics. All the natural sciences, as well as engineering and medicine, served as sources for this project.

The children are encouraged to "mess around" and capture the spirit of science, the chance of discovery, and the reward of investigation. The project gives the teacher inexpensive apparatus to use and a style of teaching that emphasizes great chances for the children to direct their own learning (Rogers and Voelker).

Program evaluation, in a formal sense, was never a strong point in this program. The writers felt that observing the children's responses to the presented materials would give an experienced teacher the clues needed to continue or change the program as needed. However, over the past few years, several research studies have uncovered some quantitative information about the successful type of learning the ESS project encourages.

SCIS, developed in 1974, was the last of the nationally adopted programs to be completed. The purpose of this project is to give students an early introduction to the basic methods and philosophies of science. This introduction is needed if children are to sort out and understand the facts they absorb in their early schooling. This purpose is described as the development of scientific literacy for children (Lockard). One aspect of the program includes a sufficient knowledge and understanding of the fundamental scientific and process-oriented concepts for effective participation in twentieth century life. A second aspect involves the development of a free and inquisitive attitude and the use of rational procedures for decision making. The emphasis on scientific literacy was effectively performed. In a study performed on different curriculum materials, Knecht reported a consistent agreement of SCIS materials with the definition of scientific literacy as defined in the NSTA position paper, "Science for the Seventies," and inconsistent results with commercial textbooks curricula.

Four conceptual schemes (i.e., matter, energy, organisms, and ecosystems) are taught. These are divided through each grade level into a biological cycle and a physical cycle. The early childhood education and kindergarten unit titled "Beginnings" uses the basic science skills of observation, classification, and communication, and measurement in an open approach to science. Using a variety of activities in the classroom and outdoors, children are given experiences with color, shape, size, texture, odor, sound, size, quantity, position, and organisms. A significant part of the unit is the evaluation activities at the end of the unit which help in diagnosing each child's behavior. The first-year units are "Material Objects" and "Organisms." In "Material Objects" the child explores physical properties of common objects in the classroom leading to properties of matter in different forms, concepts of material, concepts of serial ordering, and introduction to systems and interactions. In "Organisms" the child investigates through activities in and out of the classroom concepts dealing with birth, death, decay, feeding, digestion, food web, detritus, and diversity of organisms. The second-year units are Interaction and Systems plus Life Cycles. The third-year unit encourages the children to observe and experiment using science skills with increasingly more complex phenomena (SCIS Sample Guide).

Within the past two years, the project developers have turned their attention to evaluation. There is a series of group tests now available with many of the units. There is also an individualized learning adaptation of this material. Research has at present investigated a few aspects of this project. In the area of science skills, children involved in SCIS classroom lessons performed significantly better when compared with children who used a textbook program (Weber). The skills studied were observation, classification, measurement, experimentation, interpretation, and prediction. Also, observable differences were noted in the manner in which both groups of subjects approached solutions to process-oriented tasks. The SCIS students were more aggressive, diverse, persistent, and reactive in this work and products. In addition to skills, the conservation reasoning of young students can be affected through SCIS lessons. In one research study SCIS first-grade students outperformed non-SCIS students in total gains on every conservation task administered (Stafford and Renner). Experience in SCIS first-year units also helped children lacking preschool education to gain in conservation skills.

In another study, Stafford concluded that the rate of attainment of conservation skills in kindergarten children is significantly enhanced by experiences provided by first-grade SCIS units. In the area of achievement transfer, effects appear to be an important result of early science experiences. Almy found that progress in beginning reading was related to performance in conservation tasks. Comparison of a commercial reading readiness program with SCIS first-grade units demonstrated this earlier finding (Kellogg). Greater gains were noted in five of six reading subtest areas including word meaning, listening, matching, alphabet, and numbers.

Studies done with older children using SCIS materials also indicate significant transfer effects in the areas of mathematics application, social studies skills, and paragraph meaning (Coffia). These results indicate that science experiences like those in the SCIS units tend to help children utilize and develop higher powers of thinking more effectively than those children who have not had this experience.

Changes in teacher behavior toward student involvement, student creativity, and higher level questioning may also be an important effect of well-designed science classroom experiences (Wilson; Porterfield).

Several less widely adopted science projects are available to kindergarten, first-, second-, and third-grade teachers (Lockard). Some examples include the Conceptually Oriented Programs in Elementary Science (COPES) which is intended to give children an understanding of the nature of matter at various levels of sophistication from grades K–6. The Elementary School Science Project—Utah State University (ESSP—USU) provides qualitative and quantitative experiments for children from five to seven years of age. Two of the very few preschool projects are those developed by the University of Colorado, namely, the Elementary Science Advisory and Research Projects and the Pre-Primary Science Program (Zeitler).

Textbook publishers have a few activity-oriented early childhood science programs available for teachers. *Experiences in Science* is one in which first-grade children can explore heat and cold, young animals, lights and shadows, the earth, and the sun and weather and plants in spring (Tannenbaum et al.). *Sense and Tell* is an early childhood program dealing with basic science skills with emphasis on observing (Marshall et al.). The Early Childhood Curriculum—a Piaget-Program—is a nursery school and kindergarten program designed to foster the development of logical thinking processes (Lavatelli). Activities for four to six year olds include classification, number, measurement, space, and seriation.

Conclusions

The inevitable questions must be asked. Is it now possible to construct an early childhood curriculum containing an effective science component? What does the preceding tell us about a day-to-day science program? In order to answer these and similar questions, two important assumptions need to be stated. First, if we accept the definition of science stated in these pages, that is, science is mainly a method of achieving and to a much lesser degree a useful set of achievements, then we find that science is being taught to young children. Teachers do encourage children to notice color and shape, for example. They give children "cooking" and "mixing" types of experiences. Therefore, what is needed to implement a full-fledged science program in preschool education is an expansion of current activities and a direct attempt on the part of the teacher to plan connected lessons that allow the child to learn by observing, measuring, inferring, comparing, and classifying. Instead of focusing on things to learn, the teacher should focus on skills to acquire. These skills have the built-in advantage of helping the child learn about the world around him, even when the teacher is not present.

Second, day-to-day science experiences should alert us to teaching things that are appropriate for young children. Some science-type activities employ a subtle logic that children may be able to use. It appears that teachers of young children are very concerned about those things that might be too hard for the children, but seldom does one hear much discussion about those concepts, skills, and activities that are too easy. In both cases, the child learns very little. The concept itself, the materials in an activity, or the directions about how to use the materials may prevent learning. When the child handles materials in a science class, the teacher is free to make many observations about the ease and difficulty of concept formation.

Teachers of young children might use a commercially available curriculum or construct a science program of their own. Usually, teachers should take an eclectic look at the available programs. The students' interest, availability of materials, and time are essential in planning a science program.

Much still needs to be done to help teachers implement science programs. More research on children's observing, inferring, communicating skills, and concept forming is needed. Yet, evidence does indicate that the science methods now being utilized can give children an exciting experience with the world around them. The problems of everyday life in the future are probably beyond comprehension. Since we cannot identify these problems, we must at least give the generation of the future ways of solving a variety of problems about the world in which they now live.

References

Almy, Millie, et al. *Young Children's Thinking. Studies of Some Aspects of Piaget's Theory.* New York: Teachers College Press, 1969.

Atkins, J.M. "A Study Formulating and Suggesting Tests for Hypotheses in Elementary Science Learning." *Science Education* 42 (1956): 414–22.

Ausubel, D.P. "Facilitating Meaningful Verbal Learning in the Classroom." *Arithmetic Teacher* 15 (1968): 126–32.

———. *The Psychology of Meaningful Verbal Learning.* New York: Grune & Stratton, 1963.

———. "The Use of Advance Organizers." *Journal of Educational Psychology* 51(1960): 267–72.

Ballow, M. "A Study of the Science Interests of Students in Grades I, II, and III." Unpublished data of Educational Field Study. Colorado State College, 1951.

Barufaldi, J. "Observation and Comparison Tasks Using Ordinary and Novel Objects." NARST Abstracts, Ohio State University, 1972.

———. "The Performance of Children on Visual Observation and Comparison Tasks." NARST Abstracts, Ohio State University, 1973, p. 37.

Bennett, L.M. "Teaching Science Concepts to Preschoolers." *School Science and Mathematics* 69 (1969): 731–37.

Benson M.P. "Early Childhood Education." *American Education* 4(1968):7–13.

Blin-Stoyle, R.J. "The End of Mechanistic Philosophy and the Rise of Field Physics: Turning Point in Physics." New York: North Holland Publishing Co., 1959.

Boulanger, F.D. "The Effects of Instruction in the Concept of Speed." Paper presented at National Association for Research in Science Teaching meeting, Chicago, April 1974.

Brandwein, P., et al. *Concepts in Science.* New York: Harcourt Brace Jovanovich, 1966.

Brown, G.B. *Science: Its Method and Its Philosophy.* New York: W.W. Norton & Co., 1950.

Brownouski, J. *Science and Human Values.* New York: Harper & Row, Publishers, 1965.

Bruner, J.S. "The Act of Discovery." *Harvard Education Review* 31(1961):21–32.

———. *The Process of Education.* Cambridge: Harvard University Press, 1960.

———. "The Process of Education Revisited." *Phi Delta Kappan* 52(1971):18–21.

Butts, D.P. "The Degree to Which Children Conceptualize from Science Experience." *Journal of Research in Science Teaching* (1963):135–43.

Butts, D.P., and Jones, H. "Inquiry Training and Problem Solving." *Journal of Research in Science Teaching* 1(1966):21–27.

Bybee, R., and McCormack, A. "Applying Piaget's Theory." *Science and Children* 8(1970): 14–17.

Caldwell, B.M. "The Rationale for Early Intervention." Paper prepared for Early Childhood Conference. New Orleans, Louisiana, December, 1969.

Camp M. "The Relationships between Selected Conservation Tasks and Drawings Made from Memory by Primary School Children." Paper delivered at NARST Meeting. Chicago, 1972.

Campbell, N. *What Is Science?* New York: Dover Publications, 1952.

Capie, W., and Jones, H.L. "An Assessment of Hierarchy Validation Technique." *Journal of Research in Science Teaching* 8(1971):137.

Carr, A.B., and Emlaw, J. "Factor Affecting the Implementation of the 1972 Laboratory Approach to Science Teaching in Grades K–3." NARST Abstracts (1972):131–32.

Case R. "Implications of Piaget's Theory of Child Development for Curriculum." Paper delivered at NARST Meeting. Chicago, 1974.

Charlesworth, and Zahn. "Reaction Time as a Measure of Comprehension of Effects Produced by Rotation Objects." *Child Development* 37(1966):253–68.

Chittenden, E.A. "Piaget and Elementary Science." *Science and Children* 8(1970):9–15.

Coffia, W.J. "The Effects of an Inquiry-centered Curriculum in Science on a Child's Achievement in Selected Academic Areas." Doctoral dissertation, University of Oklahoma, 1971.

Cole, L. *A History of Education: Socrates to Montessori.* New York: Holt, Rinehart & Winston, 1950.

Colton, T., and Butts, D. "The Role of Classification Skills in Children's Acquisition of Concrete Operational Thought." NARST Abstracts, Ohio State University, 1971.

Comber, L.C., and Keeves, J.P. *Science Education in Nineteen Countries—International Studies in Evolution I.* New York: John Wiley and Sons, 1973, pp. 298.

Conant, J.B. *On Understanding Science.* New York: Mentor Books, 1951.

Crumbs, G.H. "Performance versus Verbal Ability." NARST Abstracts (1974), p. 151.

DeLancy, B.A. "Some Problems Associated with Paper-and-Pencil Test of Conservation for Length." *Child Development* 38(1967):869–75.

Denner, B., and Sheldon C. "Sensory Processing and the Recognition of Forms in Nursery School Children." *British Journal of Psychology* 58(1967):101–4.

Dewey, J. *Democracy and Education.* New York: The Macmillan Co., 1916.

Duckworth, E. "Piaget Rediscovered." *Journal of Research in Science Teaching* 2(1964): 172–75.

Durrell, C.V. *Readable Relativity.* New York: Harper Torchbook, 1960.

Educational Policies Commission, NEA, AAAS. "Education and the Spirit of Science." *The Science Teacher* (1966), pp. 18–20.

Empfield, C.O. "Learning and Cognition in a Verbal and Visual Task." NARST Abstracts, Ohio State University (1974), p. 219.

Felen B.K., and Moser, G.W. "Information Theory Applied to the Analysis of Problem Solving Using the Parallel Circuit Model." NARST Abstracts, Ohio State University (1971), p. 55.

Fish, A.S., and Goldmark, B. "Inquiry Method: Three Interpretations." *The Science Teacher* 33(1966):13–15.

Flavell, J.H. *The Development Psychology of Jean Piaget.* New York: D. Van Nostrand Co., 1963.

Frank, P. *Modern Science and Its Philosophy.* New York: Collier, 1961.

Furth, H.C. "Concerning Piaget's View on Thinking and Symbol Formulation." *Child Development* 38(1967):819–26.

———. *Piaget and Knowledge.* Englewood Cliffs: Prentice-Hall, 1969.

Gagné, R.M. *Conditions of Learning.* New York: Holt, Rinehart & Winston, 1970.

———. "Elementary Science: A New Scheme of Instruction." *Science* 151(1966):49–53.

———. "The Learning Requirements for Inquiry." *Journal of Research in Science Teaching* 1(1963):144–53.

Galbally, J.R. "Effects of a Science Inquiry Program on the Development of the Skill of Classification." NARST Abstracts, Ohio State University, 1974, p. 41.

Galey, M. "The Development of Inquiry through the Use of Television." NARST Abstracts, Ohio State University, 1971, p. 217.

Gallagher, J.J. "A Comparison of Individual and Group Instruction in Science." NARST Abstracts, 1970, pp. 138–39.

Garigliano, L. "The Relation of Wait Time to Student Behaviors in Science Curriculum Study Lesson." NARST Abstracts, Ohio State University, 1972, pp. 122–23.

Garone, J.E. "Acquiring Knowledge and Attaining Understanding of Children's Scientific Concept Development." *Science Education* 44(1969):104–7.

George, K.D. "Science for the Preschool Child." *Science and Children* 6(1968):37–38.

George, K.D., and Dietz, M.A. "How Do Children Classify?" *Journal of Research in Science Teaching* 8(1971):277–83.

George, K.D., et al. *Elementary School Science Why and How,* Lexington, Mass: D.C. Heath & Co., 1974.

Gil, A., ed. *The Relevance of Education.* New York: W.W.Norton & Co., 1971.

Glaser, R.; Reynolds J.H.; and Fullick, M.G. "Studies of the Use of Programmed Instruction in the Intact Classroom." *Psychology in the Schools* 3(1966):318–33.

Greenfield, P.; Bruner, J.; Oliver, R.; Reich, L. *Studies in Cognitive Growth: A Collaboration at the Center for Cognitive Studies.* New York: John Wiley & Sons, 1966.

Griffiths, J.A., et al. "Methodological Problem in Conservation Studies." *Child Development* 38(1967):841–48.

Gruen, G. "Notes on Conservation: Methodological and Definitional Consideration." *Child Development* 37(1966):977–83.

Hall, G.C. "Teacher-Pupil Behaviors Exhibited by Two Groups of Second-Grade Teachers Using Science." NARST Abstracts, Ohio State University, 1970, pp. 325–34.

Harding and Jones. "Organizer Influence on Children's Answers to Questions of Physical Causality." NARST Abstracts, 1970.

Hibbard, K.M. "Concept Attainment and Verbal Predictive Ability for Primary Grade Children." NARST Abstracts, Ohio State University, 1973, pp. 116–17.

Hibbard, K.M., and Novak, J. "Specific Content Knowledge as a Primary Component of a Model to Describe Learning by Young Children." NARST Abstracts, Ohio State University, 1972, pp. 100–101.

Howe, R.W. and Butts, D.P. "The Effect of Instruction on the Acquisition of Conservation of Volume." NARST Abstracts, Ohio State University, 1970.

Inhelder, B., and Piaget, J. *The Early Growth of Logic in the Child.* New York: Harper & Row, Publishers, 1964.

Jenkins, J.A. "Elementary School Science Programs: Pupils and Teacher Attitudes." NARST Abstracts, Ohio State University, 1972, pp. 79–80.

Kellogg, D.H. "An Investigation of the Effect of the Science Curriculum Improvement Study's First Year Unit, *Material Objects,* on Gains in Reading Readiness." Doctoral dissertation, University of Oklahoma, 1971.

Kemeny, J.G. *A Philosopher Looks at Science.* New York: D. Van Nostrand Co., 1959.

Kilpatrick, W.H. *The Montessori System Examined.* Boston: Houghton Mifflin Co., 1914.

Klein, C. "Differences in Science Concepts Held by Children from Three Social-Economic Levels." NARST Abstracts, Ohio State University, 1970, pp. 128–29.

Knecht, P.S. "A Model to Facilitate the Assessment of Epistemological Quality in Elementary Science Programs." Ph.D. dissertation, Michigan State University, 1974.

Kohlberg. L.A. "Early Education: A Cognitive-developmental View." *Child Development* 39(1968):1013–62.

Kuhn, D. "Science Teaching, Concept Formation and Learning Theory." *Science Education* 56(1972):189–96.

Lansdown, B., and Dietz, T.S. "Free versus Guided Experimentation." *Science Education* 49(1965):210–13.

Larat, M. "Teaching Primary School Science." *The Australian Science Teachers' Journal* 14(1968):23–25.

Lavatelli, C.S. *Early Childhood Curriculum—A Piaget Program.* Boston: American Science and Engineering, 1971.

Lawson, C.A. "The Life Science Program of the Science Curriculum Improvement Study." *American Biology Teacher* 29(1967):185–90.

Livermore, A.H. "Science—A Process Approach." *Science and Children* 1(1964):24–25.

Lockard, J.D., ed. "Science and Mathematics Curricula Developments Internationally." The ninth report of the International Clearinghouse on Science and Mathematics curricular Developments, AAAS and Science Teaching Center of University of Maryland, 1975.

Lowery, L., and Allen, L.R. "Visual Resemblance Sorting Abilities among First-Grade Pupils." *Journal of Research in Science Teaching* 6(1969):248–56.

Macbeth D.R. "Classificational Preferences in Young Children—Form or Colors." NARST Abstracts, Ohio State University, 1974, p. 24.

Macbeth, D., and Fowler, S. "The Extent to Which Pupils Manipulate Materials and Attainment of Process Skills." NARST Abstracts, Ohio State University, 1972, p. 55.

McClure, S.L. "The Application of Cognitive Dissonance to Children's Acquisition of Piaget's Conservation of Mass." NARST Abstracts, Ohio State University, 1971, pp. 215–16.

Marshall et al. *Sense and Tell.* Glenview, Ill.: Scott, Foresman and Co., 1969.

Maslow, A.H. *The Psychology of Science.* New York: Harper and Row, Publishers, 1966.

Matthews, C.C.; James, A.; Shymansky, J.A.; Penick, J.P.; and Good, R.G. "Studies of Learning Environments and Outcomes (Project LEO)." NARST Abstracts, Ohio State University, 1975, pp. 146–48.

Moe, D. "What Is Science?" *School Science and Mathematics* 6(1964):453–58.

Nagel, E. *The Structure of Science.* New York: Harcourt Brace Jovanovich, 1961.

Namy, E. "Intellectual and Academic Characteristics of 4th Grade Gifted and Pseudogifted Students." *Exceptional Children* 34(1967):15–18.

Neimark, E.D., and Lewis L. "Development of Logical Problem Solving." *Child Development* 39(1968):527–36.

Newport, J. "Process: Ends or Means or Both?" *Science Education* 56(1972):139–41.

Nizova, A.N. "Natural History in the Primary Grades." *Soviet Education* 7(1965):23–27.

Novak, J.D. "A Model for the Interpretation and Analysis of Concept Formation." *Journal of Research in Science Teaching* 3(1965):72–83.

NSTA Committee on Curriculum Studies. "School Science Education for the 70s, A Position Paper." *Science Teacher* 38(1971):46–51.

NSTA Curriculum Committee and the Conference on Science Concepts. "Theory into Action in Science Curriculum Development." Washington D.C.: National Science Teachers Association, 1964.

O'Brien, T.C., and Shapiro, B.J. "Problem Solving and Development of Cognitive Structure." *Arithmetic Teaching* 16(1969):11–15.

Oelerich, M.L. "A Study of the Observation Ability of Kindergarten Children in Science Experiences Involving Plant Specimens." Ph.D. dissertation, University of Iowa, 1969.

Osiyale, A.O. "Primary School Science in Africa: An Experiment in Education." *ESI Quarterly Report.* Spring/Summer 1966, pp. 74–77.

Padillo, M.J., and Smith, E.L. "The Teaching and Transfer of Seriation Strategies Using Non-Visual Variables with First Grade Children." NARST Abstracts, Ohio State University, 1975, pp. 44–47.

Pearson, K. *Grammar of Science.* New York: Meridian Books, 1957.

Pedersen, F.A., and Wender, P.H. "Early Social Correlates of Cognitive Functioning in Six-Year-Old Boys." *Child Development* 39(1968):185–93.

Peterson, R., and Lowerey, L. "A Study of Curiosity Factors in First Grade Children." *Science Education* 52(1968):4.

Peterson, R.W. "Assessing Curiosity and Problem-Solving Behaviors among Children." NARST Abstracts, Ohio State University, 1972, pp. 158–59.

Piaget, J. "Development and Learning." *Journal of Research in Science Teaching* 2(1964): 176–78.

Pierce, L.R. "Effect of Early School Experiences on the Learning of Science Concepts." Ph.D. dissertation, Stanford University, 1968.

"Plowden on Primary Schools." *Times Educational Supplement* 2695(1967):97–100.

Poole, H., and Feldhusen, J. "Prediction of First Grade Science Achievement." NARST Abstracts, Ohio State University, 1972, pp. 87–88.

Porterfield, D.R. "Influence of Preparation in Science Curriculum Improvement Study on Questioning Behavior of Selected Second and Fourth Grade Reading Teachers." Doctoral dissertation, University of Oklahoma, 1969.

Ramsey, G.A., and Howe, R.W. "An Analysis of Research Related to Instructional Procedures in Elementary School Science." *Science and Children* 6(1969):25–36.

Ransom, W.E. "Effect of Science: A Process Approach on Creative Thinking and Performance in Selected Processes of Science in the Second Grade." Ph.D. dissertation, Syracuse University, 1968.

Raven, R.J. "The Development of Classification Abilities in Culturally Disadvantaged Children." *Journal of Research in Science Teaching* 5(1967–68):224–29.

Raven, R., and Guerin, R. "A Piaget-Based Development Model for Criterion-Based Assessment." Paper delivered at NARST meeting. Chicago, 1974.

Riechard, D.E. "A Decade of Preschool Science: Promises, Problems and Perspectives." *Science Education* 57(1973):437–51.

Robinson, J.T. "Science Teaching and the Nature of Science." *Journal of Research in Science Teaching* 3(1965):37–50.

Rogers, R.E., and Voelker, A.M. "Programs for Improving Science Instruction in the Elementary School." *Science and Children* (1970):35–43.

Science 5/13. London: Macdonald Educational, 1972.

Science Curriculum Improvement Study, SCIS Sample Guide. New York: Rand McNally Company, 1970.

Schulman, L.S., and Tamir, P. "Research on Teaching in the Natural Sciences." In *Second Handbook of Research on Teaching,* edited by R.M.W. Travers. Chicago: Rand McNally & Co., 1973.

Schwab, J.J. "Inquiry, the Science Teacher, and the Educator." *The School Review* 68(1960): 176–94.

Stafford, D.G. "The Influence of the First Grade Program of the Science Curriculum Improvement Study on the Rate of Attainment of Conservatives." Doctoral dissertation, University of Oklahoma, 1969.

Stafford, D.G. and Renner, J.W. "SCIS Helps the First Grader to Use Logic in Problem Solving." *School Science and Mathematics,* 1971, pp. 159–64.

Suchman, J.R. "The Illinois Studies in Inquiry Training." *Journal of Research in Science Teaching* 2(1967):230–32.

———. "Learning through Inquiry." *Childhood Education* 41(1965):289–91.

Sunal, D.W. "The Planetarium in Education, An Experimental Study of the Attainment of Goals." Doctoral dissertation, University of Michigan, 1973.

Sundberg, N., and Ballinger, T. "Nepalese Children's Cognitive Development." *Child Development* 39(1968):969–85.

Taba, H. "Learning by Discovery: Psychological and Educational Rationale." *The Elementary School Journal* 63(1963):308–16.

Tannenbaum, H. et al. *Experiences in Science.* New York: Webster Division, McGraw-Hill Book Co., 1967.

Trojcak, D. "Five Stages of Instruction for Sequencing Science Activities." *Science and Children* 9(1972):28–29.

Uhlhorn, K.W. "Pictures of Scientists as Drawn by Children and Their Concept of Science." NARST Abstracts, Ohio State University, 1970 pp. 132–33.

Walbesseo, H., and Carter, H. "The Effect of Test Results of Changes in Task and Response Format Required by Altering the Test Administration from an Individual to a Group Format." *Journal of Research in Science Teaching* 7:1–8.

Weber, M.C. "The Influence of the Science Curriculum Improvement Study on the Learner's Operational Utilization of Science Processes." Doctoral dissertation, University of Oklahoma, 1971.

Webster Science Catalog, Manchester, Mo.: Webster Division, McGraw-Hill Book Co., 1968.

Weinbrenner, L.B. "Science Classificatory Dimension and Rules Used by Children." Ph.D. dissertation, University of Wisconsin, 1969.

Wilson, J.W. "Differences between the Inquiry-Discovery and the Traditional Approaches to Teaching Science in the Elementary School." Doctoral dissertation, University of Oklahoma, 1967.

Wohlwill, J.F., and Lowe, R.C. "Experimental Analysis of the Development of Conservation of Number." *Child Development* 33(1962):152–67.

Xerox Curriculum Catalog. New York: Dept. C, Xerox Corporation, 1968.

Zapata, A.G. "An Instrument to Measure the Science Interests of Grade School Children." *Studies in Science Education* 1(1973):14–18.

Zeitler, W.R. "Preliminary Report on a Pre-Primary Science Program." *School Science and Mathematics* 5(1969):417–25.

Zigler, E. "Cognitive Processes in Development of Children's Appreciation of Humor." *Child Development* 37(1966):507–18.

chapter six

Mathematics

Martin L. Johnson

John W. Wilson

How many more?

Mathematics programs currently available for young children are quite diverse in rationale, philosophy, and content. Much of this diversity is due to the attempts of program developers to answer the following questions:

1. What mathematics *can* children learn?
2. How *do* children learn mathematics?
3. What mathematics *should* children learn?

In addressing the last question Glennon and Wilson suggest that three positions (or theories) can be taken; namely, a logical position, a psychological position, and a sociological position. Advocates of each of these positions can be found among those who view themselves as "early-childhood educators."

Proponents of the logical position state that the curriculum is determined by the inherent logical structure of the discipline. In the case of mathematics this structure can be used to design well-organized, sequential tasks that can be presented to children. The logical structure of mathematics takes precedent over other considerations such as whether five year olds should be taught operations with negative integers. The fact that neat instructional packages can be developed that lead children into these ideas somehow justifies including this approach in our curriculum. Gagné has provided much insight into the notions of task analysis and developing learning hierarchies. With this information, and with the structure of the discipline of mathematics, mathematical content once seen only in the upper grades and sometimes only in senior high school is now presented in kindergarten and primary grades.

A second approach, the psychological approach, to what the mathematics curriculum should contain is to begin with a knowledge of children and how they learn and develop a program that places the responsibility upon the children to select to learn the mathematics they view as important or that they want to learn. This position is made clear by A.S. Neill:

> We have no new methods of teaching, because we do not consider that teaching in itself matters very much. Whether a school has or does not have a special method for teaching long division is of no significance, for long division is of no importance except to those who *want* to learn it. And the child who *wants* to learn long division *will* learn it no matter how it is taught. (Neill, p. 5)

This second approach suggests that the curriculum will be determined by what the children feel they need to know.

The advocates of the sociological position argue that the curriculum should consist only of the mathematics the child will need to exist in society or in real-life situations. Such a position in its strictest sense leads one to develop a program based on what mathematics is being used "at the moment" with little emphasis on whether what is being taught will be useful in future years. A leading spokesman for this position is Guy M. Wilson who stated:

> The schools should no doubt develop arithmetic somewhat beyond the present actual needs of children, but certainly not beyond the needs of adults. Common adult usage should be the limit of any arithmetic undertaken for drill or mastery in the grades and general high school. (Wilson, p. ix)

Glennon and Wilson suggest that the question of what should be in the curriculum is too important to be left to any one group (i.e., the mathematicians, the psychologists, or the sociologists). The curriculum should reflect the viewpoints of each of the positions to result in a somewhat balanced curriculum.

Well-defined philosophies have been established in an attempt to answer the questions, What mathematics can children learn? and How do children learn mathematics? The positions taken can be thought of as representing a continuum when compared on the questions stated above. At one extreme we find the strict task-analysis approach of the behaviorists. At the other extreme are the naturalists who advocate that no structure be imposed on the learning task or immediate environment since the child will learn what he *feels* to be important. Somewhere between these positions are the viewpoints of the cognitive developmentalists; they believe that the child must interact *both* mentally and physically with his environment and this may take place as a result of a structured or unstructured learning task. Most research and curriculum materials in mathematics for preschool and primary children are directly related to these three positions. However, the viewpoints of great educators such as Pestalozzi, Gagné, Ausubel, and Dienes seem to include some aspects of all the mentioned positions; however, each has influenced mathematics education in his own way. In the next section the theoretical positions of the behaviorists, the cognitive developmentalists, and the naturalists will be discussed as they relate to the three questions posed in the beginning paragraph.

Theory, Research, and Curriculum Projects

The Behaviorists

For the behaviorists, learning, in the purest sense, is an observable change in one's behavior. While variations and differences can be found among the philosophies and theories of behaviorists such as Hull, Watson, Thorndike, Skinner, and Englemann, one common thread that runs throughout these theories is a concern for bringing a specific behavior under the control of a specified antecedent and/or consequent stimuli (praise, rewards, etc.) The critical issue becomes one of discriminating between relevant and irrelevant stimuli. In other words, if we do not concern ourselves with consequent stimuli, we can determine which antecedent stimuli causes the child to give a certain response. If the antecedent stimuli are controlled, the desired response can be obtained by a reinforcement system of rewards such as praise, candy, stars etc. Englemann (1969) suggests that a system of reinforcement can help in defining the set of relevant stimuli and in providing motivation to elicit the desired behavior. Englemann states quite forcefully that "the child will perform the actions that are specified by the tasks only if he receives a greater payoff for these behaviors than he does for other types of behaviors that are available to him at the moment" (Englemann, *Conceptual Learning*, p. 81). This position is widely accepted by leading authorities on behavior modification techniques and appears to have far-reaching implications to teaching mathematics to children.

With reference to the questions posed earlier, the behaviorists give little attention to what should be taught. The position they take is that if the content (or terminal behaviors) can be specified, a way can be found to train the child to give these behaviors. Specifically, if the wish is for a child to solve algebraic equations in the third grade, a set of antecedent and/or consequential stimuli can be found for this behavior. Children learn by being exposed to numerous stimuli and, through a process of discrimination, abstract the relevant set. Operating from this frame of reference, there appears to be no limit to what a child can learn, since if learning does not occur it is the fault of the sequence of stimuli, not a fault of the child. In some sense, this approach seems to support the well-known hypothesis of Bruner that "any subject can be taught effectively in some intellectually honest form to any child at any stage of development" (Bruner, p. 33). The task is to find the relevant set of stimuli. It is not left to chance that the child will be exposed to the relevant stimuli since the teacher's role is to *teach* facts, concepts, and principles through carefully planned sequences of tasks. The teaching is primarily didactic. Englemann (1966, 1969a, 1969b) has proposed strategies for teaching arithmetical facts, concepts, and principles that reflect examples of these didactic procedures.

As far as discovery is concerned, Englemann states "the discovery techniques advocated by most new math programs have no place in an elementary teaching program" (Englemann, 1969b, p. 252). He points out that a strategy of teaching concepts must include both positive and negative instances (Englemann, 1969a). For example, if the child is to learn the concept "triangle," he must be shown large, small, equilateral, isosceles, and scalene triangles and told that they are all triangles. The child should also be shown squares, rectangles, octagons, and other plane figures and told that they are *not* triangles. By considering both the positive and negative instances, the child will come to react to the correct set of stimuli for the concept "triangle."

Dienes takes the position that in order for the child to abstract a concept, he needs to meet the concept in many embodiments. Hence, the child not only needs many instances of the concept but also needs "multiple embodiments" of it as well. Shumway investigated the effect of negative instances on the forming of mathematical concepts with 120 eighth-grade students. The concepts treated were from areas of geometry, and exponents and operations, and included topics such as closure, commutativity, associativity, identity elements, and distributivity. After each concept was defined, the experimental classes received both positive and negative instances while the control classes received only positive instances. The experiment lasted sixty-five days; the total number of instances studied for a given concept was equal for both experimental and control classes. Shumway concluded that the use of negative instances helped to control the common error of overgeneralizing. The question of optimum number of positive and negative instances is still open for investigation.

A literature search reveals much research on behavior modification and its effect on learning in general. However, little of this literature is addressed to the learning of mathematics by preschool and primary children. In an effort to disprove Piaget's hypothesis that children must reach a certain stage of development before they can solve problems requiring formal operational thought patterns, Englemann (1967) sought to show that culturally disadvantaged and culturally advantaged preschoolers could be trained to solve a criterion problem analyzed as requiring formal operational thought. The component skills necessary for the criterion problem were taught to the ten children in the sample. The test results revealed that seven of the ten children trained were able to solve the problem, yet six of the seven had not reached even the Piagetian stage of concrete operations. Englemann concluded that the ability to handle formal operational problems was a function of instruction and not a function of development.

Englemann extols the expository method of teaching mathematics. The mathematics education literature has numerous reports on research that attempted to determine the merits of an expository verses a discovery method of teaching, sometimes referred to as "drill" versus "meaningful," although it is not intended that the teaching methods of the behaviorists be viewed only as drill methods. In a very early study, Brownell and Chazal sought to answer the question, "What contribution, if any, does drill make to raising the level of children's performances in arithmetic, to promoting growth in mature forms of arithmetic thinking?" (Brownell and Chazal, pp. 17–28) Brownell interpreted drill to mean those teaching procedures through which the pupil is led to say appropriate verbal formulas and to read and write number symbols and statements over and over without change. The sample for this study consisted of sixty-three children beginning the third grade. All of the children had learned two hundred addition and subtraction combinations, having addends less than nine and sums less than eighteen, through drill procedures in grades one and two. Ten days after coming into grade three, all of the children were given a written test on the one hundred addition combinations.

On the basis of their performance on this test, Brownell and Chazal interviewed thirty-two children and asked them to think out loud about how they solved the combination. During the next two months, they held two additional interviews; the first was held after each child had been drilled on the combinations and the second, after a month in which no drill was given. Among the conclusions stated by Brownell and Chazal are the following: "First, drill, as it was administered in this study, does not guarantee that children will be able immediately to recall combinations as such. The reason lies in the fact that drill as given by teachers does not necessarily lead to repetition on the part of the pupils. Second, in spite of long-continued drill children tend to maintain the use of whatever procedures they have found to satisfy their number needs. Third, drill makes little, if any, contribution to growth in quantitative thinking by supplying maturer ways of dealing with numbers" (Brownell and Chazal, pp. 17–28).

Brownell does not claim that there is no place for drill in the teaching of arithmetic but rather procedures that promote understanding of a concept should precede practice on that concept. The findings of Brownell suggest that the behaviorist position that a child "knows" a concept whenever he has a name for it and can distinguish between examples and nonexamples is open to question and is a researchable hypothesis. Brownell also investigated the learning of mathematical operations and raised questions about the effect of previously learned skills on more complex tasks in mathematics.

Programs Based on the Behaviorist Approach. One mathematics program that reflects the behaviorist philosophy is the Distar Arithmetic I Program. This program, developed by Englemann and Carnine and marketed by Science Research Asscciates (SRA), has as one of its goals to teach preschool-primary children what the statements of arithmetic are and how one goes about answering them. A quote from the teacher's manual effectively describes the Distar Program.

> Distar Arithmetic I teaches the basic rules about arithmetic that are needed if the children are to have a solid basis for remembering and classifying facts. The children take a step at a time. They do not move in the program until they have mastered the steps that are needed for the operations that are to come. They are systematically taught the symbols, conventions, and operations that enable them to solve a broad range of problems. (Englemann and Carnine, Teacher's Guide, p. 7)

The mathematics content of the Distar Arithmetic I Program contains the mathematics that is viewed as being essential for primary children. The content begins with number counting as the logical beginning point. This is different from primary programs that begin with one-to-one correspondence and then proceed to counting. Arithmetic symbols, such as the equal, plus, and minus signs, receive much attention. Addition is introduced as the first binary operation; the child is taught how to begin with a number and what happens when you add one, then two, etc. Later, when subtraction problems are introduced in the form of missing addends (referred to in the program as algebra problems), the child is taught to solve the problem by counting from five to seven; taking into account what the equal sign means and trying to make each side equal.

Other content topics covered are line counting, more and less, counting by two's, and algebra subtraction story problems. While the content covered in the Distar Arithmetic I Program is designed for the preschool-primary child, programs for advanced children have also been proposed by Englemann (1969b).

The instructional approach throughout the Distar Arithmetic I Program is purely expository. The teacher is provided with lesson plans, and little variance from the proposed plans is recommended. A total of 220 different plans are presented; some are applicable to group teaching and others are designed for individual sessions. It is suggested that the teacher reward children who demonstrate acceptable behavior and also attempt to get full participation from all children in each presentation. The program consists of both teacher and student material. The teacher material consists of five presentation books: Preskills and Books A, B, C, and D. The student material consists of 170 take-home activities in perforated multibook form. This program, referred to as an "Instructional System," offers a complete package to the teacher.

The Cognitive Developmentalists

The cognitive developmentalist is concerned with the way in which children develop cognitive structures and what factors influence this development. The developmentalist does not view the child as being under the control of selected stimuli, but rather he sees the child as one who has the freedom to choose which of the various stimuli surrounding him he wishes to respond to. Piaget has emerged as the dominant figure among the cognitive developmentalists. Piaget proposed a developmental theory that attempts to explain the development of a person's intelligence from birth to adolescence. Piaget's theory, while unique in several respects, is not completely divorced from other epistemological positions in that he views learning as a function of experience (Hunt; Bruner).

Piaget's theory is of interest to those who develop mathematics programs for children since much of his research was addressed to the learning of concepts of number, length, weight, etc., all quantitative concepts. Much of his theory gives insight into how children learn mathematics and the factors influencing how the child learns. Piaget revealed many critical points in the development of children where their thinking differed tremendously in quality. The stages of development are identified based on the following junctures:

1. Sensorimotor stage (0 to 2 years)
2. Preoperational stage (2 to 7 years)
   a. Preconceptual thought (2 to 4 years)
   b. Intuitive thought (4 to 7 years)
3. Operational stage (7 to 16 years)

a. Concrete operational thought (7 to 11 years)

b. Formal operational thought (11 to 16 years)

Piaget identified types of mathematical reasoning that can be expected of children at each stage. Furthermore, he argued that learning is influenced by four factors: maturation, social experience, physical experience, and equilibration.

In general, Piaget is concerned with the way reasoning patterns develop and how learning occurs. With reference to mathematics learning, Piaget states that prerequisite to understanding arithmetical operations is the ability to conserve number. One can conserve when he realizes that certain properties remain invariant under many transformations. In the case of number, four objects remain as four objects regardless of their spatial arrangement. Piaget (1950, 1952, 1956, 1960) reported that the child conserves number, length, weight, and area at different times from five to twelve years of age; primary children are able to conserve number and length. While age designates are not definitive, the developmental sequence from number to length, etc., is somewhat fixed. Within each area, the sequence from nonconservation to a transition period to true conservation is constant.

Much has been written about classification and seriation actions, the ability to use transitivity of set and length relations, and proposed relationships between and among these operations (Beth and Piaget; Piaget, 1970; Inhelder and Piaget, 1969; Inhelder and Piaget, 1958; Ripple and Rockcastle, 1964). The Piagetian research can be classified as belonging to one of two nondisjoint groups: (1) those studies that sought to replicate Piaget's work and (2) training studies that used a wide variety of theoretical and methodological approaches in an attempt to determine if the acquisition times of conservation, transitivity, operational seriation, etc., as proposed by Piaget were sensitive to training and designed to seek out relationships among and between certain variables in the theory. The relationship between seriation behavior and transitivity, conservation behavior and whole number addition, and classification actions and forming of sets has been of particular interest. The two categories listed represent, to a large extent, the progression of thinking in Piagetian research since Piaget's theory became popular. We turn now to studies in the first category.

Estes administered a series of Piagetian tasks to fifty-two four- to six-year-old children in an attempt to determine if children in America exemplified the same stages of thinking as the children in Piaget's sample. The tasks were mainly conservation of number tasks designed in the "classical" sense; that is, two sets having the same cardinalities were displayed, one designated as belonging to the experimenter, the other to the child. The experimenter asked the child, "Do we have the same amount (number) of objects?" After the child gave an affirmative answer, the experimenter rearranged one set and asked the child, "Do we have the same now, or do you have more than me, or do I have more than you?" Then the child was asked, "Why?" One task involved balls of clay and match sticks. The subjects were asked to make a straight line on the edge of a piece of cardboard using match sticks and clay. Estes found nothing to support Piaget's developmental sequence of conservation behavior. Furthermore, Estes reported that economic level did not seem to be a factor in the results. While no statistical analyses are presented, this study is one of few that did not support Piaget's work.

Dodwell replicated Estes' study with a sample of 250 children. The findings reported were completely different from those reported by Estes. Dodwell concluded that the three stages of cognitive development described by Piaget were found. Dodwell also confirmed Piaget's hypothesis that young children do not possess a concept of number, even though they may be able to count.

Hyde carried out a cross-cultural study with groups of European (mostly British), Arab, Indian, and Somali children, all six to eight years of age. All of the children were given a battery of Piagetian number and quantity tasks. Hyde found that in general all subjects showed the same type of responses to number problems as Swiss children, developmental changes in responses were largely as Piaget had indicated, and European subjects generally performed at a higher level than their non-European peers. Hyde also found a number of subjects who departed from the predicted sequence by conserving weight but not quantity, volume but not weight.

Elkind (1961b) replicated one of Piaget's experiments in an attempt to determine if the ages at which children conserved mass, weight, and volume were the same as proposed. His sample consisted of 175 children, 25 each from kindergarten to the sixth grade. Each child was presented with two balls of clay that were identical in size, shape, and weight. To determine the child's knowledge of mass, the experimenter asked, "Do both balls have the same amount of clay? Is there as much clay in this ball as in this one?" After the subject agreed that the two balls were equal, the experimenter asked the child to predict if they would have the same amount of clay if one ball was rolled into a hot dog shape. After the child's prediction, the experimenter actually rolled one ball into a hot dog shape and asked the child for another judgment. He also asked the child to justify his answer. The same procedure was followed for weight and volume. Elkind reported that the conservation of mass did not usually appear before ages 7 or 8, conservation of weight did not usually appear before ages 9 or 10, and conservation of volume did not in most cases appear before the age of 11. These findings were consistent with Piaget's. Further support for both Piagetian stages of conservation development and order of acquisition was reported in studies by Lovell and Ogilive, Elkind (1961a), Feigenbaum, and Wohlwill.

Among the reasons Piaget gave for a lack of conservation in young children are their inability to use reversible thinking and to overcome the perceptual attributes of conflicting situations. Some researchers are beginning to look for different factors that may influence conservation. Zimiles and others (1965) examined the role of a set of variables on number conservation in kindergarten and first-grade children from different backgrounds. The general conclusion was that the ability to distinguish between spatial and numerical cues is an important factor in developing conservation behavior.

Liedtke and Nelson reported that bilingualism has favorable effects on intellectual functioning. In this study fifty monolingual and fifty bilingual first graders were given conservation of length tests. The mean score for the bilingual group was significantly higher than the mean score for the monolingual group. This study was conducted in an attempt to determine if Piagetian-type observations could be used as an assessment of intellectual capacities. It is expected that Piagetian-type tasks will be used for this purpose in the near future.

Taranto and Mermelstein attempted to clarify the nature of number conservation tasks involving variations in length, area, and volume. They hypothesized that a child's success on the number conservation tasks would follow the order proposed by Piaget of acquisition of conservation of length, then volume, and then area. The sample consisted of eighty children from four to seven years of age. The authors report that the hypothesis was not confirmed.

The majority of the research reports that conservation of number is present in children around seven years of age. Mehler and Bever reported that number conservation behavior could be detected in their sample of children who were two years four months or two years seven months of age. While this finding was certainly contradictory to Piaget's findings, it did raise the following question: If different methods of assessment are used, will conservation behavior be detected earlier than previously thought? Achenbach replicated this study and concluded that the Mehler and Bever findings appeared to be an artifact of experimental procedure and not an indication of true conservation behavior. Failure to replicate Mehler and Bever was also reported by Willoughby and Trachy.

The different findings related to conservation reported in the above sections all reflect attempts to replicate Piaget's research. It is clear that some consideration must be given to the methods used in gathering data so intelligent interpretations of these data can be made. This topic has generated much attention by researchers (e.g., Rothenberg; Elkind, 1967; Gruen, 1966; Zimiles, 1963).

The second category of Piagetian studies attempt to answer the question of the effect of training on the acquisition of conservation of number and on the development of logical operations such as seriation and transitivity. A series of studies by Smedslund approached the conservation problems by involving children in conflict situations. Smedslund (1961a) sought to determine if children who were trained to conserve weight would give answers of the same quality as those children who were "normal" conservers whenever faced with a conflicting situation involving conservation of weight. In this study a number of five- to seven-year-old children were given pretests on conservation of weight. On the basis of their performance, the subjects were classified as being a normal conserver or a nonconserver. The nonconservers were given two training sessions with empirical controls of conservation of weight on a balance. On a posttest the trained subjects showed evidence of conservation of weight. These subjects along with those who were "normal" conservers were then given problems referred to as extinction trials. In a sample extinction trial, the subject was shown two plasticine objects and told they weighed the same. One of the objects was changed in shape and a piece was taken away inconspicuously. The child was then asked to make a judgment about the weight, after which the objects were placed on the balance where it was seen that one was heavier than the other.

Smedslund reported that none of the subjects who had acquired the principle during the experimental sessions showed any resistance to extinction whereas about half of the subjects who had acquired the principle in the "normal" way did not change to give nonconserving answers whenever situations with strong perceptual conflicts were present. The point is it was not possible to predict a child's extinction abilities from his initial explanation of conservation.

In another study, Smedslund (1961b) used two procedures in an attempt to induce a child's concept of conservation of weight. Smedslund's sample consisted of forty-eight five to seven year olds who were partitioned into two experimental groups. One group was given thirty-two reinforced trials on conservation of weight; the form of one of the two plasticine balls was altered and the child predicted if the two plasticine balls still weighed the same. The second group received reinforced practice on an addition/subtraction procedure where addition to or subtraction from an object or group was made. Smedslund reported little success in changing nonconservers to conservers and the procedures appeared to be effective only with those children who already showed some evidence of conservation.

Beilin used four training procedures with 170 kindergarten children in an attempt to teach number and length conservation. The four procedures were (1) nonverbal reinforcement, (2) verbal orientation reinforcement, (3) verbal rule instruction, and (4) equilibration. Beilin reported an improved performance in conservation of both number and length for each training procedure; however, the group that differed significantly from the control group was the VRI group. This method was purely didactic and involved telling, as follows in the case of length, "Whenever we start with a length like this one (pointing) and we don't add any sticks, but only move it, it stays the same length even though it looks differently. See, I can put them back the way they were, so they haven't really changed" (Beilin, p. 326). Even with this improvement on number and length conservation, no improvement was found on a transfer test of area conservation. Beilin also concluded that children in the transition stage between nonconservation and conservation benefited the most from the training.

Gruen (1965) in his study on the effects of direct training found results similar to those of Smedslund's. Gruen found that whenever the cognitive-conflict training was preceded by a verbal pretraining session, conservation of number was facilitated. He also suggested that focusing one's attention on the relation between the two sets of conflicting elements may be an important aspect of the acquisition of conservation of number.

Sigel, Roeper, and Hooper chose to use a method involving multiple classification, multiple relationality, and reversibility in an attempt to induce number conservation. The sample was composed of ten children from ages four years three months to four years five months who were divided into experimental and control groups of five subjects each. They determined that none of the children could conserve number. The training sessions involved making comparisons and classifying objects on the basis of similarities and finding ways objects differed. Some notions of reversibility were also included in the training sessions. On posttests involving conservation of substance, liquid substance, and weight and volume, three of the five children conserved substance, two conserved liquid substance, and two conserved weight. Children were also able to verbalize their ideas on a high level. The authors argue that this method of training involves ideas prerequisite to conservation of number, such as compensation and reversibility as proposed by Piaget. Similar results were found using classification procedures by Shantz and Siegel and multiple strategies by Baptiste.

The results of the forementioned studies must be viewed as encouraging. However, little success in changing conservation responses using many of the already mentioned training procedures has been reported by Smith, Mermelstein and Meyer, Wohlwill and Lowe, and Murray (1968).

Many other training procedures are worthy of mention. Harper and Steffe carried kindergarten and first-grade children through a series of twelve lessons designed to help them in the recognition and conservation of numerousness. The lessons involved the concept of one-to-one correspondence, perceptual rearrangement, as many as, more than, fewer than, additions, and subtractions. The authors concluded that the lessons were successful in enhancing the childrens' ability to conserve numerousness. Scott investigated the hypothesis that the ability to recognize numerousness as a property of a set is prerequisite to the conservation of numerousness of sets. He presented eleven lessons to kindergarten and preschool children in an experimental group. He found little increase in the performance of the experimental group on a conservation of numerousness posttest.

Piaget (1952) suggested that a concept for number develops from many sources, that is, one-to-one correspondence, classification and seriation behaviors, and knowledge of mathematical relations. Many researchers have focused their attention on how children learn equivalence and order relations. Examples of equivalence relations are "as many as" and "as long as" used in forming groups (or sets) while "more than" and "shorter than" are examples of order relations.

Ginsberg investigated the learning of "more than" by preschool children by using approaches requiring the child to make comparisons and state which of two pictures had the greater number of objects. Group one used only sets consisting of circles. Group two used pairs of objects that were alike in each pair but types of objects varied between the pairs. Group three used unlike objects. For each group, forty-two trials were conducted per day for three days or until each child could respond correctly eight times. Ginsberg concluded that concept learning in young children was most effective when the concept was introduced in a simple context, as in group one. In another study, Ginsburg (1971) reported that nursery school children can learn simple mathematical concepts and that the concept of "more than" was more easily understood than the concept "less than."

Weiner reported that children understand "more" before they understand "less." He found that two and three year olds related "more" to the idea of "many."

Uprichard compared experimentally all the possible learning sequences of the set relations "equivalence," "greater than," and "less than." Using the three relations, six possible sequences can be generated; they are EGL, ELG, GEL, GLE, LEG, and LGE. Thirty-two nursery school children in the sample were randomly assigned to these six sequences forming six experimental groups. There were also two control groups. All groups consisted of four subjects. Uprichard was concerned with determining the most efficient learning sequence for preschoolers. The efficiency of a particular learning sequence was evaluated in terms of the time needed to learn the three relations and the amount of transfer this learning facilitated. The experimental groups were involved in numerous activities requiring the identification and reproduction of sets of numerosity three, four, five, and six. The children were instructed in small groups for twenty-five minutes a session, three sessions a week. The results of this study suggest the following:

1. The most efficient instructional sequence appropriate for preschoolers in learning the set relations "equivalence," "greater than," and "less than" appears to be "equivalence," "greater than," "less than."
2. "Less than" is not a difficult relation for the child to acquire if "equivalence" and "greater than" are first acquired.

3. Preschoolers can be trained to conserve the one-to-one correspondence between sets containing three, four, five, and six elements.
4. There appears to be a hierarchical relationship among the set relations "equivalence," "greater than," and "less than."
5. Preschoolers have the capacity to acquire the set relations "equivalence," "greater than," and "less than" for the numbers three, four, five, and six.

Young reported that culturally disadvantaged preschoolers could learn and retain conservation of number, weight, volume, area, and mass, even when taught to do so by an inexperienced classroom teacher. In both of the above mentioned studies by Young and Ginsberg the instructional groups consisted of from four to six subjects. Murray reported that a training strategy involving social interaction was quite effective with nonconservers.

A few researchers have investigated acquisition of length conservation. Gilbert attempted to determine the effect of training on the ability of kindergarten children to conserve length. The training consisted of three twenty-minute sessions aimed at the understanding of the property of length. Results indicated that training was a significant variable, with girls making greater gains than boys. Carey and Steffe found that the performance of four- and five-year-old children on conservation and transitivity of length relations can be improved by direct training procedures. Callahan and Passi reported that no statistical relationship could be found between the ability to conserve length and the conceptual tempo of the kindergarten and first-grade children that was consistent with Piaget's research.

Kincaid investigated the effectiveness of training middle-class three and four year olds classification and seriation operations. The twenty-four children in the sample were placed into two age groups: mean ages three years eight months and four years five months. Each group was subdivided into three groups, each containing four subjects; the three groups consisted of a seriation training group, a classification training group, and a control group. At the end of the training session, Kincaid administered six seriation tasks, seven classification tasks, and three conservation tasks to the children. The results showed significant treatment and age-treatment interaction with the high age seriation group indicating superior performance.

The classification training procedures were not effective in improving classification performance or in improving ability to transfer learning to the conservation tasks. Schafer used cue fading and reinforcement to instruct children for performance at Piaget's stage three seriation behavior. He divided thirty-four kindergarten children into two groups; the experimental group was given training to induce their ability to insert an object into an ordered set of objects. Schafer reported that the training procedures were successful in inducing seriation; however, they were not successful in inducing ability to transfer to new materials.

Using eighty-one first- and second-grade children, Johnson attempted to improve their concept of length seriation and length classification by training. The experimental subjects were involved in a ten lesson unit consisting of activities that focused on grouping on the basis of "same length" and placing objects in series using "longer than" and "shorter than." Johnson reported that the training was successful in giving the children an algorithm for length seriation but that the training had little effect on the children's ability to classify on the basis of length or on the ability to conserve length. It was also reported that little improvement was found in the ability to use the transitive property of the relations on which the seriations or classifications were based.

As has been indicated, the mathematics research generated by Piaget's developmental theory has one common theme, how do children learn basic ideas that are prerequisite to an understanding of number? While much of the research has dealt with the child's ability to conserve number, few researchers have attempted to find what relationship conservation ability has to performance in arithmetical and geometrical tasks commonly found in elementary mathematics programs. A few studies related to this idea demand attention.

Van Engen and Steffe investigated what effect the perceptual aspects of the situation would have on the ability of first graders to use the set-union model for addition. They used a sample of one hundred children, fifty boys and fifty girls. The experimenter presented each child with two collections of hard candy and stated, "Here are two piles of candy," pointing to each one. The experimenter then pushed the piles together and stated, "I put them together and made one pile." The child was then asked if he would prefer to take the one pile or the two initial piles to his friends, or did it make a difference. The piles of candy consisted of varying amounts so the child worked with groups of ten and fifteen, three and two, four and five, and twenty-five and twenty-five. After the candy items were administered, each child was given a paper and pencil test involving nine basic addition facts. One interesting result of this study was that ninety-nine of the one hundred children could correctly perform the paper and pencil task: $3 + 2 =$ ___. Yet only fifty-four of the one hundred would say that the amount of candy remained invariant and it did not make any difference whether the one pile or the two initial piles were taken. One interpretation the authors gave for this finding was that the children had not abstracted the concept of sum of two numbers from physical situations but had memorized the addition combinations.

In an attempt to relate conservation performance with addition performance, Steffe studied the performance of 132 first-grade public school children grouped by conservation levels on addition problems involving various types of problem-solving tasks. He found that children who had the lowest conservation abilities performed significantly less well on the problems than children in the other levels. LeBlanc reported similar findings on a test of subtraction. LeBlanc also stated that the child's conservation level related better to problem-solving performance than IQ.

The research generally supports Piaget's theory of cognitive development. Relationships between developmental level and performance on arithmetical operations are beginning to demand attention from top researchers in an effort to make Piaget's research findings applicable to practical situations. This kind of research is needed to give direction in curriculum development. We now turn to available materials that either reflect the Piagetian philosophy or are concerned with developing logical thought patterns through an activity approach.

Programs Based on the Cognitive Developmentalist Approach. The materials of the Nuffield Mathematics Teaching Project are designed for those early childhood programs in which an activity-based curriculum is preferred. This project, started in 1964 under the direction of Geoffrey Matthews has as its aim to produce a contemporary course in mathematics for children aged five to thirteen. The materials produced by the project are all in the form of books for the teacher. The first of these was entitled *I Do and I Understand,* and it summarizes the philosophy and aims of the program. The other books fall into three categories: Teachers' Guides, Weaving Guides, and Checkup Guides. The Teachers' Guides cover three main topics: computation and structure, shape and size, and graphs leading to algebra. The development is spiral with the same concept encountered at different stages.

The books do not cover any specific time span but rather develop themes and ideas and therefore show the teacher how to allow one child to progress at a different pace from another. The Teacher Guides contain direct teaching suggestions with examples of both mathematical and nonmathematical situations appropriate for in or out-of-school discussions.

The Weaving Guides are single concept books that give detailed instructions or illustrations about a particular topic such as desk calculators or of a project that shows how various topics of mathematics can be integrated. The Checkup Guides contain "checkups" that can be used to evaluate the children's progress. Since the activities suggested are far from traditional, the "checkups" have been designed for individual administration. Most of the "checkups" are Piagetian tasks.

The emphasis throughout the program is on "how to learn, not on what to teach." It remains the task of the teacher to design or implement the ideas given in the teachers' guides. No lesson plans are given to the teacher, but explicit accounts of sequential development of ideas occur frequently. The teacher is encouraged to allow the child to manipulate objects, classify objects, and have a variety of concrete experiences as forerunners of the abstract ideas of mathematics. For example, children will pair shoes with socks and dolls with doll houses as the concrete basis for the idea of a "mapping" and later of the domain and range of a function. The mathematical content for the primary years begins with prenumber ideas such as one-to-one correspondence between sets, classification and seriation, set relations and comparisons, operations of addition and multiplication, and much emphasis on measurement and geometry. Throughout the development of the content, all topics are woven together so the child can see mathematics as a unified way of thinking about the world and not as a collection of separate subjects.

The Fundamentals Underlying Number (FUN) Program is designed to help children acquire concepts for sets, numbers, and relations (Wilson and Uprichard). The program consists of a series of games emphasizing one-to-one correspondence, greater than, less than, and equivalence. The material consists of a large spinner cloth, set boards, blocks, and plastic cubes. All activities are presented in the form of two kinds of games: "find it" games and "make it" games.

In a "find it" game the set boards of a specific pattern are placed in designated slots on the spinner cloth. Each child (usually a group of from three to six can participate) has a set board of a specific pattern. The spinner is turned, and the teacher picks up the set board indicated by the spinner and asks, "Who has a set that matches (or is equivalent to) this one?" The child's task is to determine if his set board matches the one held by the teacher or to find the correct board. The "make it" games are played in a similar fashion; however, when a board is designated by the spinner, the players try to make a set of blocks that is equivalent to the sample.

Throughout the program, heavy use is made of the principle of transitivity; that is, if set A is equivalent to set B and set B is equivalent to set C, then set A is equivalent to set C. The program attempts to help the child grasp this important principle; however, whether or not transitivity of equivalence is developed is still a researchable question. The FUN objectives are developed in a spiral fashion allowing a concept to be introduced at one level and treated in more depth at another. By following the program, the child moves from one-to-one correspondence to counting to whole number operations. At the present time, Unit I, dealing with sets, numbers, and relations is available; Unit II dealing with sets, numbers, and operations is being developed.

The Dienes Mathematics Programme attempts to help children learn sophisticated mathematical ideas by giving them a large number of varied experiences that embody the mathematical ideas. Directed by Zoltan P. Dienes, the content has great emphasis on logic, geometric transformations, and nondecimal numeration systems. The rationale behind this selection of content is Dienes' belief that a child can learn arithmetic topics incidentally through a variety of mathematical experiences.

The materials developed that are used in the various content areas are Dienes Logiblocks, States and Operators, and Dienes Multibase Arithmetic Blocks. Throughout the program Dienes suggests six steps leading to formal abstractions; they are free play, games, abstraction, representation (diagrams), symbolism (arithmetical language), and axiomatization (axioms, theorems, proofs). It is Dienes' philosophy that the child should be presented with many opportunities to explore, using many different materials to develop a common idea; this is referred to as the Multi-Embodiment Approach. Books listing games and activities and direction for use of the material are available for the teacher. Users of the Dienes material should keep in mind that the intent of the developer is to teach mathematics, not arithmetic.

The Cuisenaire Program was developed by M. Georges Cuisenaire and Caleb Gattegno. The program attempts to develop mathematical ideas through operations involving measurement and ratio. The material used in the program is the Cuisenaire rods, a set of ten rods equal in cross section to one square centimeter but differing in length and color. The length ranges from one to ten centimeters with the colors of white, red, purple, light green, yellow, dark green, black, brown, blue, and orange. Cuisenaire's philosophy of teaching stresses that the child must be actively involved and must involve as many senses as possible. The content of the Cuisenaire program could be considered as being somewhat traditional, beginning with comparisons of rods (later comparisons of numbers) and progressing to carrying out the basic operations of rational numbers. Teacher guides, workbooks for students, and independent discovery cards are available for users of this program.

The curriculum writing groups responsible for much of the material referred to as "new mathematics" devoted their efforts to developing programs for senior and junior high schools; however, they developed some elementary and early childhood units. The Minnesota Mathematics and Science Teaching Project (MINNE MAST) developed a set of coordinated units in science and mathematics for kindergarten and grade one. The coordinated units tend to fuse the disciplines of science and mathematics and attempt to release the child's creative abilities. Many of the units require processes of observing, describing, and classifying. The unit titles for kindergarten are Watching and Wondering, Curves and Shapes, Describing and Classifying, Using Our Senses, Introducing Measurement, Numeration, and Introducing Symmetry. Grade one units cover these topics: Observing Properties, Numbers and Counting, Describing Locations, Introducing Addition and Subtraction, Measuring with Reference Units, Interpretations of Addition and Subtraction, Exploring Symmetrical Patterns, and Investigating Systems. The mathematical units for grades two through five extend the ideas of the K–1 program; however, there are separate units for mathematics that are not coordinated with science. Some of the ideas used as the foundation for the second-grade mathematics program are as follows:

1. Conservation—those properties of objects or sets that remain unchanged while rearrangements are taking place.
2. One-to-one correspondence—used to give an operational definition of the relations "more" and "less."
3. Linear order—use of the relations "more than" and "less than" as applied to sets, number, length, and volume. Transitivity is also stressed.
4. Number representation—begins with equivalent sets and uses story problems to motivate counting. Also involved is the assigning of number names to sets.

Many of the ideas from research are now being used by textbook writers as they attempt to develop sound primary programs. The *Essential Modern Mathematics, Primary Program* published by Ginn and Company is an example of a textbook-oriented program. The three levels of the Primary Program, Levels A, B, and C, are based on the psychological principles of Piaget and others and are written with the way children learn in mind. Every lesson provides for hands-on experiences for the children and is complete with objectives listed for the teacher, materials needed for the lesson, and possible additional experiences for the children. The program is developed around the topics of matching (color, size, shape, kind), classifying (by color, size, shape, kind), patterns, sets (comparing, counting, joining and separating), addition and subtraction, numeration and place value, measurement, and problem solving and geometry. These topics are spiraled throughout the development of the program.

Most programs reviewed in this section emphasize the set approach to learning number concepts involving one-to-one correspondence and set relations such as "more than" and "less than." Many base their selection of content and methodology on research findings while others seem to be guided by the logical structure of mathematics as a discipline. All seem to suggest that more research is needed to provide sound bases for curriculum development.

The Naturalists

Advocates of this position see the child as the center of the curriculum and the motivating factor for all work. They view the teacher as a guide, not a taskmaster. This philosophy of teaching is expressed by Rousseau in the following statement:

> Teach your scholar to observe the phenomena of nature, and you will soon raise his curiosity; but if you would have it grow, do not be in too great a hurry to satisfy the curiosity. Put the problems before him and let him solve them himself. If ever you substitute authority for reason, he will cease to reason and be a mere plaything of other people's thoughts. (Rousseau, pp. 228–29)

While some modern proponents of this position, like Neill, must be viewed as extreme, the common thread found throughout the writings of the naturalists (see Gutek; Dewey; Boyd) is that the curriculum for the primary child should be developed from the interests of the child. In the case of mathematics, this approach has at different times in history given support to the "incidental learning" theory of arithmetic. That is, the introduction, development, maintenance, and extension of mathematical content and skills were a function of the incidental need for them in connection with what was usually an activity unit; since no systematic program of mathematics instruction per se would usually be included, the arithmetic that was taught suffered from being unorganized.

The naturalist conclusion that children will not learn and hence should not be taught until they are ready to learn led to many discussions of readiness and whether introduction of topics should be postponed (Brueckner; Betz; Washburne). While most modern mathematics educators have more or less concluded that incidental learning will not produce favorable results in mathematics, this philosophy still influences the way mathematics is taught in large numbers of preschool programs. This approach has contributed little toward both the research on mathematics learning and on developing mathematics curricula materials. Perhaps this is understandable since proponents of the naturalist approach ascribe to the credo "we teach children, not mathematics" (Berman; Hymes).

Further Considerations

The research and projects reviewed in this chapter point out the need for answers and direction in the teaching of early childhood mathematics. For those questions that can be answered empirically, the challenge for future researchers is clear: design and carry out research studies that will provide definitive answers from which sound, workable mathematics programs can be developed. What are some further areas of concern? To begin with, some projects presently existing emphasize product, others stress process, while some advocate the development of the affective domain. Can programs be developed that attempt to integrate product, process, and affect? This, of course, causes us to examine the goals of our mathematics program. Is the main goal that our children acquire mathematical knowledge or mathematical understanding or that they develop knowledge with understanding? How do we improve attitudes toward mathematics? Will the current movement toward learning mathematics in a "math lab" aid in this regard? Does a child's improved self-concept contribute as much to successful mathematics learning as successful mathematics learning contributes to a child's self-concept? What do teachers do in a classroom to help children organize their thinking? What is the role of didactic teaching? discovery teaching? Just how much is meaningfully learned by a kindergarten child who is taught by a purely expository approach? On the other hand, are kindergarten children capable of "discovering" the mathematical ideas we feel to be important for that grade? How do we integrate the various methods of teaching into one that gives maximum results?

With reference to mathematical content, just what is appropriate and important for primary children? Do we teach topics, e.g., negative integers in the kindergarten, to children just because we know they can learn them? It has been the tendency of curriculum developers to continually "push down" mathematics topics from high school to elementary to preschool. Where do we draw the line on this activity? Should topics from transformational geometry, topology, and advanced set theory be a part of the preschool curriculum? What about the learner? Have we given him due consideration? Can we use Piaget's findings about learning of quantitative ideas of number, length, weight, and volume in both the assessment of knowledge and development of programs?

How serious should we take the multiple embodiment theory of Dienes? Can it be determined that concepts are formed more meaningfully if the child has many embodiments of it? In this same regard, does the idea of multiple embodiments provide a justification for the use of manipulative materials in the primary class? If a child needs both positive and negative instances of a concept to help with the abstraction, is there an optimum number of such? Will this number vary with the different learning styles of the children? Will it vary with the concepts?

This list is but a sample of the questions concerning curriculum, method, and learner variables whose answers would contribute to the knowledge in the field. Other lists of pertinent questions appear elsewhere (see Brown and Abell; Pingry). Probably the most important questions have not yet been asked. That challenge is yours!

References

Achenbach, T.M. "Conservation below Age Three: Fact or Artifact?" Paper presented at the Proceedings of the 77th Annual Convention of the American Psychological Association, 1969.

Baptiste, H.P., Jr. "The Effect of an Equilibrated Methodology on the Acquisition of the Concept—Conservation of Quantity. Ph.D. dissertation, Indiana University, 1969. Ann Arbor, Mich: University Microfilms, No. 70-7967.

Beilin, H. "Learning and Operational Convergence in Logical Thought Development." *Journal of Experimental Child Psychology* 2(1965):317-39.

Berman, L.M. *Not Reacting but Transacting: One Approach to Early Childhood Education.* College Park: University of Maryland, Center for Young Children, 1972.

Beth, E.W., and Piaget, J. *Mathematical Epistemology and Psychology.* Dordrecht, Holland: D. Reidel Publishing Co., 1966.

Betz, W. "The Reorganization of Secondary Education." In *The Place of Mathematics in Modern Education* (Eleventh Yearbook of the National Council of Teachers of Mathematics). New York: Teachers College Press, 1936.

Boyd, W. *The Educational Theory of Jean Jacques Rousseau.* New York: Russell & Russell Publishers, 1963.

Brown, K., and Abell, T. *Analysis of Research in the Teaching of Mathematics* (OE Bulletin 1965, No. 28). Washington, D.C.: U.S. Government Printing Office, 1965.

Brownell, W. "The Effects of Practicing a Complex Arithmetical Skill upon Proficiency in Its Constituent Skills." *The Journal of Educational Psychology* 2(1953):65-81.

————. "An Experiment on 'Borrowing' in Third-Grade Arithmetic." *Journal of Educational Research* 3(1947):161-71.

————. "Rate, Accuracy, and Process in Learning." *Journal of Educational Psychology* 6(1944):321-37.

Brownell, W., and Chazal, C. "The Effects of Premature Drill in Third-Grade Arithmetic." *The Journal of Educational Research* 29(1935):17–28.

Brueckner, L.J. "The Development of Ability of Arithmetic." In *Child Development and the Curriculum* (Thirty-eighth Yearbook of the NSSE). Bloomington, Ill.: Public School Publishing Co., 1939.

Bruner, J. *The Process of Education.* New York: Random House, 1960.

Callahan, L., and Passi, S.L. "The Relationship between the Ability to Conserve Length and Conceptual Tempo." *Journal for Research in Mathematics Education* 2(1971):36–43.

Carey, R., and Steffe, L.P. *An Investigation in the Learning of Equivalence and Order Relations by Four- and Five-Year-Old Children* (Research Paper No. 17). Athens, Ga.: University of Georgia Press, 1968.

Cuisenaire, M.G., and Gattegno, C. *Numbers in Color.* Mount Vernon, N.Y.: Cuisenaire Company of America, 1954.

Dewey, J. *How We Think.* Lexington, Mass.: D.C. Heath & Co., 1933.

Dienes, Z.P. *Mathematics in the Primary School.* Melbourne: Macmillan and Co., 1964a.

———. *The Power of Mathematics.* London: Hutchinson Educational Ltd., 1964b.

Divers, B.P. Jr., "The Ability of Kindergarten and First-Grade Children to Use the Transitive Property of Three Length Relations in Three Perceptual Situations." Ph.D. dissertation, University of Georgia, 1970.

Dodwell, P.C. "Children's Understanding of Number and Related Concepts." *Canadian Journal of Psychology* 14(1960):191–205.

Elkind, D. "Children's Discovery of the Conservation of Mass Weight and Volume: Piaget Replication Study II." *The Journal of Genetic Psychology* 98(1961a):219–27.

———. "The Development of Quantitative Thinking: A Systematic Replication of Piaget's Studies." *The Journal of Genetic Psychology* 98(1961b):37–46.

———. "Piaget's Conservation Problems." *Child Development* 38(1967):15–27.

Englemann, S. *Conceptual Learning.* San Rafael: Dimensions Publishing Co., 1969.

———. *Preventing Failure in the Primary Grades.* Chicago: Science Research Associates, 1969.

———. "Teaching Formal Operations to Preschool Advantaged and Disadvantaged Children." *The Ontario Journal of Educational Research* 9(1967):3.

Englemann, S., and Carnine, D. *Distar Arithmetic I, An Instructional System.* Chicago: Science Research Associates, 1969.

Englemann, S., and Englemann T. *Give Your Child a Superior Mind.* New York: Simon & Schuster, 1966.

Essential Modern Mathematics, Primary Program. Boston: Ginn and Co., 1970.

Estes, B.W. "Some Mathematical and Logical Concepts in Children." *Journal of Genetic Psychology* 88(1956):219–22.

Feigenbaum, K.D. "An Evaluation of Piaget's Study of the Child's Development of the Concept of Conservation of Discontinuous Quantities." Paper presented at the American Psychological Association Meeting. New York, 1961.

Gagné, R. *The Conditions of Learning.* New York: Holt, Rinehart, and Winston, 1965.

———. "Factors in Acquiring Knowledge of a Mathematical Task." *Psychological Monographs* 76(1962) No. 7 (Whole No. 526).

Gilbert L.E. *An Introduction of Length Concept to Kindergarten Children* (Report from the Project on Analysis of Mathematics Instruction). (Educational Resources Information Center ED036335) Washington, D.C.: Office of Education, 1969.

Ginsberg, R. *Investigation of Concept Learning in Young Children. Final Report.* (Educational Resources Information Center ED030498) Washington, D.C.: Office of Education, Bureau of Research, 1969.

———. *Mathematical Concept Learning by the Pre-School Child. Final Report.* (Educational Resources Information Center ED065171) Washington D.C.: National Center for Educational Research and Development, 1971.

Gruen, G.E. "Experiences Affecting the Development of Number Conservation in Children." *Child Development* 36(1965):963–79.

———. "Note on Conservation: Methodological and Definitional Considerations." *Child Development* 37(1966):977–83.

Gutek, G.L. *Pestalozzi and Education.* New York: Random House, 1968.

Harper, E.H., and Steffe, L.P. *The Effects of Selected Experiences on the Ability of Kindergarten and First-Grade Children to Conserve Numerousness.* (Technical Report No. 38) Madison: University of Wisconsin Press, 1968.

Hunt, J.M. *Intelligence and Experience.* New York: The Ronald Press Co., 1961.

Hyde, D.M. "An Investigation of Piaget's Theories on the Development of the Concept of Number." Ph.D. dissertation, University of London, 1959.

Hymes, J.L., Jr. *Teaching the Child under Six.* Columbus: Charles E. Merrill Publishing Co., 1968.

———. *The Growth of Logical Thinking from Childhood to Adolescence.* New York: Basic Books, 1958.

Inhelder, B., and Piaget, J. *The Early Growth of Logic in the Child.* New York: W.W.Norton & Company, 1969.

Johnson, M.L. "The Effects of Instruction on Length Relations on the Classification, Seriation, and Transitivity Performances of First- and Second-Grade Children." *Journal for Research in Mathematics Education* 5(1974):115–25.

Kincaid, C. "A Study in Training Nursery Children on Logical Operational Skills." Paper presented at the annual meeting of The American Educational Research Association, New York, February 1971.

LeBlanc, J.F. "The Performances of First-Grade Children in Four Levels of Conservation of Numerousness and Three IQ Groups when Solving Arithmetic Subtraction Problems." Ph.D. dissertation, University of Wisconsin. Ann Arbor, Mich.: University Microfilms No. 68–711, 1968.

Liedtke, W.W., and Nelson, L.D. "Bilingualism and Conservation" (Study was conducted at University of Alberta). (Educational Resources Information Center ED030110), 1968.

Lovell, K., and Ogilive, E. "A Study of the Concept of Conservation of Subtraction in the Junior High School." *British Journal of Educational Psychology* 30(1960):109–18.

Matthews, G. "The Nuffield Mathematics Teaching Project." *The Arithmetic Teacher* 15(1968):101–2.

Mehler, J., and Bever, T. "Cognitive Capacity of Young Children." *Science* 158(1967):141–42.

Mermelstein, E., and Meyer, E. "Conservation Training Techniques and Their Effects on Different Populations." *Child Development* 38(1967):39–52.

Minnesota Mathematics and Science Teaching Project. Minneapolis: University of Minnesota Press, 1961.

Murray, F. "The Acquisition of Conservation through Social Interaction." Paper presented at annual meeting of the American Educational Research Association, New York, February 1971.

———. "Cognitive Conflict and Reversibility Training in the Acquisition of Length Conservation." *Journal of Educational Psychology* 5(1968):531–42.

Neill, A.S. *Summerhill.* New York: Hart Publishing Co., 1960.

Piaget, J. *The Child's Conception of Number.* New York: Humanities Press, 1952.

———. *Genetic Epistemology.* New York: Columbia University Press, 1970.

———. *The Psychology of Intelligence.* New York: Harcourt Brace Jovanovich, 1950.

Piaget, J., and Inhelder, B. *The Child's Conception of Space.* London: Routledge and Kegan Paul, 1956.

Piaget, J.; Inhelder, B., and Szemenska, A. *The Child's Conception of Geometry.* New York: Basic Books, 1960.

Pingry, R. "Summary of Discussion. Proceedings of National Conference on Needed Research in Mathematics Education." *Journal of Research and Development in Education* 1(1967): 44–47.

Ripple, R., and Rockcastle, V., eds. *Piaget Rediscovered. A Report of the Conference on Cognitive Studies and Curriculum Redevelopment.* Ithaca, N.Y.: Cornell University Press, 1964.

Rothenberg, B.B. "Conservation of Number among Four- and Five-Year-Old Children: Some Methodological Considerations." *Child Development* 40(1969):383–406.

Rousseau, J.J. *Emile.* Translated by B. Foxley. London: J.M. Dent and Sons, 1911.

Schafer, L.E. "Inducing Stage III Seriation Capabilities in Kindergarten Children through Cue Fading and Reinforcement." Ph.D. dissertation, Michigan State University. Ann Arbor, Mich.: University Microfilms No. 72-22, 282, 1972.

Scott, J. *The Effect of Selected Training Experiences on Performance on a Test of Conservation of Numerousness. Report from Phase 2 of The Prototypic Instructional Systems in Elementary Mathematics Project.* (Educational Resources Information Center ED036334) Washington, D.C.: Office of Education, 1969.

Shantz, C., and Sigel, I. *Logical Operations and Concepts of Conservation in Children, a Training Study. Final Report.* (Educational Resources Information Center ED020010) Detroit: Merrill Palmer Institute, 1967.

Shumway, R. "Negative Instances and Mathematical Concept Formation: A Preliminary Study." *Journal for Research in Mathematics Education* 2(1971):218–27.

Sigel, I.; Roeper, A.; and Hooper, F. "A Training Procedure for Acquisition of Piaget's Conservation of Quantity: A Pilot Study and Its Replication." *British Journal of Educational Psychology* 36(1966):301–11.

Smedslund, J. "The Acquisition of Conservation of Substance and Weight in Children; III. Extinction of Conservation of Weight Acquired 'Normally' and by Means of Empirical Controls on a Balance." *Scandinavian Journal of Psychology* 2(1961a):85–87.

———. "The Acquisition of Conservation of Substance and Weight in Children: VI. Practice in Problem Situation without External Reinforcement." *Scandinavian Journal of Psychology* 2(1961b):203–10.

Smith, I. "The Effects of Training Procedures upon the Acquisition of Conservation of Weight." *Child Development* 39(1968):515–26.

Steffe, L.P. *The Performance of First-Grade Children in Four Levels of Conservation of Numerousness and Three IQ Groups when Solving Arithmetic Addition Problems.* (Technical Report No. 14) Madison: University of Wisconsin Press, 1966.

Taranto, M., and Mermelstein, E. *A Study of Number Conservation with Tasks Which Vary in Length, Area, and Volume. Final Report.* (Educational Resources Information Center ED064147) Washington, D.C.: National Center for Educational Research and Development, 1972.

Uprichard, E. "The Effects of Sequence in the Acquisition of Three Set Relations: An Experiment with Preschoolers." *The Arithmetic Teacher* 17(1970):597–604.

Van Engen, H., and Steffe, L.P. *First-Grade Children's Concept of Addition of Natural Numbers.* (Technical Report Number 5) Madison: University of Wisconsin Press, 1966.

Washburne, C. "The Work of the Committee of Seven on Grade Placement in Arithmetic." In *Child Development and the Curriculum* (Thirty-eighth yearbook of the NSEE). Bloomington: Public School Publishing Co., 1939.

Weiner, S.L. *On The Development of "More" or "Less."* (Education Resources Information Center ED073839) Bethesda, Md.: National Institute of Health, 1972.

Willoughby, R., and Trachy, S. "Conservation of Number in Very Young Children: A Failure to Replicate Mehler and Bever." *Merrill-Palmer Quarterly of Behavior and Development* 17(1971):205–9.

Wilson, G. *Teaching the New Arithmetic.* New York: McGraw-Hill Book Co., 1951.

Wilson, J., and Uprichard, E. *Fundamentals underlying Number.* Boston: Teaching Resources Corporation, 1972.

Wohlwill, J. "A Study of the Development of the Number Concept by Scalogram Analysis." *Journal of Genetic Psychology* 97(1960):345–77.

Wohlwill, J., and Lowe, R. "An Experimental Analysis of the Development of the Conservation of Number." *Child Development* 33(1962):153–67.

Young, B. "The Efficacy of a Mathematics Readiness Program for Inducing Conservation of Number, Weight, Area, Mass, and Volume in Disadvantaged Preschool Children in the Southern United States." Paper presented at the annual meeting of the American Educational Research Association, New York, February 1971.

Zimiles, H. "A Note on Piaget's Concept of Conservation." *Child Development* 34(1963):691–95.

———. "The Development of Differentiation and Conservation of Number." (Educational Resources Information Center ED003345) New York: Bank Street College of Education, 1965.

CHAPTER SEVEN

ART

Carol Seefeldt

Why do children draw?

Art seems to belong to young children. Wherever groups of children gather, there are art activities. Children intent on scribbling designs on paper with large chunky crayons; engrossed in spreading bright colored tempera paint over large sheets of newsprint; or patting, pushing, and pounding moist clay are seen across the nation in Head Start classrooms, child-care centers, private nursery schools, or public kindergartens and primary classrooms. From the very beginnings of early childhood education, art has held an honored position. The Froebelian kindergarten, which first introduced children to a variety of art activities, began a long tradition of including art in the preschool program. Even during the sixties, when emphasis was placed on cognitive and academic skill development, art activities did not lose their revered place in the curriculum for young children.

Art and young children are a natural combination. The uninhibited child, anxious to explore his environment, experiment with materials, understand his world, communicate ideas, feelings, and emotions, finds drawing, painting, modeling and constructing intriguing and gratifying experiences.

Teachers of young children seem to enjoy children's art nearly as much as the children. Interested in child growth and development, anxious to provide an optimum educational environment for children, and concerned about each individual child, teachers see art as a valuable and integral part of their program.

Usually untrained as an artist, the teacher of young children views art as a generalist rather than as an artist. He knows that the values and purposes of art are many. Through art, the children have opportunities to develop intellectually as they use symbols to express their ideas and learn to perceive colors, textures, and shapes. Eyehand-muscle coordination is strengthened as the children cut with scissors, scribble, or paint. Children gain social skills as they work together to construct a block building, share paper scraps to make a collage, or plan a mural. Emotional and mental health is fostered as children release tensions through finger painting and working with clay or wood.

Art is often thought of as the glue that holds the preschool-primary program together. Social studies concepts, ideas from children's literature, and scientific concepts all find expression through art as children draw their perceptions of a field trip, paint a picture to illustrate a story they've heard, or paint the butterfly emerging from a cocoon.

Few would deny the value and contributions art brings to young children and the total preschool-primary program. However, few teachers have as their goal the development of art as a body of knowledge as well as a series of activities. The National Art Education Association's major objectives that the child be able to see and feel visual relationships, make art, study works of art, and critically evaluate art are rarely identified as the objectives of art education in the preschool-primary classroom (Linderman and Herbolz). Although research has demonstrated that four-year-old children can gain the following concepts, few teachers have incorporated these goals into their art program (Schwartz and Douglas).

1. Art is a means of nonverbal communication.
2. The art product is the result of the artist's idea.
3. The artist uses what he sees, thinks, and feels to create art.
4. There is a great variety of materials available to the contemporary artist.

Rather, teachers of young children are more likely to identify the goals of their art program in terms of helping children to express ideas and feelings, release emotions, explore new media, and foster creativity. Congruent with these goals, teachers often interpret their role as that of a provider of materials and builder of a secure environment that will allow children the freedom to explore, create, and experiment. "The role of the teacher in art activities is to create an environment that fosters optimum growth, a setting that is challenging and stimulating (Leeper, p. 339). Other early childhood educators encourage teachers to "prepare a secure environment which offers art activities suited to the developmental needs and levels of the children. Advice on matters of technique have no place in the art of young children. Indeed it is likely to affect their development adversely. Given the right environment and offered the right experiences, the creative expression of young children will flourish" (Ebbeck and Ebbeck, p. 88).

The usual art program in the preschool reflects these suggestions. Children are presented with a wide variety of media and permitted to experiment and explore the possibilities of these media. Teachers often encourage children to talk about their work, and they compliment children on their art products. These practices are firmly

rooted in child development theory and are consistent with the developme
of child art.

Theories

The Developmental Theory

Although there are a number of cogent theories of child art, the developmental
theory, which advises against direct instruction or any interference with children's
personal expression, has been most widely accepted in early childhood education.

As early as 1885 Ebenezer Cooke drew attention to the successive stages of development found in children's drawings and advanced the theory that children drew in
accordance with their general development. Since that time the developmental stages
found in children's drawings have been well and widely documented. There is general
agreement, even among those who advocate a variety of theories, that children's drawings do follow a general pattern of progression. Drawings of children appear to
progress through the following stages:

1. The use of circular, ovoid and sticklike representations of people and things
2. The creation and representations of people and things
3. The creations and repetition of basic representational formula, including
   representations of space and motion
4. An increasing degree of visual correspondence
5. The shape, color, and spatial location of objects during the upper elementary
   years
5. A type of realism in adolescence

Lowenfeld, revered art educator and author of *Creative and Mental Growth*, is
perhaps the most widely known advocate of the developmental theory. Lowenfeld
categorized the stages of growth in children's art as

1. Scribbling Stage, ages 2–4. The first stages of self-expression.
2. Preschematic Stage, ages 4–7. First representational attempts.
3. Schematic Stage, ages 7–9. The achievement of a form concept.
4. Gang Stage, ages 9–11. The dawning realism.
5. The Stage of Reasoning, ages 11–13. Pseudo realistic stage.

Lowenfeld describes these stages as the unfolding of a genetic program. Each of the
stages is believed to be a part of the natural and normal aspects of human growth and
development. Children, he claimed, must pass through one stage before they can
achieve another. Changes in the level of stages are contingent upon changes and
growth in the child's total development, that is, his affective, intellectual, social, and
physical growth. The form and content of a child's drawing is believed to be totally
dependent on his particular stage of social, emotional or intellectual development.
The child's experiences and values are believed to be represented in his art. No
external teaching is required for a child to pass from one stage to the other.

Reflecting the naturalistic, neo-Rousseauian point of view, the developmental theory has received the wholehearted endorsement of early childhood educators. Having received a great deal of child development theory as a part of their education and still following in the tradition of Froebel, who saw the teacher as a gardener, one who brings forth what the child possesses, rather than as an instructor, teachers of young children have logically incorporated the developmental theory of art into the curriculum.

Most of the developmental theorists do advocate the role of the teacher as that of a guide (Lowenfeld; Read; and Kellog, 1969). Read wrote, "The logical role of the teacher is one of a guide, attendant, inspirer, psychic midwife" (Read, p. 206). Lowenfeld stated, "Generally speaking, the activity of self-expression cannot be taught. Any application of an external standard, whether of technique or form, immediately induces inhibitions and frustrates the whole aim. No proper stimulation of the child's creative activity can be given without a thorough knowledge of what changes can be expected at various developmental stages in the child's subjective relationship to an environment" (Lowenfeld, p. 12).

Kellog, who also advances a developmental theory of child art, and who has compiled children's earliest scribbles in *What Children Scribble and Why,* also believes that children should be left alone, without any interference from an adult. "Children left alone to draw what they like, without the interference of adult guidance, usually develop a store of gestalts, which enable them to reach the culminating stage of self-taught art. From there, if they are especially gifted, they may develop into great artists, unspoiled by the stenciled minds of well-meaning adults. Few children, however, are given this opportunity, and most relinquish art after the first few years in school" (Kellog, 1969, p. 21). Adults who coach their children to draw real-life objects are not helpful, but according to Kellog, are actually harmful. "The child's purpose is not that of drawing what he sees around him, rather he is probably a very experienced master of self-taught art, concerned primarily with the productions of esthetic combinations that are the envy of adult artists. In fact, Picasso said that adults should not teach children to draw but should learn from them" (Kellog, 1969, p. 12).

These philosophies prevailed in early childhood education until the 1960s. During the sixties, the educational climate dictated a call for curriculum reform in every area. Bruner wrote *Toward a Theory of Instruction,* and compensatory education flourished. A general direction away from the child development approach to education occurred. Somehow, with the emphasis on the economically disadvantaged child, the structure of curriculum and cognitive development, the concept of teaching by providing a challenging environment, waiting for children to develop according to a normal, predestined pattern no longer seemed tenable. During this time of articulating objectives, identifying disciplines, and being accountable, many art educators became highly critical of the developmental theory of children's art.

McWhinnie wrote, "Certain forces abroad in the land today make the uncritical acceptance of the Lowenfeld position no longer desirable. These forces are a drive for excellence in education and the reemphasis on subject matter content in all subjects, the current disfavor towards the child-centered school, and the increase in sophistication of the research in creativity and perception which makes some of Lowenfeld's assumptions no longer tenable" (McWhinnie, 1963, p. 36).

This type of criticism of the developmental theory grew out of a concern for the teaching of content in art and led to the development of several art curriculum projects. The Aesthetic Education Curriculum Project, the Stanford Kettering Project, the Mifflin Title II Curriculum Project, and others attempted to identify the content of art. These curriculums emphasized the subject matter of art, the history of art, and the critical evaluation of art.

In the 1970s the same art educators, alarmed by the emphasis on content, discipline, and subject matter, have called for another look at the developmental theory as expressed by Lowenfeld. "Because of Lowenfeld's humanness, his sense of social justice, and his role as a social engineer, his ideas have new meaning for the 1970s. Someone with his orientation is now needed to redirect art education towards a greater concern for the individual and social ends and move it away from the excess of concern with the cognitive goals and discipline centeredness" (McWhinnie, 1972, p. 11).

The Cognitive Theory

"The child draws what he knows, not what he sees" (Luquet 1913) is the phrase most often used to exemplify the cognitive theory of child art. Expanding on this theory, Goodenough wrote that "to little children, drawing is a language—a form of cognitive expression—and its purpose is not primarily esthetic" (Goodenough, 1926, p. 14). Goodenough, and others advocating the cognitive theory of child art, believe that explanations of children's art must go beyond the fields of simple visual imagery and eye-hand coordination and take into account the higher thought processes.

According to the cognitive theorists, drawings of the young child are not dependent on the general developmental level of the child but rather are representative of the child's concept formation. Distortions of size and shape, inaccuracies, and perplexities found in children's drawings are believed to be the result of their lack of understanding and knowledge of the world around them. As children gain in understanding, grow, and have more experiences, they increase their fund of concepts, and likewise, their drawings and paintings increase in detail, complexity, and accuracy.

Goodenough argues that the ability of a child to form concepts is an intellectual ability, requiring that the child recognize similarities and differences among a group of objects or ideas. If a child can make these distinctions and is able to recognize instances of a class when he confronts it, he has attained a concept of that class (Goodenough and Harris). "The child's drawing of any object will reveal the discriminations that he has made about that object as belonging to a class, that is, a concept. In particular, it is hypothesized that this concept of a frequently experienced object, such as a human being, becomes a useful index to the growing complexity of his concepts" (Goodenough, 1926, p. 35).

Based on this hypothesis, Goodenough, by analyzing the amount of detail that appears in a child's drawing of a man, and later Goodenough and Harris demonstrated that they can indeed obtain an index of a child's intellectual maturity simply by asking the child to draw a picture of a man and then evaluating that drawing on a set of specified criteria. A survey of the research on the validity of the Goodenough-Harris Draw-A-Man Test as a useful measure of nonverbal intelligence yields substantial support to the theory that children draw what they know. Although the validity of the Goodenough-Harris Draw-A-Man Test is not the question, the numerous research studies correlating the Goodenough-Harris with a variety of other intelligence tests including the Stanford Binet, the Wechsler Intelligence Scale for Children, and the Primary Mental Abilities Tests yield correlations of .55 to .80 and do serve to give credibility to the concept that children draw what they know.

Recently a large, nationwide study of over 7,000 children, ages 6 to 11, was conducted to examine the intellectual maturity of children in the United States. The Goodenough-Harris Draw-A-Man Test was utilized as the assessment measure. Although this study was concerned with an analysis of the intellectual maturity of noninstitutionalized children in the United States, it did validate the theory that children, with age, increased experiences, and more complete concepts, draw with progressively more detail and realism.

Another measure of children's intelligence that utilizes art work is the Lantz Easel Age Scale. The Easel Age Scale is also based on the theory that children paint what they know. This scale that analyzes children's spontaneous easel paintings along the dimensions of form, detail, meaning, and relatedness of the painting has satisfactory correlations with the Goodenough Draw-A-Man Test. Although it is not as widely used as the Goodenough, or as well known, it is thought to be an acceptable measure of quantitative intelligence.

On the other hand, there is evidence, again based on the Goodenough-Harris Draw-A-Man Test, that might serve to question the theory that children draw what they know. Medinnus, Bobitt, and Hullett demonstrated the susceptibility of the Draw-A-Man Test to rapid alteration. This study illustrated that when children had the opportunity to construct a puzzle figure of a person, they were able to significantly increase their scores on the Draw-A-Man Test. The authors drew the conclusion that if scores on the Draw-A-Man Test can be altered so easily without changing performance on other measures of IQ, then the theoretical relationship between the test and the knowledge of the children can be questioned.

McWhinnie (1971) cautions that although the Draw-A-Man Test has been proven to be a potent and vital research tool, care must be taken in the design and execution of research studies utilizing it as an assessment measure. A review of the research on figure drawings led McWhinnie to conclude that the Draw-A-Man Test is extremely sensitive to a number of variables that are usually uncontrolled in research studies. Variables such as the effect of the art media used, the color of the paper, and cognitive style were found to significantly affect children's execution of their drawing of a man.

Supported as it is by the research, the cognitive theory of why children draw appears to have validity. It does seem to explain the simplicity of forms found in very young children's art and the increasing details and realism that occur as the child grows and has increased contact with his environment. However, there are critics of the theory. Feldman claims that this theory does not explain the differences between artistic and inartistic children of the same intelligence, nor does it sufficiently recognize that concept formation depends on and follows sensory experience. According to Feldman, it does not recognize that representation must involve the creation of a visual image or percept that can satisfy a present or a recalled set of sensations.

The Psychoanalytic Theory

"Children draw what they feel, their art comes from deep down inside," is an expression that has been used by art educators and lay people alike to explain children's art. Firmly based on the concept of an unconscious, a type of mental activity that people are not even aware of, this theory of child art postulates a relationship between children's emotional and psychological development and their art. Children's art products are thought to be a reflection of their emotions and expressions of their deep, unconscious feelings rather than reflections of their knowledge or concept development or general development.

According to this theory, a child draws himself as a large circle with sticks that represent arms and legs, not because he is unaware of the fact that he has shoulders, a neck, or a stomach, but because the circle represents a force deep within the child as a symbol for the womb, the breast, or some other emotionally loaded object. The progression from a circle to realistic representation is explained as a growth process. As the child grows, his conscious thought suppresses the powerful force of the unconscious, and he is able to draw and paint more realistically.

Psychoanalytic thought has greatly influenced early childhood education. The contributions of Anna Freud, Lois Barclay Murphy, and Katherine Baker Read, advancing psychoanalytic theory, contributed to the early childhood educator's acceptance of the psychoanalytic theory of child art. Many of the art education practices of the preschool-primary teacher today are based on this theory of child art. The preschool teacher's love of finger paint, clay, and fluid tempera is based, at least in part, on the concept that these materials allow for a full release of the child's inner feelings and emotions and thus provide a valuable opportunity for the release of tensions and expression of emotions.

Believing that children's art is a reflection of the unconscious and is a preverbal mode of expression, Alschuler and Hattwick studied preschool children's easel paintings. On the assumption that there is a relationship between the child's personality as manifested by his social behavior and the form and content of his painting, Alschuler correlated styles of painting with personality traits. Some of the conclusions Alschuler and Hattwick drew from their study of children's easel paintings as reflections of personality were as follows:

1. Children who have strong emotional lives also tend to exhibit strong preferences for certain colors and express themselves with color and mass rather than with line and form.
2. Children who focus on line and form rather than on color show greater self-control, more concern with external stimuli, and higher reasoning behavior.
3. Children who constantly favor warm colors tend to be free in their behavior and display warm, affectionate relations; they are sympathetic with others, cooperative in play, and make relatively good adjustments.
4. Children who consistently focus on colors tend to be restrained or pressed in their inner feelings.

Alschuler and Hattwick further concluded that the child's treatment of space in his painting could be considered as a sample of the child's usage of his total environment. The relationship between the use of colors and various painting procedures such as overpainting, making of crosses, long strokes, color placement, and usage were also explored.

Support for the psychoanalytic theory of children's art comes from various sources. Clinical psychologists have increasingly used human figure drawings in their work to gain indications of personality. The field of art therapy also uses drawings and paintings as indicators of deep personality traits (Naumberg; Machover; Kris; and Hammer).

Empirical research has also given validity to the psychoanalytic theory. A dated, yet classic, study by Reichenberg indicated that positive toned affective states, when experimentally induced, did influence children's drawings to higher ratings by judges. Britain manipulated children's affect by criticizing their toy block buildings. Britain found that the children who had received the critical treatment produced drawings that were rated as constricted and impoverished. On the other hand, children who received positive, supportive, and warm comments during a play session produced drawings that were rated as expansive and elaborate.

Gardner, in a study of over 2,000 boys, demonstrated that there are significant differences in the drawings of boys from various cultures and groups and between those rated high and low on hostility measures. Burns and Kaufman used children's drawings for psychological diagnosis. They categorized the children's drawings of their families in terms of significance of objects, position on the page, omissions, barriers, and force fields. They identified thirty-seven classes as having significance.

The relation between children's art and personality has intrigued other researchers. Lantz, in discussing the Easel Age Scale, noted the need for a category for those paintings that seemed to be the result of emotional states rather than predictors of intelligence. Even Goodenough, articulating the cognitive theory of child art, admitted that there are drawings that seem to reflect a child's idiosyncratic view of his world and his experience; however, she cautioned against the validity of utilizing such drawings as measures of children's personalities on the basis that the validity coefficients of the children's drawings with personality measures were too low to be considered meaningful (Goodenough, 1926).

Research studies also seem to encourage caution in concluding that children's art is a reflection of deep feelings and emotions. Manzalla, exploring the relationship between children's drawings and personality, postulated that children's feelings of self would influence their art work. He found no significant differences in children's art work that could be attributed to their emotional state. Lingren attempted to identify emotional indicators in human figure drawings of children who were rated as shy and aggressive. Ninety-seven pairs of children, ages five to twelve, were matched for age, sex, and IQ. No significant differences appeared to characterize the drawings of the children who were rated as shy or aggressive.

The Toronto Board of Education conducted a large-scale study of children's drawings of their classrooms (Rogers and Wright). A taxonomic approach led to the conclusion that children's drawings as a whole are measures of skill execution and are more reliable as predictors of drawing intelligence than they are of mood, attitude, or personality.

Experimenting with the effects of frustration on nursery school children, Thomas attempted to place children in a frustrating situation. He postulated that the frustrated children would reveal their emotional state in their paintings. An experimental group was placed in a room and shown toys and boxes but was not allowed to play with them. The control group was taken to the room, but they were allowed to play with the materials and attractive toys. Upon an analysis of the children's paintings, Thomas found no significant differences between the two groups. It was suggested that the frustrating situation was not intense enough to be reflected in children's paintings or that emotions are not reflected in child art.

Given the conflicting research on the validity of the psychoanalytic theory of child art, the conclusions of Alschuler and Hattwick seem cogent. From their study of personality and children's paintings, they concluded that children's art could be useful as one source of data that might indicate behavior patterns or personality; however, they warned that children's art work cannot be used with confidence to predict behavior or personality (Alschuler and Hattwick).

The Perception Delineation Theory

In her book, *Preparation for Art,* June King McFee advanced yet another theory of art. McFee bases her theory on concepts from the behavioral sciences and claims that art is based on several factors, rather than just one. The factors she identifies are

1. The readiness of the child. This includes the child's physical development, intelligence, perceptual development, response sets, and cultural dispositions he has acquired.
2. The psychological environment in which he is to work. This includes the degree of threat or support existing in this environment and the number and intensity of rewards or punishments.
3. Information handling. This factor is affected by the child's ability to handle detail, his intelligence, his ability to handle asymmetrical detail, and the categories he possesses for organizing.
4. Delineation skills. This includes the child's ability to manipulate media, his creative ability, and his ability to design qualities of form.

McFee believes that art education is a multi-faceted phenomenon. She identifies the content of art as drawing, painting, sculpture, etc., and claims that art education is design in its broad ramifications—it is art as historical impact; it is art criticism; it is also cultural communication. In order to teach art, a person must have a highly developed understanding of both individual and cultural living and their relation to learning.

The base for McFee's art curriculum is built on the premise that a culture, an environment, has a very definite effect on the artistic achievements of children. She claims that today's society, because of its complexity as well as mobility, has placed children from many subcultural groups in the classrooms of our schools. She believes that the teacher should help the children find avenues of maintaining their own subculture through art.

Eisner stated that McFee's theory, based as it is on four broad factors that would affect nearly any human activity, is "comprehensive and useful as a theory of child art—indeed, artistic learning in general—for it is reasonable to assume that these four factors will need to be taken into account" (Eisner, 1972, p. 93).

The Perceptual Theory

Arnheim, in his book *Art and Visual Perception,* states that children draw what they see rather than what they know or feel. Coming from a Gestalt frame of reference, Arnheim believes that perception develops from whole to parts by means of a process called perceptual differentiation. Children do not see objects as the sum of the observed parts; rather they see perceptual wholes or total images structured by the brain on the basis of retinal impressions. All viewers as perceiving organisms have certain basic requirements; these requirements are expressed by Gestalts as laws, that is, needs of the organism for completeness, closure, or unity.

For Arnheim, seeing is a visual judgment and is not affected by the intellectual capacity of the individual. According to him, "The oldest, and even now most widespread, explanation of children's drawings, is that since children are not drawing what they are assumed to see, some mental activity other than perception is responsible for the modification. It is evident that children limit themselves to representing the overall qualities of objects, such as the straightness of legs, the roundness of a head, the symmetry of the human body. These are facts of generalized knowledge, hence the famous theory according to which the child draws what he knows rather than what he sees" (Arnheim, p. 128).

Explaining why children's drawings do not include all they see, Arnheim stated, "But this is not the whole answer. Unquestionably children see more than they draw. At an age at which they easily tell one person from another and notice the smallest change in a familiar object, their pictures are still undifferentiated. The reasons must be sought in the process of representation" (Arnheim, p. 130).

Arnheim claims that the child, in attempting to re-create a perceived object on a two-dimensional sheet of paper, must use his ingenuity. He states, "Thus seeing the shape of the human head means seeing its roundness. Obviously, roundness is not a tangible perceptual thing. It is not materialized in any one head, or in any number of heads. There are shapes, such as circles or spheres, that represent roundness to perfection. Even these shapes stand for roundness rather than being it, and a head is neither a circle nor a sphere. In other words, if I want to represent the roundness of an object, such as the head, I can use the shapes actually given it but must find or invent a shape that will satisfactorily embody the visual generality 'roundness' in the world of tangible things. If the child makes a circle stand for a head, that circle is not given to him in the object. It is a genuine invention, an impressive achievement, at which the child arrives only after laborious experimentation" (Arnheim, p. 131).

Arnheim believes that perception is learned or at least can be improved through training in visual discrimination. However, he does not describe how instruction might facilitate or hamper children's perceptual and hence drawing development.

Knowledge of perception and Gestalt theory seems required to comprehend Arnheim's theory fully. Eisner stated that "the view that Arnheim advances is useful for thinking about the relationship between drawing and perception, and it relates to a variety of theoretical work . . . the views are not, however, experimentally sound, nor does Arnheim provide systematic quantitative descriptions of data to support his assertions. We do not know, from his work, the extent to which the characteristics of children's drawings can be altered, nor do we know why individual differences emerge in drawing among children" (Eisner, 1972, p. 83).

The Cognitive Developmental Theory

There is perhaps no content area that the work of Piaget has not influenced, and his theoretical and experimental work has implications for the development of another theory of child art. Piaget relates children's art to their ability to understand the permanent existence of objects, for unless the child understands objects that have a permanent existence, he has no imagery through which he can evoke the past and anticipate the future in the absence of present objects.

Children, according to Piaget, must be able to evoke what is absent or past in order to think about it, and this evocation requires a symbol to stand for what is not here and now. Representation is the means by which human beings organize their experience of the world in order to understand it further. Such representation requires symbols, and imagery is one way of symbolizing the world, with language being another (Piaget, 1955).

Representation gradually becomes not only imagery but rather images that inhere within certain relationships, including spatial relationships, which are increasingly understood and reproduced in the child's expressions (Brearley). Adopting terms originally used by Luquet, Piaget calls the stages of development of children's understanding of pictorial space (1) synthetic incapacity, (2) intellectual realism, and (3) visual realism. Synthetic incapacity is the stage found during the preschool years and is characterized by partial and fragmented images. The inaccuracies that occur in children's art during this stage are believed to be due to the fact that children neglect spatial relationships of proportion, distance orientation, and perspective; this neglect results in a failure to synthesize image elements.

Intellectual realism, the second stage, is consistent with the cognitive theory of art. The child, during this stage, draws what he knows, not what he sees. The child who draws a dog with four legs to one side does so because he knows that a dog has four legs, rather than the two he can see.

The third stage, visual realism, appears around the age of nine or ten and is characterized by drawings that indicate the child now knows more. He does not necessarily know more about the world around him, but he now understands the relationships of objects to their spatial coordinates.

Brearley claimed that these stages are a matter of development but that development is related to two types of experiences. One type of experience is sensorimotor in which the child learns how to pick up blocks and control a paint brush or crayon; the other type of experience is that which brings content to the child's expression. Brearley advocated the exploration of materials and the provision of a wide variety of raw materials. "Children need experience with materials to acquire skill in using various media, but there are other sorts of experiences which are crucial, for they are the experiences which give content to children's expressions" (Brearley, p. 40). Brearley believes that the type of art a child produces will depend directly on the variety, richness, and intensity of experiences to which he is exposed. Conditions favorable to stimulating child art are seen as being a combination of providing the proper tools and materials, the time to gain skill in the use of the tools and materials, and a "wide spectrum of experiences, but also a sequence of experiences, which relate to each other and which lead to increasing depth of understanding" (Brearley, p. 41).

Empirical Research and Curriculum Trends

Art education presents a fertile, relatively untouched, and yet hostile field for researchers. Until the 1950s little research in art education was conducted; and since that time, the research has been largely piecemeal, with few, if any, comprehensive reports or organized investigations bringing together existing research information. Clifford wrote, "Art education also depended upon a discipline of unabashed, qualitative valuation; opposition to analysis and inquiry seemed strong among practicing artists who also taught" (Clifford, p. 7).

Several factors have hindered empirical research in the field of art education. Artists, not trained in research or the behavioral sciences, are largely unconcerned with research. The very nature of art also makes it difficult to evaluate or research, and the expressive vocabulary of art—form, color, space, line, texture—are equally difficult to handle in a research design. The prevailing theories of Lowenfeld, Read, and others, who advocated a naturalistic, developmental approach to art, also hindered the development of research, for why should anyone want to research something that is natural and follows a normal pattern of development?

D'Amico believed that researching the art of young children would be improper and irrelevant. Scientific inquiry would be irrelevant because children's art was believed to be a result of emotional feelings; it would be improper because probing would destroy the unique characteristics of art. Burns and Kaufman added that "the findings of these studies are singularly devoid from any real relationship to creative behavior and real understanding of art" (Burns and Kaufman, p. 427). Yet the research conducted, however meager in quality and quantity, when coupled with the theoretical positions of art educators, does have implications for the development of art programs for young children.

Selecting Media

The theoretical approaches developed to describe why children draw or paint as they do have provided the preschool-primary teacher with implications for the selection of media. Alschuler and Hattwick maintained that easel painting with flowing bright tempera, large brushes, and large paper, provided a perfect medium for children to express their emotions and feelings. They suggested that materials such as crayons, requiring finer control, led children to be concerned with finished products or with external standards.

Arnheim and Schaefer-Simmern, who advocated the perceptual theory of child art, suggested that the media a child uses have serious consequences. According to these educators, the broad brushes, fluid paints, and finger paints, so revered by the psychoanalytic school of thought, might actually restrict the child's artistic potential. Arnheim believed that the fluid paints and wide brushes might actually hinder the child from clarifying his observations of reality and negate his learning to create order. Eisner, in discussing typical early childhood practices, stated, "The task of painting with fluid tempera paint, on an upright surface, using nonresilient brushes on newsprint, is a task that would frighten the most mature artist; yet it's one that young children are faced with daily" (Eisner, 1972, p. 160).

Lowenfeld also believed that certain materials are not appropriate for young children. He stated that the widespread use of finger paints in preschools was not justified. Children who are just learning to use tools need to be encouraged to use tools and to develop an interest in tools; they should be encouraged to control their muscular activity rather than to mess around. He suggested that the most appropriate materials for young children would be crayon and plain paper.

However, many early childhood teachers, imbued with the naturalistic and psychoanalytic theory of child art, find satisfaction in providing many more materials than just crayons for children. Many teachers, on the basis that the child needs to be introduced to many stimulating and different media, strive for the wide and diverse use of a variety of media in the classroom. In the never ending search for innovation and in an attempt to provide the optimum environment for children's development, teachers continually ask, "What can I do tomorrow? We painted yesterday; I can't do that again." Student teachers, seeking to please their supervisors, search for still one more medium to give to the children. In fact, many preschool programs are evaluated on their effectiveness by the number and type of different media given to the children. Barkan aptly describes this situation by stating, "The more media they provide, the better they think they are; the more varieties of media their children experience, the better they assume the learning to be. Most teachers are on a perpetual hunt, not only for more media, but also for new ones" (Barkan, p. 426).

According to Eisner, instead of being preoccupied with introducing new media to their children, teachers should strive to understand the role of the teacher and the complexities involved in artistic learning and the development of art curriculum that have well-thought-out aims, objectives, content, and instructional support. Eisner believes that when teachers do not know how skills can be developed with paint or clay, they have hardly any alternative but to continually introduce the children to new media.

Children who are continually introduced to new media are never able to gain skills in the use of any one medium or to see the opportunities present in any media. Visitors in the Far East note that young children cut block prints that are far advanced of those cut by children in the United States. Young children in the Orient are introduced to block carving early in their life and are allowed to continue developing their skill and proficiency. Unless children have the opportunity to gain this type of control over a medium, they will never achieve the skills required to use that material as a means of artistic expression.

Several research studies are available that lend credence to the idea that media can influence the child's artistic expression. Preschool classrooms are rarely equipped with pencils because many educators believe that young children's muscles are not developed enough to use a pencil. Badri investigated the hypothesis that novel experiences, such as holding a pencil, might inhibit the drawing ability of rural children who were unfamiliar with them. He found that a child's experience with a pencil did affect the child's later drawings. Those children who had previous experiences with pencils did figure drawings that had a greater differentiation of form and human schemata than those children without previous experiences.

Koppitz investigated children's figure drawings and their personality correlates under conditions of pencil and crayon. She compared the drawings made with pencil with those made with crayon and found little difference in the two when they were scored for developmental characteristics using the Goodenough-Harris Draw-A-Man Test. However, she did find significant correlations between the medium used and the emotional factors present in the drawings when they were scored by the Machover Scale. The crayon drawings, with different colors and strokes, were believed to contain more emotional indicators.

Salome conducted an analysis of kindergarten children's drawings using colored pencils and crayons. The results of his study demonstrated that there are no significant differences in the amount of detail children included in their drawings as a result of using either the pencil or crayon. Most of the children delineated larger shapes in their crayon drawings than they did in their pencil drawings, and most of the children filled more space on a piece of 12" x 18" paper when drawing with crayons rather than with pencils. The lines that the children produced in the crayon drawings were more definite, bolder, freer, and heavier than those they produced in the pencil drawings. Salome concluded that children can draw with pencils or crayons and that the theory of meeting the child's developmental needs by providing him with large crayons for drawing can be questioned.

Questioning the validity of the use of the wide paint brush for easel painting in kindergarten, Seefeldt (1973) analyzed easel paintings executed with wide and narrow brushes using the Lantz Easel Age Scale. The paintings executed with narrow brushes invariably included more detail, design, and complexity than those paintings done with wide brushes. The paintings completed with narrow brushes included facial features, wheel spokes, designs and patterns on clothing, and often had a complete, complex theme. Children were observed to determine if those who were rated as being more mature would select narrow brushes if given a choice. No preference was noticed, and children, when given a choice, picked whatever brush was closest to them. It was concluded that at least for five-year-old children a variety of brush sizes should be available for easel painting. It was also concluded that the narrow brush, rather than inhibiting children's free expression, actually allowed them to create and express themselves with paint fully.

Teaching Techniques

The developmental and psychoanalytical theories of Alschuler, Kellog, Read, and Lowenfeld left little doubt as to the role of early childhood educators. A teacher, following the advice of these art educators, provided materials, wiped up spills, freed children for creative expression, and offered encouragement. Teaching, direct or even indirect, was not a part of the art program.

As early as 1946 Dubin demonstrated that children's artistic expression can be improved through the use of discussion techniques. Dubin, in this early and classical study, worked with nursery school children. Identifying a series of stages in the literature used to describe children's art, she placed children's paintings into the classes of scribbling—unnamed, scribble named, diagram, design, and presentation. Dubin identified the particular stages at which children in the experimental group were working; through discussions about their work and with questions of various types, she was able to move these children up to the next stage of painting. Dubin concluded that the simple technique of discussing children's art products could increase their artistic development.

Rand employed more direct teaching techniques that were designed to improve children's ability to copy forms. Theoretically, Rand postulated that copying requires at least two important abilities: visual analysis and drawing rule utilization. In this study Rand designed two training methods to improve preschool children's ability to analyze figures and to utilize drawing rules. These two types of training were compared in terms of their effects on figure discrimination and copying accuracy. Training in drawing rule utilization resulted in improved copying accuracy but did not improve discrimination ability while training in visual analysis resulted in improved discrimination ability but no improved copies. Increased improvement in figure discrimination was related to decreased copying accuracy. Rand concluded that utilizing drawing rules is essential and that adequate visual analysis is a necessary, but not sufficient, prerequisite to the production of adequate copies.

Nelson and Flannery also studied the effects of specific instruction on children's drawing ability. They found that first-grade children's skills in drawing a simple figure can be improved through specific task instruction. The most effective instructions directed the child to attend to the shape of the figure instead of to the total figure. The children receiving no instruction tended to draw a less differentiated and more global perception of the figure-group relationship. Asking the children to criticize their own work was somewhat productive of desired changes but was not as useful as specific task instruction. Two types of instruction, that is, repeated practice and attention to the proportions of the shape copied, produced decrements in the children's drawing scores. The conclusions of this study were that the drawing behaviors of children are more cognitive in nature than they are sensorimotor, as specific task instruction was most effective.

Several other research studies stem from the postulation that training in visual discrimination can improve the drawing skills of children. Eisner (1972) spoke of the value of instruction in developing children's visual perceptual skills, and Arnheim, believing that children draw what they see, also suggested that children can learn visual perceptual skills.

Salome and Reeves conducted two pilot studies in order to determine the effects of perceptual training on children's drawings. The first study consisted of practice in visual discrimination and the second consisted of drawing lines of varied direction and shapes including contour direction, changes in angles, peaks of curvature, and lines due to abrupt color changes. The results of the study, as measured by scores on Early Childhood Embedded Figures Tests and drawing tests, indicated that the training did affect greater differentiation in children's drawings of a truck and appeared to be a significant factor in explaining the experimental group's higher level of performance on the Early Childhood Embedded Figures Test. The authors concluded that in view of the significance of these findings, continued investigation was in order.

Examining the effects of a training program on visual perception, Seefeldt (1974) randomly assigned five-year-old children to three treatment groups. She gave a series of lessons designed to teach the concept of texture, rough and smooth, to the first and second experimental group. In addition to learning to recognize texture upon seeing it, the children were taught to discuss texture in the art work of others and to incorporate texture into their own drawings. The first group received one lesson, approximately fifteen to thirty minutes in length, for ten consecutive days. A graduate student conducted the lessons. The second group received one thirty-minute lesson, once a week, for a period of ten weeks. The school's art teacher conducted these lessons. The third group, the control, received no treatment. The children receiving the ten-week training sessions were observed to discuss texture in their work when in the kindergarten classroom; they continually incorporated a great amount of texture in their spontaneous crayon drawings as well as the pre- and posttest. The results of this study indicated that children in each of the experimental groups gained significantly in their ability to talk about texture in the art work of others and in their art work and to use texture in their own crayon drawings. It was concluded that teaching children to be aware of texture in the environment, encouraging them to discuss it in art works of others, using texture in their own work was valid for five-year-old children.

Taylor and Trujillo conducted a study to determine the effects of a prototype environment, certain selected stimuli of a multi-sensory cognition system, the training of learning facilitators in the use of discovery techniques and questioning strategies, and the use of the cognition system on the (1) aesthetic quality of art products, (2) concept formation with the elements of design, and (3) the critical aesthetic judgmental abilities of four-year-old children.

The study revealed that gains in the overall aesthetic quality of the art products of the experimental group can be attributed to the prototype environment. Based on the findings it was concluded that there were significant changes in the quality of tempera paintings for the experimental group over trials, gains in concept formation but no measurable gain in subjects' ability to make critical aesthetic judgments. Because of the volunteer nature of the sample, the authors concluded that the study should be replicated with a random sample. However, they believed that the prototypic multi-sensory environment, developed to facilitate exposure to and learning of art concepts, could be further developed.

Motivation

How often do teachers hear young children say, "I can't draw, show me," or see the familiar tulip, tree, and house picture? Many art educators agree that when children are properly motivated, these inadequate responses to art disappear. Motivation, a strong teaching tool, is advocated by Linderman and Herbolz. Children, they claim, cannot be expected to pour forth ideas without some type of prior stimulation. Consistent with the cognitive as well as the developmental theory of Lowenfeld, motivation, as a technique for teaching art, is receiving acceptance in early childhood education.

Linderman and Herbolz maintain that teachers can motivate students by including visual aids, firsthand materials, and sensory experiences to support their verbal discussions. They group motivation techniques into the following three main categories:

1. Artistic motivation includes all of those things that increase perceptual awareness, aesthetic sensitivity, and skills with art media.

2. Intellectual motivations have as their aim the development and enrichment of children's concepts for natural and man-made objects.
3. Imaginative motivations help the child to develop his imagination, inventiveness, and originality.

The effects of various types of motivation are being investigated by Eisner, who claims that motivation is also a strong research tool. Eisner noted that the amount of detail and ingenuity displayed in children's art work after they have had an opportunity to role play is greater than when they are exposed to other motivation procedures. He claims that role playing, such as acting like a wave crashing upon the shore or a bird lofting through the sky, tends to increase the presence of certain artistically valued proponents in children's art work.

McWhinnie (1971), calling motivation a set variable, a specific task instruction, demonstrated how it influences the aesthetic quality of children's drawings. Groups of young children were asked to do two drawings of a tree. The first drawing was made after asking the children to draw a tree, and the second was completed after the children had been shown pictures and paintings of trees and then instructed to draw the best tree possible. In over 90 percent of the cases, the first tree drawings were typical stereotyped trees whereas the second drawings were far more differentiated and complete.

Although not necessarily considered as a work investigating motivation, a study conducted by Schwartz and Douglas presented a unique motivational experience for four-year-old children. This study was designed to determine the effects of a training program on children's understanding of artistic concepts. Schwartz and Douglas demonstrated that through the sharing of ceramic works, discussing the technique the artist used to make the piece, and identifying other materials the artist could have used to make the same thing, children can gain artistic concepts. In addition to gaining an understanding of art, the children's own work with clay increased in a number of ways. After they examined various ceramic pieces and participated in discussions of the works, focusing on what the object was, who made it, how it was done, and whether they could do the same thing, the children's attention span, when working with clay, expanded to over an hour, and their clay products increased in dimensionality, complexity, and detail. In addition, the children in the experimental group made significant increases in their verbalizations.

It might be concluded from these studies that the use of the effect of motivation on children's art provides a fruitful area for research. How different motivational techniques influence children's art and how a preschool-primary teacher might use motivation to increase children's artistic concepts and expression are questions that require answering.

Planning to Teach

Early childhood educators, whose philosophy of education is usually based on the child development approach, have often considered the use of behavioral objectives as being antithetical to their basic philosophy. To teach by identifying outcome behaviors of students, especially when applied to young children's artistic experiences and expressions, seems totally inappropriate to many early childhood teachers.

In the wake of cybernetics and information theory, the use of behavioral objectives has permeated education in the past decade. During this time, the fallacies and weaknesses of behavioral objectives have been identified. Often the writing of objectives seemed like just one more meaningless exercise with little real value. Objectives could also become so trivial as to be useless to the teacher. Furthermore, the teacher of art is not necessarily interested in predicting the performance of children, making behavioral objectives appear totally inappropriate.

However, Walbaesser, Rashid, and Eisner (1972) believe that objectives have a place in art education. While cautioning that the usefulness of behavioral objectives is greatest when they are treated "with discretion, rather than with passion" (Eisner, 1972, p. 155), they stated that objectives could be appropriate when used with those activities that are intended to predict outcomes. Further, when teachers utilize behavioral objectives, they should continue to recognize the great amount of unplanned experiences that cannot be identified ahead of time.

A great deal of work is necessary for teachers to utilize objectives fully in art. Teachers need to understand the content of art, its goals and structure, as well as possess knowledge of children's art concepts and an understanding of the skills they already have.

The Southwest Regional Laboratory (SWRL) is currently developing a year-long kindergarten art program (KAP). This program will later be expanded to grade six. An early step in the development of the SWRL instructional materials was to identify the skills possessed by children. Two areas of concern were the focus of the program. The first was the extent to which children entering kindergarten had mastered psychomotor skills, such as holding a pencil, tearing a piece of paper along a line, or copying a shape or line; the second was related to the children's knowledge of art terminology and identification of colors, shapes, textures, and lines. The results of this pilot study led to the modification of the objectives of KAP. Those skills which children had already mastered were decreased in importance in the curriculum; those that few had obtained were strengthened; and those that were found to be difficult were given increased attention.

One source of behavioral objectives available for teachers of art is found in *A Guide to Art in Florida's Elementary Schools,* Bulletin 77. This guide introduces the general objectives of art education which lead a child to (1) see and feel visual relationships, (2) produce works of art, (3) know and understand about art objects, and (4) produce works of art. The guide breaks each content area into educational and instructional objectives. An educational objective dealing with color is, "The child will be able to perceive, discuss, and use color in their work and that of others" (Florida Guide, Bulletin 77, p. 10). The instructional objectives are, "The child will be able to make a design out of an arrangement of colors using repetition, pattern and line forces. The child will be able to mix the primary colors to make secondary colors. The child will be able to use the emotional qualities of colors and shapes to convey a specific mood or feeling" (*A Guide to Art in Florida's Elementary Schools,* Bulletin 77, p. 20).

Objectives certainly have a place in art education, and the cautious use of them might focus the teacher's attention to the many possibilities for teaching art. Also, as objectives identify the behavior expected to result from teaching, they might assist the teacher in evaluating the children's progress in art.

Art and General Education

Art is a valuable subject for young children. If child art is related to growth of perception, concept formation, and emotional state, then it holds tremendous power in the curriculum for young children. However, rising costs, accountability, and new priorities have dictated that school systems examine their expenditures. Often art becomes the first area of the curriculum to be questioned.

Art teachers have long recognized the value of art in the development of skills in other content areas, and now there are several research studies to support the claim that there is a strong relationship between art education and achievement in general.

Mills, postulating that art education could play an important role in reading by helping the child to differentiate letters and words, analyzed the effectiveness of art instruction upon the area of reading readiness. He employed a classical paradigm of control and treatment groups, randomly selected, and pre- and posttesting on the Metropolitan Reading Readiness Test. The treatment consisted of ten art lessons for ten consecutive days. During the treatment, the main objective was to attempt to influence the treatment group to include more details in their drawings. The procedure consisted of questioning and making statements concerning the topic of the art lesson. The results indicated that the children who received the art training achieved significantly higher scores on five subtests of the Metropolitan Reading Readiness Test. The findings, according to the author, suggest that children's reading development can be improved through art lessons that stress the inclusion of details.

Postulating that work in art would favorably affect a child's self-concept, provide courage for nonverbal children to attack other highly verbal educational procedures, and provide an important area for affective development and expression. Cohen explored the effects of an art program that followed children through kindergarten, first, second, and third grade. In this study sessions related to perception, self-concept, expressing feelings, and thinking about the environment were presented to the children. The author concluded that art is a valuable tool for increasing children's self-concept, verbal skills, and perceptual abilities. She concluded, "We need to help teachers to develop their sensibilities and to pass this awareness on to their children. Teacher training should stress the interrelatedness of knowledge, avoiding the fragmented kind of teaching which can result in fragmented people. In many cases, art can act as a sort of cement, binding understandings in social studies, literature, and science into an integrated whole" (Cohen, p. 181).

Recognizing the value of art to the general curriculum, Project IMPACT, originally funded under the Educational Professional Development Act Teacher Retraining Authorization, is an effort to demonstrate that the arts are the ideal and indispensible vehicle for humanizing the education of children and teachers. Five project sites have been selected to implement programs designed to incorporate arts into the regular school program. The fundamental purpose of IMPACT projects is to demonstrate that school activities in those areas of creative human endeavor called the arts can transform the traditional curriculum into one which emphasizes the integration of art into the mainstream of human experience, aids students in becoming sensitive to the qualitative aspects of their own experiences as sources for artistic idea, explores the similarities and differences in the ways professionals in the arts develop their ideas, and challenges students to make effective use of their creative resources. Evaluation at the end of the second year of the project reinforced the concept that IMPACT was successful in fulfilling its objectives. School districts involved in the project have planned to continue and expand it, even without funding support. The arts, they claim, seem to serve as a focus for humanizing the curriculum and to provide a vehicle for change.

Conclusion

In the past, art education for young children has been strongly influenced by the theories of Lowenfeld, Alschuler, and Read. As a result, the art program today generally consists of providing a rich, stimulating environment, a variety of media for the child to explore, and freedom for experimentation. It has usually been considered inappropriate to do any direct teaching of art, for any interference is believed to negate the child's freedom and creativity.

Now, however, the work of Eisner, McFee, and other influential art educators, when coupled with the results of the meager research, does provide direction for early childhood teachers. It seems possible for teachers to draw on the past, keeping all that is valued from each of the theories of child art, and yet go beyond that past. Understanding that there is a body of knowledge in art that can and should be passed on to the children, teachers can, without destroying their concern for the individual, humanness, self-expression, and creativity, lead children to fuller artistic expression.

References

A Guide to Art in Florida's Elementary Schools, Bulletin 77. Tallahassee, Fla.: State Department of Education, 1969.

Alschuler, R. and Hattwick, L.B. *Painting and Personality: A Study of Young Children.* Chicago: University of Chicago Press, 1947.

Arnheim, R. *Art and Visual Perception: The Psychology of the Creative Experience.* Berkeley: University of California Press, 1954.

"Arts Impact: Curriculum for Change: A Summary Report." Washington, D.C.: Office of Education, U.S. Department of Health, Education, and Welfare, March 1973.

Badri, M.B. "The Use of Figure Drawing in Measuring the Goodenough Quotient of Culturally Deprived Siamese Children." *Journal of Psychology* 72(1967):205–7.

Barkan, M. "Transition in Art Education." In *Readings in Art Education,* edited by E.W. Eisner and D.W. Ecker. Waltham, Mass: Blaisdell Publishing Co., 1966.

Brearley, M. *The Teacher of Young Children: Some Applications of Piaget's Learning Theory.* New York: Schocken Books, 1970.

Britain, S.D. "Effect of Manipulation of Children's Affect in Their Family Drawings." *Journal of Projective Techniques and Personality Assessment* 34(1970):234–37.

Burns, R., and Kaufman, S.H. *Kinetic Family Drawings: An Introduction to Understanding Children through Kinetic Drawings.* New York: Brunner/Mazel, 1970.

Clifford, G.J. "A History of the Impact of Research on Teaching." In *Second Handbook of Research on Teaching,* edited by R.M. Travers. Chicago: Rand McNally & Co., 1973.

Cohen, E.P. "Does Art Matter in the Education of the Black Ghetto Child?" *Young Children* 24(1974):170–82.

D'Amicao, V. "Art Education Today: Millennium or Mirage." *Art Education* 7(1966):46–53.

Dubin, E.R. "The Effect of Training on the Tempo of Development of Graphic Representations of Preschool Children." *Journal of Experimental Education* 15(1946):166–73.

Ebbeck, T.N., and Ebbeck, M.A. *Now We Are Four.* Columbus, O.: Charles E. Merrill Publishing Co., 1974.

Eisner, E.W. *Educating Artistic Vision.* New York: The Macmillan Co., 1972.

———. "Evaluating Children's Art." In *Art and Education,* edited by G. Pappas. New York: The Macmillan Co., 1970.

———. *Teaching Art to the Young: A Curriculum Development Project in Art Education.* Stanford: Stanford University Press, 1969.

Feldman, E.B. *Becoming Human through Art.* Englewood Cliffs, N.J.: Prentice-Hall, 1970.

Gardner, H.W., "A Cross-cultural Comparison of Hostility in Children's Drawing." *Journal of Social Psychology* 19(1969):291–92.

Goodenough, F.L. *Measurement of Intelligence by Drawings.* New York: Harcourt Brace Jovanovich, 1926.

Goodenough, F.L., and Harris, D. *Children's Drawings as Measures of Intellectual Maturity.* New York: Harcourt Brace Jovanovich, 1963.

Hammer, E. *Expressive Aspects of Projective Drawing: Clinical Application of Projective Drawings.* Springfield, Ill.: Charles C. Thomas Publisher, 1958.

Intellectual Maturity of Children as Measured by the Goodenough Harris Draw-A-Man Test. PHS, Publication Number 1000, Series 11, No. 105. Rockville, Md.: U.S. National Center for Health Statistics, 1970.

Kellog, R. *Analyzing Children's Art.* Palo Alto, Calif.: National Principle Books, 1969.

———. "Understanding Children's Art." *Psychology Today* 1(1967):16–25.

Koppitz, E. "A Comparison of Pencil and Crayon Drawings of Young Children." *Journal of Clinical Psychology* 72(1967):205–7.

Kris, E. *Psychoanalytic Explorations in Art.* New York: International Universities Press, 1952.

Lantz, B. *Lantz Easel Age Scales.* Los Angeles: California Test Bureau, 1955.

Leeper, S.L. *Good Schools for Young Children.* New York: The Macmillan Co., 1968.

Lindermann, E.W., and Herbolz, D.W. *Developing Artistic and Perceptual Awareness.* Dubuque, Iowa: William C. Brown Co. Publishers, 1974.

Lingren, R.H. "An Attempted Replication of Emotional Indicators in Human Figure Drawings by Shy and Aggressive Children." *Psychological Reports* 29(1971):35–38.

Lowenfeld, V. *Creative and Mental Growth.* New York: The Macmillan Co., 1947.

Luquet, G.H. *The Drawings of a Child.* Paris, France: F. Alcan, 1913.

McFee, J.K. *Preparation for Art.* 2d ed. Belmont, Calif.: Wadsworth Publishing Co., 1970.

Machover, K. "Personality Projections in the Drawings of the Human Figure." *Journal of Educational Research* 64(1971):370–74.

McWhinnie, H.J. "Lowenfeld Revisited." *Creative Crafts,* (Fall 1963): 35–37.

———. "Reviews of Recent Literature on Figure Drawing Tests as Related to Research Problems in Art Education." *Review of Educational Research* 41(1971):115–31.

————. "Viktor Lowenfeld: Art Education for the 1970s." *Studies in Art Education* 4(1972): 8–13.

Manzella, D. "The Effects of Hypnotically Induced Change in the Self-Image on Drawing Ability." *Studies in Art Education* 4(1963):59–70.

Medinnus, J.R.; Bobbitt, D.; and Hullet, J. "Effects of Training on the Draw-A-Man Test." *Journal of Experimental Education* 35(1966):62–63.

Mills, J.C. "The Effect of Art Instruction upon a Reading Development Test: An Experimental Study with Rural Appalachian Children." *Studies in Art Education* 14(1973):4–9.

National Art Education Association. "The Essentials of a Quality School Art Program. A Position Statement." *Art Education* 26(1973):21–25.

Naumberg, M. "Studies of 'Free' Art Expression of Behavior Problem Children in Adolescence as a Means of Diagnostic Therapy." *Nervous Mental Disorders.* Monograph No. 71. New York: Cooledge Foundation, 1974.

Nelson, T.M., and Flannery, M.E. "Instruction in Drawing Technique as a Means of Utilizing Drawing Potential of Six and Seven Year Olds." *Studies in Art Education* 8(1967):58–65.

Piaget, J. *The Child's Conception of Reality.* London: Routledge & Kegan Paul, 1955.

————. *The Psychology of Intelligence.* London: Routledge & Kegan Paul, 1932.

Rand, C.W. "Copying in Drawing: The Importance of Adequate Visual Analysis versus the Ability to Utilize Drawing Rules." *Child Development* 44(1973):47–53.

Rashid, M.V. "Introduction: Behavioral Objectives." In *Children and the Arts,* edited by D. Devers. Washington, D.C.: Central Atlantic Regional Education Laboratory, 1967.

Read, H. *Education through Art.* New York: Pantheon Books, 1943.

Reichenberg, H.W. "Changes in Children's Drawings after a Gratifying Experience." *American Journal of Orthopsychiatry* 23(1953):501–17.

Rogers, R.S., and Wright, E.N. "A Study of Children's Drawings of Their Classrooms." *Journal of Educational Research* 64(1971):370–74.

Salome, R.A. "A Comparative Analysis of Kindergarten Children's Drawings in Crayon and Colored Pencil." *Studies in Art Education* 72(1967):205–7.

Salome, R.A., and Reeves, D. "Two Pilot Investigations of Perceptual Training of Four- and Five-Year-Old Kindergarten Children." *Studies in Art Education* 13(1972):3–9.

Schaeffer-Simmern, H. *The Unfolding of Artistic Activity.* Berkeley: University of California Press, 1948.

Schwartz, J.B., and Douglas, N.J. *Increasing the Awareness of Art Ideas of Culturally Deprived Kindergarten Children through Experiences with Ceramics.* Final Report Project Number 6-8647. Washington, D.C.: U.S. Department of Health, Education, and Welfare, 1967.

Seefeldt, C. *An Investigation of the Effects of a Program Designed to Increase Visual Perception of Texture in Young Children.* College Park, Md.: University of Maryland, 1974.

————. "The Validity of the Exclusive Use of the Wide Paintbrush in the Five-Year-Old Kindergarten." *Studies in Art Education* 14(1973):48–54.

Taylor, P.A., and Trujillo, J.L. "The Effects of Selected Stimuli on the Art Products, Concept Formation, and Aesthetic Judgmental Decisions of Four-Year-Old Children." *Studies in Art Education* 14(1973):57–67.

Thomas, R.R. "Effects of Frustration on Children's Paintings." *Child Development* 22(1951): 123–32.

Walbaesser, H.J. "The Construction of Behavioral Objectives." In *Children and the Arts,* edited by D. Devers. Washington, D.C.: Central Atlantic Regional Educational Laboratory, 1967.

CHAPTER EIGHT

Music

Shirley J.
Shelley

Let's make music.

For many years the Music Educators National Conference (MENC) has been concerned with the musical experiences of the preprimary child and advocated that a child's entire musical development is influenced by these experiences (Flagg). The basic philosophy of *music for every child and every child for music* has permeated the profession but, in actuality, has not been practiced, specifically with the Head Start and Disadvantaged Children's Programs (Adkins and Greenberg). This, of course, has been partially caused by the fact that Head Start programs as a rule have been disassociated with the public schools. When the Early Admissions Program, the forerunner of Head Start, was first initiated in the Mt. Royal Elementary School in Baltimore City, the music resource teacher was told not to participate. Fortunately, this policy was changed, and today the classroom teacher and music teacher work together.

Institutions of higher education are still emphasizing the training of music educators for kindergarten through high school levels, yet they are slow not only in providing but requiring method courses for preprimary level. Special method courses for the early childhood specialist are not in abundance and frequently are taught in conjunction with a multi-media arts or creative activities course (Mankin).

A review of the professional journals of music and early childhood reveals a paucity of literature dealing with the young child and music. One could conclude that incompatibility has existed between the two disciplines and appears to be the result of traditional thinking caused by training rather than choice.

It is encouraging to note that sessions dealing with music and the preschool child are currently being given special attention at the music educators' conferences and that some of the consultants leading these sessions are specialists in early childhood education. Likewise, music education specialists are being asked to participate in various early childhood conferences. This is how it should be, for each is vitally dedicated to helping the young child reach his fullest potential and capacity for learning, whether it be in the arts or other related areas. By combining efforts, the ultimate goal will be reached sooner.

Articles concerning music and the preschool child are beginning to appear more frequently in journals, and one of the newest publications of MENC is *Music in Early Childhood* (Andress, Heimann, Rinehart, and Talbert). Writings by pioneers in the field of nursery and music education are being rediscovered. An impressive list includes the writings of Thorn, Johnson, Coleman, Cole, McCall, Sheehy, Driver, Nelson and Tipton, and Dykema and Cundiff.

The intent of this chapter is to reflect the current thinking of the music education profession, to review the research and writings pertaining to music and the preschool-primary aged child, and to identify some of the current influences on music education. As a result of the discussions, some suggestions for the classroom teacher and the implementation of music experiences for the young child will be included.

Current Thinking of Music Educators

Aesthetic education that cultivates aesthetic behavior has always been a concern of the arts, but it often has been neglected in actual classroom practice. Emphasis on music education, as aesthetic education, came into prominence in the 1960s. Broudy, at the Tanglewood Symposium, stated:

> A cultivated taste is better than a raw one . . . One of the stumbling blocks to aesthetic education is the relentless pressure on the child to be literal, factual, and scientifically terse. (Broudy, p. 11)

At the 1970 biennial meeting of the music educators, held in Chicago, the first conference within a conference was held. The conference was a joint effort of the Music Educators National Conference and the Central Midwestern Regional Educational Laboratory, St. Louis, Missouri. CEMREL, as it has come to be known, came into existence as the result of people in art, music, theatre, and dance education working cooperatively with the Office of Education. Their prime purpose is to explore ways of strengthening aesthetic education in the schools, and its efforts are directed toward the development of instructional systems to meet these needs (Bloom).

> Programs of music education conceived as aesthetic education stress sensitive, intelligent, and creative development of musicality through the fundamental avenues of expression: creativity, performance, and response. (Kneiter, p. 19)

Kneiter further identifies the five characteristics of the aesthetic experience, namely, focus, perception, affect, cognition, and the cultural matrix; he believes that all five occur simultaneously.

A child's musical development is primarily dependent upon his being actively involved in making music. When given the opportunity to improvise, compose, create, and recreate, he acquires various behaviors that will enable him to identify, discriminate, analyze, observe, discover, recall, relate, compare, and rearrange. He accomplishes this through the process of perception (see Figure 1).

If we think about perception and understand what happens in the process, then we are aware that within perception we find interaction between learning and thinking. We can also find the roots of imagination and judgment if we can accept recognition as a primitive form of judgment and the beginning of conceptualization. Perception is the basic element of cognitive development (Forgus).

It is through various activities and experience with music that the child acquires knowledge and skills. Pitts believes:

> Children have a *feeling* for the meanings of music. However, because what they feel is sensory and nonverbal in character, children need assistance in becoming aware of the musical values that are in their singing voices, their rhythmic bodies, and their eager hands and fingers, as well as in their special curiosities and likings. Growth—musical or otherwise—is an active, not a passive, process. A child learns to sing by singing; he learns to move expressively by moving; he learns to play an instrument by manipulating a given instrument; and he learns to *think* in musical terms by 'acting out' the music that is in himself in as many appealing and enjoyable ways as possible. (Pitts, p. 80)

Review of the Research and Writings

When reviewing research literature and writings, two problems exist: what should be reported, and how should they be categorized? There is a tendency to lose sight of objectivity when faced with the review of a particular study of which certain aspects conflict with one's pedagogical or philosophical beliefs. However, it is the responsibility of the writer to report all available studies. There are also times when a question arises as to the validity of a particular study.

Kwalwasser made a strong appeal to music educators to become involved in scientific research. Frazen questioned the actual application of the scientific method in many music research studies. Should those studies that were measured by observational techniques be discarded? The struggle and frustrations of music research pioneers in coping with the testing procedures for three and four year olds are evident in their writings. How old is three? Some studies were discontinued or proved unfruitful due to the fact that the child was unable to understand the task at hand (Seashore).

Hissem as well as Vance and Grandprey, using the observational method, obtained useful information when the testing was part of the normal nursery school program. Vance and Grandprey stated that any method used in determining a young child's musical capacity must be concrete, capture his interest, and be within his attention span. Williams believed that the observational method was valid when it was handled under proper conditions by a competent individual (Williams, 1932, p. 69). It

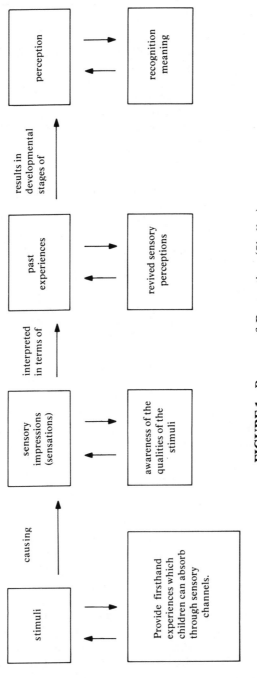

FIGURE 1 Process of Perception (Shelley)

is also interesting to note that few studies are confined to either the preschool- or primary-aged child. However, some studies concerned with elementary school children may contain useful information.

Klemish has found a solution to the problem. She stated that, although several studies may not be identified as true research, some may contribute to the understanding of how a child learns and develops musically, while others may contribute to innovative practices and supply instructional resources. It is with this viewpoint in mind that both observational and scientific studies are included, and they may or may not be confined specifically to the preschool- or primary-aged child.

Perceptual and Conceptual Development

Several researchers have investigated a multiplicity of items in order to determine the child's perceptual and conceptual capacities. Petzold concluded that an aural understanding of musical elements is a prerequisite to the musical growth of the child. In a longitudinal study lasting six years, Petzold (1969) concluded that if serious consideration is not given to the development of aural understanding when the child is young, his musical development will be seriously inhibited. He also recommended that children learn how to think musically and be able to analyze and evaluate the inherent qualities of music.

In applying Piaget's principle of conservation, Pflederer devised musical tasks which represented an attempt to embody the principle of conservation of meter, tone, and rhythm. The answers of a majority of the eight year olds reflected that they were in the intermediate stages of conservation whereas the answers of the kindergarteners were more characteristic of preoperational thought. In finding solutions to rhythmic tasks involving conservation of meter, the children often resorted to clapping, swinging, tapping, counting, and singing to themselves. "These overt activities were a manifestation of sensorimotor intelligence where action guides thought" (Zimmerman, p. 18). She recommended that a child be given a wide range of musical experiences before he is asked to intellectualize these experiences. Musical problems to be solved must be within the limits of the child's understanding (Pflederer, 1964, p. 266). In a follow-up study involving children of ages five, seven, nine, and thirteen, Pflederer and Sechrest examined types of responses denoting nonconservation and conservation for each of the age groups. They found a startling lack of proper vocabulary when applied to musical understanding or identification.

Zimmerman and Sechrest as well as Hair reported that although tempo variation and the addition of harmony can produce faulty perception, young children are capable of some comprehension of fairly complex musical concepts. It should also be noted that five year olds do relatively well in recognizing repetition of an original stimulus but tend to lose perspective when the stimulus is modified. In agreement with Petzold (1969), they suggested that the child reaches a plateau of auditory perception at approximately age nine and that the need for auditory experiences for the young child in developing musicality is crucial.

Although a study of Andrews and Deihl involved fourth-grade children, it holds significance and implications for music with the young child. In their attempt to develop a technique for identifying concepts of music elements (i.e., pitch, duration,

and loudness) in children, they designed the *Battery of Musical Concept Measures.*
They concluded that children first develop the concept of loudness followed by durations and then pitch. The data, although not conclusive, substantiate earlier studies
in that some children confuse the three terms *high, loud,* and *fast* with the three terms
low, soft, and *slow.* Kyme devised some techniques to solve these problems. Having a
child blow across the top of a bottle containing water can produce a sound. As the
water level is lowered, the sound chamber becomes deeper, and the child discovers
that the pitch of the sound is lower. The child is able to relate to the bassoon as being
a low-sounding instrument since it has the longest sound chamber of the woodwinds.
He is also able to understand the meaning of the word *bass* as being low.

By deepening a child's perception of the structure and style of music, Raley found
that new concept formation contributed to an increased aesthetic sensitivity. He suggested various musical learnings which a primary grade child should experience in
order to formulate new concepts.

Schultz developed a test to measure the child's ability to listen and identify various
elements of music (e.g., melody, rhythm, tempo, timbre, mode, and key change). (Apel
defines timbre as meaning the quality or color of a tone; e.g., the difference between
the sound of the same pitch played on a violin and a trumpet.) His subjects were children in grades two through eight. One of his recommendations was that further investigation of the relationship between musical preferences and the development of
musical concepts was needed since some of the children appeared ready to grasp an
understanding of the structure of music as early as the second or third grade. Fullard
concluded that preschool children are capable of identifying through programmed
techniques the timbre of specific orchestral instruments.

A comparative study of preschool twins and singletons concerning the emergence
and development of music responses and their vocal capabilities was made by Alford.
The children's gross and imitative responses and free-play activities to music stimuli
were observed over a two-year period. Two of his conclusions were that all subjects
exhibited response to music throughout the entire period; however, they exhibited a
gross response to piano, orchestra, and choral stimuli more frequently than imitative
responses. Age level appears to influence the emergence and development of music
responses.

The following is a list of suggestions for the teacher based upon a review of the
research literature pertaining to perceptual and conceptual development:

1. Help children discover all types of sounds: environmental, mechanical, and
   musical.
2. Guide children in understanding that some sounds can be repeated and that
   other sounds may be in contrast: high and low, loud and soft, long and short.
3. Use visual aids, various instruments, and other materials to provide experiences that will help the children grasp the meanings of high-low, loud-soft,
   long-short.
4. Turn a xylophone on end or use step bells to help children understand direction
   of melody.
5. Use the technique of echo clapping and singing melodic fragments in a

"seesaw" fashion in order to help the children develop tonal and rhythmic memory.

6. Play a familiar melody or fragment on the resonator bells or piano; repeat it rhythmically on a variety of instruments; help the children realize that the rhythm is still the same.
7. Help the children understand duration; use a gong or triangle in contrast with a tone block or rhythm sticks.
8. Help the children distinguish between the sound of a violin and a trumpet; find recorded musical examples to demonstrate the timbre of the instruments.
9. Use a variety of recorded music that features a specific instrument in playing a particular theme within a composition.
10. Use instrumental and electronic recordings that illustrate how some composers are able to create environmental sounds (e.g., a storm, horse's hoofs).
11. Use proper vocabulary; a five year old after experiencing fast and slow can understand the meaning of tempo.

Vocal Development

Bentley believes that a child sings before he talks and labels the sounds that are uttered during infancy as *lalling*. As the child begins to use words and phrases, he acquires facility in speech, his tonal inflection decreases, and the vowels become shorter; thus, he has learned to speak through singing.

Spontaneous Expressive Singing. Parents and teachers who are well acquainted with young children are aware that they often sing melodic fragments. These fragments are usually in the form of a chant and generally accompany some form of physical movement (e.g., pounding a hammer, rocking a doll, scooting along on a wheel toy, walking, or hopping). Moorhead and Pond observed that chants were expressions of a fact or thought and imitative of the imaginary part of child's play. They found that children like to repeat the same sounds over and over; for example, "Hello lunch box," "Hello pineapple juice," "Hello . . ." (Moorhead and Pond, I, p. 9). The melodic content usually consisted of a repeated tone or began with a repeated tone and ended with a descending third. As to the rhythmic content, it often began in 2/4 and ended in 6/8 time.

It is common knowledge that children all over the world sing the minor third; it has been labeled the natural chant of childhood (see Figure 2).

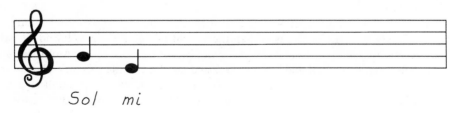

FIGURE 2

The writer observed a little boy approximately four years old walking hand in hand with his mother completely oblivious to the crowded walkway improvising his chant:

FIGURE 3

It is obvious that children love the sound of language, and a wise teacher encourages this feeling and utilizes the chants in the classroom by writing them down, identifying each with the proper child's name, and sharing them with the other children. Benefits derived from such a technique encourage the child's vocal improvisation, nurture his self-concept, and acquaint him with early stages of reading words and melodic direction. Hissem used improvisational techniques in her testing.

Three year olds usually do not show a preference for tonality and favor higher notes in spontaneous vocalization (Jersild and Beinstock, 1931). Moorhead and Pond observed that "the child shows us that he desires instinctively, not the trivialities of melodies built upon scalewise progressions, but the more angular vitality of primitive music" (Moorhead and Pond, 1941, p. 16). It is interesting to note that Williams (1932) found that four year olds who often sang incorrect intervals within the actual melody frequently ended up on the correct ending pitch; in other words, they maintained a feeling for the tonal center or tonality. In support of Williams' findings Krestaff believes that a child's initial awareness of tonal order as an organized means of musical expression and communication comes into being during his fourth year.

The Child's Ability to Sing Songs.   The child's first repertoire of songs is acquired by imitation and is classified as rote songs. The ability to sing accurately is dependent to a degree on aural discrimination of pitch and intervals. Music is tone, and it is perceived through the ear. Some early investigators tested only pitch discrimination while later investigators tested children's discrimination of intervals, phrases, and melodies.

Jersild and Beinstock (1934) in testing three year olds concluded that they sang narrow intervals of seconds and thirds (e.g., middle C to D and C to E) more readily than the wider intervals of fourths and fifths (e.g., middle C to F and C to G). Children preferred singing within the range of middle C to A, a sixth above middle C (see Figure 4). Drexler, using children of ages three to six, found that they could manipulate descending intervals more easily than the ascending ones. She also found that the difficulty in ability to carry a melody is most significant between the ages of three and four and five and six. Duell and Anderson tested children in the primary grades and concluded that 30 percent were unable to discriminate differences so small as a half step (e.g., C to C#) while only 4 percent were unable to discriminate differences as large as a sixth (e.g., C to A).

As previously mentioned, children frequently misunderstand the terms *high* and *low.* Hitchkock found that three year olds confuse *high* and *low* with *big* and *little.*

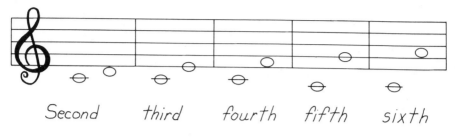

FIGURE 4

Jeffrey attempted to program the child's response in an overt behavioral task. He taught the child to push one or two buttons corresponding to two different tones. The training method helped the child learn the initial task but did not provide transfer to new pitches.

Other investigators (Monroe; Smith, 1914; Wolner and Pyle; Petzold, 1963), on the premise that a phrase or melody contains a rhythmic structure as well as melodic material, approached the problem from the standpoint that if children could accurately reproduce a phrase or melody by singing, they were able to differentiate pitch. Petzold (1963) concluded that the presence of rhythm had no appreciable influence upon the child's perception of the melodic items. He suggested that auditory perception of phrases precedes auditory perception of larger musical units.

Children, as a rule, prefer a lower range than has been traditionally advocated. Jersild and Beinstock (1931) concluded that when given the opportunity to choose their natural starting pitch, children prefer a lower pitch and sing more readily. Hattwick reported this finding in testing first and second graders and concluded that publishers had ignored research findings. A sampling of 350 songs representative of 8 song books in use at the time revealed the tessitura (singing range) to be E above middle C to E flat fourth space. A lower tessitura has recently been appearing in some of the elementary school music texts. However, studies by de Yarman and Wilson continue to support Hattwick's findings.

Kirkpatrick concluded that children prefer a starting pitch of D flat above middle C and have extensive ranges from F below middle C to E fourth space (see Figure 5). However, as reported earlier, children utilize the higher range in spontaneous singing but prefer a lower range when singing songs.

The Influence of Training on the Child's Voice. The influence of training versus maturation on the vocal development of children has been another favorite topic of researchers. There is conflicting evidence that early vocal training is advantageous. There is also disagreement as to whether the method of training is dependent on maturation.

Williams (1932, p. 79), using a group situation with supplementary individual instruction, concluded that the training of young children was handicapped by lack of motivation and maturation. Updegraff, Heiliger, and Learned, using small group instruction, found that when half of the children were singled out for simple and intensive short periods of training which emphasized individual attention, their improvement in singing ability, interest, and aptitude was superior. Smith (1963)

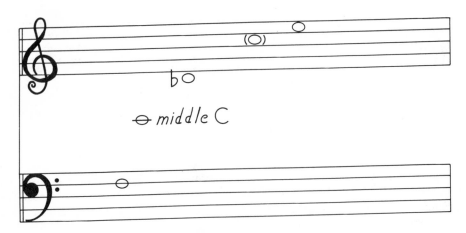

FIGURE 5

attempted to train entire groups of nursery school children and concluded that group vocal training is appropriate for young children and that training, not maturation, affects vocal development. His findings suggest that training in the lower range of middle C to A a sixth above middle C is more suitable in helping young children learning to sing; he recommends postponement of training in the upper range of G above middle C to C or D a fifth above G until the intermediate grades (see Figure 6).

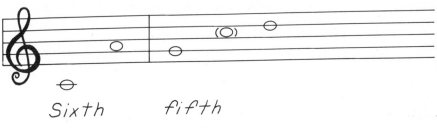

FIGURE 6

As to sex differences, he is perhaps the first to conclude that boys are usually slow beginners in the nursery school, but with training can catch up with girls around the fifth grade (Smith, 1968).

A follow-up study by Boardman with kindergarten, first-, and second-grade children who had participated in Smith's study revealed that at the second-grade level no significant difference occurred in the vocal accuracy between those who had received earlier training as compared with those who had not. She concluded that preschool training accelerates but does not otherwise improve normal developmental processes.

The Child Who Has Difficulty Learning How to Sing.   There are many children who have difficulty in singing and upon reaching adulthood are convinced that they are hopeless. Wolner and Pyle conducted a significant study of training although it was not concerned with the preschool child. Their subjects were three boys and five girls who had received musical instruction in the Detroit Public Schools for five, six, or seven years and had not learned to distinguish one pitch from another and could not sing. With intensive individual training, approximately sixteen hours over a period of eighty days, they found a marked increase in all the subjects' ability to distinguish pitch. They suggested that the failure of such children in ordinary school instruction may be due to failure of method. The belief that an inability to distinguish pitch was due to some native structural defects that could not be affected by training was not correct.

Hartsell stresses the point that teachers must refrain from labeling children as nonsingers, out-of-tune singers, and monotones. Stene provides support for this opinion and projects ways to correct children's difficulties in learning how to sing.

Investigating the singing problems of elementary school children, Gould (1969) concluded that kinesthetic aspects of the discovery of the singing voice by the child and his developing skill in using and controlling this new found voice are essential to improvement in singing. The study established two basic principles: the child must learn to hear his own voice in speaking and singing and to control the high and low pitches, and he must be able to sing in unison with either another voice or instrument and to learn the sound and feeling as his voice matches the pitches he hears.

Surveying 9,000 children's choices of songs, Blyer concluded that children prefer songs whose texts concern the known interest of their age group and that the music must reflect the thought and emotions involved.

The following is a list of suggestions for the classroom teacher based upon the review of the research literature pertaining to vocal development:

1. Encourage children to improvise; sing about the happenings in the classroom or on the playground.
2. Use the tape recorder to record the child's original song or chant; provide an opportunity for the child to listen to his own voice.
3. Help children write down their chants and original melodies. Utilize their suggestions and ideas for scoring (lines or dashes could show melody direction, pictures or children's drawings can be used for word meaning); transfer to actual words and musical notation when you feel they are ready.
4. Provide an opportunity for the child to sing along with a singing record or the teacher's voice.
5. Help the child learn how it feels to sing.
6. Use many songs that have a limited number of pitches as the child begins to learn songs; for example, *John the Rabbit* (Nelson and Tipton, p. 63) in which children sing "Yes mam" throughout the song on the same pitch, *Jingle Bells, Merrily We Roll Along.*
7. Choose songs whose tessitura is between middle C and A a sixth above middle C.
8. Vary the beginning pitch level; at times allow children to start on their own natural pitch level.

9. Utilize songs that have a broader range as children progress in their ability to sing; help them "stretch" their voice range.
10. Sing songs that have repeated words, phrases, and rhythmic patterns.
11. Play melodic phrases on resonator bells; help children acquire skill in playing phrases on the bells.
12. Encourage the children to create melodies and chants to accompany their movement; add instruments for percussion accompaniment.
13. Encourage the children to use a contrasting voice inflection, utilize poetry (e.g., Mother Goose), and imitate sounds (e.g., a siren, the sound of a young kitten crying, the sound of a fog horn).

Motor and Rhythmic Development

A child's ability to synchronize body movements or manipulate instruments with rhythmic stimuli is to a large degree dependent upon his perception of rhythm and the level of his motor ability. The studies that are available in this area are few in number. Investigators appear to have used two approaches in measuring the child's rhythmic capacity. One approach was to have the child freely respond through body movement or some form of rhythmic activity to a musical stimulus; the second approach concerned the child's ability to imitate or match a definite rhythmic pattern in response to a musical or mechanical stimulus. Baldwin and Stecher in a tapping experiment used the kymograph to record preschool children's performance ability to keep in time to a march played on a phonograph. The performance of two of the children who were three years old revealed that rhythmic ability does not depend on age. They further concluded that response to a rhythmic stimuli may lapse for a short time and then be recovered. Some children tapped the steady beat while others tapped the melodic rhythm.

A study by Heilein concluded that to judge a child's rhythmic capacity by observing his spontaneous moving to music is unreliable. One child who displayed an excellent sense of motor rhythm in a free-locomotor type response to music was totally unable to synchronize his movement with the beat when marching on the rhythm platform. The lack of synchronization was indicated on the kymograph that had recorded the child's footsteps and the underlying beat of the music. Heilein refers to the inability to respond accurately as "arhythmic," and he says that the term *rhythmic response* is a speech inaccuracy (Heilein, p. 221).

Tempo as a significant factor was reported in studies by Hulson; Jersild and Beinstock, 1935; Williams, 1932. Preschool children are more capable of responding accurately when a fast tempo is used. In a tapping experiment in which children responded to the ticking of a clock, Sievers concluded that elementary school children are more accurate in duplicating simple rhythmic patterns at a fast tempo.

Vance and Grandprey recommended that children below the age of three should not be tested since there is a possibility of measuring maturity rather than aptitude. In testing the ability of three year olds to duplicate rhythmic patterns, the children were more successful with those patterns that started with quarter notes rather than half notes. This supports Gardner's findings in that the number of taps, their arrangement, and the item's position in the test has bearing on the ability to duplicate the pattern. He also found that in skill development some six year olds were as proficient as some of the subjects reaching adolescence.

The influence of age and maturation versus instruction on rhythmic synchronization ability was investigated by Groves. In testing primary-aged children, he concluded that age and maturation were more significant than training.

On the premise that teachers have limited resources in considering children's musical needs, Christiansen undertook a curriculum study involving nursery, kindergarten, and first-grade children. By systematic observational techniques, she recorded their body rhythmic activities in response to pronounced rhythmic music. She also considered the young child, the social setting of the modern school, and the pronounced rhythmic music. Some of her findings and recommendations were that the nursery school child is capable of showing preference for certain types of music such as instrumental music that is characteristic of the contemporary sound, there is only a slight difference between boys and girls in total responsiveness, and children should be given continuous opportunity to experience music experimentally and creatively through body movement as it is highly desirable for social-emotional growth and provides a satisfying means of creative expression. At this age a child's motor activity is still the primary response to most stimuli (Christiansen, p. 178).

Jersild and Beinstock (1935) believed that there may be a large discrepancy between a child's interest in rhythmic activities, his ability to improvise original movements, and his accuracy in keeping exact time with a music stimulus. They recommended that work in the area of motor rhythm should not concentrate on teaching a child how to keep perfect time to a specific meter, tempo, or musical pattern. A child should be encouraged to move spontaneously and to get in touch with the "feeling" for rhythm; by so doing, he would among other things improve his balance and muscular control in motor response to various rhythmic stimuli (Jersild and Beinstock, 1935, p. 97).

The following is a list of suggestions for the teacher based on a review of the research literature pertaining to motor and rhythmic development:

1. Encourage children to create their own rhythmic patterns; let them experiment with all types of percussive and melodic instruments.
2. Try to match the various rhythms that children create through body movement with various instruments.
3. Let them explore the various ways they can move their bodies in response to various rhythmic stimuli.
4. Use children's names, nursery rhymes, and poems; have children play the word rhythms on instruments and by clapping hands or tapping the body.
5. Help the children understand repetition of words or sounds.
6. Use a simple form of scoring for various rhythms; let children make suggestions.
7. Have children create body movement that expresses the rhythmic content of poetry and speech.
8. Use various recordings that demonstrate mood, rhythmic patterns, melodic direction, and form; encourage children to respond to the characteristics of the music.

9. Encourage children to respond to instrumental recordings using various instruments in accompaniment and matching various rhythmic patterns.

10. Help children begin to discriminate in choosing suitable instruments for simple orchestration; the triangle may be suitable for "Sleep Baby Sleep" while drums and sticks may be more appropriate for a Sousa march.

Related Topics

Influence of the Home Environment.   An infant in a crib or playpen often responds to music or other stimuli through some form of rhythmic activity (e.g., rocking, shaking his hands, or a combination of both). His total body is involved, and the feeling appears to come from deep within the child; he obviously enjoys the feeling of motion. The young child who is exposed to a broad spectrum of musical sound, which could include a parent singing, perhaps while the child is being rocked, listening to records, the chance to pound on toys or objects, pushing musical sound toys, or shaking rattles, will acquire tonal and rhythmic awareness very young in life. Taubmann and Elliot stress that the parents' natural involvement in music has a direct influence on the child's developing a positive attitude toward music, while the presence of a musical environment has a direct bearing on the child's musical aptitude.

Shelton concluded that a trait of the musical child is that he employs music spontaneously in his play and sings frequently at home (Shelton, p. 41). He also reported that there is a definite relationship between a child's early desire and opportunity to experiment with instruments and his first-grade ability.

Near the end of the nursery school years, a young child who has had many musical experiences, including an opportunity to experiment with musical sounds, turns his attention toward the solution of intellectual problems (Bailey). Inquiry and the working out of practical problems seems to be intensified in the six year old. As he creates melodies he tackles the problems of reading and writing music and simple orchestration. "He creates music as he creates models or pictures, and so he learns to use his growing knowledge of the mechanics of music" (Bailey, p. 108).

Teaching a Child to Read Music.   A child's ability to learn to read music is determined by his readiness to read. The teacher and the child often use lines, drawings, hand and body movements, numbers, and other psuedo-type symbols in musical notation to illustrate melodic direction, rhythmic patterns, and form (Dykema and Cundiff, p. 269). Klemish (1970) identified this approach as one method of teaching first-grade children to read music as compared with a second method using the music staff and symbols. Results of the study included that the approach in method one is better for developing aural skills (e.g., identifying melodic direction, aural matching, aural/visual matching and singing patterns) whereas method two is better for developing visual and writing skills (e.g., recognition, dictation, dictation with numbers, and visual matching). She further reported that children in the first grade can learn to read tonal patterns and that music reading skills should be introduced on the basis of the child's readiness to read.

Woskowiak developed programmed music reading games involving certain principles of Dalcroze, Kodaly, and Orff. She concluded that programmed games may be effectively used for teaching music reading skills; children are capable of acquiring concepts of high-low, loud-soft, and fast-slow; and children can comprehend the difference between basic note values due to their physical response and ability to play rhythmic patterns on various instruments.

Current Influences on Music Education

The principles and practices of Dalcroze, Kodaly, Sazuki, and Orff continue to have a strong influence on the musical education of children in the United States. This is evidenced by the rapid increase of articles, books, workshops, summer institutes, and new methods of adaptation that are available today. Their approaches, although interrelated, were not founded for the same reason.

Dalcroze, the Swiss educator, formulated his principles of methodology early in his teaching career as a result of his students' inability to perform rhythmic patterns correctly. He observed that they were capable of interpreting such patterns through body movement, and it was on this premise that he founded his method. Although it developed into three components, namely, eurhythmics (rhythmic movement), solfège (singing a melody with syllables), and piano improvisation, his basic approach was to experience rhythm through body movement. Dalcroze believed rhythm was the fundamental driving force in all of the arts (Landis and Carder).

A young child walking at a natural pace can begin to grasp the idea of pulse or beat. By running, twisting, and stretching, he can begin to understand tempo, duration, and mood. Improvisation at the piano or instruments such as the drum can be played as an accompaniment in matching the child's rhythm. As music is introduced, the child learns to adapt his rhythm to the music. His aural acuity is being challenged and his listening skills developed.

Willour believes that this approach also develops coordination and encourages large muscle movement. It contributes to eye-hand-body coordination so necessary to other academic areas, helps the child learn how to associate sounds and symbols, and trains his eyes to follow left to right.

Kodaly, the Hungarian composer and musicologist, advocated music as a way of life for the Hungarian people, and he hoped to accomplish his mission through a unified system of music education based on the child developmental approach (Choksy). Kodaly was very demanding that children should be exposed to authentic Hungarian folk music, and it was through his efforts combined with those of Bartok that much of this music is available today (Edwards). He believed that training for musical literacy should begin with the very young child and that all should learn to read and write music.

It is interesting to note that his method begins with the interval of the minor third (the natural chant of childhood). After the child is able to aurally recognize and reproduce this interval, he then becomes acquainted with the visual representation of it. The child learns to sing by using syllables (e.g., the minor third is always *sol mi* in whatever key the child may sing). Kokas stresses that solmization, however, is not a system of symbols used to reinforce the memory of the tonal intervals; she proposes that the symbols recall for the child the emotional reactions of movement, play, dancing, and laughter, associated with songs and games, which in turn challenges and motivates the child to acquire skills in writing and reading music. The child comprehends rhythmic duration symbols by using word rhythms that match the visual symbol (Choksy). As the child develops, the musical content becomes more complex.

Suzuki, the Japanese violinist and teacher, believes that the "mother tongue" method is the most natural way to teach a child. Children everywhere in the world speak their own language fluently. The child acquires this skill through a constant repetition of sounds between parent and child and progresses naturally through daily practice. The parents may skillfully build up enthusiasm in the child which results in the child's developing a positive self-concept (Suzuki, p. 1).

Because of these beliefs, he began teaching very young children how to play the violin. Due to his success with three year olds, he founded the Talent Education Institute in 1948. At this school the preschool child is first exposed to music by listening to it and begins to play the violin by the rote method. A parent accompanies the child to the lessons and learns along with the child in order that the parent may guide and encourage the child throughout his training. The only prerequisite for admission to the Talent Education Institute is that the child speaks the Japanese language.

Suzuki believes that every child is influenced from the moment of birth by his environment and that every child can be developed. "Musical ability is not inborn" (Suzuki, p. 8). The results of his work of forty years provides convincing support for his philosophy (Kendall).

Orff, German composer and educator, believed that in order for music to be meaningful to the young child, it must be connected with movement, dance, and speech. In other words, music is meaningful only in active participation. This he identified as "elemental music" (Orff). As mentioned previously, a child often accompanies himself by singing or chanting while involved in some form of physical movement. Orff believed that the musical education of a child should begin during this time of spontaneous free expression. Like Kodaly he felt the melodic starting point should be the minor third. He also felt that the child's improvisational skills could be developed by combining poetry, movement, and instruments. He believed that the prime purpose of music education is the development of the child's creative faculty and thus is accomplished by helping the child acquire improvisational skills (Landis and Carder).

Other Influences

The Pillsbury Foundation School, Santa Barbara, California, was founded in 1937; it enrolled children ages two through six. Heterogeneous groupings were determined by children choosing their own activities and playgrounds. At the suggestion of Dr. Leopold Stokowski, the school was founded to discover the child's natural form of musical expression and to determine means of developing his musical capacities, particularly in the area of spontaneous creation. The experiment was based on the premise that in order for the child to produce his own music, he needs freedom to explore sounds that are appropriate to his interests and purposes. Technical help in acquiring skills was given only when a child showed readiness and need for it (Moorhead and Pond, 1941).

The report of observations, musical experiences, original work by the children, techniques, materials, instruments, and various findings are recorded in four pamphlets by Moorhead and Pond and Moorhead, Sandvik, and Wight. One significant conclusion of this study is that the serious study of musical techniques may be undertaken by the young child provided he has ample opportunity for uninhibited creative experiences with sound by which he gains musical understanding, the desire for a richer musical experience, and the acquisition of skills (Moorhead and Pond, 1944, p. 13).

The Contemporary Music Project for Creativity in Music Education was sponsored by MENC and the Ford Foundation in 1964. The project was designed to acquaint music teachers and children with contemporary music, encourage creative music activities, and help children acquire improvisational skills. Music teachers attended weekly seminars that were conducted by the composer in residence and explored contemporary music and the inherent compositional techniques of the music. Two cities, Baltimore and San Diego, were selected for the project. Baltimore, however, was the only one that involved children in kindergarten and first grade. Pilot teachers were responsible for finding suitable ways of introducing contemporary music to children. Improvisation and the utilization of contemporary compositional techniques were used to help the children acquire skills in composing and arranging original compositions and percussion scores.

Among other contributions, the younger children developed sound stories (e.g., "Pots and Pans Symphony" and "Goldilocks and the Three Bears") and created original melodies for poetry. The creative rhythmic movement and dances of the first- and second-grade children were "their most original and distinctive contribution" (Contemporary Music Project, p. 15).

The Manhattanville Music Curriculum Program (MMCP) (1965–1970) was sponsored by the Arts and Humanities Program of the Office of Education, DHEW. CEMREL assisted in the early stages of the research and development of the curriculum. The program was designed to provide sequential learning experiences with requisite materials appropriate for children of primary through high school age. An adaptation of part of this project concerns the preschool-primary child (Biasini, Thomas, and Pogonowski). MMCP Interaction is a process-oriented curriculum. Emphasis is placed on sounds and music in an aural form for the young child. It focuses on helping the child develop his creative abilities through various developmental processes of music exploration.

A Gift

The previous discussion has been totally concerned with the musical development of the preschool-primary child. A question remains, Who will teach the child? We have a diversified approach to teaching special subjects across the country. One system adheres to the specialist coming into the classroom, or the children going to the music room, two or three times a week for approximately twenty minutes. Another system supports the idea of the self-contained classroom in which the classroom teacher is responsible for all subjects. The optimum is that children experience music throughout the day every day.

Many classroom teachers have a fine musical background and enthusiastically share music with their children, whether they are totally responsible for the program or share it with a music specialist. But what about the teacher who is terrified by the thought of having to teach music and says. "I can't sing"? Somewhere in his early experiences with music, he developed a negative attitude. Perhaps it emerged in a classroom, in a home situation, or in a college music course. As Mager says, "Things surrounded by unpleasantness are seldom surrounded by people" (Mager, p. v).

The beauty of young children is their willingness to love, to give, and to share. The teacher who says to her children, "Who knows a song that we can all sing together?" and follows it by saying, "I need some help because I never learned to sing," will perhaps be a little surprised that the children will take this in their stride, not the least upset; immediately some will say, "I know a song," while others will spontaneously begin singing a favorite song.

A teacher who can chant, find a beginning pitch on a xylophone or an autoharp, or is willing to use singing records can help children learn to sing, although singing is only one small part of the child's musical development. A teacher who can share poetry, the beautiful sound of language, new sound sources, and fine recordings with his children; who encourages sensitive expressive movement and improvisation with instruments, body, and voice; but most important, who helps children discover how "to *play* with music" will help children become musical.

A teacher expends a tremendous amount of energy helping children develop self-worth, but what about his own self-concept? Jersild (1952) uses the term *self-understanding*. When the teacher begins to realize how many children he will shepherd through each year of his teaching career, and if he is convinced the young child's music experiences will influence his total musical development, than he can do nothing other than say, "I don't know if I can, but I will try."

References

Adkins, D.C., and Greenberg, M. *Music for Preschool Accompanied by Songbook.* (OEO Final Rep. No. 9929) ED060948. Washington, D.C.: U.S. Government Printing Office, 1971.

Alford, D. "Emergence and Development of Music Responses in Preschool Twins and Singletons. A Comparative Study." Ph.D. dissertation, Florida State University. Ann Arbor, Mich.: University Microfilms, No. 66–5439, 1966.

Andress, B.L.; Heinmann, H.; Rinehart; C.A.; and Talbert, E.G. *Music in Early Childhood.* Washington: Music Educators' National Conference, 1973.

Andrews, F.M., and Deihl, N.C. "Development of a Technique for Identifying Elementary School Children Musical Concepts." *Council for Research in Music Education* 13(1968): 1–7.

Apel, W. *Harvard Dictionary of Music.* Cambridge: Harvard University Press, 1964.

Bailey, E. *Discovering Music with Children.* London: Methuen & Co., 1958.

Baldwin, B.T., and Stecher, L.I. *The Psychology of the Preschool Child.* New York: Appleton-Century-Crofts, 1925.

Bentley, A. "Measurement and Development of Musical Abilities." *Journal of Research in Music Education* 17(1969):41–46.

Biasini, A.; Thomas, R.; and Pogonowski, L. *MMCP Interaction Early Childhood Music Curriculum*. Bardonia, N.Y.: Media Materials, Inc. No date.

Bloom, K. "Development of Arts and Humanities Program." In *Toward an Aesthetic Education*. Washington: Music Educators National Conference, 1971.

Blyer, D. "The Song Choices of Children in the Elementary Grades." *Journal of Research in Music Education* 8(1960):9–15.

Boardman, E. "An Investigation of the Effect of Preschool Training on the Development of Vocal Accuracy in Young Children." Doctoral dissertation, University of Illinois. Ann Arbor, Mich.: University Microfilms, No. 64–8354, 1964.

Broudy, H.S. "The Case of Aesthetic Education." In *Documentary Report of the Tanglewood Symposium*, edited by R.A. Choate. Washington, D.C.: Music Educators National Conference, 1968.

Choksy, L. *The Kodaly Method*. Englewood Cliffs, N.J.: Prentice-Hall, 1974.

Christiansen, H. "Bodily Rhythmic Movements of Young Children in Relation to Rhythm in Music." No. 736. New York: Teachers College Press, 1938.

Cole, N.R. *The Arts in the Classroom*. New York: The John Day Co., 1940.

Coleman, S.N. *Creative Music in the Home*. New York: The John Day Co., 1939.

Contemporary Music Project. *Experiments in Musical Creativity*. Washington, D.C.: Music Educators National Conference, 1966.

de Yarman, R.M. "An Experimental Analysis of the Development of Rhythmic and Tonal Capabilities of Kindergarten and First-Grade Children." Reviewed by Robert E. Nye, *Council for Research in Music Education* 29(1972):28–32.

Drexler, E.N. "A Study of the Development of the Ability to Carry a Melody at the Preschool Level." *Child Development* 9(1938):319–22.

Driver, A. *Music and Movement*. New York: Oxford University Press, 1947.

Duell, O.K., and Anderson, R.C. "Pitch Discrimination among Primary School Children." *Journal of Educational Psychology* 58(1967):315–18.

Dykema, P.W., and Cundiff, H.M. *School Music Handbook*. Evanston: Summy-Birchard Co., 1955.

Edwards, L. "Hungary! Musical Powerline to the Young, the Great Animating Stream of Music." *Music Educators Journal*, 57(6), 38–40.

Elliot, R. *Teaching Music*. Columbus, O.: Charles E. Merrill Publishing Co., 1960.

Flagg, M. "Music in Early Childhood Ages Two to Six." In *Music Education Source Book*, edited by H.N. Morgan. Chicago: Music Educators National Conference, 1947.

Forgus, R.H. *Perception*. New York: McGraw-Hill, 1966.

Fullard, W.G. "Operant Training of Aural Musical Discriminations with Preschool Children." *Journal of Research in Music Education* 15(1967):201–9.

Frazen, B. "It Is Research?" *Journal of Research in Music Education* 17(1969):13–15.

Gardner, H. "Children's Duplication of Rhythmic Patterns." *Journal of Research in Music Education* 19(1971):355–60.

Gould, A.O. "Developing Specialized Programs for Singing in the Elementary School." *Council for Research in Music Education* 17(1969):9–22.

Gould, O. *Developing Specialized Programs for Singing in the Elementary School*. (OEHEW Final Rep. No. 5-0241) Washington, D.C.: U.S. Government Printing Office, 1961.

Groves, W.C. "Rhythmic Training and Its Relationship to the Synchronization of Motor-Rhythmic Responses." *Journal of Research in Music Education* 17(1969):408–15.

Hair, H. "The Effect of Training on the Harmonic Discrimination of First-Grade Children." *Journal of Research in Music Education* 21(1073):85–90.

Hartsell, O.M. *Teaching Music in the Elementary School Opinion and Comment.* Washington, D.C.: Association for Supervision and Curriculum Development, NEA, 1963.

Hattwick, M.S. "The Role of Pitch Range." *Child Development* 4(1933):281–91.

Heilein, C.P. "A New Method of Studying the Rhythmic Responses of Children Together with an Evaluation of the Method of Simple Observation." *Pedagogical Seminary and Journal of Genetic Psychology* 36(1929):205–28.

Hissem, I. "A New Approach to Music for Young Children." *Child Development* 4(1933): 308–17.

Hitchcock, A. *The Value of Terminology in Children's Descriptions of Changes in Pitch Direction.* Master's thesis, University of Minnesota, 1942.

Hulson, E.L. "Tempo in Rhythm for Young Children." *Childhood Education* 6(1929):78–80.

Jeffrey, W.E. "Variables in Early Discrimination Learning: II. Mode of Response and Stimulus Difference in the Discrimination of Tonal Frequencies." *Child Development* 29(1956): 531–38.

Jersild, A.T. *In Search of Self.* New York: Teachers College Press, 1952.

Jersild, A.T., and Bienstock, S.F. "Development of Rhythm in Young Children." *Child Development Monographs* No. 22. New York: Teachers College Press, 1935.

———. "The Influence of Training on the Vocal Ability of Three-Year-Old Children." *Child Development* 2(1931):272–91.

———. "A Study of Children's Ability to Sing." *Journal of Educational Psychology* 25(1934): 481–503.

Johnson, H.M. *School Begins at Two.* New York: New Republic, 1936.

Kendall, J.D. *The Suzuki Violin Method in American Music Education. What the American Music Educator Should Know about Shinichi Suzuki.* Washington, D.C.: Music Educators National Conference, 1973.

Kirkpatrick, W.C. "Relationships between the Singing Ability of Prekindergarten Children and the Home Musical Environment." Doctoral dissertation, University of Southern California, 1961.

Klemish, J. "A Comparative Study of Two Methods of Teaching Music Reading to First-Grade Children." *Journal of Research in Music Education* 18(1970):355–59.

———. "A Review of Recent Research in Elementary Music Education." *Council for Research in Music Education* 34(1973):23–40.

Knieter, G.L. "The Nature of Aesthetic Education." In *Toward an Aesthetic Education.* Washington, D.C.: Music Educators National Conference, 1971.

Kokas, K. "Kodaly's Concept of Music Education." *Council for Research in Music Education* 22(1970):48–56.

Krestaff, A.D. "The Growth of Musical Awareness in Children." *Council for Research in Music Education* 1(1963):4–10.

Kwalwasser, J. "What Can Children Teach Us about Teaching Children?" *Music Educators Journal* 21(1934):21, 23–24.

Kyme, G. "The Appropriateness of Young Audience Music Program for Primary Grade Children." *Journal of Research in Music Education* 19(1971):366–72.

Landis, B., and Carder, P. *The Eclectic Curriculum in American Music Education: Contributions of Dalcroze, Kodaly, and Orff.* Washington, D.C.: Music Educators National Conference, 1972.

McCall, A. *Timothy's Tunes.* Boston: Boston Music, 1944.

Mager, R.F. *Developing Attitude towards Learning.* Palo Alto: Fearon Publishers, 1968.

Mankin, L. "Are We Starting Too Late?" *Music Educators Journal* 55(1969):36–40.

Monroe, W.S. "Tone Perception and Music Interest of Young Children." *Pedagogical Seminary and Journal of Genetic Psychology* 10(1903):144–146.

Moorhead, G.E., and Pond, D. *Music of Young Children I. Chant.* Santa Barbara, Calif.: Pillsbury Foundation Studies, 1941.

———. *Music of Young Children II. General Observations.* Santa Barbara, Calif.: Pillsbury Foundation Studies, 1942.

———. *Music of Young Children III. Musical Notation.* Santa Barbara, Calif.: Pillsbury Foundation Studies, 1944.

Moorhead, G.E.; Sandvik, F.; and Wight, D. *Music of Young Children IV. Free Use of Instruments for Music Growth.* Santa Barbara, Calif.: Pillsbury Foundation Studies, 1951.

Nelson, M.J., and Tipton, G. *Music in Early Childhood.* New York: Silver Burdett Co., 1952.

Orff, C. "The Schulwerk. Its Origin and Aims." Translated by A. Walter. *Music Educators Journal* 49(1963):69, 70, 72, 74.

Petzold, R. "Auditory Perception by Children." *Journal of Research in Music Education* 17(1969):82–87.

———. "The Development of Auditory Perception of Musical Sounds by Children in the First Six Grades." *Journal of Research in Music Education* 2 (1963):21–54.

Pflederer, M. "The Responses of Children to Musical Tasks of Conservation." *Journal of Music Education* 12(1964):251–68.

Pflederer, M., and Sechrest, L. "Conservation Type Responses of Children to Musical Stimuli." *Council of Research in Music Education* 13(1968):19–36.

Pitts, L.B. "Music Comes Alive." In *Music Education Source Book Number Two,* edited by H.N. Morgan. Washington, D.C.: Music Educators National Conference, 1955.

Raley, A.H. "Developing Musical Concepts in the Primary Grades." Doctoral dissertation, Columbia University. Ann Arbor, Mich.: University Microfilms, No, 67–9453, 1969.

Suzuki, S. "The 'Mother Tongue Method' of Education and the Law of Ability." Paper presented at a meeting of the Japan Institute of Educational Psychology, October 1973. Available at the MENC Historical Center, University of Maryland, College Park, Md.

Schultz, S.W. "A Study of Children's Ability to Respond to Elements of Music." Doctoral dissertation, Northwestern University. Ann Arbor, Mich.: University Microfilms, No. 70–154, 1969.

Seashore, C.E. "Motor Ability, Reaction Time, Rhythm, and Time Sense." *University of Iowa Studies in Psychology* 2(1899):64–84.

Sheehy, E.D. *There's Music in Children.* New York: Henry Holt, 1946.

Shelley, S.J. "Developing Sensory Perception in 3, 4, and 5 Year Olds." Paper presented at the meeting of the Music Educators National Conference, Washington, January, 1969.

Shelton, J.S. "The Influence of Home Musical Environment upon Musical Response of First-Grade Children." Doctoral dissertation, George Peabody College for Teachers. Ann Arbor, Mich.: University Microfilms, No. 66–4419, 1965.

Sievers, C.H. "A Study of Rhythmic Performance with Special Consideration of the Factors Involved in the Formation of a Scale for Measuring Rhythmic Ability." In *Measurement of Musical Development, University of Iowa Studies in Child Welfare,* edited by G.D. Stoddard. 7(1932):108–72.

Smith, F.O. "The Effect of Training in Pitch Discrimination." *Psychological Monograph* 16 (1914):67–103.

Smith, R.B. "The Effect of Group Nursery School Music Training on Later Achievement and Interest in Music: A Ten-Year Progress Report." Paper presented at the meeting of the Music Educators National Conference. Seattle, March, 1968.

———. "The Effect of Group Vocal Training on the Singing Ability of Nursery School Children." *Journal of Research in Music Education* 11(1963):137–41.

Stene, E.J. "There Are No Monotones." *Music Educators Journal* 55(1969):46–49, 117–21.

Taubmann, H. *How to Bring Up Your Child to Enjoy Music.* New York: Hanover House, 1958.

Thomas, R.B. *Manhattanville Music Curriculum Program* (OEHEW Final Rep. No. 6–1999) ED045865. Washington, D.C.: U.S. Government Printing Office, 1970.

Thorn, A. *Music for Young Children.* New York: Charles Scribner's Sons, 1929.

Updegraph, R.; Heiliger, L.; and Learned, J. "The Effect of Training upon the Singing Ability and Musical Interest of Three-, Four-, and Five-Year-Old Children." *University of Iowa Studies in Child Welfare* 14(1938):83–131.

Vance, T.F., and Grandprey, M.B. "Objective Methods of Ranking Nursery School Children on Certain Aspects of Musical Capacity." *Journal of Educational Psychology* 22(1931): 577–85.

Williams, H.M. "Studies in the Rhythmic Performance of Preschool Children." In *The Measurement of Musical Development, University of Iowa Studies in Child Welfare,* edited by G.D. Stoddard. 7(1932):32–66.

———. "Studies of Vocal Control of Pitch of Preschool Children." In *The Measurement of Musical Development, University of Iowa Studies in Child Welfare,* edited by G.D. Stoddard. 7(1932):67–91.

Willour, J. "Beginning with Delight." In *The Electric Curriculum in American Music Education: Contributions of Dalcroze, Kodaly, and Orff,* edited by B. Landis and P. Carder. Washington, D.C.: Music Educators National Conference, 1972.

Wilson, D.S. "A Study of the Child's Voice from Six to Twelve." Reviewed by Bessie Swanson, *Council for Research in Music Education* 34(1973):54–60.

Wolner, M., and Pyle, W.H. "An Experiment in Individual Training of Pitch Deficient Children." *Journal of Educational Psychology* 24(1933):602–8.

Woskowiak, L.F. *Programmed Music Reading Games for First Grade Utilizing Certain Principles of Dalcroze, Kodaly, and Orff.* Paper presented at the meeting of the Music Educators National Conference. Anaheim, March, 1974.

Zimmerman, M.P. *Musical Characteristics of Children.* Washington, D.C.: Music Educators National Conference, 1971.

Zimmerman, M.P., and Sechrest, L. "Brief Focused Instruction and Musical Concepts." *Journal of Research in Music Education* 18(1970):25–36.

CHAPTER NINE

Play

Bonnie Tyler

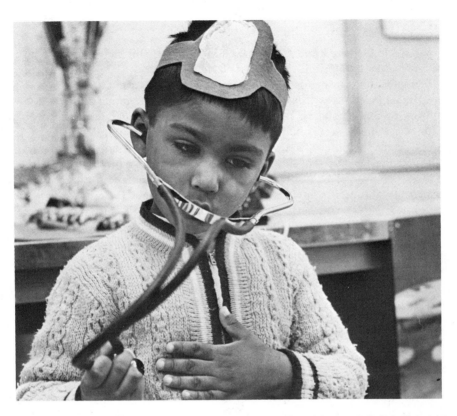

Play, like love, defies description.

Introduction

Play, like love defies description. Yet, according to the poet, man is never more human than when he plays. If this is true, it would seem imperative that we discover what play is all about and proceed to cultivate it from a very early age.

The most concise conceptualization of play in the literature related to children's play behavior identifies it as the opposite of work. In fact, it has been noted by some students of animal behavior that since animals do not work, they cannot be said to play. In expanding on this nonwork definition of play, other writers have designated its "useless, nonproductive nature" as the primary differentiating characteristic. Spencer, for example, posited a relationship between creative play and aesthetic activity, reasoning that neither is a useful activity. In contrast to this point of view, other writers have emphasized the *critical* role of play in personality development. Even among these writers, however, there is little agreement as to the function play serves. Frank attempted to establish play as a meaningful activity in its own right, stating his arguments in an article succinctly entitled "Play is Valid." Others see play as valid only when meaningful, constructive activities are incorporated into the play process. Thus, Kagan emphasizes the cognitive function of play when he suggests that "long periods of play are important between mother and child in which thought processes, no matter how primitive, are rewarded" (Kagan, p. 275).

Finally, some theorists neither deny the usefulness of a concept of play, nor do they expound on its function. Rather, they throw the concept out, noting that it is too loose to be of much use in modern psychology (Schlosberg). Or as Huizinga concludes, "The fun of playing resists all analysis and all logical interpretations" (Huizinga, p. 3).

Perhaps some resistance arises from the difficulties encountered in trying to describe and analyze play activities as being separate and apart from child behaviors. Since most behavior of children is called play, how then do we differentiate our subject matter, or for that matter, why do we feel the need to? In spite of the fact that the description of play and the analysis of its functions are difficult, it is nevertheless essential that efforts be made to describe play behavior systematically and to determine the potential role of play in the home and school in facilitating the child's development. The material to be presented in this chapter will be divided into three sections:

1. Theoretical bases for explaining play behavior
2. Literature and research findings relevant to children's play
3. Implications of this information

Theories of Play

In an early theory of play, probably the first, Schiller (1791) classified play as a form of art—a product of pure imagination. No motive other than the goal of enjoying the freedom allowed through play and through escaping reality was attributed to play activity. Nearly a century later, Spencer (1873), described play as an expression of excess energy, agreeing with Schiller that it was aimless activity. While many parents and teachers today would readily second the motion that children need to let off steam, this theory is not generally accepted as a sound theoretical base for explaining play activity.

Hall's explanation of play was derived from his initial theoretical assertion that a child passes through all the developmental stages that the human race before him has survived. Similarly, as the child's play skills develop, he experiences all the prehistoric periods man has known. Play then serves as a vehicle for the very young child to try out primitive urges; as the child matures, these urges become tamed to a state of social acceptability.

In a later, more utilitarian theory, Groos suggested that play is a preparation for work in the adult world. According to Groos, play is instinctual and, while at first awkward and undifferentiated, can be trained in the child through experience. He saw in play the exercising of specific instincts along with related motor patterns, resulting in incomplete play activity—a rehearsal that would have significance later in adult life. This idea of play as practice for later life is still seen as one of the significant functions of play activity, particularly when the role of imitation is stressed.

Buhler, like Schiller, pinpointed the importance of play in the satisfactions derived from the play itself and from the originating of the activity, rather than in the end result. In other words, even though the child frequently changes activity in mid-stream, without reaching his first goal, he is still satisfied. In Buhler's theory, *all* activities are enjoyable, in and of themselves. While quite descriptive, unfortunately this broad theory does not explain why the child plays what he does when he does; nor does it explain why nonplay activity (e.g., work) is not enjoyable in many instances.

Psychoanalytic theorists view play as an avenue through which the child can express emotions and satisfy desires that are denied in his real, everyday life. For the child, play is the vehicle for expressing his inner state, as well as the outlet for his instinctual forces. On the one hand, playing out emotional experiences helps the child assimilate disturbances, while at the same time reduces the shock of potentially traumatic experiences. Thus, unpleasant events are repeated in play because reenactment helps to reduce the negative feelings that accompanied them. In play, however, the child is the controller, rather than the victim, of the situation.

While traditional psychoanalysts view play as a way of escape into an imaginary world where the child can achieve wish fulfillment, later analysts theorize that the child is forced by the material world to see reality in play. Thus, when anxieties and hostilities become too strong, the child seeks out real people and real-life situations in an effort to regain his self-confidence. Whether the child perceives play as part of an imaginary world or as a real-life situation, the psychoanalyst believes that the child distinguishes play from reality and is able to cross over from one to the other by utilizing props from the real world to create his own world, consisting of those things most pleasurable to him.

Play therapy is one derivative of the psychoanalytic interpretation of the function of play. In a play therapy setting, the therapist provides suitable play materials and a permissive, noninterfering climate in which the child is allowed to express feelings and to release emotional energy. The rationale for this approach is that in a free-play situation, the child's fears and anxieties are minimized, allowing him to come to grips with reality on his own terms.

Another systematic, although not always consistent, theory of play is presented by Piaget. His contribution to a theory of the development of play derives from his studies of child cognitive development in which he stresses two processes: (1) assimilation in which the child interprets new experiences in familiar terms, and (2) accommodation in which the child changes his behavior to incorporate new information that experience has given him. For Piaget, play in the very young child involves only pure assimilation where a familiar play activity is repeated indefinitely. The motivation here is the satisfaction derived from the activity itself—"activity for activity's sake." Sometime during the first year of life, the child combines several play activities so that the repetition takes on variations. According to Piaget, the pleasure the child gains here comes from "ordering" the activities himself. Thus, once a child has learned to turn a button or push a toy, he will repeat the movements again and again, each time getting satisfaction from having mastered the activity and having caused it to happen. Unfortunately, Piaget's definition of play as pure assimilation confines the young child's activity to repetitious behavior and eliminates the possibility of creativity or change. Sutton-Smith feels that for Piaget play exists in childhood because the very young child cannot think; it serves, in a sense, as compensation for this inadequacy (Herron and Sutton-Smith). While Piaget does see play as serving the function of "ego continuity" for the young child, he makes it clear that this function has nothing to do with the thinking process.

Piaget describes the child's play during the twelve- to eighteen-month period as involving active, systematic exploration; after this period, symbolic play begins. Symbolic play parallels the development of representational thinking where several things happen—substitute behaviors occur so that one object can be substituted for another (e.g., a handful of dirt is "as if" it were mashed potatoes); an image takes the place of an absent object; and symbols or signs (e.g., words) are incorporated in the child's thinking to stand for objects. Symbolic and make-believe play allow for practicing the images and symbols that the child has accumulated and help him express the feelings that have accompanied his experiences. Imitative play, which occurs primarily as role playing or reenacting familiar events, represents the child's efforts to remember the past. The very young child often imitates people in his environment, repeating their facial gestures, noises, etc. After the age of two, however, imitative behavior occurs in the absence of a model or familiar stimulus. According to Piaget, all of this symbolic play, both imaginative and imitative, is egocentric, distorting reality in the direction of meeting the child's needs. At the same time, make-believe play, utilizing familiar objects and situations, provides opportunities for the child to sort out and organize his feelings about people and his impressions of the world at a time when abstract symbols are not yet available.

In contrast to the Piagetian idea of egocentrism in the play of the young child, some writers feel that imitative play is an active effort on the child's part to become a part of the adult world. Thus, instead of manipulating reality to match his ego and meet his own unique needs, as Piaget theorizes, the child is making every effort to conform to his memory of a past situation and to duplicate the role played by the adult, including the feelings that accompany the actions.

From the ages two to four, Piaget sees the child continuing in symbolic or make-believe play; however, now the play is closely linked to intellectual growth. Since language is developing during this period, symbolic play flourishes. It should be noted that all research findings do not support Piaget's view that language and symbolic play develop in a parallel fashion. Clearly, some children who have developed language skills at this age have not developed the ability for symbolic play. Evidently something more than a language factor is involved in mastering the complex of skills that make up symbolic play.

In the period between four and seven years, symbolic play comes closer to reality, according to Piaget. The child imitates actual experiences more probably because of his becoming more social and sharing more experiences with others. Following this period, play becomes more elaborate and organized. Games with rules take the place of individual make-believe play, so that new elements (e.g., cooperation, logic as base of decisions, collective discipline, and codes of honor) enter into play activity. Again, Piaget sees this stage of play activity tied closely to the level of intellectual development at this age.

In summarizing Piaget's attitude toward play, it seems clear that he does not see it as a vital concept in human development. He gives only minimal attention to its function in childhood and presents conflicting statements regarding the role of play in later life, in one instance suggesting that it serves no critical function in adulthood and consequently drops out completely. While the timetable he defines for play development is somewhat similar to his schedule for intellectual development, he does not explain the relation between the two. And although he defines play as a function of cognition and as an integral part of the development of intelligence, he does not explain what that function is or how the two are integrated.

Like Piaget, Erikson sees play as developmental, following a clear sequence that roughly parallels Piaget's stages. At first, play centers on body sensations, corresponding to Piaget's sensorimotor stage. In the second stage, play involves mastering a small world of objects. Piaget labels this symbolic play. Erikson's third stage, sharing with others, parallels Piaget's rule games. More importantly, Erikson goes beyond the sequential development of play to an emphasis on its function in coordinating the growth processes in the child—self, body, and social; play allows for "hallucinating" mastery, while at the same time provides a situation for practicing and coping. Typically, the child uses play to reenact difficult experiences, helping him to regain lost confidence and to reinstate feelings of mastery or achieve higher levels of mastery.

As for the learning theorists' explanation of play, it is assumed that most writers in this camp share Schlosberg's notion that play can be explained by the same principles of learning that are applicable to other categories of behavior. Thus, the child "generalizes" from one play stimulus to similar stimuli, his "threshold" for play activity varies, "selective reinforcement" shapes play behavior, and so on. While these "laws" of learning help to account for the whys and wherefores of repetitive play activity, there are other more complex aspects of play behavior that the learning theorist attempts to explain. For example, how does one account for play occurring when there is no apparent reinforcement for the child? Harlow et al. explain this unrewarded "inquisitive" behavior in animals by invoking an exploratory drive, while Berlyne describes a concept of novelty to explain the satisfaction children derive from exploratory play behavior. A similar concept is that of the need for mastery, discussed by Murphy et al. and used to explain the motivation underlying such play activities as a child engaging in solitary play for long periods of time. In these instances, striving for the goal of mastery or anticipating the surprise of novelty provide adequate internal motivation for maintaining play behaviors. However, once the novelty has worn off, and the task is mastered, these activities become less attractive.

Social learning theorists have given little attention to play and its role in the child's development. This is especially surprising in the case of Bandura and Walters, who emphasize the importance of the role of imitation in the acquisition of behavior, yet ignore its role in the symbolic play of the child.

In general, it would seem that developmental theories have tended to attach minimal importance to the role of play. However, more recently the function of play has been assigned greater significance, particularly in the development of the very young child.

Review of the Literature

In surveying the literature on young children's play activity, one is struck by the amount of empirical material relevant to this area produced in the twenties and thirties. In fact, some writers of that era even ventured into discussions of the play activities of adults! One of the most interesting early empirical studies of play behavior was published in 1905 by Chase and entitled "Street Games of New York

City." Realizing that questionnaires often produce inaccurate data, this researcher chose to walk the streets of the tenements for two years and record the games played, the number of children playing, and the level of interest shown. Strangely enough, as Chase had expected, none of the ten most popular games being played on the streets appeared on the lists made by these children of their favorite outdoor games.

Studies similar to Stone's are included in three reviews of play literature published prior to 1941 by Marshall, Hurlock, and Britt and Janus. The studies included in these reviews will not be discussed here. To this writer's knowledge, there are no reviews of current play literature available at present, although two recent books on play have extensive bibliographies. These two outstanding books are *Child's Play* by Herron and Sutton-Smith and *The Psychology of Play* by Millar. The former is a compilation of readings covering a period of seventy years, while Millar's book represents her current thinking, which is both scholarly and practical, on the meaning of play.

The literature reviewed here will be divided into sections according to specific areas being investigated. These include the following:

1. The function of play
2. The relation of play to cognitive development
3. Creativity and play
4. Cross-cultural differences in play behavior
5. Stages of play development
6. The facilitation of play behavior

The Function of Play

Here again, we run into the perennial conflict over whether or not play should serve a purpose. Some writers stoutly maintain that once play leaves the category of useless behavior and becomes purposive and productive, it is no longer play. However, when one examines the "play for play's sake" point of view, the difficulty encountered in describing play without assigning some attributes to it becomes apparent. Consequently, the tendency has been to define the function of play as providing an "assist" in areas such as cognitive, emotional, and social development as well as an opportunity for the child to experience "mastery"—all of this under the guise of pleasure or "fun." Sutton-Smith maintains that this conceptualization is an attempt to justify play in terms of a "payoff" and is no longer a viable approach. Rather, he feels the more recent trend is toward dealing with the intrinsic function of play (i.e., the meaning of play as found in the satisfaction a child feels from spontaneously and expressively responding to his own experience).

Other writers feel that the role play serves in socializing the child is its major function. Murphy et al. attribute much of a child's motivation toward an activity to the excitement or fun that it provides. They suggest that pleasurable play leads to more pleasurable play, thus providing a source of alternative activities when one choice is thwarted. DesLauriers and Carson agree that the child must have pleasurable satisfaction if he is to be adequately socialized, emphasizing the critical nature of human contact for providing essential sensory and emotional stimulation. Approaching this "growth through pleasure" thesis from the opposite direction, there are a significant number of studies that support a relationship between the absence of pleasure and the failure to develop normally (Skeels; White, Castle, and Held; Rheingold; Brodbeck and Irwin). Clearly a playful or pleasurable climate facilitates growth, while its absence has the opposite effect on the child.

It has been suggested that the ease with which a child separates from his mother in early childhood is to a large extent dependent upon how playful their interactions have been; if he has found pleasure in his relationship with her, he will expect to find pleasure in others (Mahler; Pine and Furer). Autistic children who have failed to establish a positive, pleasurable relationship with their parents are described as reacting to treatment that is characterized as playful, exciting, and fun. The crucial element for achieving a response in these children seems to be the creation of a pleasant situation for them (DesLauriers and Carlson).

As for the school's role in socializing the child through play, Frank feels that children today are exploited through pressure for academic achievement and cognitive learning; he feels that schools ignore the need for skills in "living" and "social life." He feels these latter skills are learned through activities such as play; this feeling is shared by Rosecrans and Branch who see play as an opportunity for the child to begin his adaptation to the outside world as well as his preparation for an adult role. Empirical evidence for the socializing function of play is provided by Redl's study, which shows improvement in social behavior of children as a result of their playing games that demand the exercise of self-control. Similarly, Hartley et al. studied interpersonal relations of children within an operating school program by making intensive diary recordings of their play activity. These researchers were interested not only in how play facilitates socialization in the child, but more specifically, the role of play in enabling the child to "translate impulses, feelings, and fantasies into action—to play out some of his problems" (Hartley et al., p. 4). In addition, they attempted to define the contribution of play to healthy personality development of young children. Unfortunately, only the first chapter of this book deals with interpersonal relations and the mental health aspects of play. The remaining chapters present detailed discussions of specific areas of play: dramatic play, block play, water play, clay, graphics, finger painting, music, and movement.

Has there been significant variation in the degree of sociability in children's play over time? Replicating a study of first-grade play norms completed in the late 1920s, Barnes found that preschool children entering first grade today are less socially oriented in play activities than were children of the same age forty years ago. He suggests as possible explanations the greater exposure to mass media and the smaller family size. Whatever the explanation, it is clear that one must look beyond maturational factors for an understanding of children's play patterns.

Millar, discussing the function of play, notes that some writers define play as an attitude, rather than an activity, that describes the mood of the child. The implication is that the mood will characteristically be a positive one since play is pleasurable. While play may describe mood, the notion that it is typically positive breaks down when one observes the play activity of children for even a short time, during which a child may be serious, furious, absorbed, or sad as he proceeds in his play activity. Millar maintains that play is too complex to be assigned a single function. Rather, she feels that it is essential to observe the whole gamut of play behaviors and systematically study the functions of both the physiological and psychological aspects. She describes its complexity by stating, "Play is paradoxical behavior. Exploring what is familiar, practicing what has already been mastered, friendly aggression, sex without coition, excitement about nothing, social behavior not defined by a specific common activity or by social structure, pretence not intended to deceive: this is play" (Millar, pp. 255–56).

In an effort to avoid the pressures on children for early rote learning, a group of preschool teachers designed a "mini-curriculum plan" to foster cognitive learning within the spontaneous play of young children (Anker et al.). Their approach is based on the rationale that the function of play is to provide a vehicle for the child to gain self-confidence and competence for learning. Thus, sorting and number concepts are learned effectively in the housework corner or in the block area. The design of their mini-curriculum and examples of how it operates are described in the article, "Teaching Children as They Play" (Anker et al.).

Socialization of children into sex roles is at present a popular area for research, in part due to the increased activity of the women's liberation movement. While these studies will not be reviewed here, it should be noted that the consensus of the findings in this area is that the type of play activities reinforced for the child is clearly sex linked and relates to the development of masculinity and femininity in children.

The Relation of Play to Cognitive Development

There is a paradox implied in the title of Evelyn Sharp's book, *Thinking Is Child's Play*. The usual drudgery characteristic of thinking does not allow it to be a part of play in any way; yet the play of children can, and often does, create thoughtful responses. In this book, Sharp describes games for preschoolers that are derived from Piaget's description of cognitive processes and require logical reasoning for a solution. Sharp's rationale is that play provides the optimal arena for the child's thinking processes to operate because it involves manipulating physical objects. She feels that experiences with real objects are better than those with pictures or words for developing rational thinking.

The manipulation of physical objects was also involved in a study by Dansky and Silverman. They predicted that preschool children who were permitted to play freely with four types of objects would subsequently score higher on a test involving alternate uses of those objects than children who were not given this opportunity. Children in the play group did name significantly more nonstandard uses than children who previously used the objects in an imitative context or than children who had not seen the objects. The authors concluded that play activity can facilitate associative fluency.

Some writers feel that the concept of novelty plays a crucial role in cognitive growth (Kagan et al.; Elkind; Hunt). They believe there is an optimal level of incongruity between incoming information and information already assimilated by the child. This same pattern would be true for play with an optimal level of familiarity between incoming play stimuli and already assimilated stimuli. Boredom results from too little incongruity or too much familiarity and stress from too much incongruity. The optimal amount of incongruity or familiarity produces motivation to learn or play. The concept of novelty is also relevant to free-play activity in that the child can seek his own level, trying out new behaviors or new combinations of behaviors that are neither too stressful nor too tedious, often through symbolic or imaginative play.

Keister is strongly in favor of letting very young children function on their own as they play. She feels that the most significant learning is accomplished when children are left alone in a stimulating environment. Cognitive emphasis (e.g., a curriculum) introduces too much pressure and complexity in the child's life. The babies and toddlers she works with are free to satisfy their natural curiosity; the staff is available to talk, show, explain, read, or respond in some way when they are sought out.

A similar viewpoint is expressed in Murphy's chapter in *Play and Development* (Piers). Murphy distinguishes between the passivity of watching IV and the physical activity of play where the child is free "to impose something, some structure, some pattern, on the environment" (Piers, p. 121). While these patterns are individually determined by the wishes, worries, and angers of the child, they also reveal "puzzlements, questions, and a need to clarify experience, to make a cognitive map, or to improve on nature" (Piers, p. 121). In other words, like Keister, Murphy feels that cognitive development is a significant part of spontaneous play.

There are further empirical data on the outcomes of allowing freedom in the play situation. Suzuki, reporting on the effectiveness of guidance of play for preschool children in Japan, found that children who played without instruction were superior in creativity to children who played with instruction. On the other hand, when preschoolers in an American day-care setting were divided into two activity schedules, required versus optional activities, their participation continued as high when they were required to follow a schedule of activities in sequence as when they were free to choose activities (Doke and Risley). The authors noted that a child was never forced to wait before moving on to the next activity and there was always an abundance of materials in each required activity (a significant factor in itself). When these conditions were met, high levels of participation continued without allowing freedom of choice.

Certainly not all teachers feel that free play is the optimal play condition for children. Some maintain that aimless play should be replaced with educational play. Both Painter and Haggitt feel that a child's education should begin with directed play long before the preschool years. Painter tested a program of daily activities for infants and young children that she feels parents should start by the time the child is four or five months old. Her play schedule, which begins with motor and sensory stimulation, is to be presented to the child in the context of serious but happy educational play. Haggitt feels that the goals of preschool teaching should be to develop the personality of the child, including learning to express feelings, to try out social relationships, to utilize learning skills, and to expand the child's language.

If play behavior is closely related to the child's cognitive development, it might follow that the level of play could be used as an indicator of the level of cognitive skill. Maw and Maw found that play behavior in their subjects correlated highly with their information seeking in general. Similarly, in a study of ghetto four year olds, the correlations between psychiatrists' competence judgments, teachers' ratings, and psychological test scores indicated a consistency in a child's functioning from these varied perspectives (Borowitz, Hirsch, and Costello). The authors suggest that a child's actual effectiveness and feelings about his competence can be generalized to all areas, including play.

Courtney sees play as involving cognitive tasks such as making decisions and choices. He feels these activities provide valuable practice for the child in becoming self-directed and allow him to function later in life without being dependent on external reinforcements. For Vigotsky, the cognitive function of play is primarily the use of symbolic activity that carries the child back and forth from imaginative situations to real ones through the reproduction of real meanings and rules in the context of play.

The make-believe or "as if" aspect of play involves, in cognitive terms, representational or symbolic thinking. If a child has the ability to adopt a representational set in play—to pretend "as if" things are the way he wants them to be—it seems feasible to infer that he will think representationally at the concept level. Learning theorists, however, do not agree on accepting such a conclusion.

Creativity and Play

Several investigators have studied ability in children and related it to playfulness. In an article by Sutton-Smith in the book *Child's Play,* the author explores the hypothesis that play is related to cognitive variation seeking (i.e., creativity) (Herron and Sutton-Smith). More specifically, he suggests that play activity broadens a child's experiences and thus increases the number of responses available to him. Jersild reports that the child's ability to imagine or create appears at least as early as his ability to talk; some children show skill in imagining before they are able to talk, according to Jersild. While actual experiences are the source of much imaginative play, toward the end of the preschool period and during the primary school years, imaginative activity consists primarily of private fantasies and daydreams.

Smilansky challenges Jersild's conclusion that imaginative play is available to all children, regardless of age. Her data, gathered on immigrant groups in Israel, indicate that these children do not engage extensively in imaginative play—in fact, many of them not at all. Smilansky's data will be presented in more detail in the discussion on cross-cultural differences in play.

Lieberman empirically supported a positive relationship between creativity and play activity with kindergarten subjects. Children in his group who were rated as the most playful also showed more creative skill, indicated by their abilities on tasks such as suggesting novel ideas for the use of familiar toys. In a later study, in which he attempted to conceptualize a quality of play, Lieberman found that through a factor analysis of data on children, a single factor of playfulness did emerge.

One form of creative play in childhood is the imaginary companion. While there has been little systematic research on this phenomenon, one recent study attempts to determine the factors associated with this behavior in the preschool child (Manosevitz, Prentice and Wilson). While familial and individual factors were investigated, the primary concern was with data related to play activities. The findings indicated that significantly more of the children who had imaginary companions were described as self-initiating in their play at home. In addition, play in the homes of these children was described as quiet for fewer of them than for children without an imaginary companion. The authors suggest that the child who has an imaginary companion may be more able to involve himself in play activities; this in turn may be due to greater creative abilities. It might be noted that, as reported by their parents, there were no differences between the two groups in how well the children got along with other children. Also, children who had imaginary companions took part in significantly more different activities with family members than did children with no imaginary companions.

Cross-cultural Differences in Play Behavior

Findings of the majority of studies investigating cross-cultural variations in play indicate clear-cut differences in children's play activity from one culture to another as well as differences from one social level to another within a culture. The most extensive research has been done by Smilansky and by Eifermann, studying different groups in Israel. Smilansky worked with school children from socioculturally underprivileged levels made up primarily of immigrant groups from the Middle East and North Africa. Many of these children had been unable to meet the standards demanded by the Israeli schools and consequently were failing scholastically. As a result, they tended to lose their initiative and concentration and develop a negative attitude toward school. Experimental programs were instituted at the kindergarten level in an effort to develop the abilities of these children. Smilansky's involvement was in the area of sociodramatic play. The rationale behind the use of this technique was that it helped a child see meaningful relationships among his learnings and experiences, which to this point lacked continuity (i.e., The thinking of these children tended to be either repetitious or completely disconnected). Through dramatic imaginative play, in an almost lifelike situation, it was felt that the child could talk about his experiences, act out his feelings, and interact with peers in the kind of play situation that Smilansky had previously found enjoyable for most children. She also included in her study a group of nondisadvantaged children.

As this study progressed, Smilansky became aware that most of her subjects had had no experience with imaginative play during their preschool years. Rather, the sequence of play development for them included motor play that was followed by imitative play and rule games, with no imaginative play interspersed, as is the more common pattern. Smilansky felt that this lack accounted for the inability of the disadvantaged children to participate in sociodramatic play. Her investigation then changed from using sociodramatic play as a means of promoting intellectual development to observing the differences between the two groups and to determining how to develop play abilities in the underprivileged group. Having redefined her problem, Smilansky devoted the remainder of her book to analyzing in detail the differences in play behavior between the two groups of children and to describing sociodramatic play and its function. In addition, she discussed theoretical explanations for these differences and described her program for training the culturally deprived children to participate in sociodramatic play. In the final chapter, Smilansky reports the results of this training.

Eifermann, also working in Israel with preschool and primary school children used only a socioeconomic criterion to categorize the children as either disadvantaged (lower class) or nondisadvantaged (upper class). She found that disadvantaged children ages six to eight in the low school (the Israeli version of Head Start) do develop the ability to participate in symbolic play and take part in such play more often than their nondisadvantaged peers. She interpreted these data to mean that disadvantaged children reach the peak of symbolic activity at a later age than other children; her views are in contrast to Smilansky's interpretation that maintained that symbolic play did not occur at all, or if so, only minimally, in disadvantaged children. The explanation of later development of symbolic play activity has been suggested to account for the absence of imaginative play that has been observed to some extent in children in Head Start programs in the United States. With these children, the predominant play activities have been sensorimotor and kinetic.

A thorough analysis of children's behaviors and their parents from disorganized, lower-class families is presented in the book, *The Drifters* (Pavenstedt). While these authors describe extensive use of imitative behavior in these children (e.g., gestures, facial expressions, activities, choices), they point out that there is almost a complete absence of imagination in the children's behavior. "Imitation has a 'carbon copy,' literal quality in that what is imitated most readily are the concrete features of a person or situation" (Pavenstedt, p. 129). In other words, this imitative behavior is restricted to observable, external characteristics of another person without perceiving the meaning or sharing the feelings of the outward expression. Further observations reveal that identification develops from an aggressive tie to parents, so in play the children act out the parents' aggression that they have had to experience passively. "In play they assume adult roles in which they yell, curse, and punish . . . they tend to recreate in nursery school the aggressive relationship they have known at home. Thus, there is little comforting, protecting, or tenderness in their caretaking play with dolls" (Pavenstedt, p. 136). The severe limitations in the imaginative play of these children is demonstrated by the repetitive nature of their aggressive play and its stereotyped quality.

As for the effect of child-rearing practices on play activity, Ghahramani, in a study of children and their parents in southern Iran, reports a complete absence of play between parents and children, with the children turning to peers for play activity. The author does not discuss the consequences of the lack of adult-child play activity. In contrast to the Iranian pattern, Butler describes a pattern in the Eskimo culture of complete indulgence of Eskimo children by adults, who maintain a very gentle and permissive attitude toward all children. There is much playfulness between parents and children, and what are usually considered punishable "crimes" in the American culture are laughed at by Eskimo parents who see them as natural and expected childhood behaviors. Whiting conducted an extensive study of child-rearing patterns in six societies. Her data included descriptions of the differences in play activities and toys available to the children in these widely scattered communities. One significant finding of this study was the variation among cultures in the amount of fantasy and imitative play in children; the variation ranged from complete absence in some societies to very complex and varied symbolic play in others.

Other cross-cultural comparisons reveal additional differences in play-related behaviors. Working with boys in a preschool setting, Kniveton and Pike observed that middle-class boys played with a greater number of toys than lower-class boys. In addition, constructiveness of play seemed to be a function of the interaction of social class level, intelligence, and time in the play situation; this last factor becomes relevant as constructiveness decreased with time, probably due to boredom. Baughman and Dahlstrom concluded from a study of black families that when parents show no playfulness with their children and when pleasure is not a part of their daily lives, their children are not as well socialized as other children.

In comparing play responses of children in Asia and North America, Murphy concluded that children in both cultures develop the capacity to play out their own time-space pattern (i.e., They reenact familiar experiences, such as family situations) (Piers). While extremely deprived children from disorganized homes are also active at repeating familiar household tasks in a play setting, they do not manipulate vocabulary, show curiosity, or plan and carry out the plan. They do enjoy sensory play, which involves manipulating material (e.g., water, clay); and after becoming familiar with a setting such as a preschool, they will try out new play behaviors and put together combinations of old activities.

The Carmichaels observed extreme leniency in the behavior of teachers in Japanese kindergartens where the children responded very spontaneously in their play. In addition, these researchers may have discovered one cross-cultural game consistency; they came across kindergartners in Japan who enthusiastically played the rock-scissors-paper game!

In spite of some differences in interpretation of cross-cultural data regarding imaginary play (cf. Smilansky and Eifermann), it seems clear that play behaviors vary cross-culturally and that the type of play activity a child engages in is to a large extent a function of his cultural background. Agreeing with this conclusion, El'Konin gives particular emphasis to the role of the adult culture as does Marshall, who feels that play behavior varies according to the parental reinforcements received by the child. As Millar sums it up, the differences in the variety and intensity of play activities in different countries is mainly a function of "the diversity and richness of the cultural lives of the adults in the different societies" (Millar, p. 248).

Stages of Play Development

Typical studies of play behavior in the twenties and thirties were concerned with characteristic play activities at different ages or stages of development. Gesell's initial studies fit into this period. In the paper by Hurlock, referred to earlier, many of these studies are reviewed. She points out that there is no aggreement among writers as to dimensions of so-called play stages (i.e., how many there are, when they occur, or how long they last). This is just as true now as it was in 1934 when she wrote the paper. More recently, efforts to conceptualize the play activities of children into stages have often been directed toward a specific theoretical orientation. Two in particular stand out. The first is the alignment of play development with Freud's interpretation of the stages of psychosexual development in the child, and the second is the incorporation of play behaviors into Piaget's description of cognitive development in children. Both the psychoanalytic interpretation and Piaget's description of play are discussed in detail in Millar's chapter, "Play in Psychological Theories" (Millar). Erikson's theory of play combines these two points of view, although the distinctive sequences he sees in children's play tend to parallel to some extent Piaget's developmental sequence more than the psychoanalytic sequence.

Harlow follows a stage developmental plan, although to a lesser extent than Piaget or the psychoanalytic theorists, as he describes the role of play in the development of affectional behaviors. Noting that play proceeds according to a definite maturational pattern, he describes age-related play behaviors in humans and monkeys, emphasizing the critical role of play in growth toward normal heterosexual affectional behavior. As he puts it, "The path to passion is paved with play" (Harlow, p. 45). Millar likewise describes a maturational pattern in the development of social play; the sequence begins with solitary activity, progresses to parallel, associative, and coopera- tive play, and culminates in group or gang activity.

While the preceding writers attempted to describe definitive maturational play stages, others discuss play in the context of very general age categories. For example, Children's Bureau pamphlets, directed toward a parent audience, are divided into three stages: *Infant Care, Your Child from One to Six,* and *Your Child from Six to Twelve.* In *Infant Care,* play is discussed in the section, "Four to Eight Months," and is confined to suggestions about the types of toys that are safe and the kinds of games that are exciting for the child. In *Your Child from One to Six,* the role of play in the life of the toddler (ages one to three) is discussed with practical hints about where he can play, equipment, and safety. The section on three and four year olds includes a general description of play behavior at this age plus an extensive list of aids for play. In *Your Child from Six to Twelve,* specific play activities are discussed only mini- mally; rather, emphasis is placed on team and group play and the importance of peer group interaction at this age.

In the book *Children and Their Peers—First Steps in the Social World,* Jersild traces the development of social behavior in children from infancy through preschool. He makes the point in discussing stages of play behavior that the child's ability to take part in the play and games preferred by his age group will have a critical effect on his social relationships, whether he is in an early or late stage of play development.

The development of characteristics such as control and handling of impulsivity is related to stages of play development. Strommen studied the impulsive behavior of both boys and girls in preschool, kindergarten, first, and third grades using the Simon Says game. She found that the task of control involved in this game varies in difficulty by age and by sex, so after periods of practice everyone improved except the pre- schoolers and kindergarten boys.

The findings presented here related to stage explanations of play behavior suggest that if such a concept of play development is to be utilized, both maturation and socialization factors must be incorporated into the explanation of how, when, and where play behaviors occur.

The Facilitation of Play Behavior

Evidence has been presented that suggests that play does not come naturally to children, particularly spontaneous, imaginative play. Rather, it flows out of an environment that supports it. The lack of a capability for free, imaginative play suggests a deprivation situation as its source. In the literature reviewed here, several writers have made at least indirect approaches to dealing with the absence of such skill, suggesting ways in which imaginative play might be made a part of a child's repertoire. Hartley, Frank, and Goldenson, in their book *Understanding Children's Play* give emphasis to the importance of the teacher's attitude in facilitating the child's learning how to play. Each chapter contains not only a discussion of the value of an activity for the child and its meaning for the teacher in understanding the child but also the effect the teacher's attitude toward this activity (e.g., attitude toward aggressive use of blocks, attitude toward clay, etc.) has on the child.

As discussed earlier, Smilansky designed a program in which she developed the dramatic play skills of disadvantaged children. Her goal was to provide these children with the experiences they missed, particularly with parents, which she feels are critical to the development of effective play skills. In her book, Smilansky details the procedure followed in testing the effectiveness of different methods of adult intervention aimed at facilitating the ability of these children to take part in sociodramatic play. Her findings provide information about the critical role of basic play techniques as a prerequisite for the child's absorbing new learnings and experiences.

Feitelson concluded that the ability to play imaginatively can readily be taught to young children. She supervised college students conducting "play teaching" sessions with children from homes where play activities had not been encouraged. After nine weekly one-hour sessions, there were significant changes in interest span, intensity of play, and initiative in creative play.

Wooten, Wood, and Barnes observed that the play behavior of emotionally disturbed preschoolers was delayed compared to that of normal children. Both groups were observed in a health clinic. To study this difference, observers noted the play activity of the normal children while the two groups were playing together and guided the behavior of the disturbed children in that direction. These authors reported that in a short time the disturbed children reached a more mature level of play than that of the nondisturbed children. Ross reported similar results with educable mentally retarded children who were taught skills related to games and sports in the context of play situations during a six-month training period. While the retarded children scored much lower than an average group at the beginning, after training there was no statistical difference between the scores of the retarded children and those of the average group.

The results of one recent study do not support the efficacy of teaching the skill of creativity. Suzuki studied the effects of guidance on the play behavior of preschool children in Japan. While an experimental group played under instruction, a control group played without instruction. Both groups used the same toys and played in the same room. While the play behavior of both groups improved in such attributes as liveliness, consistency, and enjoyment, the noninstruction group was superior in creativity. These results suggest that instruction has a disturbing effect on creative expression during free play, while instruction and noninstruction are equally effective in facilitating other play-related behaviors.

Implications of Research Findings

The Function of Play

In discussing the function of play, it was noted that even with fairly young children a distinction is made between play and behavior of a nonplay nature; some writers insist that for play to serve its proper function it has to be identified as completely different from work. Thus, behavior tends to fall into one of two major categories—either fun and play or work and study—the former taking on a halo of pleasantness, the latter a shackle of unpleasantness. This dichotomy is clearly illustrated as my nine-year-old neighbor boy describes his educational history to me, "In nursery school they taught me to play; in kindergarten they taught me to share; since then, it's been nothing but work!"

This is not to say that a distinction should not be made between work and play activity; this is legitimate, and often essential. However, the implication of such a dichotomy is that there is a rigid distinction between the two concepts, making it difficult to perceive any overlap, even though deliberately seeking overlap. Thus, the teacher thinks in terms of *work* periods and *play* periods; the parent clearly defines the *work* activity that is to precede the *play* activity. In addition, one is usually seen as pleasant, the other as unpleasant. Such either-or thinking does not necessarily have to occur but probably will occur because of the initial assumption of work and play as opposites. Thus, our built-in predisposition to perceive play as capricious and frivolous places severe limitations on our flexibility in utilizing play, particularly beyond the preschool level. Our built-in predisposition to perceive work as serious and tedious reduces the potential for deriving pleasure from this distasteful activity. A further implication of this work-play dichotomy is that if and when there is a change in emphasis in education away from a "work" orientation, the primary thrust should not be in the direction of curriculum revision but more importantly in a revision of teachers' attitudes toward accepting play as a legitimate and productive arena for learning. In the past, many innovative programs have gone on the rocks not because of inadequacies in the programs but because of teachers' attitudes of uncertainty about them.

The trend toward giving importance to the *intrinsic* function of play was discussed earlier. What are the implications of this trend? It seems clear that play activity does produce intrinsic satisfactions, as children do play for long periods of time in the absence of identifiable extrinsic reinforcements. However, in this writer's opinion, if play is to be thoroughly understood, one must go beyond using the dimension "intrinsic satisfaction" as a complete explanation for why play occurs. Rather, play behavior must be observed and analyzed in an effort to define operationally the intrinsic satisfaction. In other words, as investigators and teachers, we need to know more specifically the goal the child is achieving in play or the need that is being satisfied. Several theorists have come up with solutions to this problem; the concept of mastery as a goal has been used to explain prolonged activity in a play situation, while the concept of novelty as a need to be satisfied has been used to explain exploratory behavior. Having defined such specific needs or goals, play activities can then be structured, play environments designed, and curricula revised to facilitate the child's achieving these goals and meeting these needs. Such changes might include games that allow for mastery, classrooms that maximize opportunities for exploratory behavior, and curricula that allow for novel approaches.

The Relation of Play to Cognitive Development

What are the implications of findings related to cognitive development and play? Since studies demonstrate a close relationship between play behavior and cognitive development in the child, the earlier a child starts to play, the sooner his education begins. Unfortunately, the relaxed learning climate of play is short-lived, gradually shifting to a new orientation labeled "achievement." Thus, the playful quality of the play-learning environment is replaced by a more noticeable achievement-oriented learning environment structured by selective reinforcements supplied by adults.

Within this new climate, several new dimensions emerge: a behavior is now right or wrong; the child succeeds or fails; behavior that yesterday produced laughter may now be punished; freedom to choose to play or not to play may be lost as a specific goal enters into the picture. Play activities that were spontaneous may begin to fall into the category of work, so that playing at helping Mommy with the dishes is now a regular duty or the game of playing with numbers is now schoolwork.

The learning that takes place in the work context, however, is felt to be more effective, or of greater importance, than learning in a play context. This is a somewhat erroneous perception. The data relevant to cognitive development indicate that all areas of functioning in children are facilitated by activity that is of a pleasant or playful nature; there are no findings that suggest that growth, development, or learning are nurtured by a "serious" climate (i.e., one characterized by strictness, determination, conformity, or adherence to structure). In other words, if adults and children play together or laugh, talk, and respond to one another, the children will probably grow up to be responsive and aware adults. If the adults are constricted, humorless, frightened, and conscientious, but dissatisfied, their children will probably reflect these characteristics. This is not to suggest that all learning will be exciting and fun or that all learning situations must be three-ring circuses of children and teachers joyfully cavorting together; it *is* to suggest that educators' priorities, attitudes, and reward systems are mixed up. The typical school day that prescribes six class periods and one period is out of balance; the teacher who takes his work "seriously" and strives to produce serious students has little feeling for learning; and the school system that prizes quiet and orderliness over laughter and spontaneity is missing the boat! If a playful, pleasurable climate facilitates learning and growth, as the data indicate, we can base our approach to education on the assumption that there is excitement in learning for both the student and the teacher. Going a step further, if we assume that play *is* learning and that a classroom is meant to be full of playful learning, or learningful play, then as teachers we will begin to see the connection between play and math, between grammar and play.

Creativity and Play

The findings relative to creativity and play show a significant relationship between the two. In other words, the most creative children tend to be the most playful, suggesting that these two characteristics develop together, possibly in response to similar stimuli. One implication of this relationship is that a child's playfulness and thus his creativity can be enhanced by broadening his experiences so that new alternatives become available to him. Implicit in this wider range of behaviors are more opportunities for learning to make decisions and for dealing effectively with choices. In addition, the findings which show that direct efforts to teach imaginative play have been effective are especially significant in working with young children whose past experiences have not fostered imaginative or creative play. While provision of free playtime facilitates the child's trying out imaginative play, some children require direction and practice in using the skill. The implication here is that teachers themselves will have to learn how to play imaginatively and to master the art of teaching others the skill. This learning is based on the premise that the teacher enjoys imaginative play and feels it has significance for the child.

Cross-cultural Differences and Play

Probably the most important implication of the cross-cultural data on play is the finding that play does not come naturally to children. If they play at all, it is because they have been exposed to a playful environment. Consequently, there will be children in the classroom who have never played and who will have difficulty coping with new experiences that are playful and fun, in contrast to their more familiar experiences that have been hostile and aggressive. Again, the knowledge that play behaviors can be taught is relevant.

Stages of Play Development

An important implication of the findings regarding stages in play development is that the maturation factor must be considered in assessing readiness for play activities, primarily in terms of the limitations it sets on a child's learning specific skills and controls. As shown in Strommen's study, preschool children are not developmentally ready for games involving impulse control. On the other hand, play serves an important function as a socializer at all stages of development. Research findings emphasize the influence of pleasure and playfulness as facilitators of the socialization process. If any one factor is going to make or break a child as he plows through the developmental stages, it is his interactions with people, which may be satisfying or disastrous. For most children, the first contact outside the family is in a play situation —day-care center, nursery school, family group care situation, or kindergarten. Here the teachers have the opportunity to make this first nonfamily socialization experience a positive one for the child through happy, nonthreatening play activities. Of special significance for the teacher of the preschool child are the findings that show that significant learning occurs in free-play situations, particularly when there is adequate equipment for the child to try out different modes of activity. While the child is exploring and experimenting, the play activities he chooses provide the teacher with clues about his feelings toward others and toward himself as well as an indication of the amount of confidence he has in his abilities.

The implications of viewing play as an opportunity for socialization through practicing real-life and adult roles are significant for education. However, the use of play in this way has been confined primarily to the early years when play is considered legitimate in the classroom. Even then, play is confined to a restricted range of real-life situations (e.g., setting up a cardboard grocery store or post office). At a later stage of play development, some teachers expose their students to the democratic process by conducting elections; others allow juries of children to make decisions for the class, usually regarding how a child shall be punished. Beyond these rather classic situations, there are meaningful ways in which play can be utilized in the classroom for practicing adaptive behaviors—experimenting with expressing feelings, testing limits of assertiveness, making decisions and choices, and above all, practicing skills for getting along with other human beings.

The Facilitation of Play Behavior

The findings related to facilitation of play behavior in general support the conclusion that play behavior, imaginative and otherwise, can be taught. The implication is that while all children have the potential for playing, more information is needed about effective methods of teaching different types of play behavior to different types of children. For example, what is an effective approach for teaching lower-class, disadvantaged children to participate in imaginative play? And how can educable mentally retarded children most effectively learn to follow rules of games? Answers to these and similar questions can be obtained only by observing many different teachers *teaching* many different ways and watching many different children *learning* many different ways.

In summary, while there is no agreement among theorists and practitioners as to the primary function of play, there is agreement among all who have studied, observed, or played with children that many things happen when children play— socialization proceeds, learning occurs, feelings are expressed, imagination runs wild, mastery is experienced, problems are solved, fantasies are played out, and adult roles are practiced. Play does not come naturally, however; consequently, there are variations from one culture to another in the ways children play, just as there are differences among social levels within a culture in typical play behaviors. While a specific type of play activity may be less common in one group than in another (e.g., imaginative play is frequently not a part of the lower-class child's play), the skill involved in that activity can usually be taught. One implication of this knowledge for the field of education is that the tremendous potential inherent in play is not utilized. The school defines its role as a promoter of learning and approaches the task in a narrow, constricted way. And even though we know that learning is facilitated by a playful, pleasant atmosphere, as educators we are unable to incorporate this information into our thinking. Hopefully, we will be able to broaden our perspective to make room for more playful activity in the classroom and bring fun back into learning.

References

Anker, D.; Foster, J.; McLane, J.; Sobel, J.; and Weissbourd, B. "Teaching Children as They Play." *Young Children* 29(1974):203–13.

Bandura, A., and Walters, R. *Social Learning and Personality Development.* New York: Holt, Rinehart & Winston, 1963.

Barnes, K. "Preschool Play Norms: A Replication." *Developmental Psychology* 5(1971):99–103.

Baughman, E., and Dahlstrom, W. *Negro and White Children: A Psychological Study in the Rural South.* New York: Academic Press, 1968.

Berlyne, D. *Conflict, Arousal and Curiosity.* New York: McGraw-Hill, 1960.

Borowitz, G.; Hirsch, J.; and Costello, J. "Play Behavior and Competence in Ghetto Four Year Olds. *Journal of Special Education* 4(1970):215–21.

Branch, M. "Play and Equipment" Proceedings of In-Service Training Course for Staff. Christchurch, N.Z., 1972.

Britt, S.H., and Janus, S. "Toward a Social Psychology of Human Play." *Journal of Social Psychology* 13(1941):351–84.

Brodbeck, A., and Irwin, O. "The Speech Behavior of Infants without Families." *Child Development* 17(1946):145–56.

Buhler, K. *The Mental Development of the Child.* London: Kegan Paul, 1937.

Butler, J. "Enepût: A Hot Idea from the Eskimos." *Day Care and Early Education* 1(1973): 16–18.

Carmichael, L., and Carmichael, R. "Observations of the Behavior of Japanese Kindergarten Children." *Psychologia* 15(1972):46–52.

Chase, J. "Street Games of New York City." *Pedagogical Seminary* 12(1905):503–4.

Courtney, R. "Education Is Play." *Childhood Education* 49(1973):246–50.

Dansky, J., and Silverman, I. "The Effects of Play on Associative Fluency in Preschool-Aged Children." *Developmental Psychology* 9(1973):38–43.

DesLauriers, A., and Carlson, C. *Your Child Is Asleep: Early Infantile Autism.* Homewood, Ill.: Dorsey Press, 1969.

Doke, L., and Risley, T. "The Organization of Day-Care Environments: Required vs. Optional Activities." *Journal of Applied Behavior Analysis* 5(1972):405–20.

Eifermann, R. *Determinants of Children's Game Styles.* Jerusalem: Israel Academy of Sciences and Humanities, 1971.

Elkind, D. "Piagetian and Psychometric Conceptions of Intelligence." *Harvard Educational Review* 39(1969):219–37.

El'Konin, D. "Symbolics and Its Function in the Play of Children." *Soviet Education* 8(1966): 35–41.

Erikson, E. *Childhood and Society.* New York: W.W. Norton & Co., 1950.

Feitelson, D. "Learning to Play." *Early Child Development and Care* 16(1972):202–23.

Frank, L. "Play is Valid." *Childhood Education* 45(1968):443–40.

Freud, S. *An Outline of Psychoanalysis.* Translated by James Strachey. New York: W.W. Norton & Co., 1949.

Gesell, A. *The Mental Growth of the Preschool Child.* New York: The Macmillan Co., 1925.

Ghahramani, M. "Child-rearing Practices in the South of Iran." *Pennsylvania Psychiatric Quarterly* 9(1969):43–48.

Groos, K. *The Play of Man.* New York: D. Appleton, 1901.

Haggitt, A. "The Basis of Teaching the Preschool Children." Proceedings of In-Service Training Course for Staff. Christchurch, N.Z., 1972.

Hall, G. *Youth: It's Education, Regimen and Hygiene.* New York: Appleton-Century-Crofts, 1907.

Harlow, H. *Learning to Love,* San Francisco: Albion Publishing Co., 1971.

Harlow, H.F.; Harlow, M.; and Meyer, D.R. "Learning Motivated by a Manipulation Drive." *Journal of Experimental Psychology* 40(1950):228–34.

Hartley, R.; Frank, L.; and Goldenson, R. *Understanding Children's Play.* New York: Columbia University Press, 1952.

Herron, R., and Sutton-Smith, B. *Child's Play.* New York: John Wiley & Sons, 1971.

Huizinga, J. *A Study of the Play Element in Culture.* Translated by R.F.C. Hull. London: Routledge and Kegan Paul, 1949.

Hunt, J.M. "How Children Develop Intellectually." In *Readings in Human Development,* edited by H. Bernard and W. Huckins, Boston: Allyn & Bacon, 1967.

Hurlock, E. "Experimental Investigations of Childhood Play." *Psychology Bulletin* 31(1934): 47–66.

"Infant Care." Children's Bureau Publication No. 8, 1963.

Jersild, A. *Children and Their Peers: First Steps in the Social World.* Englewood Cliffs, N.J.: Prentice-Hall, 1960.

Kagan, J. "Inadequate Evidence and Illogical Conclusions." *Howard Educational Review* 39(1969):274–77.

Kagan, J.; Henker, B.; Hen-Tov, A.; Levine, J.; and Lewis, M. "Infant's Differential Reactions to Familiar and Distorted Faces." *Child Development* 37(1966):519–32.

Keister, M.E. *The Good Life for Infants and Toddlers.* Washington, D.C.: National Association for the Education of Young Children, 1970.

Kniveton, B., and Pike, C. "Social, Class, Intelligence, and the Development of Children's Play Interests." *Journal of Child Psychology and Psychiatry* 13(1972):167–81.

Lieberman, J. "Playfulness and Divergent Thinking: An Investigation of Their Relationship at the Kindergarten Level." *Journal of Genetic Psychology* 107(1965):219–24.

Mahler, M. *On Human Symbiosis and the Vicissitudes of Individuation. Vol. I: Infantile Psychosis.* New York: International Universities Press, 1968.

Manosevitz, M.; Prentice, N.; and Wilson, F. "Individual and Family Correlates of Imaginary Companions in Preschool Children." *Developmental Psychology* 8(1973):72–79.

Marshall, H. "Children's Plays, Games, and Amusements." In *A Handbook of Child Psychology,* edited by C. Murchison. Worcester, Mass.: Clark University Press, 1931.

Marshall, H., and Shwu, C. "Experimental Modification of Dramatic Play." Paper presented at the American Psychological Association, New York, 1966.

Maw, W., and Maw, E. "Personal and Social Variables Differentiating Children with High and Low Curiosity." Cooperative Research Project No. 1511. University of Delaware, 1965.

Millar, S. *The Psychology of Play.* Baltimore: Penquin Books, 1968.

Murphy, L., et al. *The Widening World of Childhood.* New York: Basic Books, 1962.

Painter, G. *Teach Your Baby.* New York: Simon & Schuster, 1971.

Pavenstedt, E., ed. *The Drifters.* Boston: Little, Brown and Co., 1967.

Piaget, J. *Play, Dreams and Imitation in Childhood.* New York: W.W. Norton & Co., 1962.

Piers, M., ed. *Play and Development.* New York: W.W. Norton & Co., 1972.

Pine, F., and Furer, M. "Studies of the Separation-Individuation Phase: A Methodological Overview." In *Psychoanalytic Study of the Child, Vol, XVIII,* edited by R. Eissler, A. Freud, H. Hartmann, M. Kus. New York: International Universities Press, 1963.

Redl, F. "The Impact of Game Ingredients on Children's Play Behavior." Fourth Conference on Group Processes. New York: Josiah Macy, Grant Foundation, 1958.

Rheingold, H. "The Modification of Social Responsiveness in Institutional Babies." *Monographs of the Society for Research in Child Development* 21, No. 2, 1956.

Rosecrans, C. "Play—the Language of Children." *Mental Hygiene* 52(1968):367–73.

Ross, S. "Effects of an Intensive Motor Skills Training Program on Young Educable Mentally Retarded Children." *American Journal of Mental Deficiency* 73(1969):920–26.

Schiller, F. *Essays, Aesthetical and Philosophical.* London: George Bell, 1875.

Schlosberg, H. "The Concept of Play." *Psychology Review* 54(1957):229–31.

Sharp, E. *Thinking Is Child's Play.* New York: Avon Books, 1969.

Skeels, H. "Adult Status of Children with Contrasting Early Life Experiences." *Monographs of the Society for Research in Child Development* 31, No. 3, 1966.

Smilansky, S. *The Effects of Sociodramatic Play on Disadvantaged Children.* New York: Appleton-Century-Crofts, 1973.

Spencer, H. *Principles of Psychology.* 2d ed. New York: Appleton-Century-Crofts, 1871.

Strommen, E. "Verbal Self-Regulation in a Children's Game: Impulsive Errors on 'Simon Says.' " *Child Development* 44(1973):849–953.

Suzuki, Y. "The Study of Physical Play in Preschool Children—An Analysis of the Characteristics of Child Behavior." *Bulletin of the Yamagata University* 5(1971):31–48.

Vygotsky, L. "Play and Its Role in the Mental Development of the Child." *Soviet Psychology* 5(1967):6–18.

White, B.; Castle, P.; and Held, R. "Observations on the Development of Visually Directed Reaching." *Child Development* 35(1964):349–64.

Wooton, M.; Wood, S.; and Barnes, K. "Shaping Preschoolers' Play Behavior in the Child Health Conference Waiting Area." *Canadian Journal of Public Health* 61(1970):10–16.

Whiting, B., ed. *Six Cultures: Studies of Child Rearing.* New York: John Wiley & Sons, 1963.

Your Child from One to Six. Children's Bureau Publication No. 30, 1969.

Your Child from Six to Twelve. Children's Bureau Publication No. 32, 1968.

CHAPTER TEN

MOVEMENT

Lydia A.
Gerhardt

Let your feet lead you through the space.

The Practice of Movement Education—Three Styles

Style 1

S is pushing his friend around the room in a child-sized doll carriage. Passing the easel, the back wheel grazes one leg causing the easel to move slightly. "Look what you made me do!" the angry painter shouts. S angrily kicks through the air at the painter. The painter cries, "Teacher!" The teacher responds, "What's the trouble over here?" The sequence is retold after which the teacher replies, "It sounds like S made you angry when he bumped into the easel. It would be better to tell him, 'Watch where you are going.'"

S leaves pushing the carriage into the doll corner where he announces, "Now we're home. Pretend it's time to eat. I'll cook dinner." He flings open the cupboard door, gathers up some dishes and pours them onto the table. Several dishes roll off and rattle to the floor. "Are you still feeling angry?" the teacher inquires. S replies, "I'm going to work now." Heading for the workbench, he snatches up a small piece of wood and drops it into the vice. With a rapid cranking of his right hand he closes the vice, ending the action by leaning over the handle and lifting his feet off the floor momentarily. He wipes his brow. "That was hard work," the teacher observes. Children nearby are feeding carrots to the guinea pig. He glances over at the activity and mumbles something to himself while reaching up for a saw that is hanging on a rack over his head. Putting the saw on the edge of his wood, he begins to saw slowly and when he sees that a notch has formed, he changes to short, firm, and rhythmic strokes. "I think you like sawing," the teacher comments. When the piece crashes to the floor, S drops the saw on the bench, picks up the fallen piece, and carries it over to take his turn stroking the guinea pig.

Later in the day S participates in a music and movement experience. "I'm a fish." "I want to be airplanes." "Can we play 'Ducky Dawdle'?" The children request favorite activities. "Let's be airplanes first, then fish, and then sing 'Ducky Dawdle,'" the teacher suggests. "Get your airplanes ready!" S runs around the circle with his arms outspread with his friends. Then he joins the "fish" swimming in a pool and opens his mouth for bread that the teacher throws to the "fish." While singing "Ducky Dawdle," S waddles in a squatting position, clapping his hands near his lower back. Before going outside, the teacher plays a favorite record. "You can do any kind of dance you want," she offers. S hops on one foot, turns himself around and ends by jumping loosely up and down. "That was a lovely dance," the teacher observes. On the playground S joins some friends riding tricycles. To reverse direction, he frequently stands straddling the tricycle and drags it around with one hand on the back of the seat and the other on the handlebar. When climbing the jungle gym, he easily alternates both hands and feet. "You're a good climber," the teacher remarks. "It feels good to be so high," she adds. While working with his friends on a hollow block structure, S carries blocks against his chest. When he moves short planks, he wraps one arm over and around, while he uses the other arm to support the plank in front of his body.

Looking at S's movements through the day, one might note that he experienced pushing (carriage), kicking, flinging, gathering and bending (with the dishes), sawing, pressing, cranking (vice), stroking (guinea pig), flying like an airplane, swimming, hopping on one foot and jumping, carrying (hollow blocks and planks), and numerous other movements. In what ways is S being educated through his own body movements? To what educational ideology does his teacher subscribe?

Style 2

B is tracing geometric forms in her workbook. Her teacher reminds her, "Remember B, after you trace each shape, copy it in the space underneath." Noting that B is pressing extremely hard and rounding the corners, she decides to give her some extra practice so she fills another sheet with additional shapes for B to trace. "Trace them gently," she reminds B, "and make the corners very square." B continues to press unnecessarily hard, but she makes her corners more angular. When the teacher comes around again, she says, "That's better B. Now try the next page. On this page you must draw a straight line between the two things that go together (rabbit and carrot; child and tricycle; cup and saucer).

Later in the day, the teacher helps the group to set up five large motor tasks: a balance beam, hoops in a 2–1–2–1–2 pattern, three-foot uppercase letters (*S, T, O*), angels in the snow, and large rubber balls. The class is divided into five small groups. B begins on the balance beam; she walks with arms spread wide, takes baby steps, and carefully watches her feet. When she accidently slips off, she goes back to begin again. Her teacher reminds her, "Look straight ahead at the fire extinguisher." B makes it to the other end on the third attempt but only by taking a large slip step and jumping off quickly. "That's better, B, but don't rush it," the teacher comments. Then B's group goes to make "angels in the snow." Her friend tells her, "Slide this arm (right) and this leg (left)." All four limbs slide along the floor. B jumps up saying, "Now it's your turn," to her friend. She tells her friend, "Slide this arm (left)." From there B's group goes to the hoops. Here the children know that they are supposed to jump into the first two hoops with both feet (one in each hoop), then hop on one foot in the single hoop, jump with two feet in the next two hoops, etc. B manages the first jump into the first pair of hoops, one foot in each hoop but then trips on the edge of the hoops and has to begin again. By stepping on several hoops and totally missing two others, she makes it to the end. "Do it carefully," the teacher reminds her. "Don't hurry." Next are the letters. B traces each letter (often stepping off the line) using baby steps and reciting, "An *S* goes one way and then it goes the other way." "A *T* is made with a straight line across and a straight line down," etc. Finally, B's group moves to the balls. "Bounce your ball changing hands like this," the teacher directs as she demonstrates. Once B manages to alternate hands for two bounces. She prefers to use her right hand and is more successful bouncing it as many as four times this way. The materials are put away and the teacher sits down at the piano. "Let's skip before we have our story," she suggests. The group recognizes the skipping music and begins to travel around the room in a variety of hop-step-run combinations. B step-hops on one foot.

In reexamining B's movement, one finds that she has drawn lines forward, backward, and side to side. The lines have gone toward her body, away from her body, and across her midline as well as around in an oval and circle. B has walked alternating feet on a balance beam for four steps followed by a slip step and a jump off the end. She has tried opposition in the "angels in the snow" game but moves all four limbs together. The teacher has recorded that she hurries to finish the hoop-hopping task and steps on several hoops. She also notes that B could alternate hands twice while bouncing a ball. In what ways is B being educated through her own body movement? How does her experience differ from S's movement experience? To what educational ideology does B's teacher subscribe?

Style 3

C and some friends are building a two-story bus depot. She has carried armloads of quads and doubles (unit blocks) to the building site. She carefully arranged a flat foundation and suggested that the depot be two stories high. They used quads to build latticelike sides; this was C's idea. After they placed quads on the top to form a roof, C went for cylinders and little triangles. "These will be the decorations," she announces. She carefully balanced each triangle on a narrow cylinder. L asks C, "How will the buses get out?" C replies, "An elevator, stupid!" L complains, "No, buses can't fit in an elevator." "Yes, they can. It's a big bus elevator," replies C. "OK, on a ramp then. We need a ramp," C suddenly blurts out after several moments of contemplation. The teacher interjects, "Is there any other way to get buses from the top of a two-story bus depot to the bottom? You might like to look in this book for some other ideas." She hands C a book. Several pictures of a spiraling roadway spark a discussion about building a round ramp. C makes a pile of six doubles and tries to balance some curves on it. "They keep sliding off," she complains. "Why do you suppose this happens?" the teacher asks. Then she brings three triangular blocks to the group. "You seem to have a problem. Do you think you can use these to build a ramp?" she asks. C shouts, "I know." She begins to experiment. Eventually, she finds that by supporting the two long triangles on a double, she can connect the smaller triangle to make a continuous surface (see Figure 7). With further experimentation, the ramp begins to grow.

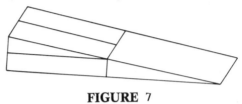

FIGURE 7

L starts to push a car up the ramp, "No! This is the *out* ramp," states C emphatically. "They can go in *and* out," replies L. "No, it's not big (wide) enough," argues C. A later argument arises about how the buses get from the ramp into a tunnel. And then there is a discussion about how passengers get to the platform to get on the buses. "After juice time we'll walk over to the bus station and try to find out all of these things," the teacher suggests.

It is time for movement activities. The children remove their shoes and socks. "When you are ready, move into a space and practice your own movement idea," the teacher directs. Soon the space is filled with children hopping, jumping, rolling, crawling, twisting, and trying to do cartwheels. C is rolling backwards over her right shoulder. It is clear that this is a very familiar activity to all of the children. "Get ready to . . . stop," the teacher says gently but firmly. Everyone freezes in a total body shape. C is balanced on four fingers of each hand and one foot. "I see some new ideas," the teacher observes. "There's a lovely twisted and stretched shape. Some people are in hard-to-balance shapes. And there's a very low spread shape. Let's try it some more. This time think about the shape your body is making as it moves. Ready? Off you go." She repeats this pattern several times. The children are again stopped in an interesting shape. "Now, from where you are, change your shape until you have a shape with important knees." C stands and then thrusts out both knees so that she is in an asymmetrical squatting position. "Now make your knees disappear," the teacher directs. C straightens her knees. "Now make a new knee shape." This time C tips over to support herself with one hand on the floor and lifts one leg off the floor. "Everyone, have one more try. Travel through the space with important knees. You might like to try some spiraling ways, some hopping ways, or even some ways that take your knees away from your body and toward your body. Ready? Off you go." After further exploration, the teacher directs, "Sit down and listen to this music. We're going to use it to make a knee dance." She plays a portion of a lively folk dance and encourages the children to move their bodies while sitting in one place on the floor. "Now, stand up and make a beginning knee shape. This is going to be a dance about knees. Ready? Are you near the floor, or are you near the ceiling? In what way are your knees important? Ready?" She puts the music on, and the children begin to dance. As the music gradually comes to an end, the teacher turns down the volume and reminds the children, "Find a way to end your dance with important knees." "Do you know what I was?" C asks. "No, what did the music make you think about?" the teacher inquires. "I was a grasshopper!" C replies.

In reexamining C's movement experience, one finds that she carried armfuls of blocks, carefully balanced triangular blocks on cylinders, arranged quads to form a surface floor and ceiling. She tried to balance curved blocks on a stack of doubles to make a ramp and discovered it wouldn't work. With the teacher's help she figured out a way to build a ramp using the triangular blocks. During the movement experience, C rolled backwards over her right shoulder and tried to balance on one foot and eight fingers. She thrust out both knees asymmetrically to "make her knees important." She straightened them to "make them disappear." Then she balanced herself on one hand and one foot in a new knee shape. When asked to travel with important knees, C found a way to lift her knees alternately and turn in circles. She noticed that D made "roundy round" patterns (spirals) on the floor. During the knee dance to music she tried traveling backwards, sideways, and hopping from side to side. She discovered that her knees can make a sound and that she can "hop-skip" with important knees. In what ways was C being educated through her own body movement? How does her experience differ from that of S's and B's? To what educational ideology does her teacher subscribe?

The teachers of S, B, and C reflect three of the divergent theories, methodologies, and ideologies that permeate today's early childhood classrooms, more particularly young children's movement education. Before analyzing the theoretical underpinnings of each child's movement experience, we will look briefly first at the historical roots and current research underlying today's practice and then at the potential role movement education can play in young children's education.

Historical Trends

The pendulum reflecting the importance of the child and his physical-motor development as well as the theoretical base on which the child's physical education should be designed has swung in many dimensions through history. The classical Greeks emphasized harmony of body and mind as they tried to balance mental, physical, and spiritual factors in human development. During the Middle Ages the child and his physical development took a back seat, unbalancing the body-mind harmony in favor of spiritual development through aesthetic awareness. The reawakening of interest in the classics during the Renaissance brought about an interest in the child and a study of his needs; the child was the starting point of education, and child study became a reality. From the period of the Enlightenment to the twentieth century, physical education was seen as training to enhance optimum physical development, again reflecting both disharmony of body and mind, and separation between those aspects of development.

The twentieth century brought about a repetition and modification of earlier trends as psychological research tried to describe sequences in physical and psychological development. Subsequent focus turned to processes underlying human growth and development. Analysis of separate aspects of development in the 1930s proved inadequate, so the concept of the "whole child" was formulated in the 1940s. Since this theoretical formulation also proved unsatisfactory because it did not explain particular developmental problems, a concept of individual differences was developed with a heavy emphasis on the child's social and emotional development. In the 1960s Sputnik seemed to be responsible for a sudden concern for intellectual development. America had to beat Russia to the moon and in order to do this had to train scientists.

Current emphasis not only reflects historical trends (i.e., "harmony of body and mind," "aesthetic awareness," "the whole child," *and* "individual differences") but also recognizes the complexity of the human organism's interaction (i.e., body, mind, and feelings) in his unique environment. Both physical education and early childhood education literature of the late sixties and early seventies draws on multiple disciplines to explain and justify new theoretical underpinnings.

Multi-disciplinary Views Emerge

It seems that as physical educators, psychologists, and early childhood educators search for new insights into the role of movement in human development, each group is drawn to research in other disciplines. Since the turn of the century, American physical educators have been struggling to produce a rationale for their existence as an academic discipline. During the first sixty years of the twentieth century, scholars periodically focused their attention on the psychological, sociological, and physiological variables and their implications for physical activity. Brown and Cratty attempted to coordinate this trend through a multi-disciplinary overview of relevant facts, theories, and techniques derived from the academic disciplines related to the study of man in action. Their selected authors have drawn from fields such as biochemistry, kinesiology, physiology, neurology, sociology, and anthropology and have attempted to analyze and synthesize the pieces of current knowledge that contribute to physical education. Their growing understanding of the complexity of physical activity in human development is revealed in their present literature that articulates the role of

1. Biochemistry in understanding metabolic pathways and enzyme activity;
2. Neurology in understanding the transmission of visual-sensory information including spatial and temporal sensation;
3. Anthropology in understanding man as a biocultural organism;
4. Sociology in understanding the social phenomenon of sport;
5. Kinesthesis as a physiological and perceptual-illusory phenomenon;
6. Psychology in the understanding of perceptual-motor phenomenon.

Emerging from this analysis are ideas related to perception, perceptual-motor development, visual-motor coordination, and intellectual-motor relationships. Cratty (1967) made further attempts to uncover the complexities in movement behavior and motor learning through an analysis and synthesis of relevant literature on perception, learning theory, and principles of human growth and development. From this approach he elucidated the role of movement in the total educative process, pointing to perceptual-motor functioning within the human personality and specifically to the interrelationships between movement behavior and classroom functioning (Cratty, 1969, 1970). His thinking seems to derive from his work with exceptional children as the last half of *Perceptual-Motor Behavior and Educational Processes* is devoted to curriculum planning for perceptually handicapped, orthopedically handicapped, mentally retarded, and neurologically impaired children. More recently, he has attempted to develop concrete techniques for teachers based on the theory that mind and body are inseparably linked. It is interesting to note that none of this physical education literature is concerned with the very young child.

While physical educators have increased the depth of their understanding of physical activity in human development, psychologists have reviewed interdisciplinary literature to increase the depth of their understanding of physical activity in human development. Their needs have derived from observations of children with learning difficulties who characteristically have motor awkwardness and poor gross and/or fine motor movements. Physical training programs designed to improve coordination have frequently resulted in increased scores on measures of academic and intellectual achievement (Conner; Godfrey, 1964; Smith).

A multi-disciplinary approach to physical activity is also supported by the psychologist, Kephart, whose work with exceptional children has led him to develop body movement training programs (Kephart; Roach and Kephart). In his attempt to identify the basic skills that underlie classroom achievement, he draws from his own observations of children performing simple tasks that he feels elucidate their underlying components. He speaks of motor bases of achievement, perceptual processes, form perception and space discrimination, concluding with sensorimotor and perceptual-motor training activities. Like Cratty, he has worked primarily with teachers and children in special education who seem to benefit from his training. More recently, he has collaborated with the physical educator, Godfrey, to write about movement education which they define as "that aspect either of physical education or classroom education which deals with development and training in basic movement patterns as differentiated from movement skills" (Godfrey and Kephart, p. 19). Their focus, like Cratty's, deals with psychomotor and perceptual-motor development and behavior rather than with physical fitness, organic vigor, muscle building, and competence in sports and games. They state, "Movement education is the foundation component of both physical education and general education" (Godfrey and Kephart, p. 19). Each emerges from and builds on a foundation of movement education. They speak of "motor patterns" as the internal neurological processes and "movement patterns" as the external observable performance or behavior of the internal process. With the exception of Kephart's work, none of this psychological literature is concerned with the very young child.

Early childhood educators, too, have begun to search in other disciplines for new understandings of the role of body movement in human development. As recently as 1970, the National Association for the Education of Young Children (NAEYC) and the American Association for Health, Physical Education, and Recreation (AAHPER) initiated what has become an annual conference concerned with the young child and his physical education. The content of the first conference summarized in *The Sig-*

nificance of the Young Child's Motor Development revolved around four stated purposes:

1. To help develop clearer insights concerning the significance of physical activity in the early years of childhood.
2. To examine the existing body of knowledge from research and experience regarding the motor development of young children.
3. To explore the relationship of motor development to other aspects of development (i.e., emotional, social, and intellectual).
4. To present some ideas for an appropriate environment to facilitate the motor development of young children.

Moving and Knowing which describes the role of body movement in conceptualization is also an interdisciplinary document (Gerhardt, 1973). Through an analysis and synthesis of the literature from anthropology, biology, genetic epistemology, philosophy, neurophysiology, psychology, art, dance, and education, a conceptual framework for the relationship between movement and conceptualization is built.

Components of Movement—Attempts to Analyze

While looking for a rationale in a multiplicity of disciplines, physical educators have simultaneously focused their attention on the components of human movement. Recent theory seems to be rooted in analyses similar to that originally defined by Laban in his earliest books, *Effort* and *Modern Educational Dance,* published in England after World War II. Current articulation of his principles of movement falls under four headings:

1. The body (What the body can do: locomotion, elevation, turns, rising/sinking, advancing/retreating, opening/closing, etc.)
2. Effort (How the body moves: strong/light, sudden/sustained; direct/flexible; bound/free, etc.)
3. Space (Where the body moves: near/far, high/deep, right/left, straight/angular/ curved/twisted, etc.)
4. Relationships (Relationships of body parts to each other, individuals to each other, groups to each other)

All English literature concerning movement education is organized using this framework. Although current American physical education literature reflects similarities to Laban's principles of movement, it organizes the principles differently and hence views them differently. Mosston (1965) presents materials for teaching through an integration of physical attributes (i.e., strength, agility, flexibility, balance, rhythm, endurance), body parts (i.e., calves, shoulders, back, etc.), and kinds of movement (i.e., running, jumping, throwing, bending, swinging, etc.). He arranges these developmentally from the simple to the complex by referring to their physiologic and kinesthetic characteristics. Like Mosston, Schurr speaks of the factors of "movement study" including qualities of movement (i.e., time, force, body shape, flow, and space), body actions, and relationships. She considers these factors in her subsequent discussion of locomotor movements (e.g., slide = step + hop; skip = walk + hop) and nonlocomotor movements such as bends, stretches, pulls, pushes, lifts, and swings. Stanley used Laban's four basic categories but described their components differently. Frostig and Maslow's analysis falls under two large headings: attributes of movement and creative movement, more closely paralleling Mosston's work. Hanson, on the other hand, sees Laban's effort factors as roots of "elements of movement," then "basic movement," and finally "fundamental skills" (Barrett). She apparently does not find Laban's other four categories useful.

Despite the discrepancies described, it is interesting to note that Laban's principles of movement not only seem to have emerged first but also are permeating American movement analyses today. From my personal experiences with Laban's principles in ongoing movement study, movement explorations with young children, and teaching movement for preservice and inservice teachers, I have found them increasingly more useful. They provide a structure for observing movement behavior and for planning and organizing both functional and expressive movement experiences.

What Is Movement Education?

Movement education is a "coming to know" through one's own body movement. The human organism learns to move as he moves to learn. Hence, my definition is rooted in growth and development, an ongoing process. Through body movement, the human organism develops

1. A sense of self;
2. An ability to collaborate socially;
3. An aesthetic sense;
4. Gradually more complex ways of using his body;
5. An ability to think and engage in symbolic representation.

Movement Education and the Development of a Sense of Self

Through our interactions with the environment, we form a picture in our mind of what our body is, what it can do, and how each part is inextricably interwoven into the whole. As our muscles relax and contract in response to the movement tasks we set before ourselves, auditory, visual, tactile, aural, olfactory and kinesthetic messages unite to form a body unity, a body schema, a body image.

According to Erikson, the five to eight year old is developing a sense of initiative. His self-image is a function of his earlier development of a sense of trust and a sense of autonomy. Through endless repetition in his attempts to grasp objects, roll himself over, and finally creep and walk, the infant comes to trust his body to do his bidding. He builds his sense of self-reliance and adequacy which Erikson calls autonomy as he is given opportunities to make decisions. He expresses this autonomy when he decides whether to sit or stand, whether to approach a stranger or run from him, whether to accept food or reject it, and whether to use the toilet or to wet himself. He must learn both control and release if he is to function in a social world. He must express his feelings as he learns to understand the feelings of others. The young child's "sense of initiative" is characterized as it is built by his ability to imagine, to make contact with other children, and to explore his spatial world. Body movement is key to developing a "sense of self," for it is through movement that the child builds his body image. Sensing one's body weight contributes to "sense of self" particularly as one shifts that weight onto parts of the body that are unaccustomed to supporting that weight. The child comes to feel different combinations of body parts as he shifts his weight from part to part. It is the parts that make up the whole and the continuing sensations received, that invite awareness of whole to part and part to whole, working to build the "whole me." The power of "I can" is confidence. Within the structure the teacher provides, the child aspires to, selects from, compensates for, focuses on, relates to, and integrates his sense of self in space. The nature of his body image is significantly related to his ability to function in the world. According to Kephart, "His body is the zero point, or point of origin, for all movements and for all interpretations of outside relationships; these movements and the relationships will be disturbed if the body image is disturbed" (Kephart, *The Slow Learner,* p. 52). His body image is intricately woven with his laterality (the sensing of the sidedness of his body) and directionality (his sensing of the relationships of the parts of his body to objects in space). Hence, body movement is key to developing a stable space world and sorting out the stuff of the world whether it be direction in space, differentiation of shape or size, components of mathematics, reading, science, and social knowing. Body awareness emerges only after a multiplicity of experiences which enable the child to perceive the parts as well as the whole. Depth of understanding comes from the richness of movement experience in a broad range of body tasks and challenges. The quality of his body image is directly related to the quality of the child's ability to perceive relationships in space-time, including perception of his own body in space-time, and later in perception of objects and symbols in space-time.

What can you say about the development of a sense of self through the movement opportunities provided for S, C, and B?

Movement Education and the Development of Social Collaboration

Through his movement, the newborn infant builds his first social relationships. In his mother's arms he is shaped as he shapes her, and a relationship begins. As he becomes more mobile, again it is movement which arouses his mother to remove him from the top of the kitchen table; he moves to strike out at an adult who thwarts his explorations; and he moves to hug his baby brother.

In a room in which every child is moving independently, each child's space becomes a dynamic space. He is forced to make time-space judgments, adapting his movement to the dynamic space created by his peers. In short, he builds awareness of others in space as he builds increasing control of his body in movement. Further, through his own body movement he learns to deal with children who are aggressive, children who assume leadership, children who respect him, children who deny him his goals, children who share love, and children who are angry. Observations of peers who find new ways to complete a task builds respect, empathy, and understanding of one's own skills as well as those of others. Sharing perception of others' (movement) ideas builds roots of democracy. In effect, the child "listens" to others' ideas through movement, his most immediate and well-developed sensory tool.

What can you say about the development of social collaboration through the movement opportunities provided for S, C, and B?

Movement Education and the Development of an Aesthetic Sense

An aesthetic sense emerges from experiences that stimulate the senses, inspire the imagination, and provide opportunities for expression. The child's environment from his home, his classroom, his school, his community, and the world must help him to differentiate visual, auditory, tactile, aural, olfactory, and kinesthetic data. The natural world of trees, shells, rocks, bark, flowers, plants, insects, birds, and mammals must be available for his direct sensory exploration. In addition, the child needs help in focusing his attention on shape, texture, color, balance, form, rhythm, harmony, flavor, pitch, tone, line, and structure. Not only must he have opportunities which impress the senses but he must further have opportunities to organize these impressions in expressions of his own new forms.

Initially, differentiation of experience needs to be rooted in self; the body itself has form and shape, texture, internal and external rhythms, balance, and line. It can create sounds, shapes, rhythms, and ideas. Such expressions need to be organized and structured. Movement allows the child opportunities to organize his feelings, ideas, and responses; the quality of this organization will reflect the quality of the environment he has experienced. His environment needs clarity, organization, and aesthetic ordering if the child is to clarify, organize, and aesthetically express his feelings and ideas.

What can you say about the development of aesthetic awareness through the movement opportunities provided for S, C, and B?

Movement Education and the Development of Gradually More Complex Ways of Using the Body

It is generally accepted that efficient use of the body has a beneficial effect on the general health and physical well-being of an individual; it is equally accepted that poor body dynamics with its accompanying lack of muscle tone, lowered threshold of fatigue, and lessened available mechanical energy has a bad effect on general health. In addition, the quality of body movement is intrinsically related to circulation, respiration, elimination, and the functioning of the nervous system and endocrine glands.

Being able to move in increasingly complex ways is dependent upon both maturation and learning. One of the most rapid forms of development taking place during the early years of life is that of control over the different muscles of the body. From an uncoordinated, helpless infant, a child becomes an independent and integrated member of the world by the age of five or six. Proceeding from head to toe in cephalo-caudal fashion and from the center of the body out to the extremities in proximo-distal fashion, the young child progresses from lifting his head to rolling over, to crawling, to sitting, to creeping, and finally to standing and walking. Given opportunity to practice, the five to six year old learns to stand on one foot, hop, jump, gallop, and finally skip. Control seems to emerge from both readiness for body learning and the stimulation the environment provides. Despite obvious individual differences in children growing up in similar environments, it seems clear to me from my observations of children's movement that the complexity of their motor skill is directly related to the complexity of their movement experiences. Children need to be guided if they are to find the many ways there are to express in movement their ideas about storms, strength, war, gentleness, fear, or joy. Likewise, they need guidance if they are to find the many parts of their body on which they can travel. Teachers can provide experiences which invite children to explore more complex ways of moving. You see children quite at home supporting their weight on their hands, traveling on unusual body part combinations, finding curled up or stretched out ways to travel along an apparatus, and finding different ways of getting on and off apparatus. Providing time and space and apparatus is only the beginning. Teachers need to know the learnings inherent in the materials they provide as well as the learning styles of each child so that they can help each child move ahead. Tasks, such as "Find different ways of traveling in a stretched out shape," allow the beginner to walk stretching his arms and legs to the side while tipping his weight from side to side in starlike fashion. It allows the skilled mover to do left and right cartwheels. "Find different parts of your body that can support your weight as you travel" allows the beginner to crawl on his hands and knees, while the more skillful child can travel on one hand and one foot. Such tasks are *structured*, helping the child to focus his attention, but *open* as there are many possible solutions.

What can you say about the potential for developing more complex ways of using one's body in the movement opportunities provided for S, C, and B?

Movement Education and the Development of Thought and Symbolic Representation

"It is from actions that words flow" (Bartlett, p. 216). Piaget said, "It is primarily preverbal sensorimotor activity that is responsible for the construction of a series of perceptual schemata, the importance of which in the subsequent structuring of thought cannot, without oversimplification, be denied" (Piaget, p. ii). He also stated, "Verbal or cognitive intelligence is based on practical or sensorimotor intelligence which in turn depends on acquired and recombined habits and associations" (Piaget, p. 1).

One needs to spend only a short period of time observing children in action to discover that indeed movement is a reflection of thought. As a child runs to the top of a hill, pauses, and then rolls down the hill, it can be said that his action is a reflection of thought. He has focused his attention. He made a decision. Perhaps he evaluated the nature of the turf—it was soft. Or he remembered from a previous time that it felt good to roll on this hill but it was the other hill that had all those uncomfortable bumps on it. The child who places a series of blocks in a pattern to make a tower reveals a "spontaneous knowing" of pattern as well as of structure, components of mathematical and language symbolization (Vygotsky). The child who draws a picture of his daddy returning from a business trip on a plane shows that he has an image of a particular experience. As he goes on to describe a particular airline, the luggage rolling rack, and the escalator to the taxi stand, he further reveals that his movement has contributed to his conscious perception of a sequence of events, and he can recreate them in symbols at a point later in time. Movement to the airport has contributed to his imaging, and experience with language provides the words to describe that experience.

Intellectual development is characterized by a continuous play from action to images to words to images to actions (Gerhardt, 1973). The actions of constructing with clay, building a birdhouse at the woodworking table, walking through the woods in search of "mini-beasts" for the terrarium each contribute to the images necessary for intellectual development. Words alone are empty symbols with meaningless points of reference. The word *fly* is that much richer if one has experienced flying through the air from a box on the playground, the unwanted flies at a picnic, butterflies, horseflies, air travel, or the "Flight of a Bumblebee." As the child stretches into a wide shape or contracts it into a narrow shape, he uses his most immediate and natural point of reference to feel narrow/wide shape. As he kinesthetically feels his weight supported on different parts of his body, he comes to know his own "body weight," which will become his point of reference for judging the weight of objects outside his self. As he climbs up on a jungle gym, rung by rung, he reflects a spontaneous sensing of distance—a body sensing, a movement sensing. Describing his own movement in words (e.g., "I climbed up." "That's a big step.") deepens his understanding and contributes to his development of scientific concepts such as climbed, up, big, and step (Vygotsky). Hence, body movement is key to developing "concepts in formation" (Minor).

Yes, it is from actions that words flow. The astronauts practice their mission through actions as well as words; the anthropologist goes to the dig for his information; the farmer crumbles the soil in his hands to evaluate its worth. It is movement which gets the human organism in touch with his environment. Moving and knowing are inseparable as moving feeds knowing and knowing is reflected in movement (Gerhardt, 1973).

What can you say, now, about the potential for developing thought and symbolic representation inherent in the movement opportunities provided for S, C, and B?

Which Ideology for Education through Body Movement?

Now we are ready to examine the movement experiences of S, B, and C. In what ways was each child being educated through his own body movement? To what educational ideology does each teacher subscribe?

A Romantic View

In reexamining the description of S's movement experiences, it is easy to find his teacher's concern for his inner experience. He values his student's feelings and reflects them back to him. "Are you still feeling angry?" he inquires. "That's fun, isn't it?" He is concerned with the child's immediate perceptions; he exemplifies an existentialist epistemology. The child asks to become an airplane. The teacher supports his request. He provides freedom for S to find happiness and be himself; he allows time and space for S to climb up the jungle gym and time to spin on a swing. "That's fun, isn't it?" he observes. S's sense of self is the core of the curriculum he designs for him. He must be given freedom to find happiness, freedom to be himself, freedom to mature. His role is to provide an environment which will allow S's inner "good" abilities and social virtues to unfold and S's inner "bad" to come under control. Motor skills and movement achievements are purely a means to his happiness and good mental health. The teacher says to S, "I think you like sawing." The maturationist, according to Kohlberg, believes that cognitive and social-emotional development proceed somewhat differently. Cognitive unfolding is largely inborn while emotional development is vulnerable to fixation and frustration by the environment. Although intellectual components are acknowledged, knowledge or truth rests in self-awareness or self-insight (Kohlberg and Mayer).

Such an ideology is not uncommon in early childhood literature concerning movement. Speaking of music and movement in the introduction to her book, *Discovering Music with Young Children,* Bailey writes:

> The modern way of regarding the education of young children is to consider what type of happy growth and flowering they can achieve, in the best conditions which we can supply. The core of the idea is that this growth is spontaneous and that we, the adults, must watch it happening and be guided ourselves by its force and direction at each state of development and in each field of knowledge.

Hartley, Frank, and Goldenson in their chapter "Music and Movement" list the values of this combined medium as

1. It affords release from crippling impulses by stimulating primitive and infantile movement and attitudes by relieving instinctual tensions and expressing "shapless emotion" and by evoking deeply buried fantasies.
2. It helps the child sublimate his aggressive and destructive urges and channel disorganized energy in socially accepted ways.
3. The effect of releasing emotion and achieving order and self-control through rhythm gives the child "harmonious contact with himself," and through this, increased integration of body and mind and enhanced self-acceptance.

Further, they articulate the role of the teacher as one requiring active participation:

> She can be used by the children in any way that fits their needs. She can play a cherishing role for those who need "mothering" and are too shy to ask for it, or she can be a wild menace which is, in the end, overthrown and outwitted by the children. As long as she remains within the group, she also offers support to those who are not yet ready to sustain continuous contact on their own. (Hartley, Frank, and Goldenson, p. 337)

Although more recent publications reflect some move toward a more comprehensive grasp of the role of movement in children's growth and development, outdoor play is heavily valued for its role in building self-confidence, building attitudes about self, and developing large motor skills. Read heads her discussion, "Sensorimotor Competencies: Concept Formation" but goes on to say that a child builds self-confidence through muscle control. She also states that the child's postures and the way he uses his body reveal attitudes about himself.

Rudolph and Cohen speak about children's discovery of "weight" and their own strength through the use of pulleys; the importance of having ladders of two or three heights to accommodate different children and different areas of reaching; and balls that are different in size, color, texture, weight, with which children can cause the motions of rolling, twirling, spinning, throwing, and falling in various directions, and catching and bouncing at various speeds. But their strongest argument for including motor activities in kindergarten programs seems to be:

> five year olds must have a chance to exercise their growing muscles, especially the large ones, and to use their abundant energy. They must have the opportunity for continued practice to develop coordination and mastery of a variety of activities and skills because the confidence and satisfaction that follow mastery of one's own body give a child a feeling of total well-being and adequacy as a person. (Rudolph and Cohen, p. 287)

This ideology strongly supports the child's development of a sense of self and to a large degree the development of the child's ability to collaborate with his peers. However, his ability to use his body in increasingly complex ways, his development of an aesthetic sense, and his ability to think and engage in symbolic representation all take a subordinate position. The latter may emerge from a strong sense of self, but the romantic ideology sees them at best as secondary concerns, which will simply be by-products of maturation.

A Cultural Transmission View

B's movement experience is quite different. Her teacher is concerned with her external, measurable behavior, that is, her performance. Does she make a "square" corner? Can she make a straight line? B must conform to what the teacher values—"round," not oval circles; looking straight ahead while walking on the balance beam even if you fall off; bouncing the ball using alternate hands. B must conform to the teacher's structure —her shapes, her way of hopping, her perception of an *S*. The cultural transmitter believes that his "primary task is the transmission to the present generation bodies of information and/or rules or values collected in the past" (Kohlberg and Mayer, p. 453). The child is viewed as a machine into which stimulus-energies from the environment must be transmitted and/or stored, retrieved, and recombined. Cognitive learning necessitates a statement of desired behaviors or goals. Such behaviors or goals rest in the "value premise of social relativism—the doctrine that values are relative to, and based upon, the standards of the particular culture and cannot be questioned or further justified" (Kohlberg and Mayer, p. 468). The teacher's role is the direct transmission of knowledge, skills, and social and moral rules of a culture. The child can learn at his own rate, but there is a culturally given body of knowledge that he must acquire albeit in a particular sequence (Kohlberg and Mayer).

Such an ideology is more difficult to find in early childhood literature dealing with movement, but it is not difficult to find in psychological literature and physical education literature. Programs with perceptual-motor or movement training in their title seem to be programs based on cultural transmission ideology.

Although perhaps useful for movement observation, Kephart's Perceptual Survey Rating Scale is designed to "point up areas of weakness in the child's perceptual-motor development" (Kephart, *The Slow Learner,* p. 158). Furthermore, Kephart's "training activities," though advocated for "aiding the development of more generalized skills," are specific (i.e., chalkboard training, sensorimotor training, training ocular control, and training form perception) and have clearly spelled out secondary skills to be developed. For example, in using a balance beam, the child must first learn to "walk forward, then backward, then sideways, and finally turning and bouncing" (Kephart, *The Slow Learner,* pp. 218–19). Directionality is taught on a chalkboard in a follow-the-dots form beginning with short distances and gradually increasing the distances between succeeding dots; the teacher places a new dot only after the child has connected the last dot. Angels-in-the-snow is taught in a sequential pattern; the teacher begins by asking the child to move both legs apart as far as he can, keeping his knees stiff and progressing toward the use of different combinations of legs and arms (Kephart, *The Slow Learner,* pp. 230–33). Similar programs are described by Connor, Godfrey, and Cratty.

Herkowitz described additional perceptual-motor training programs. Through the use of specially designed equipment such as copper tubing hoops rubber banded together; plywood squares, circles, and triangles large enough to crawl through; a swinging bridge for crawling over; and a bed spring; Herkowitz describes a perceptual-motor training program to improve the gross motor abilities of preschoolers. Smith's training program for kindergarten children includes specific ways of jumping in and out of a circle. He directly teaches "over-under," "through-between," and "outside-inside" concepts through the use of jumping and animal walks.

This ideology puts the child's sense of self and his ability to collaborate with his peers in the background. The development of particular movement skills is paramount. There is "a" way, that is the teacher's way, society's way, to use one's body. Independent thinking and symbolic representation are relegated to memory and channeled conformity. The teacher must "teach" society's forms and patterns. The child is trained to perform, not educated. Although definitive answers have yet to be found, it seems that such training programs may have a role to play for children with severe perceptual-motor problems and/or children who have fixated movement patterns despite opportunities designed to unlock their rigidities.

A Developmental-Interaction View

C's teacher seems to value the cognitive-affective interaction of the child in his environment. The teacher acknowledges the child's view by saying "That's another way (to get buses down from a higher level)." But she also helps C view the problem from many angles by stating "You might like to look in this bus book and see if there are any other ways or ideas." When the blocks slide off the support, she acknowledge's C's frustration and provides a clue to an alternative method. The teacher says, "You seem to have a problem. Do you think you can use these (triangles) to build a ramp?" During the movement experience she also structures the environment but looks for and values each child's perception and mode of responding. "Now try different ways of traveling with important knees. . . . Try taking them low near the ground for a while. . . . Now try taking them high near the ceiling. . . . Let's look at a few of these interesting ideas." Sometimes the task is extremely open (e.g., "When you are ready, move into the space and practice your own movement idea."). Sometimes it is more closed (e.g., "Get ready to . . . stop."). But there is always structure, a clear expectation. Ordering, reasoning, problem solving, and development is different for each child; yet the content (e.g., bus stations, ways of traveling with important knees) is the same. This progressive view of education acknowledges both internal states and external behavior. Progressive teachers are familiar with stages in mental development and attempt to discover not only the stage each child is in but how particular experiences help each child to reflect new integrations of his thought. The progressive educator is interested in sequence of development, that is, a longitudinal view of children's thinking. The young child integrates his experiences despite us. It becomes the teacher's role to provide experiences which will facilitate a logical and healthy integration of tasks which require gradually more complex reasoning, problem solving, judgment, and action. More specifically, the teacher's role in designing movement experiences is to

1. Identify each child's style of thinking.
2. Identify the stage of development of each child's thinking.
3. Design particular experiences which will help each child move ahead in his thinking.
4. Know how to arouse the kind of cognitive conflict, social conflict, and disagreement which leads children to search for new understandings.
5. Provide experiences which enable the child to focus his attention on his own movement and receive "natural" feedback.

This third strand of educational ideology was originally described by Kohlberg as the cognitive-developmental point of view; called the developmental-interaction point of view by Shapiro and Biber; and education for development by Almy. A common thread, development, is clearly visible in all three terms, and that development deals with both cognitive and affective structures. Born out of a marriage of Piaget's research and Dewey's progressivism, this educational ideology discards the dichotomy of the nature-nurture controversy and speaks to an organism-environment interaction which brings about reorganization of psychological structures. Despite the common thread, clear formulations have yet to emerge. Kohlberg speaks of cognitive and affective development as parallel aspects of structural transformations undergone in development, while Shapiro and Biber speak of developmental-*interaction*. I prefer Shapiro and Biber's construction because developmental-interaction implies a complexity in the child's interaction with his total environment as well as complexity in the interaction between cognitive and affective structures.

> Development refers to the emphasis on identifiable patterns of growth and modes of perceiving and responding which are characterized by increasing differentiation and progressive integration as a function of chronological age. Interaction refers, first, to the emphasis on the child's interaction with the environment—adults, other children, and the material world, and second, to the interaction between cognitive and affective spheres of development. The developmental-interaction formulation stresses the nature of the environment as much as it does the patterns of the responding child. (Shapiro and Biber)

Such a formulation embodies numerous implications for teaching-learning and for movement education. Cognitive functions of ordering, reasoning, problem solving, and symbolic representation must be viewed in the context of the child's development of a sense of self, social collaboration, an aesthetic sense, and increasingly complex ways of using his body. It is critical that teachers recognize the interdependence of these developmental tasks, and educational practice must reflect the complexity in the interaction among them. Curriculum must recognize and stimulate the individually unique integration of each child's thinking-being, thinking-relating, thinking-feeling, and thinking-moving. Some movement education literature and practice does reflect growth toward this ideology.

For nearly twenty years Andrews' book, *Creative Rhythmic Movement for Children*, and Murray's book, *Dance in Elementary Education*, have been sources of inspiration for teachers. Written for both specialists and classroom teachers, these books make a plea for problem solving and discovery through stimulated decision making. Mosston delineates observable teaching styles in physical education along a continuum of teacher-student interaction in the decision-making process, a gradual movement from command to discovery. As this complex interaction between the teacher, the student, and the subject matter evolves in a series of teaching styles, Mosston continually refers to the effect of each style on physical, social, emotional, and intellectual channels of development. In his final chapter entitled "Problem Solving," he points to individualization in each facet of development which leads to "inclusion" of every student rather than "exclusion" of all but those who can achieve at a level commanded by the teacher. Although Andrews, Murray, and Mosston support, in part, a developmental point of view, their texts are directed to the teacher of the elementary age child. Teachers of the very young child will find their books limited. Since the needs of individual children and groups of children are unique, the best literature provides a clear structure to help the teacher design his own curriculum. *Moving and Knowing* by Gerhardt gives suggestions for individual curriculum design. It focuses on the three- to six-year-old child, builds a strong theoretical base for movement in education, and provides a structure to help the teacher design rich movement experiences for young children. Since it is directed specifically to the development of concepts of space through body movement, it speaks primarily to this fundamental learning task through the use of a broad range of carefully designed materials and experiences.

Although there is a clear need in English literature for theoretical clarification of the role of movement in education, the practice of movement education in England's primary schools seems to fit most nearly the developmental-interaction ideology. Rooted in principles of movement developed by Laban which provide a structure for planning movement curriculum and observing movement behavior, movement education practice in England enhances the young child's total development. The reader may find some of the following literature useful. Brearley's chapter on movement focuses on the young child and builds the best theoretical base I have found in English movement literature, but it does not directly help the teacher design movement curriculum. Although they provide limited theoretical foundations, the Inner London Education Authority book, *Movement Education for Infants*, Cameron and Cameron's book, *Education in Movement in the Infant School*, and Boorman's book, *Creative Dance in the First Three Grades* are directed to the teacher of the five to eight year old and provide practical suggestions for designing movement experiences. Russell's book, *Creative Dance in the Primary School*, provides both a theoretical framework and practical suggestions, but her book is concerned with the child who is five to eleven years old. With a "movement" understanding of Laban's principles of movement, Russell's lesson plan design is both useful and educationally valid.

The developmental-interaction ideology seems to satisfy all five developmental tasks described earlier. The child's perception is critical; his sense of self is tied to this perception. The child is encouraged to collaborate socially with his peers as well as with adults in finding solutions to his problems. The teacher consciously designs school experiences to help the child first differentiate his sensory perceptions and then organize these perceptions in patterns that are aesthetically satisfying to him. His curriculum brings him into direct contact with the real world for feeling, seeing, smelling, tasting, and hearing and provides material such as blocks, wood, paint, clay, and sand so that he can recreate his experience. Development of increasingly complex ways of using his body is not left to maturation or structured for him. Movement tasks are designed to focus his attention and encourage new body responses. Finally, each child's own organizations are actively elicited; his thinking is valued and his symbols are encouraged.

Some Specific Guidelines for Movement Education

The foregoing discussion was designed to raise some questions and answer others. Hopefully, it opened the reader's mind to some of the issues, theories, methodologies, and research permeating current movement education literature. The literature is both incomplete and confusing, leaving the classroom teacher with many unanswered questions. This is as it should be. Teachers must accept the challenge to actively search for new understandings. The suggestions that follow are a few guidelines for the teacher to use in this search.

First a word of caution lest you think it is suggested that American movement education must replicate English movement education. It cannot and should not. What has developed and exists in English movement education developed organically over a period of twenty-five years or more, in a context that is different from the American educational context. In addition, early childhood classrooms in America are considerably larger than English classrooms and the American pupil-teacher ratio is considerably smaller than the English pupil-teacher ratio. Numerous authorities have suggested that there are basic social and cultural differences as well. There are, however, some characteristics of quality movement experiences that American educators can take from the English movement education model.

1. Movement education in early childhood should be taught by the classroom teacher who is in the best position to know each child's characteristic growth and level of development. Physical educators who have a strong background in movement education should be used as consultants to provide workshops, literature, guidance, and moral support for the classroom teacher.
2. All young children should have guided movement experiences at least three times per week for a minimum of twenty minutes. Teachers should not only be encouraged to provide a well-rounded program of expressive movement, functional movement, dramatic movement but also to use and develop skills in movement areas of their particular interest.

3. In-service courses in movement should be available regularly for all teacher's continuous growth and development. This need could be met by physical educators who have been educated through body movement or by local colleges and universities offering courses in movement education.
4. Children should be encouraged through movement to think independently, build sensitivity to one another, express their aesthetic awareness with increasing sensitivity, and develop increasingly complex ways of using their bodies.
5. Functional movement apparatus and materials should be designed so that young children can set them up and put them away independently and so that they can be arranged in numerous architectural patterns. Such materials should be designed for both indoor and outdoor use.
6. Children should explore movement barefoot and in clothing that has no buttons, zippers, snaps, and other harsh decorations. Underwear, leotards, and knit shorts with elastic waistbands are possibilities.

As teachers we need to be in touch with our own body movement. The degree to which we understand our own body in movement is directly related to the degree to which we can understand the significance of the young child's body movement and plan meaningful movement experiences for him. The content of our understanding should include the following:

1. What the body can do—activities (locomotion, elevation, turns, gestures, rising/sinking, opening/closing, advancing/retreating, rolling, etc.), relationships of body parts to the whole body in movement, symmetrical and asymmetrical movement, simultaneous and successive movement, body shapes (e.g., arrow, wall, ball, screw)
2. How the body moves in relation to the qualitative factors of weight (strength/lightness), time (suddenness/sustainment), space (direct/flexible), and flow (bound/free)
3. Where and in what shapes the body moves—extension (small/large), level (high/medium/low), direction (high/deep, forward/backward, right/left), air patterns (straight, angular, curved, twisted), floor patterns (straight, angular, curved, twisted)
4. Relationships the body builds between and among body parts, other individuals, groups of individuals
5. The study of *functional movement*—movement directed toward a practical or external purpose (e.g., ball handling, climbing, rolling, hanging, flight, balancing, "arriving on," "on and off balancing," traveling, etc.)
6. The study of *expressive movement*—movement which communicates feeling, moods, ideas, and thus serves an inner purpose (e.g., movement accompanied with sounds, words, percussion sounds, poetry, music, etc.)
7. Techniques of *observation* and interpretation of body movement behavior and characteristic movement styles—Teachers need to be familiar with stages in motor development as well as how environmental factors contribute to motor skill. (e.g., What is the significance of rolling around each of the three body axes? What role does creeping play in walking, running, and handwriting skills? What body movement experiences does the tense, anxious child need? What

movement experiences does the child who lacks inner controls of his movement need?)

8. How *physical space and materials* contribute to movement learning—Which materials structure body movement in the vertical (up and down), horizontal (side to side) and sagittal (forward and back) planes? Which materials invite movement on different angles through space? Which materials are stable? Which ones move? Which climbing materials force the child to have both hands on the same level, and which ones force the climber to always have each hand and each foot on different levels? What textures (e.g., rope, leather, rubber, wood, sand, grass, pebbles) are available for movement exploration? Which materials invite children to arrange and design their own movement experiences? What role do large open spaces, narrow spaces, hills, platforms, high spaces, low spaces, curved spaces, and angular spaces play? What role does the natural environment play—tree stumps, brooks, hills? Of what value are materials that structure movement over/under, around/through, in/out, above/below, up/down? Why is it important to have places where children can hang upside down, slide, roll? Why is it important for children to have materials for pushing and pulling?

References

Almy, M. "Guiding Children for Life in Tomorrow's World." In *Education in Anticipation of Tomorrow,* edited by R.H. Anderson. Belmont, Calif.: Wadsworth Publishing Co., 1973.

American Association for Health-Physical Education-Recreation. *Motor Activity for Early Childhood.* Washington, D.C.: American Association for Health-Physical Education-Recreation, 1971.

Anderson, M.E. *Inventive Movement.* London: Chambers, 1970.

Andrews, G. *Creative Rhythmic Movement for Children.* Englewood Cliffs, N.J.: Prentice-Hall, 1954.

Arnold, P.J. *Education, Physical Education and Personality Development.* London: Heinemann, 1968.

Bailey, E. *Discovering Music with Young Children.* New York: Philosophical Library, 1958.

Barrett, K.R. "Learning to Move—Moving to Learn: Discussion at the Crossroads." *Theory into Practice* 12(1973): 109-11

Barsch, R.H. *Achieving Perceptual-Motor Efficiency.* Seattle, Wash.: Special Child Publications, 1967.

Bartlett, F.C. *Remembering.* Cambridge, England: Cambridge University Press, 1964.

Baylor, B. *Sometimes I Dance Mountains.* New York: Charles Scribner's Sons, 1973.

Biber, B. "A Learning-Teaching Paradigm Integrating Intellectual and Affective Processes." In *Behavioral Science Frontiers in Education,* edited by E. Bower and W. Hollister. New York: John Wiley & Sons, 1967.

Blackie, P.; Bullough, B.; and Nash D. *Drama.* Toronto: MacMillan, 1972.

Boorman, J. *Creative Dance in the First Three Grades.* New York: David McKay Co., 1969.

Borton, H. *Do You Move as I Do?* New York: Abelard-Schuman, 1963.

Bower, E.M., and Hollister, W.G., eds. *Behavioral Science Frontiers in Education*. New York: John Wiley & Sons, 1967.

Brearley, M., ed. *Teaching Young Children: Some Applications of Piaget's Learning Theory*. New York: Schocken Books, 1970.

Brown, R.C., Jr., and Cratty, B.J. *New Perspectives of Man in Action*. Englewood Cliffs, N.J.: Prentice-Hall, 1969.

Cameron, W.M., and Cameron, M. *Education in Movement in the Infant School*. Oxford, England: Basil Blackwell and Mott, 1969.

Cameron, W.M., and Pleasance, P. *Education in Movement School Gymnastics*. Oxford, England: Basil Blackwell and Mott, 1963.

Conner, O.M. "The Effect of Neuro-Muscular Activity on Achievement and Intelligence of Kindergarten Children." Ph.D. dissertation, Michigan State University, 1965.

Cratty, B.J. *Intelligence in Action/Physical Activities for Enhancing Intellectual Abilities*. Englewood Cliffs, N.J.: Prentice-Hall, 1973.

———. *Movement Behavior and Motor Learning*. Philadelphia: Lea & Febiger, 1967.

———. *Movement, Perception and Thought*. Palo Alto, Calif.: Peek Publications, 1969.

———. *Perceptual-Motor Behavior and Educational Processes*. Springfield, Ill.: Charles C Thomas, Publisher, 1969.

———. *Some Educational Implications of Movements*. Seattle, Wash.: Special Child Publications, 1970.

Department of Education and Science. *Movement, Physical Education in the Primary Years*. London: Her Majesty's Stationery Office, 1972.

Erikson, E.H. *Childhood and Society*. 2d ed. New York: W.W. Norton & Co., 1963.

Frostig, M., and Maslow, P. *Movement Education: Theory and Practice*. Chicago: Follet Educational Corporation, 1970.

Gerhardt, L.A. *Moving and Knowing: The Young Child Orients Himself in Space*. Englewood Cliffs, N.J.: Prentice-Hall, 1973.

———. "The Role of Movement in the Child's Conceptualization of Space." Ed.D. dissertation, New York University, 1970.

Godfrey, B. "Development of a Motor Therapy Laboratory." Speech delivered at the Summer Conference of the University of Michigan Graduate Department of Physical Education. Ann Arbor, Michigan, July, 13, 1964.

Godfrey, B., and Kephart, N.C. *Movement Patterns and Motor Education*. New York: Appleton-Century-Crofts, 1969.

Gordon, L.D. "Relative Importance of Various Physical Education Objectives for Grades K–2." *American Association for Health-Physical Education-Recreation Research Quarterly* 44(1973):192–96.
Columbia University Press, 1952.

Hays, J. "Creative Movement Exploration." *Journal of Health, Physical Education and Recreation* 44(1973):95–96.

Herkowitz, J. "A Perceptual-Motor Training Program to Improve the Gross Motor Abilities of Preschoolers." *Journal of Health, Physical Education and Recreation* 41(1970):38–42.

Inner London Education Authority. *Movement Education for Infants*. London: I.L.E.A., 1967.

Jordon, D. *Childhood and Movement*. Oxford, England: Basil Blackwell and Mott, 1966.

Kephart, N. *The Slow Learner in the Classroom.* Columbus, Charles E. Merrill Publishing Co., 1960.

———. *Success through Play.* New York: Harper & Row, Publishers, 1960.

Kohlberg, L., and Mayer, R. "Development as the Aim of Education." *Harvard Educational Review* 42(1972):449–96.

Laban, R. *Modern Educational Dance.* London: MacDonald and Evans, 1963.

Laban, R., and Lawrence, F.C. *Effort.* London: MacDonald and Evans, 1947.

Lowndes, B. *Movement and Drama in the Primary School.* London: B.T. Batsford, 1970.

Minor, F. "Cognitive Development: Some Pervasive Issues." *Theory into Practice* 12(1973): 78–87.

Mosston, M. *Developmental Movement.* Columbus, O.: Charles E. Merrill Publishing Co., 1965.

———. *Teaching Physical Education: From Command to Discovery.* Columbus, O.: Charles E. Merrill Publishing Co., 1966.

Murdoch, E.B. *Expressive Movement.* London: Chambers, 1973.

Murray, R. *Dance in Elementary Education.* New York: Harper and Row, Publishers, 1953.

National Association for the Education of Young Children. *The Significance of the Young Child's Motor Development.* Washington, D.C.: National Association for the Education of Young Children, 1971.

Piaget, J. *The Origins of Intelligence in Children.* Translated by M. Cook. New York: W.W. Norton & Co., 1952.

Read, K.H. *The Nursery School, A Human Relationships Laboratory.* Philadelphia: W.B. Saunders Co., 1971.

Roach, E.C., and Kephart, N.C. *The Purdue Perceptual-Motor Survey.* Columbus, O.: Charles E. Merrill Publishing Co., 1966.

Rudolph, M., and Cohen, D.H. *Kindergarten, A Year of Learning.* New York: Appleton-Century-Crofts, 1964.

Russell, J. *Creative Dance in the Primary School.* London: MacDonald and Evans, 1965.

Schurr, E.L. *Movement Experiences for Children.* New York: Appleton-Century-Crofts, 1967.

Shapiro, E., and Biber, B. "The Education of Young Children: A Developmental-Interaction Approach." *Teachers College Record* 74(1972):55–79.

Sheehy, E.D. *Children Discover Music and Dance.* New York: Holt, Rinehart & Winston, 1959.

Sinclair, C.B. *Movement of the Young Child Ages Two to Six.* Columbus, O.: Charles E. Merrill Publishing Co., 1973.

Smith, P. "Perceptual-Motor Skills and Reading Readiness of Kindergarten Children." *Journal of Health, Physical Education and Recreation* 41(1970):47.

Stanley, S. *Physical Education—A Movement Orientation.* Toronto: McGraw-Hill, 1969.

Vygotsky, L.S. *Thought and Language.* Cambridge, Mass.: The MIT Press, 1962.

Chapter Eleven

The Process Approach

Daniel C.
Jordon

Developing full human potential.

Introduction

In one way or another, curriculum has been a central concern of formal education since its inception. But as a recognized field of inquiry in the United States, it did not come into being until the 1920s. Since then it has gone through a number of "identity crises" related to such fundamental issues as the definition of curriculum itself; whether or not there is, should, or could be a theory of curriculum; who should determine what a curriculum is; how to make it socially relevant; and, assuming the legitimacy of theoretical notions concerning curriculum, how to reduce the gap between theory and practice and effect a reapproachment between theoreticians and practitioners. More recently, the struggle over the issue of what should be done to the curriculum to help equalize educational opportunity has been added to the list of concerns facing curriculum developers.

Other equally important questions have yet to be raised in any systematic way: What is the relationship between a theory of curriculum and a theory of teaching? Does the nature of learning itself have a bearing upon what is meant by curriculum? What implications for curriculum arise out of the nature of knowledge and how can one come to acquire knowledge? How comprehensive should the curriculum be?

Since the knowledge explosion is upon us and there is no way to teach anything but the tiniest fraction of man's accumulated knowledge, what criteria should be used in determining what should make up that tiniest fraction?

With a few notable exceptions, the past fifty years of curriculum development have been characterized by fragmentary and piecemeal efforts to deal with the basic issues outlined above. Educators, theorists, researchers, practitioners, psychologists, and a variety of local, regional, and national commissions have participated in these efforts. Any field of inquiry beleaguered by the continuing irresolution of so many of its fundamental issues is bound to become paralyzed. Schwab says:

> The field of curriculum is moribund. It is unable, by its present methods and principles, to continue its work and contribute significantly to the advancement of education. It requires new principles which will generate a new view of the character and variety of its problems. It requires new methods appropriate to the new budget of problems. (Schwab, p. 1)

Schwab believes that the curriculum became moribund because of an "inveterate, unexamined, and mistaken reliance on theory" and that the only way we can salvage it is to leave theoretical pursuits and concentrate on dealing in a practical way with problems and issues as they arise through the process of deliberation (Schwab, p. 1). At the same time, he advises that an eclectic approach should be used in arriving at a decision as to what ought to be done in response to a given issue or problem. By eclectic, Schwab means appropriately applying the knowledge which theories represent to different practical problems. He does not believe that the eclectic approach means combining alternative theories into one coherent theory—an achievement which, according to him, may take a hundred years. Because things are in such a bad state of affairs, he believes that educators cannot afford to wait a hundred years; it is therefore necessary for them to deal with educational problems on an ad hoc basis through the process of deliberation.

While Schwab's approach might relieve short-term tensions, it will not bring us any closer to a long-range solution to the problems surrounding the field of curriculum. On the contrary, the solution to complex curriculum issues lies essentially in the construction of a comprehensive theory, whose propositions, definitions, and explanations will function as an efficient guide to practices that lead to the achievement of specific educational objectives. If the objectives are efficiently achieved by applying the theory, the theory becomes substantiated. If not, the theory is challenged and must be modified; but that does not mean theory construction and research is unimportant.

For several years, my colleagues and I have been working on the construction of a theory of curriculum which forms a part of a comprehensive theory of education. This body of theory and the procedures for translating it into practice are known as the Anisa model (Streets and Jordan). In the course of working on the model, we attempted to deal with every one of the issues concerning curriculum development previously mentioned. There are therefore many different aspects of this work which are beyond the scope of this chapter, but the efforts we made to define curriculum in a comprehensive way and the endeavor to create a process curriculum are directly relevant. *Our experience has led us to conclude that if the field of curriculum is moribund, it is because curriculum has been defined too narrowly in terms of subject matter or content rather than in the broader context of human development. To rescue it from that condition, we believe that curriculum development must be given a broader theoretical base that takes into account the nature of development and directly reflects the idea of process.* Understanding a process approach to curriculum necessarily depends upon knowing something about human development and the nature of process. For this reason, the process curriculum of the Anisa model, which is derived from a comprehensive theory of development, can only be understood by knowing the theory to which we now turn our attention.

The Nature of Development and the Meaning of Process

Development refers to a change in an organism from one state to a more complex and highly integrated state; *process* refers to a patterned expression of energy utilization that depends on some structure in the brain that produces the pattern. Developmental change is therefore accompanied by the accumulation and integration of new structures and their associated functions. Generally speaking, new structures and their integration occur as a result of biological maturation on the one hand and learning on the other.

Developmental psychology is the primary discipline concerned with a description and explanation of changes in patterns of human behavior over time. It therefore has a special interest in process. Understanding the nature of change and process has been problematical not only for psychology but also for philosophical thought and for the world of practical action as well. While much remains to be learned about the nature of human development and the processes involved in the organism's progression from conception to death, a great deal of knowledge has accumulated that has implications for educational practice in general and for the development of a process curriculum in particular.

The following list highlights certain features of the nature of development and the meaning of process, each one of which had an important bearing upon the development of the Anisa theories of development and curriculum.

1. *Development presupposes potentiality*—Once we agree that being is not characterized by static actuality, we are impelled to consider process, and process presupposes potentiality. Anything that develops must have the potential for becoming what it eventually does become (e.g., the oak tree, not the pine tree, is potentially present within the acorn).

2. *Development presupposes some end state*—This proposition is perhaps one of the more controversial issues in development. Such an assumption immediately raises a question as to what the end state is, and many scientists and theorists object to any idea of teleology (purpose or final cause) which such an assumption entails.

3. *Development is orderly*—If the movement from one state of being to a subsequent one is orderly, processes (i.e., the functionings associated with particular structures) must be characterized by a pattern and occur sequentially.

4. *Development is progressive*—If the nature of change over time is progressive, a later developmental stage will always be different from a previous one and identifiably so on the basis of some criteria, usually complexity and level of integration.
5. *Development is cumulative and continuous*—For all practical purposes, a later state of being is the consequence of the preceding stages of development. In other words, all subsequent stages have their roots in earlier stages; something cannot come out of nothing.
6. *Development has a rhythm*—Not only are the changes comprising development orderly in terms of their spatial configuration but there is also a temporal orderliness or pattern as well. Timing is important. For instance, certain nutritional elements or experiences are more critical at certain times than they are at others.
7. *Development is irreversible*—Changes take place in succession and are irreversible. Development proceeds irreversibly in one direction. For instance, it is not possible to "unlearn" something; it is only possible to add additional learning which may have the effect of altering a behavior that emerged out of some kind of prior learning.

Using the above characteristics of development as a point of departure, we formulated a comprehensive theory of development which defines development as the translation of potentiality into actuality and equates the translation with creativity, the "universal of universals" (Whitehead). The theory accounts for the means (process) by which the translation takes place, classifies potentialities, establishes three basic categories of environment, and describes the nature of actuality in terms of value formation (see Kalinowski and Jordon). This comprehensive theory of development serves as the generative base for the construction of a theory of curriculum which deals with both process and content. It affirms that the translation of potentiality into actuality is sustained by the *organism* itself at whatever state it is in at any given moment in time, by the *environment*, and by the *interaction* between them. All three have basic implications for the definition of curriculum.

The theory establishes two fundamental categories of potentialities: biological and psychological. It cites nutrition as the key factor in the actualization of biological potentialities and fixes learning as the key factor in the actualization of psychological potentialities. While the process curriculum of the Anisa model includes nutrition and the development of biological potentialities, this chapter focuses only on the process curriculum related to the actualization of psychological potentialities (see Raman, "Nutrition and Educational Planning"). Psychological potentialities are broken down into five basic categories: psychomotor, perceptual, cognitive, affective, and volitional. Because the translation of these potentialities into actuality is regarded as synonomous with creativity in the most fundamental sense of that term, we believe that any school system intending to foster creativity must necessarily emphasize process rather than product in its conception of the total curriculum. In the model, each category of potentiality has been broken down further into important processes which by virtue of their fundamental nature are keys to large numbers of subsequent developments. These processes form the basis for the development of the Anisa process curriculum. Explanations and examples of these processes will be presented later, and their implications for practice will be explored.

If learning is the key factor in the translation of psychological potentialities into actuality, then *learning* is the *essential creative process* around which the process curriculum should be developed. Thus, understanding the nature of learning is for all practical purposes the same as understanding the nature of process and a prerequisite to the development of a process curriculum.

We conducted an extensive review and analysis of all major learning theories in hope of distilling from them a common denominator that would shed light on the nature of learning and lead to a fuller understanding of process. After an intensive effort at comparative analysis, we finally arrived at the following definition: learning is the ability of the organism to differentiate experience by breaking it down into contrastable units; to combine or integrate these contrastable elements in novel ways thereby generating new patterns of movement, perception, thoughts, feelings, and intentions; and to generalize these patterns to new situations.

Differentiation, integration, and generalization, then, constitute the essential characteristics of process; they depend on the development of particular structures in the brain and are applicable to whatever category of potentiality is being addressed. For instance, processes pertinent to psychomotor potentialities will concern *differentiation* of the movements of the various muscles of the body, their *integration* into particular movement patterns such as walking, skipping, or swimming, and the *generalization* of these patterns to a variety of other situations. If the process being developed is an important and obvious one, we sometimes refer to it as a stage. When a child, for example, is learning how to differentiate the movements of muscles which then become integrated in a particular way so that locomotion in an upright position is possible, we say that the child is at the "walking stage" that was preceded by a "crawling stage."

Because there is an infinite number of processes, some decision has to be made concerning which processes are important enough to be included in a process curriculum. Our most difficult tasks continue to be identifying the processes which seem to be critical for subsequent major developments, researching them, and expressing them as elements in the process curriculum. Some processes are evidently essential or prerequisite to the development of large numbers of additional processes, while others are not. Taking this as a given, it follows that those processes which lead to the largest number of important subsequent developments would be the ones which should be first in line for inclusion in the process curriculum. Degree of probable necessity for subsequent developments is one of the basic criteria we applied when deciding whether or not to include a particular process in the curriculum.

We use the word *process* to refer to the functioning that is made possible by some structure in the brain which is built up out of the organism's particular interactions with particular environments. Process is not to be confused with activity that is provided for a child. We reserve the phrase *interaction with the environment* to describe what the child does. It is the purpose of the process curriculum to specify what kinds of environments and what kinds of interactions with those environments are necessary for particular structures to emerge, thereby endowing the child with competence to function in terms of their associated processes. We cannot, as yet, isolate specific anatomical structures in the tissues of the brain and their analogous physiological functions on which the processes depend. We therefore infer the presence of the structures and their functioning by patterns of behavior which we can observe. However, we should not make the mistake of believing that a given structure is not there if the person does not perform a particular behavior. It is possible to know how to do something without ever doing it so that if and when it is done, it is done right the first time. In our view, an excessively behavioristic orientation to learning is like wearing blinders. Much of what is important about the nature of human development and learning is not directly observable, but just because we cannot see it is no justification for believing it does not or cannot exist. What goes on inside the head is tremendously important for psychology as a science. Thought does not necessarily have any immediate or directly related behavioral manifestations; yet few people would deny its importance.

A Comprehensive Theory of Curriculum

Ultimately, any satisfactory theory of curriculum must derive from a superordinate theory that explains the nature of the human being whom the curriculum is supposed to serve; thus a curriculum theory cannot be completely independent and autonomous. If it is not derived from a theory of development, it is likely to be unworkable because it fails to take into consideration the characteristics of man. For example, a curriculum theory that does not take into consideration characteristics such as interest, motivation, attention, and fatigue, or even more importantly, the developmental characteristics associated with the acquisition of knowledge will be doomed to failure when implemented and will survive only because other parts of the educational system compensate in some way for its deficiencies. Unfortunately, there has been no adequate theory of development from which a satisfactory theory of curriculum might be derived. This accounts for the inability of theorists up to this time to produce such a theory of curriculum.

A theory of teaching, like a theory of curriculum, can also only exist as a derivative from a theory of development. To teach is to help children learn; a successful theory of teaching must therefore be derived from a theory of development that explicates the nature of learning. In other words, if somebody is teaching, children must be learning; if they are not, then we cannot say any teaching is going on (see Streets and Jordan).

From the Anisa theory of development we have derived compatible theories of curriculum and teaching. There will no doubt be other theories of development emerging in the future, and the Anisa theory will probably undergo perpetual modification and refinement. However, the present Anisa theories of development and curriculum will suffice for our purposes of explaining a process approach to curriculum and the relationship of process to content.

On the propositions set forth by the Anisa theory of development, we based the Anisa theory of curriculum which defines curriculum as two interrelated sets of educational goals and what children do, usually with the help of peers and adults, to achieve those goals. In essence, curriculum consists of goals and a specification of interactions with particular environments to achieve those goals. For example, one set of goals concerns assimilation of information about the world in which we live; they form part of the content curriculum. Culture and direct experience are the primary sources of this information, the organization of which rests on the classification of environments as set forth in the theory of development. The other set of goals concerns the potentialities of man and the means by which they become actualized through learning; they form part of the process curriculum. Achieving these two sets of goals (i.e., content and process) results in the emergence of a personal identity—a Self. As this Self gains mastery over its environment and over the processes of its own becoming, it can take charge of its own destiny; this is the overarching purpose of the Anisa model.

The five categories of potentialities established by the theory of development provide the basic organization of the process curriculum. Designed to develop competencies in each of these areas, the process curriculum sets the guidelines for creating experiences for children that enable them to develop structures in the brain which when functioning are evidence that the child has developed a particular process. Each category of potentiality has been broken down into the processes which underlie learning competence in that area. All of the processes, regardless of the category of potentiality to which they are related, are comprised of differentiation, integration, and generalization in some combination or another. The emphasis of a process curriculum is on the "how" as opposed to the "what" of a content curriculum. For instance, the content curriculum may focus on *what* a child should be thinking about whereas the process curriculum focuses on enabling a child to learn *how* to think. The process curriculum of the Anisa model is thus organized to enable a child to know *how* to move his muscles and gain maximum control over them, *how* to perceive, *how* to think, *how* to feel, and *how* to formulate intentions and consummate them. As the child masters the basic processes in each of these areas, he becomes a competent learner—he learns *how* to learn. Learning how to learn is therefore the basic objective of the process curriculum; it is the means whereby one takes charge of one's own becoming.

It is the function of theory to guide practice toward some end. That is why the Anisa theory of curriculum not only specifies the ends but sheds light on how they are to be achieved. This is set forth by the interaction component of the curriculum theory. Detailed explanations of the content curriculum of the Anisa model and the interaction component are beyond the scope of this chapter. However, it should be noted that no curriculum theory can be comprehensive if it does not include both content and process goals and specify what the children must do in what kind of environments in order to master the processes and assimilate the contents outlined in the goals.

Design for a Process Curriculum

The major tasks in designing the Anisa process curriculum were to identify the basic processes that make up learning competence in each of the five categories of potentialities and to determine what interactions with what kinds of environments are necessary to internalize them. In the following sections, a selected number of processes from each category will be identified and briefly explained. A few of the processes will be treated more fully than the others and serve as examples of how particular activities planned for the children are related to the mastery of the processes.

The Psychomotor Process Curriculum

The general definition of psychomotor competence which follows will provide a framework for understanding each of the processes on which the psychomotor process curriculum is based.

> Psychomotor competence is an inner awareness of all of the muscles (which can come under voluntary control to whatever degree), all of the differentiated movements of body parts they are capable of effecting, and the ability to execute an infinite variety of combinations (integrations) of such movements into patterns which express purposes of the organism. By 'body parts' we mean more than head, limbs, and trunk; included are muscles which control the size of the blood vessels, muscles which move the eyes, the tongue, the lips, and the bladder and anal sphincters, the muscles producing speech sounds, muscles which comprise the genital organs, and the diaphragm which controls breathing. (Blane and Jordan)

Since various muscle movements are patterned to carry out certain functions associated with different bodily systems, we have organized the basic process underlying psychomotor competence in terms of these systems.

Vital Functions Systems

Respiratory System. Movement patterns involved in breathing involve the diaphragm and muscles controlling the movement of the ribs, throat, and nasal passages.

Circulatory System. Movement patterns involve cardiac muscle and muscles in the walls of blood vessels controlling dilation and constriction.

Digestive System. Movement patterns involve muscles used in chewing, swallowing, carrying the food to the stomach; the actions of the stomach muscles and intestines; and those involved in elimination.

Reproductive System. Movement patterns concern muscles of the female and male genitals and muscles in the uterine wall.

The movement patterns of all of the muscles involved in these vital functions systems are largely determined by reflex action and maturation rather than consciously directed learning. However, there are a variety of exercises that can increase voluntary control over them. For instance, it is possible for a person to gain control over the muscles in the walls of the blood vessels so that his high blood pressure can be voluntarily reduced through learning how to dilate them. Many of the detailed aspects of this part of the Anisa process curriculum have yet to be researched and developed. We include them here to demonstrate what comprehensiveness in planning a psychomotor process curriculum requires.

Skeletal Muscle System

Balance and posture. This refers to the ability to maintain balance and posture through movement accommodations to the forces of gravity while maintaining a position in space. Balance and posture are made up of several subprocesses as follows:

1. *Verticality*—One must have a functional awareness of different muscles and their movements in relationship to the direction of gravity and awareness of what neural muscular operations (i.e., integrations) stabilize the body with reference to this direction (i.e., verticality). This includes the awareness of which muscles are down and which ones are up and how to move the required muscles to maintain stability.
2. *Laterality*—This refers to a functional awareness that the body has sides: right and left (i.e., symmetrical laterality) and dorsal and ventral (i.e., asymmetrical laterality).
3. *Directionality*—This refers to a functional awareness of the integration of verticality and laterality and their corresponding movement patterns to maintain the organism in its relationship to the forces of gravity. Different combinations of verticality and laterality are reflected in movement patterns which are recognized as sitting, lying down, bending over, standing, kneeling, etc. Directionality does not include movement from one locality to another.

Locomotion. This refers to the ability to execute a series of muscular movements which carries the whole organism through space over time while maintaining balance and posture. The subprocesses of locomotion are

1. *Sequence*—This is the ability to organize the movement of body parts in an ordered series which can culminate in activities such as walking or running.
2. *Synchrony*—This refers to the ability to make movements of body parts simultaneously.
3. *Rhythm*—This is the ability to perform a regular succession of repeated motor actions where there are alternations of tensing and relaxing the muscles or particular groups of muscles.
4. *Pace*—This refers to the ability to establish the appropriate timing of locomotor movements given the intentions of the organism. This includes being able to speed up or slow down movements for a particular purpose.

There are an infinite number of combinations of the above subprocesses that yield different patterns of locomotion such as walking, hopping, jumping, swimming, galloping, skating, and diving.

Manipulation. This refers to the ability to handle or cause some aspects of the environment to be moved in accordance with some purpose. The subprocesses of manipulation are

1. *Making contact*—This is the ability to reach and grasp an object or to receive it by catching.
2. *Maintaining contact*—This refers to holding the object as long as required to achieve a particular purpose.
3. *Handling*—This is the ability to squeeze, rub, pierce, roll, or otherwise control the object.
4. *Termination of contact*—This refers to releasing or dropping objects or propelling them by throwing.

Manipulation occurs, of course, in conjunction with maintaining balance and posture or during locomotion. It also includes the use of objects as extensions of the body such as when one uses a hammer, a shovel, a surfboard, or a pole for vaulting.

Speech System

This system involves the control of muscle movements that cause air to be propelled through the vocal cords. Some of these movements are made by the same muscles which control the respiratory system, but there are additional voluntary elements in the case of speech, laughing, or singing. A special kind of timing and control are required when speech is introduced. Speech also depends upon one's control of muscles of the pharynx and larynx involved in the production of sound and the vocal chords which provide alteration of pitch, amplitude, and timbre. In addition, speech involves the muscles of the face, throat, jaw, tongue, and lips.

Most of the muscle movements involved in producing articulate speech come under voluntary control with maturation, and very little conscious effort is required to learn how to speak. However, children who develop speech problems may require particular exercises that enable them to make appropriate differentiations, integrations, and generalizations in relationship to the production of particular sounds. Part of the problem associated with a speech disorder may also be of a perceptual-auditory nature, or it could be the result of a failure to associate causally (i.e., integrate) a particular set of muscle movements with the particular kind of speech sound desired.

Perceptual Systems

A variety of muscles are used to support or increase perceptual acuity through different modalities. For instance, vision is related to eyelid movements, the movements of the eyeball (circular, vertical, horizontal), and lens accommodation. Olfactory perception is dependent in part upon the muscles which control breathing. Auditory perception is enhanced by posturing and/or turning the head in order to pick up the sound waves more directly. Taste is enhanced by the movement of the tongue. Stimulation of the cutaneous receptors for touch is dependent in part on other bodily movements.

The Anisa psychomotor process curriculum consists of statements of objectives pertinent to each of the processes and subprocesses outlined above and the actual exercises (i.e., interactions with particular environments) that children go through in order to develop the specific competencies desired. In most cases, not one but several processes are involved in a given activity, and they are therefore internalized collectively rather than individually. In the Anisa model, movement and dance (one element of the arts curriculum which also involves music and sound, the visual and plastic arts, theatre arts, and poetry and literature) provide the chief vehicle for the development of psychomotor competence in the early grades. In addition there are a variety of exercises, games, and sports activities which engage the whole child—his perceptual faculties, thinking, feeling, volition, as well as his psychomotor abilities. The advantage of having a process curriculum is that it attempts to make certain that nothing important is left out. In the case of special problems where a child is having coordination difficulties, for instance, it is useful to analyze the muscles involved and prescribe particular kinds of exercises that will enable the child to make the appropriate differentiations and integrations of movements and to generalize them under a variety of circumstances.

As an example, let us single out the process of directionality and discuss some of the activities that children might go through in order to achieve maximum functional awareness of this process.

Activity I

Set a particular problem for each group of children and let them work it out in their own way, as follows:

Ask the children to see how many ways they can maintain their balance by assuming a particular posture in which there is only one contact point with the floor. The most obvious solution to this problem is to stand on one foot. Since we do not ordinarily stand on one foot for very long, maintaining balance with only one contact point requires moving all other muscles in a variety of directions in order to maintain balance. This exercise enables the children to gain experience in directing the pattern of movement of muscles over which they would not ordinarily gain full control. Different levels of complexity can be introduced to meet different developmental levels. For instance, ask those children who find it too easy to stand on one foot to squat down as far as they can go and maintain their position and balance on one foot alone.

Ask for other solutions to the same problem (e.g., rolling the body up into a ball and using the back or perhaps the buttocks as the one contact point).

Activity II

Ask the children to strike a posture having only two contact points with the floor, only one of which can be a foot, and maintain balance. The solution might be to use one foot and one hand. Advanced students may use both hands. Some could use a knee and a foot, a knee and a hand, or a knee and the head, and so forth.

Activity III

Ask the children to assume a posture with three contact points, only one or none of which can be the feet.

Activity IV

Ask the children to strike a posture which involves four contact points with the floor, none of which can be made with hands or feet. They can use elbows and knees.

Activity V

The complexity of the above problems and their solutions can be increased by adding the dimension of locomotion to balance and posture. For instance, when the child tries to move maintaining only one contact point, his most obvious solution is to hop on one foot. Trying to move while maintaining balance and posture under the constraints of each problem activity requires the patterning of muscle movements in unusual ways and leads to an increased voluntary control over skeletal muscles. These problems can be very interesting and entertaining. New kinds of movement patterns can be discovered which might later be introduced into more serious choreographic efforts.

Since the Anisa theory of development cites interaction with the environment as the means by which potentiality is translated into actuality, the implications of psychomotor competence for the development of all other competencies is heavily implicated. We interact with the environment chiefly by means of moving our muscles, whether we are moving our bodies through space or interacting with the human environment through speech, gestures, or bodily contact. Furthermore, when a child activates his muscles, it is impossible for him not to be involved in what he is doing. In other words, a kind of intrinsic motivation accompanies the movement of muscles. The more the content curriculum and other aspects of the process curriculum involve the movement of muscles, the more enthusiastic the pursuit of learning is likely to be. For these reasons, the psychomotor process curriculum is given great emphasis in the Anisa model.

The integration of content with process and some processes with other processes is a paramount feature of the Anisa model. Because the number of possible combinations for children at different levels is practically infinite, descriptions of all of them cannot be written down. That is why teachers must understand the theory thoroughly, for on that basis they can generate any number of activities designed to achieve any number of particular objectives, process or content, which can be associated with the basic psychomotor objectives. For example, an important part of the content curriculum in the Anisa model concerns the names of all of the body parts, descriptions of the movements they can make, and general knowledge about the body as it relates to physical health. The vocabulary required to explain and deal with all of the movement and balance problems possible in developing psychomotor competence is extensive, and exposure to such terms helps the child enlarge his vocabulary. To sit passively at a desk and hear someone explain all of the body parts, all of the movements, or the kinds of joints we have and to memorize the vocabulary would be excessively boring; and the child would have difficulty remembering the information. But when learning such a vocabulary and information about body parts and their functioning is integrated with movement and dance, it is accomplished in a way that is simple for the child. When the child is out on the floor and involved in moving his own body, he is able to assimilate a tremendous amount of content efficiently while at the same time learn how to gain voluntary control over his muscles.

Combining vocabulary development and learning facts about the human body with the psychomotor curriculum is one thing; combining it with reasoning and mathematical thinking is another. However, it can be done. For example, the child grasps rhythm easily when he experiences the movement of body parts. Rhythm means timing and timing means a coordination of patterned durations of movement. Duration means measurement, numbers, mathematics. Classification, seriation, and conservation are important cognitive processes in understanding number relations (see "The Cognitive Process Curriculum," p. 289). Movements can be classified (smooth or jerky, slow or fast, complex or simple); they can be seriated (from slow to fast, from high to low, from fine to gross); or they can be conserved (length of arm movement is not changed when speed is altered). Movement, coupled with problems involving these cognitive processes, has important implications for establishing the cognitive base required for a full understanding of mathematics.

The Anisa process curriculum not only specifies goals but also provides the conceptual framework through which teachers can collaborate. That is, musicians, dancers, and specialists in exercise, science, and mathematics can come together to discover how their various disciplines might be expressed through integrated activities which would strengthen a variety of processes while at the same time enable children to assimilate an enormous amount of content. It is not difficult to see that there is an endless number of possibilities for providing highly motivating ways of assimilating content by integrating it with a psychomotor process curriculum.

The Perceptual Process Curriculum

Perceptual competence refers to the capacity to differentiate sensory information and then integrate that information into generalizable patterns, which constitute interpretations of reality, that enable the organism to make meaningful decisions and to act. Interpretation always concerns the organization of incoming stimuli in terms of past experience, present needs, and aspirations or intentions which involve the future. Perceptual competence rests upon an internal structuring which functions as a set of rules which generate and direct the basic processes of differentiation, integration, and generalization on which the interpretation or organization depends (Conway, 1974). Perceptual processes include those underlying vision, audition, olfaction (smell), gustation (taste), the cutaneous senses (those relating to the skin, such as pressure, cold, hot), and the vestibular senses (equilibrium).

Following is a breakdown of visual perception into a large number of processes, each one of which constitutes an element in the process curriculum dealing with visual perception. There are similar breakdowns of processes underlying each of the other subcategories of perceptual competence, but they are too extensive to be included here.

Visual Perception of Movement

This refers to seeing objects move rather than the perception of movement through kinesthetic and vestibular senses. Vision is not required to determine that the body as a whole is moving through space. Visual input while on an enclosed elevator, for example, will not be related to its movement or the movement of the body; one determines that the body is moving through vestibular and kinesthetic senses. Movement perception depends on a wide variety of subprocesses, such as those listed below.

1. *Directionality*—This is one aspect of movement perception and consists of several elements: fixation (holding an object centrally in the visual field), hori-

zontal pursuit (following movement from right to left or from left to right), vertical pursuit (following an object moving up or down), circular pursuit (following objects moving in circular motion, clockwise or counterclockwise), depth pursuit (following an object that is moving towards the eyes or away from the eyes), and combinations of the above.

2. *Duration (Time Perception)*—This is another aspect of movement perception and consists of several elements: velocity (being able to see the relative speeds of moving objects—slower/faster—and to see changes in speeds), synchrony or simultaneity (being able to ascertain that objects are moving at the same time), rhythm (being able to see a pattern in movement), sequence (being able to see a repetition of patterned units or that one thing comes after another temporally), pace (being able to see variations in the size of temporal units as represented by movement patterns even though the relationship between rhythm and sequence remains constant), and cause/effect (being able to see that one event, B, occurs only *after* a prior event, A. [This is a perceptual form of inference]).

3. *Space (Two-dimensional and Three-dimensional)*—This is a third aspect of movement perception and consists of two elements. *Figure-ground* or *form perception* encompasses several aspects: contour (being able to see the characteristics of the outer form of an object), edge (being able to locate the demarcation that forms the outer limits of an object), proximity (being able to distinguish the nearness or farness of objects in relationship to one another, such as above/below—height or verticality, left/right—width or laterality; front/back or before/behind—judgment of depth, and size/area—judgment of distances), separation (being able to discern disconnectedness among objects), closure (a filling in of gaps to create a figure [another form of perceptual inference analogous to interpolation in cognition]), continuity (being able to organize objects into a sequence [a form of perceptual inference analogous to cognitive extrapolation]), and constancy (being able to interpret the apparent changes in shape that occur when perspective changes as a function of perspective and not a change in the actual shape of an object. The visual image of both shape and size changes with shift in perspective; the objects themselves remain constant). The second element is *projective space* which is three-dimensional only and is determined by a number of cues, some of which can be perceived by one eye alone and some of which require both eyes. Monocular cues consist of proximal size (closer objects appear larger), brightness (closer objects are brighter), shading (shadows create perspective and depth), texture gradient (closer gradients are coarser in texture), linear perspective (parallel lines converge as they recede from the viewer), interposition (closer objects obscure objects behind them), and movement parallax (closer objects appear to move faster). Binocular cues consist of convergence (the closer the object, the more the eyes must turn inward toward each other) and retinal disparity (the closer the object, the greater the disparity between the images falling on the two retinas).

4. *Color*—This is yet another aspect of perception and consists of several elements: hue (being able to discriminate among different wave lengths, for example, being able to tell the difference between red, blue, yellow), saturation (being able to discriminate among complexities of light waves, determining the relative

amounts of gray present within a given hue), brightness (being able to discriminate among different amounts of light reflecting from a given object [being able to tell the difference between shades of one hue such as red, which might be broken down into pink, red, and maroon]), and contrast (combinations of all of the above).

5. *Translation of Two-dimensional Representations into Their Three-dimensional Referents*—Since a great deal of education in the classroom is mediated through two-dimensional representations of three-dimensional reality, children need particular experiences in order to make this kind of translation.
6. *Translation of Three-dimensional Reality into Two-dimensional Representations*—This occurs primarily through drawing pictures and involves knowledge of the various monocular cues, such as texture gradients, other depth cues created by shadows, diminishing size with increased distance from the viewer, etc.

As a case in point, let us examine in some detail the process of figure-ground perception, which we define as

The ability to differentiate certain features from a previously undifferentiated perceptual field and integrate these features into a figure or pattern that is distinctly separate from and predominant over the remaining information in the perceptual field. Those aspects of the field unassociated with the figure become the background, or simply ground. (Anisa, p. 1)

A large variety of simple visual discrimination tasks or games can be devised to facilitate the development of figure-ground perception. Such tasks may also serve a basic diagnostic function as well. For example, the teacher might present a picture containing a variety of different overlapping shapes and objects to the child and ask him to pick out particular shapes such as circles and triangles. More difficult exercises might include a variety of familiar shapes, such as birds, rabbits, and fish, all of which can be embedded in a confusing background of competing lines. The child can then be asked to locate each shape and trace it with a finger.

Different levels of difficulty can be introduced into any particular exercise by making the differentiations more complex or making the integration of the differentiated elements into some kind of figure that is less obvious. For instance, commonly known shapes, such as a circle or an outline of a house, are comprised of lines or elements that can be integrated into those particular figures. If, however, a more abstract or unfamiliar figure is embedded, it will be a greater challenge for a child to make the differentiations and integrations necessary to recognize the figure. As an alternative approach, an outline of the abstract embedded figure can also be drawn as a separate figure, and the child can be asked to locate it in the "ground" of a great number of intersecting lines. Here the task is more difficult because elements are arbitrarily assigned to figure or ground; there is nothing intrinsic to the abstract figure that will help the child separate figure from ground. The separation must take place in his mind as he gives salience to certain differentiated elements and then integrates them into the desired figure.

A good example of how to integrate this aspect of the process curriculum, figure-ground perception, with a science content curriculum concerning information about insects and plant life is to design activities for learning about camouflage in nature and its relation to evolution. Certain moths, for instance, have patterns on their wings which are exactly the same color and have the same configurations as the barks of certain trees. Certain worms have the colors and shapes of twigs. The praying mantis looks exactly like the grass. The visual characteristics of a large number of plants and animals evolved by virtue of natural selection precisely because of the figure-ground phenomenon. In the case of the moths, those visual characteristics which enabled them to be part of the ground rather than the figure when they settled on certain trees made it more difficult for birds to see them. Over time, the moths which were camouflaged became more numerous because fewer of them were eaten by birds. They lived longer and reproduced more, while the more conspicuous members of their own species eventually became extinct because they were eaten more frequently and therefore could not reproduce as rapidly nor as many times. A variety of related activities based on the phenomenon of camouflage can be organized. Children can be invited to draw pictures in which they hide (i.e., merge figure with ground) a given insect; or if there is enough time, they can be invited to camouflage themselves and hide, while others try to find them. The game of hiding the thimble takes on a new dimension of expertise in light of the knowledge of the figure-ground process.

More advanced skills, such as reading, also depend upon figure-ground perception. The reason most printed material is black on white is to facilitate figure-ground discrimination. Red print on a maroon background would make figure-ground perception extremely difficult. Reading music presents an even more difficult task since the musical staff, key signatures, and cleft designation are figure, distinguishable from a white background; but these figures function more as ground when notes are placed upon the staff. Thus, there are a variety of levels of complexity in figure-ground perception where some figures are ground in relationship to other figures and so on.

There are a number of variables that have an influence on figure-ground discrimination and which can be manipulated. For instance, Katz showed that a child's recognition of the figure is improved if he knows the label for that figure. Several studies indicate that complex figures tend to attract more attention than simple figures (Willis and Dornbusch). Experience or habit will cause certain elements to be differentiated from a background and integrated into a figure. For instance, the experience of looking at the human face and a habit of associating certain contours with the nose, the mouth, the eyes, and so forth, will enable the child to "see faces" in almost any complex set of lines that contain these elements (Goldstein and Mackenburg). A dark-light contrast is positively correlated with the ability to distinguish figure from ground (Lit and Vicars). Studies have also shown that if a figure does not possess integrity or cohesion, it may be easily lost in a larger figure simply because its contours provide insufficient contrast with the ground (Gottschaldt). Time is also an important variable. The duration of exposure to a perceptual field will have an influence on one's ability to differentiate figure from ground. Kahneman showed that a minimum amount of time is required if differentiation is to take place and that there is also a saturation point beyond which very little further differentiation tends to occur. In generating a particular activity as a part of this aspect of the process curriculum, teachers can individualize the experience by manipulating the variables of labeling, complexity, experience or habits, contrast, and timing. With appropriate manipulation, an experience can be made extremely simple for young children on lower developmental levels or extremely complex and more challenging for older children or higher developmental levels.

The Cognitive Process Curriculum

Cognition refers to the intellectual processes necessary for thinking and reasoning. The problem of defining the exact nature of thinking is an old one, and much work remains to be done if we are to achieve the clarity that will enable us to identify all of the fundamental processes that make up thinking and which therefore should be included in the process curriculum.

Like the actualization of all the other potentialities, thinking develops from interaction with the environment. Piaget says, "Actually in order to know objects, the subject must act upon them and therefore transform them: he must displace, connect, combine, take apart, and reassemble them" (Piaget, 1970, p. 704). Here we see the reflections of the general processes of differentiation ("displace" and "take apart") and integration ("connect," "combine," and "reassemble").Through these differentiations and integrations, internal structures are developed which form the basis of cognitive competence. The cognitive processes associated with these structures have been explored by Piaget, Bruner, and others. All of the processes are interrelated, and some serve as developmental predecessors of others. Among the processes which make up cognitive competence are the following:

Object Permanence. Apprehension of the continued existence of a stable object when the object is no longer in the immediate perceptual field (called animal inference by Bertrand Russell).

Deduction. Drawing a necessary conclusion from a given premise or set of premises; reasoning from the general to the particular.

Induction. Logical inference of the existence of a general principle from a given set of particulars; reasoning particulars to the general.

Extrapolation. Estimation of the value or nature of a variable based upon an assumed relationship with an observed range of values or particulars; inference of the next element which follows logically from a known sequence or pattern (e.g., 1, 3, 5, 7, 9, x; in this case, x can be inferred by extrapolation to be 11).

Interpolation. Inference of the value or the nature of a missing element or an empty category from the context in which it exists (e.g., The boy missed the first two balls pitched to him but _____ the third ball for a home run. By interpolation we conclude that the blank would be filled in with the word "hit.").

Implication. Logically deriving propositions from a given set of relations; implication may involve a combination of induction, deduction, interpolation and extrapolation.

Classification. Identification and abstraction of a common attribute or property from a group of objects, actions, events, or ideas and integration of these properties or attributes into a class or category which can be generalized to include all other objects, actions, events, or ideas possessing these attributes.

Seriation. The differentiation of quantitative attributes among objects along the single dimension, such as length, and the integration of these differences to form a graded pattern which can be generalized to include elements beyond the original group.

Conservation. The abstraction of qualitative and quantitative invariance of an object, substance, or idea across transformations of associated secondary qualities. Conservation is the ability to recognize that an object remains the same object despite certain transformations. For instance, a pint of water in a tall glass is the same pint of water when poured into a flat pan even though perceptually it may look like it is more.

Number Relations. Coordinating three primary logical processes, classification, seriation, and conservation, in understanding various concepts associated with the construct of number (including one-to-one correspondence, ordination, cardination, and measurement).

Analogy and Metaphor. Abstracting conceptual relations from one set of conditions and then applying them to another set of conditions as a means of achieving explanatory insight (e.g., "A hand is to a glove what a foot is to a _____." Using the process of analogy, one would very likely fill in the blank with "shoe.")

There are a large number of other processes which make up thinking, but the preceding list provides enough examples to convey the general idea of a process curriculum in the area of cognition. Let us now use classification to show how the process curriculum sets guidelines for activities that will enable a child to classify.

An individual's control over his environment and over his interactions with his environment becomes efficient when he is able to differentiate the many elements which comprise the environment and organize them in a pattern congruent with his own needs and intentions. One means by which the individual achieves this is to reduce the complexities of experience to manageable proportions by categorizing or grouping experiences with respect to some shared quality; this process is the first function of classification. The formation of entities called classes can thus be regarded as an essential ingredient of the thinking process itself (Flavell), and as Elkind points out, classification responses help to maintain the psychic economy by eliminating the need for fresh adaptation every time a new experience is encountered.

Any curriculum fostering classification processes cannot ignore the developmental sequence in which they appear. Up to this time, our knowledge of the step-by-step development in this area of cognitive growth comes mainly from the research of Inhelder and Piaget. They have identified the following stages:

1. *Simple sorting* refers to grouping objects according to a single property perceptually obvious such as color, shape, or size.

2. *True classification* refers to abstracting a common property in a group of objects and finding the same property in other objects in the group.
3. *Multiple classification* refers to grouping objects on the basis of more than one common property. Multiple classification also entails a recognition that any given object can belong to several classes at the same time.
4. *All-some relations* refers to being able to recognize a distinction between classes on the basis of a property which belongs to all members of the class and a property which belongs only to some members of the class. For instance, in a display of red squares, red triangles, and red circles, understanding all-some relationships would enable a child to recognize that all shapes are red while only some are squares or triangles.
5. *Class-inclusion relations* refers to an ability to form subclasses of objects or events while including the subclass within a larger class. For instance, in a container of wooden beads some of which are red and yellow in color, there is a subclass of red beads and a subclass of yellow beads, both of which belong to the class of wooden beads.

For those interested in an alternative listing, Koffsky used a scalographic study of classification development and presented a more detailed sequence of skill development than that presented here.

An example of the kind of experience a child needs in order to achieve one of the subprocesses of classification might prove useful. Let us assume that multiple classification is the subprocess of classification to be learned by the child. The purpose of the activity suggested is to enable a child to understand how an object classified on the basis of one attribute may belong to other classes at the same time (intersection) and/or that objects may be classified on the basis of two attributes (matrices) at the same time. The activity requires two large rings of sufficient diameter to include the following variety of objects when placed on a flat surface: four red triangles, four green triangles, four red rectangles, and four black rectangles. The child is instructed to place the rings near one another on a table or floor. He is invited to place all of the triangles inside one of the rings and then to place all of the remaining red objects inside the other ring so that the first ring can only have triangles. The second ring is allowed to have red objects only. The two rings can then be intersected, and the child can be asked which of the objects can be placed in the intersection area on the basis of this rule. If he places only red triangles in the intersection, he understands multiple classification. A similar exercise can be done using a matrix where a given object appears in both a column and a row. Rows could be set up on the basis of geometric shapes and columns could be established on the basis of color.

A teacher who understands the Anisa theories is able to integrate the process curriculum with the content curriculum. In zoology, all of the animals have to be classified; in music, particular pieces can be placed in different classifications (i.e., romantic, classical, baroque, impressionistic, etc.); in social studies, societies can be classified in terms of the basis of their economy (i.e., hunting, food gathering, agricultural, fishing, etc.); in anthropology, men are classified according to races (i.e., biologically inherited physical attributes). Understanding both science and the arts as disciplines depends upon the ability to classify; yet children are rarely taught what the process of classification is so that they understand that they are applying or making use of the same process no matter what the content might be. If they were taught the process with an emphasis equal to that given to content, what they learned about classification in zoology, for instance, would be transferable to classification tasks in social studies. It is the transferability of knowledge through the generalization of process that is the hallmark of a competent learner. Thus, from an Anisa point of view, process is the primary means of integrating the content curriculum.

The Affective Process Curriculum

Affective competence depends on the degree to which the organization of emotions and feelings predispose the child to interact with the environment in ways which support the release of further potentiality. Emotions are always associated with processes from all other categories (i.e., perceptual, psychomotor, cognitive, etc.), though in varying degrees of intensity. If the emotions are not properly organized, the functioning of other areas may also be impaired. How to feel about things, people, events, and ideas is for the most part learned but rarely "taught" in any direct or conscious way in school. Because the organization of a child's emotional life takes place through learning, it concerns the ability to differentiate feelings, to associate (i.e., integrate) them with particular objects, people, events, or ideals, and to generalize them to other environments. If this is done in a way that creates a reality-based stability in the relationship between the child and his environment, interactions will promote further growth.

We find it useful to regard emotional states as subjective assessments of the viability of the organism at any given time. Since viability depends on the integrity of the organism itself and involves its relationship to the rest of the environment, emotional states always have a direct implication for doing something about oneself or altering one's relationship to the environment in some way. If, for instance, one has learned to be afraid of some object which is not harmful and for which there is no reason to be frightened, one's relationship to that object will be unstable in the sense that it is not based on reality but on error. If being frightened is uncalled for, the subjective assessment of viability represented by the fright is inaccurate and unreliable; it leads to behavior patterns which reduce one's effectance as he interacts with the environment. "Effectance" is a word proposed by Robert White. In his discussion on competence and motivation, he writes:

> My proposal is that activity, manipulation, and exploration, which are all pretty much of a piece in the infant, be considered together as aspects of competence, and that for the present we assume the one general motivational principle lies behind them. The word I have suggested for this motive is effectance because its most characteristic feature is seen in the production of effects on the environment. (White, 1959)

Because emotions are powerful determinants of behavior, it is important that they become organized in ways that enable the organism to maintain the best possible relationship with its environment. Affective competence means having emotional reactions to situations which represent accurate assessments of viability. Behavior based on erroneous assessments will very likely lead to more pathology.

Mowrer suggests two fundamental emotions: fear and hope. In essence, they function as appraisals of viability. If we find ourselves in a threatening situation, we have the subjective experience of fear and this directs us to try out a number of things to reduce the fear. If what we try out increases the fear, we usually stop doing them and try something else until we find something that gives us a little bit of hope. The experience of hope causes us to increase our efforts along those lines until a condition of complete viability is attained.

Several researchers, such as Arnold, Black, Brown, Cofer, Hillman, Plutchik, Stronguran, and Young, have proposed paradigms for explaining the nature of emotions and how they are interrelated, but further research is required to clarify a number of unresolved issues (i.e., the difference between sensations, feelings, and emotions; relationship of physical pain to psychological pain). Even though much work remains to be done before we have a clear understanding of how emotions are organized to help create stable personalities, one thing is certain; namely, any educational system neglecting the emotional life of the child runs the risk of doing more harm than good. A person whose emotions are disorganized becomes his own worst enemy; his relationship to his environment, particularly other human beings, will be perpetually disturbed, and the general effect will be suppression of his potentialities. To be comprehensive, any process curriculum will inevitably include as one of its main goals the cultivation of a rich and stable emotional life.

Teachers can assist children in achieving affective competence primarily through the relationships which they establish with them and the clarity and consistency of feedback they provide the children as they interact with the environment. Reward and punishment, two kinds of feedback, are particularly powerful means of helping a child to organize emotions in reference to objects, people, events, and ideas. Excessive inconsistency in rewarding and punishing a child leads to conflict in the organization of emotions and therefore disturbances in behavior. A comprehensive and detailed theory concerning emotional development and the processes which comprise it awaits further research and elaboration. In the meantime, we are studying a number of processes pertinent to gaining affective competence which involve inhibiting, coping, managing, and facilitating emotions and feelings in terms of subjective aim or sense of purpose. For example, it is important to be able to cope with sadness, disappointment, or feelings of persecution, particularly if the sadness or disappointment leads to behavior that undermines the achievement of a higher purpose. Similarly, it is essential for children to learn how to manage anxiety, how to inhibit a destructive impulse, and, perhaps more significantly than we think, how to facilitate expressions of joy, happiness. and gladness on appropriate occasions (see Carney).

The Volitional Process Curriculum

Volition may be conceived as the central factor of self-causation or self-actualization of potentialities. It is intimately connected with one's growing sense of purpose and the use of goals consistent with the purpose as a general criterion for deciding how to interact with the environment. Thus, the purposive construction of experience and its role in actualizing other potentialities depends upon volitional capacity. Because purpose and intention both implicate the future, a child's positive orientation to his own future rests on the sense of power he has over it by virtue of experiencing his inner capacity to intend something and carry it through to a final consummation compatible with some purpose he has in mind. Children who grow up having no experience in setting their own objectives and pursuing the steps required to achieve them never become fully independent, responsible, and self-reliant human beings. In our view, the critical role of volition in self-actualization makes all of the processes underlying the development of volitional competence a necessary part of any comprehensive process curriculum.

We have identified three basic processes on which volitional competence rests: attention, goal setting, and will. From a Whiteheadian point of view, these processes underlying volitional competence can be regarded as progressive steps in the unfoldment of organismic purpose. In other words, will arises out of intention to achieve the goals set, the setting of goals presupposes attention which in turn presupposes purpose or interest. Keep in mind that these processes are not functionally separate elements of volition; we find justification in breaking them down into these elements only for the sake of conceptual clarity and because such differentiation provides a scheme that has more direct implications for curriculum construction (see Conway, in press). Following are fuller descriptions of each of these processes and their related subprocesses.

Attention

Many researchers (Mackworth, Broadbent, Ryan, Neisser, Norman, Vernon, Bakan, Hebb, and Conway, 1973) have generated a variety of perspectives and raised a number of important issues concerning the nature of attention. The material presented in this section draws extensively on the work of Conway who made an extensive survey of the literature in preparation for the development of the Anisa process curriculum for the development of volitional competence. From that survey, we arrived at the definition of attention as the purposive selection (differentiation) and organization (integration) of bodily movement, sensory information, feelings, thought, and memory into a single focus of conscious experience. This definition represents a general synthesis of a large number of definitions and theoretical perspectives put forward by different theorists. Although a great deal of research on attention has been carried out, there has, up to this point, been no theoretical base broad enough to integrate the wide variety of findings and make sense of the extensive body of data accumulated.

We have formulated the preceding definition in accordance with the principle that theoretical statements should illumine and explain experience but not contradict it. In that regard, we have found the works of Titchener and James useful from the experiential point of view and the work of Whitehead to be of critical importance in providing the unifying philosophical and theoretical perspective.

Titchener, taking a structuralist approach to explain attention, concentrated more on the qualities and characteristics of the stimulus being attended to (i.e., intensity, discreteness, irregularity, suddenness, novelty, rate of change). James, on the other hand, took a functionalist approach and viewed attention as a selection process determined more by the subject.

It is the taking possession by the mind, in clear and vivid form of one out of what seem several simultaneously possible objects or trains of thought. Focalization, concentration of consciousness are of its essence. It implies withdrawal from some things in order to deal effectively with others and is a condition which has a real opposite in the confused, scatterbrained state which in French is called distraction. (James, Vol. 1, p. 403)

What is it that directs us to "withdraw from some things in order to deal effectively with others" and avoid the "scatterbrained" state? Many different things can influence us to leave some things to deal with others; examples are thirst, hunger, desires, discomforts, or any of the other so-called primary and secondary drives. In man, even these things may be dominated by higher aspirations. In this regard, Whitehead's contribution establishes the rationale for accepting subjective aim or purpose as the major unifying force that is expressed in the unitary experience we call focal awareness. One of the great problems that has plagued psychological inquiry concerns the question of how many things one can hold in focal awareness, that is, pay attention to, at one time. In simple terms, the answer seems to be that the mind is capable of grasping and paying attention to any number of things, provided those things are connected in some way and make an integrated whole. If the elements are disparate and unconnected, then the mind must make a choice of one or the other. In other words, the power of differentiation or abstraction must be accompanied by the power to integrate if those differentiated elements are to come into focal awareness at the same time. The integrating factor will tend to be the sense of purpose or intention of the person. We therefore see attention as an act of constructive synthesis which reflects past experience, present needs, and future intentions.

What is the nature of synthesis? Are all of the elements synthesized held in focal awareness with equal clarity? Our experience tells us that we can be aware of some things very acutely while at the same time be only somewhat aware of other things. It appears that consciousness is comprised of different levels of attention, hierarchically organized. Focal awareness is at the peak of consciousness. It arises out of a perpetually emerging integration of a number of elements from lower levels of consciousness. For example, if we are good readers, we are focally aware of meaning that arises out of the sequence of words; on a slightly lower level of consciousness or attention, we are aware of words; below that, we are aware of the individual letters that make up the words. Reading is a complex process; its purpose is to derive meaning from a graphic code made up of letters. If letters themselves are what is in focal awareness, reading will be impossible because meaning inheres in the relationships among words and not in the letters themselves, although there are no words without letters. The purpose of reading determines the hierarchy of awareness levels. If the hierarchy is reversed, reading ceases.

Inasmuch as very little formal learning takes place unless there is an intention to learn and an ability to pay attention to the primary elements of the learning task, learning how to attend and concentrate becomes increasingly more important as the child develops. For this reason, attention occupies a central position in the configuration of processes which make up the Anisa process curriculum. While a great deal of learning can take place incidentally simply by virtue of the child's interaction with the environment, attaining higher levels of competence in all categories of potentialities, particularly those requiring exceptionally refined motor movements (e.g., playing the violin) or those that demand well-developed reasoning abilities (e.g., working out the solution to a complex and difficult mathematical problem), requires highly developed attentiveness.

Goal Setting

In arriving at a definition of goal setting, we have drawn on the works of a number of investigators (Locke, 1966; Locke and Bryan; Ryan; Franken and Morphy; Hughes; Winter et al.) who have investigated the dynamics of goal setting and their organizing effects on behavior. In the Anisa model, goal setting is defined as the process by which an individual organizes his future by differentiating events which when sequenced (integrated) appropriately arrive at that anticipated future. At the heart of goal setting is making a decision about how one's energy will be used. The word *decide* means to cut off; every decision, then, has the consequence of ruling out or saying "no" to any number of possible actions which will have to be rejected on the basis that they will not lead to the achievement of the goal being set. It is not difficult to imagine why children who grow up in circumstances in homes and in schools where they are not allowed to set goals and have very little experience in making their own decisions become indecisive in their general approach to life. Such people are inveterate procrastinators and their orientation to opportunity is to wait until circumstances and other people force a decision one way or another. They do not take an active hand in shaping their own destinies but allow the shaping to be done by forces outside themselves. Since one of the basic purposes of the Anisa model is to prepare children to take over the responsibility for determining their own destinies, it makes provision for definitive guidance in setting goals. In systems based on the model, children have daily opportunities for setting both short-term and long-term goals which they are encouraged to pursue until they accomplish them. Such an accomplishment brings about what Whitehead considers to be an essential motivating element in the general process of self-actualization, namely, self-enjoyment. Being able to decide what it is one wants to accomplish and then being able to achieve it are vital to the maintenance of mental health and stability of personality. It is the wellspring of reality-based confidence, one of the fundamental sources of self-encouragement.

Because man is fundamentally a social being, there are group or community counterparts to most of the processes we are discussing. For example, the source of group encouragement, motivation, and morale lies in members of the group participating in collective intentions and consummating them. If children are to become socially mature, they must learn how to participate in the formulation and sharing of group goals and cooperate with others to accomplish them. This aspect of the Anisa process curriculum is referred to later in conjunction with a discussion on the development of moral competence.

Will

Will is the realization of an intention or accomplishment of a goal. It is expressed in terms of three subprocesses: self-initiation, perseverence, and effecting closure.

The concept of will has been at the center of philosophical inquiry and controversy for centuries. Our tentative definition represents a synthesis of the views of many thinkers and the findings of a large number of researchers (May; James; Kenny; Polanyi; and Arieti). The implications of self-initiation, perseverence, and effecting closure for a process curriculum are extensive. They are the ingredients of autonomy and independence and can be fostered as part of any activity associated with other elements of the process and content curricula.

Once we grasp the essential nature of attention, goal setting, and will as an active process of differentiating and integrating experience around purpose, it follows that we cannot expect a child to stay at a task for any length of time if he cannot interact with the environment. The findings of empirical studies clearly demonstrate the inferiority of a passive modality of learning. A child must be able to manipulate and act upon his environment; otherwise, he will not develop high levels of attention and sense his own effectiveness, because there is very little feedback on what he is doing in the passive modality, simply because he is doing so little. Awareness of and sensitivity to feedback comes with active experience where there is an abundance of feedback. For this reason, teachers can improve the volitional capacity of their children, particularly those concerned with attentional processes, if they will demonstrate and directly involve the children in a wide variety of interactions with the environment rather than just explain to the children how something should be done but not have them do it. Learning how to pay attention, set goals, and effect closure comes from actively doing rather than passively observing somebody else's doing.

We have not devised a great number of experiences specifically for the purpose of helping children learn how to pay attention, set goals, and activate their wills, although in some cases it might be desirable to do so. Rather, since volitional effort is an intrinsic demand of all intentional learning, the pedagogical requirements for teaching the child how to attend, adopt goals, and achieve them have to be met in every learning task. Therefore, while all experiences planned as part of the Anisa process curriculum involve a variety of different processes, they always include attention, goal setting, and will. In time children learn how to arrange their own environments so that they control the level of distraction, but they also learn how to ignore irrelevant stimuli and carry on with the task in hand. A teacher can help a child to gain powers of concentration by regularly providing him with feedback on what he is doing and assisting him in understanding a need for seeking out feedback on his own. Eventually, a person can provide a good deal of his own feedback by learning how to establish criteria by which to measure his own progress. Once such criteria are established and justified, the person can compare what he is doing or producing with the established criteria and determine for himself whether or not he is satisfied with his work or whether he should try to improve what he is doing. Being able to fantasize the achievement of the goal (i.e., what it "feels like" and looks like to have achieved the goal) is important. Such fantasies function as an intrinsic source of motivation to persevere. They create the anticipation of inner satisfaction that comes when intentions are consummated in accordance with expectations. The fantasy is a projection of what it is like for there to be a good fit between what one is doing and the criteria by which goal achievement is determined. Teachers can use a variety of questioning procedures to encourage a child to fantasize in this constructive way. They can also involve children in the reading of stories whose basic themes elaborate an idea, relate the idea to specific goals, show how the main characters of the stories primarily pay attention to those things which lead them towards the goals, and exemplify the function of accurate feedback in maintaining high levels of perseverance.

Timing is also an important element in assisting children to attain volitional competence. Since children work at different rates, they finish what they start at different times. If the rhythm of the school day is dictated by bells which ring at predetermined intervals and the bells signal the termination of all activities of one kind and a shift to another category of activities, many children will perpetually experience a loss of inner satisfaction that comes from consummating their intentions. Repeatedly being robbed of such inner satisfaction undermines the attainment of volitional competence. Therefore, one of the most important things a teacher can do to assist a child in achieving volitional competence is to insist that when he begins something, he is not only allowed, but actively encouraged, to finish what he begins. In most cases, this will mean going by individual developmental time rather than clock time.

The Process Curriculum, Value Formation, and the Emergence of Personal Identity

The fundamental proposition of the Anisa theory of development, that is, the translation of potentiality into actuality is sustained by interaction with the environment, has extensive ramifications for both content and process curricula. The theory not only provides a means of classifying interactions but also classifies environments. As one might expect, interaction with different kinds of environments produces different patterns of actualized potentialities. Since a potentiality is a latent power or unexpressed energy, it is expressed as power or energy in one or more of the categories of potentialities when it is actualized. For instance, before a child learns to walk, he has the psychomotor potentiality of walking.

The model establishes three basic classifications of the environment following the ontological levels of creation as set forth by Whitehead, namely, the physical or nonhuman environment (minerals, vegetables, and animals), the human environment, and the unknown environment. The model also recognizes the existence of a fourth environment—the Self, a fusion of the other three in microcosm which emerges over time and becomes the most consistent part of its own environment. The theory of development explains how the powers or energies are structured as they come into being when potentialities are actualized. In other words, the energies which represent actualized potentialities are not randomly expressed after they are actualized; they are patterned. We call these patterns values. (For additional information, see "Self-Actualization as Value Formation: The Anisa Theory of Value" and *Biological Dimensions of the Value Theory of the Anisa Educational Model* by Raman.) Thus, as the organism interacts with the physical environment, it forms material values and on these values rest a person's technological competence. As the organism interacts with the human environment, it forms social values on which the person's moral competence rests. As the organism interacts with unknowns (e.g., his future, his own potentialities which are not fully known to him, his own mortality, etc.), he structures assumptions about the unknowns which incorporate some kind of position on ultimate unknowns. Because unknowns can only be approached on faith, we say that the interaction of the organism with the unknown environment leads to the formation of aesthetic or religious values on which philosophical or spiritual competence rests. It is important to note here that we are defining religion in a psychological sense rather than in a denominational sense. In other words, faith is a psychological phenomenon which is open to scientific inquiry like any other psychological phenomenon. Its operation in the human psyche speaks to the organism's orientation to the future, purpose, ideals, aspirations, and hopes. Seen in this light, "religious activity" is manifested in everybody's life, even if he regards himself as an atheist. The integration of a person's material, social, and religious values is the structural and functional reality of personal identity—the Self. A person's values define him. They represent how he deploys his energy and therefore manifests to everyone what he believes to be most worthwhile and least worthwhile. We refer to the patterns of energy use, that is, how a person invests the most precious asset he has, his energies, when we talk about a person's values in some abstract sense. When we say we want to get to know somebody, we are really saying that we want to know the patterns through which he expresses the energy available to him. This will tell us who he is, whether we can get along with him, and whether we will like him. The Self, defined in this way, focuses on process and dynamics and thus presents character in terms of patterned energy utilization.

When interacting with the physical environment, these patterns will lead to technological competence or incompetence. When interacting with the human environment, such patterns might be seen as responsible, irresponsible, cooperative, fair, honest, deceitful, aggressive, caring, helpful, disruptive, or hostile. These patterns define the moral competence of the Self (see Theroux). When the organism interacts with the unknown, it uses energy to form ideas about ultimate concerns. This includes the formation of an ideal Self as a part of those ultimate concerns. The patterns of energy used to form and nurture these ideas give purpose to life; they are the source of its wholeness and stability and the lure for its becoming. On these patterns rest the philosophical and aesthetic competence of the Self.

The model also explains how three basic symbol systems—mathematics, language, and the arts mediate the structuring of material, social, and aesthetic values respectively. (For a fuller discussion on the role of the arts in education, see "The Arts—Neglected Resources in Education" by Jordan.) These symbol systems are at the core of the Anisa curriculum and are the connecting links between the process and content curricula.

Conclusion

To the extent that teachers and educational administrators have felt that the field of curriculum is moribund, as Schwab expressed it, they have felt compelled to revive it by initiating a number of curriculum innovations. A substantial number of these innovations have tried to take into account the idea of development, interaction, and process. In the absence of a well-defined theory of development, most of these efforts have resulted in a concentration on providing a wide variety of materials as a means of keeping children engaged in activities, whether or not these activities lead to any particular educational objectives. Kliebard, in reappraising Tyler's curriculum rationale, even goes so far as to suggest that "the starting point for a model of curriculum and instruction is not the statement of objectives but the activity (learning experience), and whatever objectives do appear will arise within that activity as a way of adding a new dimension to it" (Kliebard, pp. 268–69).

While this move in the direction of involving children in more activity may be a good one, doing so without having objectives in mind has resulted in a neglect of content. Special attention must therefore be given to content if children in an "open" educational system where varieties of activities are optional are to glean basic information about the world in which they live and the culture of which they are a part. Children who do not assimilate such information will be at a disadvantage when compared with those who do.

Unfortunately, not only does content tend to be neglected when activities are emphasized and goals left to chance but fundamental processes may not be internalized either. We take the view that at least for a certain percentage of the child's time in the school setting, activities should be organized to achieve particular process objectives (i.e., classification, seriation, figure-ground, laterality, etc.) as well as content objectives. Optional activities which are not organized to achieve particular educational objectives may yield a limited harvest; it is possible for children to engage in activity without learning very much. Teachers and parents too easily fall into the trap of believing that a great deal of learning is taking place simply because the children are busy. While it may be true that a child who is engaged in activities is probably learning more than a child who is not, this does not release the serious educator from the obligation to make all activities function as a means of imparting content and enabling the child to internalize process. The child who is an enthusiastic participant in activities and produces many things may be regarded by a teacher as a child who is, because of so many achievements, learning at an optimum rate. Yet the evidence indicates that achieving is not necessarily the same as internalizing a process. A child may be able to give a correct response to a stimulus without understanding why it is correct. He can remember that *four* is the correct response to the stimulus question "What is two plus two?" without understanding the process of addition. For this reason, it is essential that teachers not regard products as evidence that the underlying process has been internalized.

The problem of distinguishing process from product or process from achievement is an old one in education (Werner). It is a problem which developmental psychologists, particularly through the work of Piaget, are beginning to solve. Ultimately, the most successful educational systems will be those that achieve a balance between content and process and find a way to integrate them within a single curriculum. The integration of the content and process curricula requires the differentiation of the teaching staff and their coordination through effective administration. (For a full discussion on the role of administration in staff differentiation and curriculum implementation in the Anisa Model, see Streets.) The Anisa model represents one promising effort in that direction.

References

ANISA. *Perceptual Competence: Figure/Ground Perception.* Amherst, Mass.: Center for the Study of Human Potential, School of Education, University of Massachusetts, 1973.

Arieti, S. *The Will to be Human.* New York: Quadrangle Books, 1972.

Arnold M.B., ed. *Feelings and Emotions.* New York: Academic Press, 1970.

Bakan, P. *Attention.* New York: Van Nostrand Reinhold Co., 1966.

Black, P. *Physiological Correlates of Emotion.* New York: Academic Press, 1970.

Blane, L.M., and Jordan, D.C. "Psychomotor Competence and the Anisa Process Curriculum." In *The Development of Psychomotor Competence; Selected Readings,* edited by L.M Blane. New York: MSS Information, 1975.

Broadbent, D.E. *Perception and Communication.* London: Pergamon Press, 1958.

Brown, G.I. "Confluent Education: Exploring the Affective Domain." *College Board Review* 80(1971):5–12.

Bruner, J. et al. *A Study of Thinking.* New York: John Wiley & Sons, 1956.

Carney, M., ed. *The Development of Affective Competence.* New York: MSS Information Corporation, in press.

———. *Teaching: Issues, Perspectives and Definitions.* New York: MSS Information Corporation, 1975.

Cofer, C.N. *Motivation and Emotion.* Glenview, Ill.: Scott, Foresman and Company, 1972.

Conway, P.W. "Perceptual Competence and the Anisa Process Curriculum." *World Order* 8(1974):23–25.

———. "Purpose and the Construction of Experience: A Theory of Volition and Its Implications for the Release of Human Potential." Ph.D. dissertation, University of Massachusetts, 1973.

———. "The Purposive Construction of Experience: The Role of Volition in the Curriculum of the Anisa Model." In *The Development of Volitional Competence,* edited by P.W. Conway. New York: MSS Information Corporation, in press.

Elkind, D. "Conservation and Concept Formation." In *Studies in Cognitive Development: Essays in Honor of Piaget,* edited by D. Elkind and J.H. Flavell. New York: Oxford University Press, 1969.

Flavell, J.H. "Concept Development." In *Carmichael's Manual of Child Psychology, Vol. 1,* edited by Paul H. Mussen. New York: John Wiley & Sons, 1970.

Franken, R., and Morphy, D. "Effects of Fortuitous Success on Goal-Setting Behavior of Individuals High and Low in Achievement Motivation." *Perception and Motor Skills* 30(1970):855–64.

Goldstein, A.G., and Mackenburg, E.J. "Recognition of Human Faces from Isolated Features: A Developmental Study." *Psychonomic Signs* 6(1966):149–50.

Gottschaldt, K. "Gestalt Factors in Repetition." In *A Sourcebook of Gestalt Psychology,* edited by W.D. Ellis. New York: Humanities Press, 1938.

Hebb, D.O. *Organization of Behavior.* New York: John Wiley & Sons, 1949.

Hillman, J. *Emotion.* London: Routledge and Kegan Paul, 1960.

Hughes, C. *Goal Setting: The Key to Individual and Organizational Effectiveness.* New York: American Management Association, 1965.

Inhelder, B., and Piaget, J. *The Early Growth of Logic in the Child.* New York: W.W. Norton & Co., 1964.

James, W. *The Principles of Psychology.* 2 vols. New York: Henry Holt Co., 1890.

Jordan, D.C. "The Arts—Neglected Resources in Education." In *Controversies in Education,* edited by D.W. Allen and J. Hecht. Philadelphia: W.B. Saunders Co., 1974.

Kahneman, D. "Exposure Duration and Effective Figure/Ground Contrast." *Quarterly Journal of Experimental Psychology* 17(1965):308–14.

Kalinowski, M.F., and Jordan, D.C. "Being and Becoming: The Anisa Theory of Development." *World Order* 7(1973):17–26.

Katz, D. "Effects of Labels on Children's Perception: Part of Speech Variation of Verbal Stimulus." *Perceptual and Motor Skills* 25(1967):949–52.

Kenny, A. *Action, Emotion and Will.* London: Rutledge and Kegan Paul, 1963.

Kliebard, H.M. "Reappraisal: The Tyler Rationale." *School Review* 78(1970):259–72.

Koffsky, E. "A Scalogram Study of Classificatory Development." *Child Development* 37(1966): 191–204.

Lit, A., and Vicars, W.M. "Effects of Luminance Contrast on Binocular Depth Discrimination." *Psychonomic Bulletin* 1(1967):3.

Locke, E. "A Closer Look at Level of Aspiration as a Training Procedure." *Journal of Applied Psychology* 50(1966):417–20.

Locke, E., and Bryan, J. "The Directing Function of Goals in Task Performance." *Organizational Behavior and Human Performance* 4(1969):35–42.

Mackworth, J.F. *Vigilance and Attention.* Baltimore: Penguin Books, 1970.

May, R. *Love and Will.* New York: W.W. Norton & Co., 1969.

Mowrer, O.H. *Learning Theory and Behavior.* New York: John Wiley & Sons, 1960.

Neisser, U. *Cognitive Psychology.* New York: Appleton-Century-Crofts, 1967.

Norman, D.A. *Memory and Attention.* New York: John Wiley & Sons, 1969.

Piaget, J. *Genetic Epistemology.* New York: W.W. Norton & Co., 1970.

———. *Logic and Psychology.* New York: Basic Books, 1953.

Plutchik, R. *The Emotions.* New York: Random House, 1962.

Polanyi, M. *The Study of Man.* Chicago: University of Chicago Press, 1958.

———. *Personal Knowledge: Towards a Post-Critical Philosophy.* Chicago: University of Chicago Press, 1958.

Raman, S.P. "Biological Dimensions of the Value Theory of the Anisa Educational Model." Ph.D. dissertation, University of Massachusetts, 1974.

———. "Nutrition and Educational Planning." In *Nutrition, Development and Learning,* edited by P. Raman. New York: MSS Information, 1974.

———. "Self-Actualization as Value Formation: The Anisa Theory of Value." In *Value Inquiry, Development, and Educational Theory,* edited by S.P. Raman. New York: MSS Information Corporation, in press.

Ryan, T.A. *Intentional Behavior: An Approach to Human Motivation.* New York: The Ronald Press Co., 1970.

Schwab, J.J. *The Practical: A Language for Curriculum.* Washington, D.C.: National Education Association, 1970.

Streets, D.T. "The Anisa Theory of Administration: A Science of Service." In *Educational Administration: A Practice in Need of a Theory,* edited by D.T. Streets. New York: MSS Information Corporation, in press.

Streets, D.T., and Jordan, D.C. "Guiding the Process of Becoming: The Anisa Theories of Curriculum and Teaching." *World Order* 7(1973):29–40.

Stronguran, K.T. *The Psychology of Emotion.* New York: John Wiley & Sons, 1973.

Theroux, S., ed. *Development of Moral Competence.* New York: MSS Information Corporation, in press.

Titchener, E.G. *Lectures on the Elementary Psychology of Feeling and Attention.* New York: The Macmillan Co., 1908.

Vernon, M.D. *The Psychology of Perception.* Baltimore: Pelican Books, 1967.

Werner, H. "Process and Achievement: A Basic Problem of Education and Developmental Psychology." *Harvard Educational Review* 7(1937):353–68.

White, R.W. "Motivation Reconsidered: The Concept of Competence." *Psychology Review* 66(1959):297–332.

Whitehead, A.N. *Process and Reality.* New York: The Macmillan Co., 1960.

Willis, E.J., and Dornbush, R.L. "Preference for Visual Complexity." *Child Development* 39(1968):639–46.

Winter, S.K. and Griffeth, J. "Capacity for Self-Deception." *Journal of Consulting Psychology* 32(1968):35–41.

Young, P.T. *Motivation and Emotion.* New York: John Wiley & Sons, 1961.

chapter twelve

Conclusion: Promises to Keep

Carol
Seefeldt

For their future.

Learning theories, however potent they have been in influencing the curriculum, are only one determinant of programs for young children. Spodek suggested that the proper source of a curriculum in early childhood is the set of goals which are the aims of education for children.

Early childhood education, since its very beginning, has mirrored the major goals of society. Froebel's original kindergarten was founded at a time when society was discarding the concept that children were filled with sin and required strict, unpleasant upbringing. His idea of a place where children could grow in love found ready acceptance. The major goals of early childhood education have often centered on children in need. Many programs for young children—the settlement houses, mill day-care centers, and even Montessori's children's house—were developed to care for children in need. Usually, the goals of such programs focused on providing a safe, physically healthy, and emotionally supportive environment. McMillan wrote, "The vast numbers of little children given over to all the dangers and horrors of the street, and in homes where no real nurture is possible, led us to set about the treatment and restoration of a few" (McMillan, p. 7). Program goals during the 1960s focused heavily on cognitive and academic skills and reflected society's desire to break the poverty cycle through educational experiences for young children. There are data to indicate that these programs did succeed in enhancing young children's intellectual development (Weikart et al., 1971; Gordon); however, educators are no longer so naive as to believe that a short-term preschool experience can permanently affect children's cognitive functioning.

In the past, preschool programs have been started to meet society's needs. The WPA Act of the 1930s provided for early childhood education in that it allowed unemployed teachers to find work helping children and families with child-rearing, nutrition, and social needs. The Lanham Act, passed during the Second World War, was designed to provide care for children whose mothers had returned to work to help the war effort. Parent cooperatives and some early nursery schools located at universities were organized to meet the needs of mothers and provide socializing experiences for children. The goal of other university nursery schools was to prepare teachers or mothers.

Now more than ever, early childhood educators seem intent on keeping the promises of the past. With more resources at hand, the large body of empirical research, new theories of cognitive development, and society's continued concern for the development of young children, the decade of the 1970s may be able to fulfill the promises made during the 1960s and beyond.

In an attempt to keep the promises of the past, the U.S. Office of Child Development has initiated the Improvement and Innovation (I & I) program. I & I has been launched as part of the overall improvement and innovation effort in project Head Start. The primary purpose of Head Start is to serve as a national demonstration of comprehensive developmental services for children from low-income families. Among the I & I programs now in operation are Parent and Child Centers, Health Start, Home Start, Child and Family Resource Program, and Developmental Continuity.

Goals for the early 1970s have centered on concern for all children to have the opportunity to develop the qualities of humanness. It is believed that only as children develop qualities of humanness, including the skills necessary to live with others, to adapt to a changing world, and to learn, will they be prepared for life in the twenty-first century. The concern for humanness is reflected in the attention given to the rights of children. As educators become more politically aware, they give more attention to the legal rights of children. Society's concerns for children are also reflected in current trends in curriculum development. The major goal of new curricula is to prepare children for living in a future that is characterized by rapid change and vast differences. Career education, moral development, aesthetic development, and multi-cultural curricula are a part of this trend.

Humanistic Education

The dehumanizing forces of society, mass media, urbanization, automation, and impersonal living, as well as the worldwide struggle for full realization of human dignity and integrity have led to a concern for humanizing education. "A renewed humanism is pressing urgently for education embracing the totality of human potentialities. In all its infinite complexity, education for the release of human spirit is imperative—more than ever before, we know it must begin in early childhood education" (Weber, 1973, p. 273).

Perhaps the best basis for curriculum decision lies in a basic philosophy of the humanness of man. Educating children to become whole, trusting, valuing men and women, who can educate themselves, have the desire and capacity to take responsibility for their own education, and are likely therefore, to be life-long, self-directed learners implies a value commitment to construct curriculum that is totally humanistic (Silberman, p. 5).

Translating concern for humanism into curriculum has been implemented in a number of ways. The open-education movement and the free-school movement are examples of humanistic philosophy at work. The trend toward constructing open-space classrooms is, at least in part, a result of the attempt to humanize education. In general, it appears that humanistic education includes individualizing the curriculum, that is, showing a concern for the match between each child's interests, cognitive or learning style, concept formation, rate of learning and his feelings, attitudes, emotions, and wishes.

Early childhood education does have a solid foundation for humanizing education. The child development point of view, the Gestalt and psychoanalytic theory, and the naturalistic theory of learning all have as their core a concern for the individual child. As a result, many early childhood programs are built on individual children's interests and feelings. Flexible scheduling which allows for large blocks of time for children to pursue their own interests, a large adult-child ratio which allows for individualized teaching, and an emphasis on the individual rather than the group have always been present in early childhood education. Centers of interests where children can select their own materials for learning are found in most preschool classrooms. The emphasis given to children's play has also allowed children to actively pursue their own way of learning.

The Anisa model, described by Jordan, has as its major goal the creation of a comprehensive educational system that will be unique in its power to release human potential. This model blends the knowledge of the past with a vision for the future and has culminated in the formulation of a philosophical base from which has derived a theory of development, a theory of curriculum, and a theory of teaching.

Traditional early childhood education methods reflect the same concerns for humanizing experiences. The criteria listed by Leeper et al. for evaluating a program for young children articulate these following concerns: "Was provision made for each child to have time of his own to do as he chose? Were the periods kept short when children were expected to sit in one place? Were new materials, new activities, and new situations for learning provided for each child according to his interests and growth? Did the children have the freedom to create, explore, experiment? Was time provided for necessary routines so that no child became tense or frustrated? Were the plans considered as tentative and used as a guide to depart from and to return to as the group planned, lived, and learned together?" (Leeper et al., p. 149).

Feelings have also been widely recognized as a critical variable in learning and curriculum planning. Observing the behavior of children receiving rewards for learning demonstrates how feelings can far outweigh any cognitive learning. For example, a group of children received cookies for correct responses. One child received none, and her feelings of dismay negated her attending to the correct response. Another child received two cookies and she focused her attention on those children receiving more. The children who received a number of cookies busily set about eating them rather than concentrating on the task. Teachers of young children, according to Washington, realize that it is foolish to talk about cognitive development without first assessing the learner's affective needs. Washington listed the following questions that facilitate the assessment of children's affective needs: "Does the learner make his own decision, feel secure with himself, and accept himself, his race, and ethnic group? Is the learner able to deal with inner conflicts, and does he exhibit goal-oriented behavior?" (Washington, p. 274)

Even though early childhood educators accept the notion of providing for children's feelings, individual learning, and humanistic education, they have problems implementing these goals into day-to-day curriculum. "The unresolved problems of carrying out such a curriculum on a day-to-day basis are, however, vast. It most certainly does not mean giving unlimited freedom to young children, but rather giving them help in the use of responsible freedom. A laissez-faire curriculum is not the answer. This we have learned. But we need a great deal more knowledge about how to assist children in making more effective transactions with their learning environment" (Weber, p. 274).

In spite of the problems inherent in implementing humanistic education, it appears to be a solid goal for the future. Kagan noted that when he was in school he received a grade in deportment. "What I want him to be graded on is humanism: How kind is he? How nurturant is he? Every society needs a set of people whom it can trust in and give responsibility to" (Kagan, 44). Kagan also said that the function of the school is to prepare humans to manage its capital and resources, the health of society's people, and the legal prerogatives of its people (Kagan, 1973, p. 44).

Rights of Children

Increasing awareness over the past decade has focused on the rights of children. Young children, who do not have constitutional powers and are incapable of organizing, lobbying, or articulating their own interests or needs, are without the normal constituency powers of other citizens.

Consistent with the civil-rights movement of the 1960s is society's concern with the rights of children. During the past years, children have gained civil rights against their parents, the schools, and the government. The question is not who has the authority over the child and the responsibility to discipline him, to protect him from harm, to make him attend school, receive medical care, and so on; it is now recognized that the child does have rights. During the 1970s a movement has begun that recognizes children as citizens, having all of the rights of citizens in the United States. Children have recently gained a right to a fair hearing under the juvenile justice system; children are now given an opportunity to answer charges that might serve as the basis of disciplinary action.

The Children's Defense Fund, whose primary objective is to organize for the explicit purpose of addressing the basic rights of children, employs a broad range of advocacy tools including litigation, the organization of parents and children in community groups, investigation, research, and reports of problems and conditions of institutionalized and excluded children. the Children's Defense Fund also supports child care, the implementation of federal social service, Head Start programs, and the development and enforcement of federal day-care standards.

Recognizing that there are over 600,000 single parent families in the United States with children under the age of five, and even more working mothers with children under the age of five, as well as a large number of children who experience poverty, discrimination, health, or family problems, the Children's Defense Fund has gone on record as advocating adequate child-care services for all children in need of them. Quality day care would permit all children to grow and develop in an environment free from physical and psychological dangers; the Children's Defense Fund sees this as a basic right. Day-care services could help children obtain the rights normally believed to be theirs: the right to live in places that are safe, healthy, and nurturing; to acquire knowledge and skills needed to become a competent person; to develop positive attitudes about themselves and others; and to have their health, social, physical, and educational needs fulfilled.

Marian Edelman, director of the Children's Defense Fund, believes that, through organized efforts, day care can be obtained and strengthened for children. The massive public response of over 200,000 individuals across the country to administration efforts to restrict social service child-care programs, according to Edelman, is a clear demonstration that a constituency for children can be mobilized in our country and can influence public policy issues for children.

Child Abuse

More children under the age of five die from child abuse than any other cause; yet society has consistently failed to protect young children. There has been a reluctance to become involved in child abuse cases; first, physical punishment is largely regarded in our country as the proper discipline for children, and second, the old and cherished belief with regard to the rights of parents over children has negated action in child abuse cases. "North American society has yet to recognize that the child is not the property of the parents, but a citizen in his own right" (Stolk, p. 264).

Recently, child abuse laws, clinics and organizations for parents who might abuse their children, and training for the professionals—teachers, nurses, physicians, social workers—dealing with child abuse have been developed. Early childhood education plays an important role in preventing child abuse. Frequently, parents who abuse their children have been abused as children themselves and are unable to nurture. Early childhood programs can help children to develop the ability to love, to nurture, and to express anger in acceptable ways by providing them with acceptable models of nurture and love.

Handicapped Children

Children who are classified as handicapped, that is, those who are mentally retarded, hard of hearing, deaf, speech impaired, visually handicapped, emotionally disturbed, crippled, or otherwise impaired, who by reason thereof require special education and related services, also have rights.

The rights of handicapped children to the free and unrestricted access to the benefits of all children and to the rights which every other citizen is entitled have led to various approaches to integrating handicapped children in programs for young children. Positive results for both the handicapped child and the other children arise when the handicapped child is "mainstreamed" into the regular school program.

All Head Start programs now must ensure that handicapped children receive the full range of services normally available to other Head Start children, including participation in regular classroom activities. In May 1974 Congress passed a law giving aid to states to assist in developing programs for handicapped children and incorporating the handicapped in the regular classroom; this action affirmed the rights of all children to equal educational opportunities in order that they might develop their full potential.

Child Advocacy

A Child Advocacy program has been developed under the direction of the Office of Child Development. An effective system of child advocacy is the first step toward correcting some of the deficits that exist in our nation.

Dr. Frederick Green, the first director of the Child Advocacy program, wrote: "There is a corporate responsibility of society to its young to assure optimum nurturing. In smaller, less complex, less mobile societies this responsibility was assumed within the extended family. Such is not the case in our contemporary society. Therefore, it is not unexpected that concerned, child-oriented members of our nation raise their voices in demand for a means of alleviating the plight of many of our young and their families. Today, this demand is for someone to speak for and correct the problem of this group. This someone we now call a child advocate" (Green, p. 83).

The prime objectives of the Child Advocacy program are

1. To guarantee that each child and his family receive every service that is needed to assure maximum developmental potential.
2. To coordinate the badly fragmented services that now serve this population.
3. To catalyze the development of necessary services that are nonexistent, but needed.

In essence, the Child Advocate supplements and supports existing services that are functioning effectively and assures the availability of those necessary services that are nonexistent.

Developmental Continuity

The continuity of preschool and primary school experiences has long been advocated in early childhood education. Parker and Temple, in 1925, wrote *The Unified Kindergarten and First-Grade Teaching* and called attention to the fact that educational systems in this country suffer because of a serious lack of coordination between the various units which compose them. As applicable today as it was in 1925, is Temple's statement: "In the field it has been growing more and more evident that there are children of kindergarten age who are mature enough to be treated in the way in which first-grade pupils used to be treated, and that there are first-grade pupils so immature that they cannot be subjected to the formal type of instruction of first grade; we feel that kindergarten curriculum can be merged in the education of young children ages five to seven" (Temple, p. 1).

Follow-up studies from Head Start and other compensatory preschool programs indicated that a child's development can be enhanced by his continuing educational experiences. Data compared cognitive changes for children attending four different Head Start curricula and cited data that suggested that differences among even apparently similar curriculum models can influence child performance. Unlearning the distinctive teaching style of the Bereiter-Englemann, DARCEE, or Montessori models may have been necessary before children could function well in another model when going to primary school. These studies led researchers to call for continuous, similar preschool and school experiences; they concluded that the best thing that could happen to a child was to participate in a preschool program that was followed by a compatible experience or where there has been maternal training as well as child participation.

Data describes how a continuity between preschool and primary school may be provided and identified five approaches (Data, p. 29):

1. Program continuity can be created by an outside sponsor whose curriculum is offered to both preschool and primary classes.
2. Comprehensive environmental continuity can be created by a unified preschool, preprimary, and elementary program.
3. Continuity of teaching staff should be provided from preschool to primary classes.
4. Continuity of peers created by keeping classes intact from preschool to primary grades can foster social learning.
5. Parental continuity—either as advocates or as trained child educators—is among the major benefits predicated from home-based programs.

The lack of continuity in the experiences of children as they go from preschool programs into the primary grades has led the Office of Child Development to initiate a new Head Start demonstration program entitled Project Developmental Continuity. Project Developmental Continuity is aimed at promoting greater continuity of education and child development services for children as they make the transition from pre-school to school; it is based on two assumptions: (1) growth and learning occur as gradual and continuous processes, and (2) development is enhanced when the child's program is based on a plan that takes into account the child's needs, home experiences, and planned sequences of preschool and early school intervention.

Project Developmental Continuity has developed two alternative approaches for implementing the project:

1. Preschool-school linkage programs which link Head Start and other preschool programs to existing elementary schools, providing a mechanism for bringing schools closer together in order to provide a continuous educational philosophy, sequenced curriculum, and other comprehensive services.
2. The early childhood schools approach does so through the creation of a new institution in which the preschool program merges with the elementary school.

The early childhood school would provide a continuous educational experience for children from preschool through the third grade; however, schools are encouraged to provide a sequential curriculum for all children enrolled. Whether curriculum is open, traditional, or structured, the emphasis is on coordination of educational goals across the age range of children to assure that the child consolidates his learning.

Education for the Future

Today's children are "children with tumultuous todays fated for churning tomorrows" (Hymes, p. 161). Education has always been concerned, to one extent or another, with preparing children to live and function in the future. In view of the tremendous changes that have occurred in the past decade, educators are now concerned with preparing children to live in a world that promises even more rapid and dramatic changes.

Hymes believes that a school that is essentially good for children today will prepare children to live in the future. He stated, "A good school will prepare them for the future, a good school will seek to build inner sturdiness into children. . . .a good school will teach in such a way that children rightly feel pleasure with themselves, strong, able, and self-respect. . . . a good school will seek to build great enjoyment of people. . . . it will provide experiences a child needs to live happily, and constructively, on a little planet packed with people. . . . a good school will seek to build into children a love of learning" (Hymes, p. 161).

More than any other goal, a love of learning and the ability to learn how to learn have become imperative in early childhood education. Inquiry education and problem-solving approaches have been developed in social studies, math, and science curriculum, in keeping with the concept of helping children learn how to learn.

Preschool and primary schools are heavily involved in developing strategies for teaching children to think, question, analyze, and synthesize information rather than to learn a set of facts. Toffler stated, "Tomorrow's schools must therefore teach not merely data, but ways to manipulate it. Children must learn how to discard old ideas, how and when to replace them. They must, in short, learn how to learn" (Toffler, p. 414). Children must learn the skills of classifying, unclassifying, and reclassifying information, how to evaluate information, and how to observe, draw hypotheses, test them, and draw conclusions.

Toffler believes new curriculum should be added to the program. "Instead of assuming that every subject taught today is taught for a reason, we should begin from the reverse premise: nothing should be included in a required curriculum unless it can be strongly justified in terms of the future" (Toffler, p. 409). Perhaps early childhood educators now have the opportunity to assess the type of curriculum they have been providing and add new and varied content to the program. A number of "new" curricula have been developed for preschool-primary children.

Multi-cultural Education

An awareness of the diversity in our society has led to including curriculum designed to strengthen the cultural heritage of children. Children's storybooks and basal readers are being prepared to include many cultures. The Black Child Development Institute has as a major goal the development of curriculum for young black children. American Indian and Eskimo children are finding equal recognition as their values, life styles, and experiences are being used as the basis of curriculum design.

Every classroom is a multi-cultural classroom, and all children have the same needs for recognition, security, and nurture. Multi-cultural curriculum begins with the acceptance of the child's culture, works to involve parents and community in the school's program, and strives to foster children's understandings of themselves and others.

The Elm Street School, located a few blocks from the international border dividing the United States and Mexico, has developed a multi-cultural curriculum for English- and Spanish-speaking children. Among the factors contributing to making the Elm Street School a quality setting for multi-cultural education are

1. Acceptance of the child's home language as a media of instruction;
2. Specific attention to home/school relationships;
3. Opportunity for all children to excel at the level of their abilities;
4. Extensive home/school planning;
5. An abundance of teaching material in the home or second language;
6. Clinical in-service training for staff development;
7. Extensive team planning.

Career Education

The urgency of developing future-oriented knowledge and skills required to live in the future has led to a focus on career education in the preschool and primary classroom. Recognizing the critical need for each child to become a productive member of society while achieving self-fulfillment, many state departments of education, federal programs, and authorities in the field of education have mandated beginning career education in the preschool.

It does seem that the preschool-primary classroom is the ideal place to begin educating children for a career. It is during these early years that a child's attitudes and values are being developed, and career education must begin with a child's feelings of self and attitudes toward work and play. Career education for young children should focus on attitude formation as well as acquaint children with the world of work.

Ecology

The problems of the environment, threatened with pollution, overpopulation, and vanishing species, has led to a focus on environmental education. Young children are being taught to care for their own immediate environment and to begin to develop an understanding of how each link is necessary for the survival of another link in the life chain. A curriculum that provides a bridge between science and social studies helps young children begin to delve into the intricate web of interrelatedness in nature.

Moral Development and Education

Educators have become aware of the implications of moral development in the curriculum. With Kohlberg as a guide, moral maturity is defined as behavior and feeling based on abstract principle in relation to people increasingly removed from our own identities. Kohlberg's studies suggested that children who are involved in extensive and varied social participation or responsibilities were, on the whole, more mature in their moral judgments.

The implications for early childhood education are clear. Gross stated, "The only way to train children to moral development is through exemplification. It's not enough to practice honesty and fairness in one's family or neighborhood or classroom; the world must become one's family" (Gross, p. 48).

Sex Role and Education

Due to the discrimination they have faced, women have turned their attention to the sex role stereotypes present in most curriculums for young children. Sex stereotypes are present in children's storybooks, basal readers, and other curriculum material; these materials depict mothers perpetually at work in the kitchen and the fathers out to work. These materials fail to reflect reality for many young children and perpetuate inequalities.

The Woman's Action Alliance, based in New York, has developed an early childhood curriculum as well as a number of teaching materials, such as pictures, puzzles, and games, that are free of stereotyped sex roles and are firmly rooted in reality. Involving trips to the community, the curriculum brings children in contact with a variety of people and the jobs they do. These experiences are reinforced by the teachers using the special materials. Children are encouraged to think about themselves and their role choices. The curriculum helps children see that both men and women have an active, important part in society.

Questions for the Future

Many questions remain to be answered before early childhood education can keep the promises of the past. When should children begin to attend school? Who should take the responsibility for this period of schooling? and Who should teach young children? all require answering. The goals of early childhood education are not merely to have any kind of program for children, just because that might be better than having none, but to have a diversity of programs and curricula and to develop options that will allow all young children to have the type of preschool experience best suited to their needs.

When Should Children Go to School?

Education begins at birth or perhaps even before birth as the embryo's growth and development is dependent on the mother's nourishment, protein intake, and general health. However, the question of when children should begin their schooling has not been fully answered. Hymes dreams of the day when "all young children will have the chance to begin their schooling in the 'first grade' and that his first grade will be for three year olds" (Hymes, p. v).

Many public school systems are now providing some type of educational program for three-, four-, and five-year-old children, and there are numerous private, industry-related, church, and social service child-care programs in existence. Many young children are beginning their schooling at an even earlier age. Research from several compensatory and intervention programs (Weikart et al., 1971; Schaeffer; Gordon;

Gray and Klaus) has led to the conclusion that beginning early educational experiences at the age of three is too late. Education, according to this research, should begin at birth, and the curriculum should offer infants a wide range of experiences and act as a challenge and guide for the teacher and the mother.

Although there is widespread acceptance of the value of beginning educational experiences for children before the age of three, there are several forces that argue against the benefits of early educational experiences. Moore and Moore have discussed the damaging nature of early schooling. They believe that early schooling can only serve to "accommodate the separation of the family and to reduce family responsibility instead of educating parents to retain their primary privilege and responsibility in an era when complete parenthood is urgently needed and to be supportive of the school when the child is ready to enroll" (Moore and Moore, p. 42). According to Moore and Moore, maternal attachment and deprivation studies clearly demonstrate the affective and cognitive benefits of maintaining warm, consistent home environments for young children until the age of seven or eight. Mothers, with understanding and empathy, are likely to teach their own children, and these children will grow to be more mature, cooperative, adaptable, sociable, and advanced in language skills than those who are placed in an early school situation. Other research cited by Moore and Moore to build their case against early school experiences comes from comparative studies of early and late school entrance. This research, they conclude, leads to the position that "comparative studies of early and late school entrants overwhelmingly indicate that later entrants generally excel in achievement, adjustment, leadership in general, social-emotional development, and motivation" (Moore and Moore, p. 17). Data from other countries on the effects of early admission or day care for children under the age of five, stated Moore and Moore, reveal no evidence that "day care makes a child more stable, sociable, responsible or a higher achieving citizen, but many studies clearly support the contrary view" (Moore and Moore, p. 43).

Kagan, in an attempt to validate the theory that early experiences shape the psychological structures that have a continuum that stretches and lasts into later life, found data that led him to reverse this position and to postulate that early schooling or early enriching experiences are not as valid as once believed. Kagan observed some children living in an isolated Indian village on Lake Attilan in the highlands of northwest Guatemala. "I saw listless, silent, apathetic infants; passive, quiet, timid three year olds; but active, gay, intellectually competent eleven year olds. Since there is not reason to believe that living conditions in this village have changed during the last century, it is likely that the alert eleven year olds were, a decade earlier, listless, vacant-staring infants. That observation forced me to question the strong form of the continuity assumption in a serious way" (Kagan, p. 41). Kagan's study revealed that eleven year olds in these villages performed on measures of intelligence equally as well as children in the United States. He concluded that environmental experiences exert a nontrivial influence on intellectual development but that influence seems to be more reversible and more temporary than many have surmised.

Concluding that preschool programs can not directly and finally influence intellectual growth, the work of Jencks et al. and Jensen (1969) have also been used to argue against the validity of early school experiences for children. Jencks, basing his study on a reanalysis of the Coleman data, postulated that school experiences are not effective in eliminating economic and educational inequalities in society. Jensen (1969), who compiled the results of a number of early education projects designed to increase children's intellectual functioning, concluded that such programs have failed. Jensen now advocates that education, rather than beginning early, should be based on the development of Level I and Level II abilities. Level I abilities are those associated with rote memory, while Level II are those concerned with higher thought processes. Jensen's latest research led to the conclusion that Level I abilities are closely associated with the child's racial background.

Nevertheless, there is sufficient evidence to conclude that early school experiences, in the form of infant day care, home visiting, or early school experiences, are beneficial to children and families. Children in day-care centers, according to a large body of information, do develop motivationally and in terms of skills considered essential in today's world. Results from several programs indicate that the most accurate generalization that can be drawn about the effects of day care is that the optimum time to begin education is during early infancy (Caldwell and Elardo; Keister). The greater the proportion of children in a program from environments that differed from the middle norms, the greater the results indicated an increase in cognitive function, acquisition of skills, and enhancement of social and affective variables.

Who is Responsible for This Early Education?

In many countries the answer to the question "Who is responsible for the early education of infants and children?" is clear. The goals of society often determine who assumes this responsibility and what type of experience it will be. When the goal of society is to live collectively for the good of the state, then the primary responsibility for bringing up children rests on the state; and the goals of early experience are to build citizens for the state. When communal living is the goal of a society and citizens live in a system of communal ownership of property, collectively determined economic production, and equal responsibility of all, then the care of the children is also communal. The kibbutz of Israel, where children live and are raised with their age group from birth, is the result of the social and ideological goals of the state. However, in a nation as diverse in values and cultures as the United States, and one possessing the ideological philosophy of the rights of individuals to democratic living, just who should assume the responsibility for the education of the very young is not clear. Should the federal government, state govenment, local government, church, or parents assume the responsibility for early schooling?

Today, the federal government plays a role in focusing attention on the significance of the early years, supports research, and serves to centralize the information resulting from ongoing early childhood projects. The federal government also supports programs designed for children with special needs that possibly would not find child care without federal assistance; examples of the type of programs that the federal government has assumed responsibility for are aid to dependent children, work incentive programs, provision for the care of the handicapped, and social service programs. Although it directs and sponsors projects such as Home, Health, and Head Start, the federal government takes very limited responsibility for the education of the nation's young children, in spite of the fact that early childhood education is listed as the second most important priority for the 1970s.

There appears to be a general resistance on the part of the federal government to usurp the family or local communities' responsibility to young children. An analysis of federal priorities and programs indicates that the education of young children is largely left up to the states and local communities. The Alternatives for Program Implementation in the States conference, 1971, declared that the states should support the development of programs for children under the age of six. The major thrust, however, of such programs should be

1. A strengthening of the role of the family as the first and most fundamental influence on child development;
2. The early detection of serious health and education handicaps;
3. The provision of remedial health and education programs for all preschool children who require services (Alternative Programs for Implementation for the States, p. 1).

Early childhood education, perhaps because the young child is so much a part of a family, has always focused heavily on parent involvement. Recently, more and more evidence has been accumulated which indicates that the parent is the most important variable to the success of any program. Besides the traditional methods of involving parents, such as parent meetings, parents working in the classroom and through an open-door policy, parents are assuming full responsibility for preschool programs. The Home and Head Start program have as their major goal the strengthening of the family's responsibility for the education of young children.

Believing that parents have the primary responsibility for the education of young children, the Office of Child Development has implemented a new program, Education for Parenthood. This program is based on the philosophy that the capacity of schools and other organizations to instruct young men and women in the techniques and responsibilities of motherhood and fatherhood needs strengthening. Education for Parenthood gathers talent from all existing programs now funding parental instruction. The Vocational Education Act, for example, now underwrites courses in the care and guidance of children, child development, and family relations for more than 350,000 high school students; many more courses are offered through programs funded under the Elementary and Secondary Education Act, the Higher Education Act, and the Impact Aid Program. "Parenthood instruction seems to me doubly justified—first, because young people desperately need this help in order to fulfill their role as parents and maintain the family as the vital basic unit in American social structure, and secondly, because learning about children's needs and development is an obvious and essential component of the current national drive to build a coherent, effective system of career education. Indeed, parenting is a universal and very demanding 'career' in itself" (Marland, p. 3).

Who Should Teach Young Children?

Ultimately, the curriculum depends upon the teacher. "It is undoubtedly the teacher, her outlook and convictions, that constitute the most important single factor in the shaping of the child's early school experiences" (Reichenberg-Hackett, p. 151).

Authorities in the field of early childhood education have long maintained that specific and complete training is a prerequisite to becoming an effective teacher of young children. Leeper wrote, "A preschool teacher may possess many desirable personal qualities and still not be an effective teacher of young children. Basic information, understanding, knowledge, skills, and appreciations can only be secured through training" (Leeper, p. 107). Piaget also stated that the younger the child to be taught, the more training and education the teacher should possess. He suggested that the more one wishes to appeal to the spontaneous activities of small children, the more psychological initiative is required (Piaget, 1970).

Contrary to these recommendations, many current preschool programs do not seek trained, experienced, or educated teachers. Employing teachers without formal education or prior experiences is believed to hold many benefits for preschool children. This policy has fostered a bridge between the community and the child's family; this policy has also served to meet staffing needs in flexible, economically feasible ways.

Now, however, there are teacher-training programs that attempt to prepare persons without formal qualities for the task of teaching young children. The Office of Child Development has designed the Child Development Associate (CDA) program to train persons indigenous to the community for positions as child development teachers. The aim of the Child Development Associate program is to improve the quality of care provided in preschool programs by increasing the competence of the program staff. The goal is to create a role for child development associates that will be as specific and familiar as those of nurses, doctors, and teachers (Klein and Weatherby, p. 2). A major challenge in CDA training lies in the effort to integrate two very different elements of an effective training program: (1) concentration on specific competencies and behaviors, and (2) an attempt to help trainees incorporate specific knowledge and skills into their total pattern of behavior and interaction with children. Essentially, a child development associate needs to be concerned with both the parts or specifics of day-to-day interaction with children and staff and with the whole of understanding self and children and relating to them in positive ways.

"Our society has not yet accepted the degree of responsibility for young children that is commonplace in some parts of the world. Many people have assumed that anyone can work with young children and that custodial care is all that is necessary until a child reaches school age. It is hoped that with the eventual establishment of child development associates as professionals trained in child care, we will have stimulated a nationwide commitment to quality care for young children" (Klein and Weatherby, p. 6).

Summary

What curriculum should be included in preschool-primary classrooms? What types of programs are found to be efficient and effective for young children? When should children begin school? All of these questions, and more, remain unanswered. Early childhood education is actually just beginning to be able to evaluate and reevaluate the knowledge, data, and information gleaned during the 1960s. The questions that remain unanswered, rather than becoming a disillusionment for early childhood educators, can be seen as opportunities for them to reevaluate the knowledge of the past, in order to establish new directions for the future.

Many innovations of the past arose out of a trial-and-error method and were not based on a solid theoretical foundation or were not reflective of a basic philosophy of the nature of man. The mistakes that have been made were perhaps the result of insignificant planning, short-term goals and objectives, or inappropriate goals. Now, careful planning in the various preschool-primary curricula and new directions in teacher training may lead to answers.

The vast amount of research and the development and implementation in the various curriculum content areas have provided a rich resource for educators to draw on as they determine directions for the future. The problem of the 1970s may not be the need for additional data on which to base decisions but rather a search for a way to implement and utilize the knowledge, data, and information already in existence. Educators are still attempting to implement the basic philosophy of Comenius, Dewey, Bloom, Bruner, and others who enriched education with their theories. "We must find a way of translating what we know into a powerful and comprehensive system of educational practice" (Jordan, p. 290).

References

"Alternative Programs for Implementation for the States: A Report of the Education Commission on the States." Denver: Education Commission for the States, 1971.

Brofrenbrenner, U. "Is Early Childhood Education Effective?" Paper presented to U.S. Department of Health, Education, and Welfare. Washington, D.C.: Office of Child Development, 1972.

Caldwell, B., and Elardo, P.T. "The Kramer Adventure: A School for the Future?" *Childhood Education* 50(1974):143–52.

Data, L.E. *New Directions for Early Childhood Development Programs: Some Findings from Research.* Urbana, Ill.: ERIC Clearinghouse, No. 1300 50, 1973.

Edelman, M.W. "Children's Defense Fund: An Interview with Marian Wright Edelman." *Young Children* 28(1973):260.

Frank, L. "The Fundamental Needs of the Child." *Mental Hygiene* 27(1938):353–79.

Gordan, I.J. "Early Child Stimulation through Parent Education." Final report submitted to U.S. Department of Health, Education, and Welfare, Children's Bureau. PHS R 306, PHS R 2061, June 1969.

Gray, S., and Klaus, R. "The Early Training Project: A 7th Year Report." *Child Development* 41(1970):919–24.

Green, F.C. "Child Advocacy Reflections." *Young Children* 22(1971):82–88.

Gross, W.D. "Comment:Watergate: Implications for Moral Development." *Childhood Education* 50(1974):48–54.

Hunter, M. "Public Education for Four Year Olds: To Be or Not To Be?" *Childhood Education* 49(1973):403–7.

Hymes, J. *Teaching the Child under Six.* Columbus, O.: Charles E. Merrill Publishing Co., 1974.

Jencks, C., et al. *Inequality: A Reassessment of the Effect of Family and Schooling in America.* New York: Basic Books, 1972.

Jensen, A. "How Much Can We Boost IQ and Scholastic Achievement?" *Harvard Educational Review* 39(1969):1–113.

———. "Interaction of Level I and Level II Abilities with Race and Socioeconomic Status." *Journal of Educational Psychology* 66(1974):90–112.

Jordan, D.C. "The Anisa Model: A New Bases for Educational Planning." *Young Children* 28(1973):282–89.

Kagan, J. "Do the First Two Years Matter? A Conversation with Jerome Kagan." *Saturday Review World* 1(1973):41–44.

Katz, L. *Early Childhood Revisited.* Atlanta: Tri State Administrators' Conference, June 1972.

Keister, M.E. *The Good Life for Infants and Toddlers.* Washington, D.C.: National Association for the Education of Young Children, 1970.

Klein, J.W., and Weatherby, R. "Child Development Associates: New Professionals, New Training Strategies." *Children Today* 2(1973):2–6.

Kohlberg, L. "Development of Moral Character and Moral Ideology." In *Review of Child Development Research,* edited by M. Hoffman and L. Hoffman. New York: Russell Sage Foundation, 1964.

Ksylering, M.D. *Windows on Day Care.* New York: National Council of Jewish Women, 1972.

Lavetelli, C.B. "A Piagetian Derived Model for Compensatory Education." In *Early Childhood Education Rediscovered,* edited by J.L. Frost. New York: Holt, Rinehart & Winston, 1968.

Leeper, S.L., et al. *Good Schools for Young Children.* 3d ed. New York: The Macmillan Co., 1974.

McMillan, M. *The Nursery School.* London: J.M. Dent & Sons, 1919.

Marland, S.P. "Education for Parenthood." *Children Today* 2(1973):259–66.

Moore, R.S., and Moore, D.R. "How Early Should They Go to School?" *Childhood Education* 50(1973):14–20.

Parker, C.S., and Temple, A. *The Unified Kindergarten and First-Grade Teaching.* New York: Ginn and Co., 1925.

Piaget, J. *The Origins of Intelligence in the Child.* New York: International Universities Press, 1952.

————. *The Science of Education and the Psychology of the Child.* New York: The Viking Press, 1970.

Prescott, D. *The Child in the Educative Process.* New York: McGraw-Hill Book Co., 1957.

Reichenberg-Hackett, W. "Practices, Attitudes and Values in Nursery Group Education." *Psychological Reports* 19(1962):151–72.

Schaeffer, E.S. "Parents as Educators: Evidence for Cross-Sectional, Longetudinal and Intervention Research." *Young Children* 27(1972):227–39.

Silberman, C.E. *The Open Classroom Reader.* New York: Random House, 1973.

Spodek, B. "What Are the Sources of the Curriculum?" *Young Children* 26(1970):48–60.

Stolk, N.V. "Who Owns the Child?" *Childhood Education* 50(1974):259–66.

Toffler, A. *Future Shock.* New York: Random House, 1970.

Washington, K.R. "Self-Concept Development: An Effective Educational Experience for Inner-City Teachers." *Young Children* 28(1974):274.

Weber, E. *Early Childhood Education: Perspectives on Change.* Worthington, O.: Charles A. Jones Publishing Co., 1970.

————. "Epilogue and Prologue." *Young Children* 28(1973):274.

————. "The Function of Early Childhood Education." *Young Children* 28(1973):273.

Weikart, D.P.; Rogers, L.; Adcock, C.; and McClelland, D. *The Cognitively Oriented Curriculum: A Framework for Preschool Teachers.* Washington, D.C.: The National Association for the Education of Young Children, 1971.

Weikart, D., and Lambie, D.Z. "Preschool Intervention through a Home Teaching Program." In *Disadvantaged Child, Vol. II,* edited by J. Hellmuth. Seattle: Special Child Publications, 1968.

White, B.L., LaCrosse, E.R.; Litman, F.; and Ogilive, D.M. "Preschool Project: Laboratory of Human Development." Symposium presented at the meeting of the Society for Research in Child Development, Santa Monica, March 1969.

Name Index

Subject Index

Subject Index